Women in American History

Series Editors

Mari Jo Buhle
Nancy A. Hewitt
Anne Firor Scott

Sport and Society

Series Editors

Benjamin G. Rader
Randy Roberts

Lists of books in the series Women in American History and the series Sport and Society appear at the end of this book.

Babe

Babe

THE LIFE AND LEGEND OF
BABE DIDRIKSON ZAHARIAS

. . . . .

Susan E. Cayleff

University of Illinois Press

URBANA AND CHICAGO

© 1995 by the Board of Trustees of the University of Illinois
Manufactured in the United States of America
C 5 4 3 2 1

This book is printed on acid-free paper.

Library of Congress Cataloging-in-Publication Data

Cayleff, Susan E., 1954–
    Babe : The life and legend of Babe Didrikson Zaharias / Susan E. Cayleff.
       p.   cm. — (Women in American history) (Sport and society)
    Includes bibliographical references and index.
    ISBN 0-252-01793-5 (alk. paper)
    1. Zaharias, Babe Didrikson, 1911–1956. 2 Women golfers—United
States—Biography. I. Title. II. Series. III. Series: Sport and
society.
GV964.Z3C39   1995
796.352'092—dc20
   [B]   94-35584
                                           CIP

For
Nat and Fritzie

What would happen if one woman told the truth about her life? The world would split open.

—*Muriel Rukeyser*

Contents

Preface and
Acknowledgments

I was new to Galveston Island, Texas, in the late summer of 1983. Like everyone else I was struggling to recover from the devastation of Hurricane Alicia. To blot out the heat and feelings of loneliness in my new home, I watched Babe Didrikson's life story on late night television. Her athletic wonders and hospitalizations had occurred exactly where I lived. I made a mental note to ask around the university, where I had just begun working as an assistant professor, if anyone there had known her.

Thus began a relationship that has lasted over a decade. My first queries focused on her bouts with cancer since I had ready access to former practitioners of hers and medical documentation. This led me into contact with family members, golfing peers, and Babe Didrikson Zaharias Foundation, Inc., members, who devote themselves to preserving her memory. What began as a study of her coping strategies with disease evolved into a life study of an enigmatic and blustery personality.

That I had played team sports my entire life, from elementary school tug-of-wars to high school and college track and field, field hockey, softball, and basketball—none with the skill but all with the passion that Babe brought to her games—has kept this study both personal and meaningful all these years. Today in college and city league play I still find myself daydreaming about how Babe would win for her team or, better yet, destroy the competition in one-on-one play. That she consciously avoided introspection has never bewildered me; sheer physicality has its own language.

Sports organized my life as they did hers. Each season was introduced to me in New England not only as a climatic change but as a competitive one as well; spring meant softball just as surely as fall meant field hockey. The feel of the equipment, the smell of the grass, the relentless posturing and teasing amongst teammates, and the locker-room banter were profound organizing principles in my life; I told time by them.

This is what inspired me to write this biography. Herein I offer Babe's life as she lived it and as she said she lived it. I utilized information gleaned from her previous biographies, newspaper and magazine articles, and Babe's own correspondence, which I have presented as she wrote it, merely correcting typographical errors that could be misleading. What really made writing this biography feasible, however, were numerous people who generously shared their memories and time with me. My gratitude to them is immense. I am indebted to Babe's family members and friends Thelma Didriksen, Bubba Didriksen, Jackie Didriksen, Betty Dodd, Bertha Bowen, and Sigrid Hill. Golfing peers and contemporary athletes who gave generously of their insights include Peggy Kirk Bell, Betty Hicks, Betty Jameson, Patty Berg, Bill Nary, and Gene Sarazen. Sportswriters were helpful, especially Thad Johnson and Herb Grassis. Local Galvestonians illuminated her residences there, especially Peter Moore, Dr. Rose Schneider, and Dr. James Belli. Nancy Corcoran and Ann Tibbetts shared information on their relatives. Because Babe and those who knew her were such eloquent storytellers, wherever possible I have used their exact words.

Ben J. Rogers of the Babe Didrikson Zaharias Foundation, Inc., has been a booster and ally throughout, as was his assistant Shawn Stevenson. Thad Johnson, chairman emeritus of the foundation, was also very helpful. Authorities have shared their expertise unselfishly: Edith Fitzhugh and the staff at the Babe Didrikson Zaharias Museum, Beaumont, Texas; the archivists for Babe's collection of materials at the Mary and John Gray Library, Lamar University, Beaumont, Texas, especially Annette Dye and Charlotte Holliman; David E. Montgomery, Library Manager, Tyrrell Historical Library, Beaumont, Texas; Jef C. Russell III and Laura Hayes of the Beaumont Convention and Visitors Bureau; Sheldon Rudman, owner of the sports memorabilia store Collections, Richardson, Texas; Oona Patton of the Women's Sports Foundation, San Francisco; the staff at the Amateur Athletic Union Library, Los Angeles; Patricia Olkiewicz, film specialist, and Bob Paul, committee on education, United States Olympic Committee, Colorado Springs, Colorado; the U.S. Roller Skating Federation, Oklahoma City; and Marge Dewey of the Ralph W. Miller Golf Library/Museum, City of Industry, California. Of constant assistance were the workers at the Interlibrary Loan Office at San Diego State University.

Students greatly facilitated the research process and to them I am grateful. Prime among them is Jennifer Watson of Poway, California, who was a rock and right hand through some of the grittiest work. San Diegans I would like to thank include Chris Boortz, Lisa Sampieri, Annette Dutton, Tae Abate, and Mary Kelly. Special thank-yous go to Sarah Fleming of Galveston/Minneapolis for pinch-hitting in an interview with another East Texan and to Roberta Schmitz of Honolulu, Hawaii, for her excellent assistance. Thanks too to Vicky Estrada of Galveston for her efforts. Office personnel have wrangled with the mechanics and been friends and supporters throughout. Foremost of these is Betty Jo Herman of Houston, who transcribed every word of every interview and kept my spirits up and my faith strong throughout a few lean years. I would like to thank Avis Anderson, Roberta Hobson, Polly Mason, Sharon McMahon, Claudia McMahon, Kate Burns, Amber Jayme, and Janine Hunn in San Diego for their invaluable assistance. Bill Waller of Tucson, Arizona, once again brought the surgeon-editor's knife to the manuscript and helped clarify the muddy waters.

I have benefited immensely from the skillful and thoughtful comments of two historians, Nancy Hewitt and Ben Rader. Carole S. Appel, formerly Senior Editor at the University of Illinois Press, was patient and steadfast over many years; Karen Hewitt and Richard Wentworth took over where she left off. Becky Standard, also of the press, was a superb copyeditor.

On the home front Ann M. Jetté, Barbara Siegel, Pat Rapson, and Roberta Hobson have shared the alternating excitement and distress that a project of this size elicits. Sue Gonda has been ally and comfort through the final stages. Roberta above all others has been counselor, researcher, word-processor, commentator, travel companion, grave site co-visitor, archival hound, and inseparable comfort and ally.

My parents, Nat and Fritzie Cayleff of Massachusetts, have been die-hard fans of this project and my immersion in it. And thanks, folks, for coming and cheering us on in all those games in all those sports over all those years.

Research for this project was facilitated by grants from the National Endowment for the Humanities, the Babe Didrikson Zaharias Foundation, Inc., and the San Diego State University Foundation.

While I have been enriched by and benefited from all of these helping hands, the final sculpted product, for better or for worse, is my sole responsibility. One final acknowledgment: to Babe Didrikson Zaharias for having lived her life in all its complexity, simplicity, and athletic grace.

Introduction

As a protagonist, Babe Didrikson elicits as much frustration and dislike as she does admiration and idolatry. She was a sports hero in a century when sports heroes were nearly always male; she was southern, working-class, and ethnic; she was unfeminine, coarse, and loud—all the things that make for a female antihero.

Didrikson's fame, broadcast as it was at all possible opportunities by Babe herself, was legendary. Several contemporary writers likened her recognizability and appeal to Eleanor Roosevelt's, a comparison Babe surely found suitable, pleasing, and earned. Her appeal expanded beyond that of a typical sports figure. She became a phenomenon, a personality. Her name, if not her image, became synonymous with excellence and fortitude. "You're another Babe Didrikson" resonated in the ears of a lucky few female athletes. Babe Didrikson Zaharias was a cultural hero, her household name used both as a compliment and a derisive put-down. She was a superb athlete in several sports, a medical humanitarian who went public with cancer, a co-founder of a professional women's sports association, and a larger-than-life Texan who wowed the American public with her brassiness, quick quips to the press, and unconventional behavior. She was a character. She was larger than life.

Her name, image, and impact transcended her deeds. She was like Muhammad Ali, whose magnetic presence overshadowed not only his competitors, but his era. Or like Marilyn Monroe, icon immemorial, who used and was abused by concepts of feminine sexuality. Monroe, like Babe, embraced these dichotomous ideals of womanhood for self-promotion. Both suffered and benefited immeasurably from this liaison. These three personalities' timing, deeds, and charisma raised them countless notches above the ordinary. Even above the great. They were ever aware of their power to transform and manipulate others' perceptions of them. They belonged to the rare breed of mythical trickster.

As one historian has noted, tricksters are "unconfined by social categories or real communities. Disorder defines the trickster, but so does power." Babe, the consummate trickster, "continually altered her body, created and recreated a personality. [She was] a creative force at war with convention, beyond gender."[1]

Mythologizing a Life

Babe Didrikson made a fortune out of being unique. She knew how. She tapped the American imagination and manipulated it for all of her forty-five years. Once Babe calculated how she could capitalize upon her athletic talents, personality, entertainment skills, and, fleetingly, even her androgyny, she skillfully parlayed them for every available nickel.

She created a "marketable self" for public consumption. She constantly generated a character, albeit rooted in reality, that kept cameras rolling and pencils sharpened. Her exhibitions of coarse language, thick Texas drawls, bawdy jokes, and knee-slapping antics were merely exaggerations of her own personality. Babe became duplicitous; she scripted both her lived life and her told/created life. Although they are parallel lives neither is complete without the other. The lived life was often tempestuous, isolated, and concealed. The told life was steadfast, harmonious, and laid open for everyone's consumption.

In short, she was a hustler. She essentially joined a troupe of female entertainers—circus acrobats and vaudeville performers—who put on an act and did whatever it took to secure a paying audience. Being unique came naturally to her, and most of the time she took great delight in it. She consciously and unconsciously built personas that kept her in the limelight. She knew when to fine-tune the ones she had and when to adopt new ones. Whatever the public wanted she would give.

For a brief period, Babe exploited the public fascination with Amazonian women. She did it largely unconsciously, though she quickly recognized what worked. Admittedly, she suffered for it, but her alternative was to retire from the public arena entirely and earn far less money than she could as an entertainer. Had she been "ladylike" even her sensational athletic performances at the 1932 Los Angeles Olympic Games could never have been converted into money.[2]

The greatest character constructed by Babe was the happily married, feminine, heterosexual woman. She even further sexualized this image to heighten its convincibility. She flirted, primped, bragged about steamy sexual exploits with her husband, and cautioned young women to follow the dictates of conventional womanhood. That she married George Zaharias, a professional wrestler—apart from using the marriage as a way of legitimizing a new image—was entirely consistent with her role as a performer. For she was much like the wrestlers of the era who relied upon hype and reversed sexual identities as a means of promotion. In the early years of their marriage, Babe felt more comfortable with wrestlers than with society's matronly upper crust.

Straddled across the rump of a "donkey-ball" mule, guffawing, walloping its butt, Babe was at home. It was the kind of stuff that made her kingpin—dreaded and admired—in her Beaumont neighborhood as a kid. But perched delicately on a bleacher coyly exhibiting her silk slip and hosiery to an approving sportswriter she was performing a trick. The image bore little resemblance to the confidant, outspoken, tautly muscled dynamo who posed it. Battered by the press for her boy-girl image, Babe abandoned her androgyny to present herself publicly as "feminine." Intimates reveal little congruence between the at-home Babe—in shorts, no makeup, proudly strutting her athleticism—and the public Babe—softer spoken, counseling conventionality, and primed for the pages of *Good Housekeeping.*

Yet the challenge of Babe is the "slippage" she enjoyed—publicly—between the two personas. Pained as she was by reactions to her androgynous physique and mannerisms, she also encouraged enigmatic perceptions of her. Thus she'd look the lady but crack a scorching one-liner or cut an opponent's concentration with a disorienting stunt. One was the more natural mantle but each was worn with equal enthusiasm. Her autobiography's title, *This Life I've Led,* consciously reflects her separation from herself, her duality. Babe led these two lives and pulled the expedient persona to the foreground as the situation dictated. She was both the Lady and the Tiger.

Thus the meaning of her life for American women, culturally constructed gender identities, sexuality, and American sports is profound. Susan Cahn argued persuasively in "Coming on Strong: Gender and Sexuality in Women's Sport, 1900–1960," "as women competed in a variety of athletic contests, they also participated in a deeper contest over the way gender would be organized and conceptualized in U.S. society." Social class and race relations mediated definitions of individual sports as masculine or feminine and assigned participants appropriate rules, uniforms, and equipment. Babe's youthful sports of basketball, softball, and track and field involved the taboo ingredients of "groups of women playing passionately and intimately together . . . [and] physical contact among women; and they were associated with working-class women whom the dominant culture historically defined as unwomanly. Hence they were deemed mannish and sexually inappropriate and inspired suspicion of lesbianism."[3]

Skill itself retained a masculine connotation, even as more and more women demonstrated athletic prowess. Thus competing philosophies of acceptable sports for women alongside competing concepts of acceptable athletic womanhood emerged. Babe, the premiere manifestation of this debate, "reflexively shaped societal understandings of gender, especially common sense beliefs about natural differences in men's and women's bodies, physical capabilities, activities, emotions, interests and power."[4]

Because Babe and other female athletes "developed 'mannish' bodies, [they] represented the opposite of femininity, which had increasingly become defined as *difference from* and *attractiveness to* men." Despite evidence to the contrary, dominant cultural ideals "linked sport to masculinity and male sexual virility. [Thus] women's sports signalled both gender and sexual deviance. Female athletes were literally unbecoming women: losing their womanhood and falling under sexual suspicion as well." Because of their ambiguous status, they were particularly vulnerable to homophobic attacks when "the familiar notion of the mannish athlete become a cold message about lesbianism." Yet despite these constraints, sports did offer Babe and other female athletes "a cultural arena for negotiating changes in sexuality and gender."[5]

Demythologizing a Life

Babe Didrikson died in 1956 after composing her autobiography while rebounding from a grave illness in 1954. She told a life story that, as one feminist historian studying the craft of biography noted, presented as fact established opinions of the age. She was nostalgic to revive the past and knew well that hers was an extraordinary personality and an eventful life. Babe shared these motivations with many others who choose to record their lives. She revealed no anger toward an often vicious press and public and her self-serving husband. She displayed her powerlessness in her private realm as a badge of achievement and normalcy and minimized her infuriating lack of control over athletic authorities, social class conflicts, heterosocial ideals, and disintegrating health.[6]

Babe told her life narrative in 1954–55, nearly twenty years before the acknowledged watershed in women's autobiography. Like other women who had succeeded in the public realm, at this time Babe was "forbidden . . . anger, together with the open admission of the desire for power and control over one's life (which inevitably means accepting some degree of power and control over other lives)."[7]

Babe wrote an acceptable version of a female athlete's life. It is not, at times, the life she led.

Unlike many women writers, Babe did not begin her autobiography to gain personal insight. Rather, she put it to paper to cement the immortality of the self-image she had labored so hard to create. Here truth overlaps with denial, which obscures deception and self-mockery. She did duplicate one biographical truism, however. She told her life story as a quest, a journey through obstacles leading ever onward and upward. Unlike most women, Babe moved comfortably in the world of daring and achievement throughout her tale. She did not exploit women's rhetoric of uncertainty, but she did (like many women writers) deny suffering.[8]

So to further craft her marketability and memories of her, Babe made a caricature of herself. Armed with lipstick and other feminine accoutrements, she created a smoke screen using flash and humor that bedazzled and distracted her audience from seeking greater truths. She was a consummate storyteller, using impact to outweigh insight. This ability, learned young, she applied liberally throughout her life.

Three lives are being revealed here, then. Babe's as she lived it, hers as she created it and chose to mythologize it, and my interpretation of her sleight of hand. Complex questions arise in the meshing of the three. How much had she internalized her female hustler role? To what extent was it the driving force in her life? Did Babe feel a responsibility to her fans or women's sports to create a larger-than-life, acceptable image? Had she come to believe that the myths and lies she told were actually true? The more often she told stories, and her own life was her favorite story, the more she shaped them according to her audience's cultural context. Was the "feminine" Babe familiar to her, yet uncomfortable like the Sunday clothes that look right, but scratch and chafe and induce fantasies of worn-out sweatshirts? At times it is painful to see how she unearthed contrived stories bathed in appropriateness. Evidence frequently unmasks her refusal to recover the actual memory; in several instances, she created fictitious memories for herself. Thus Babe sacrificed authenticity and avoided disruptive truths in favor of a harmonious, "normal," and consistent life history. Her friends and family, at times, helped her in this facade.

Babe's carefully constructed version of her life was further heroicized by Harry Paxton, who penned her verbal account. He admired her immeasurably and knew her to be dangerously ill and thus chose not to turn over a single psychic stone. The fact that Babe personally didn't put pen to paper, I believe, did not change the content of the book. Introspection was avoided by Babe as staunchly as was defeat; "telling" her story did not significantly alter what she chose to reveal.

Babe's later biographers, William Oscar Johnson and Nancy Williamson, a husband-wife journalist team known for portraits of athletes that appeared in the pages of *Sports Illustrated*, were only moderately successful in *"Whatta-Gal": The Babe Didrikson Story* (1975) at disclosing what she strove so diligently to conceal. In their undocumented but still largely reliable account of her life they lacked both gender consciousness and a solid cultural context.[9]

The Value of Oral Histories

Oral histories, acknowledged by feminist historians as an invaluable tool for exploring the experiences of oppressed or ignored groups, were essential in my study of Didrikson's life. The reasons are many: she built a palatable life story that intentionally blurred the truth; she wrote few letters (only a slim packet of correspondence between a sportswriter friend and her survive); she constantly posed for press cameras and so photographs—potentially rich for what they might reveal—were also staged; and she denied the centrality of her relationship with a woman partner. Given these limitations and falsities, oral histories gathered from family members, sports peers, friends, life partners, casual acquaintances, and medical caretakers became essential to telling her story. The "facts" of her life as she perceived them can be proven or disallowed by cross-checking with these other sources. Undoubtedly, "women's personal narratives are essential primary documents for feminist research." Babe's personal narrative was essential, but others gave voice to the silences she enforced and exacted during her lifetime.[10]

Several of those interviewed at length for this book had not been approached previously. The two Didriksen brothers, Louis and Bubba, went unconsulted during the creation of the 1975 movie *Babe*. They had been interviewed by Babe's sports biographers, but had revealed virtually nothing of her personal life. Nor had their spouses ever been interviewed. Thelma Didriksen, Louis's wife, provided information and insight that revealed Babe's fragilities and frustrations as she confided them only to Thelma. Ron

Didriksen, Louis's son, has assumed the mantle of Babe's legacy and was also helpful.

Other new sources of information are the medical personnel (some of whom were also her personal friends) at the University of Texas Medical Branch at Galveston, where Babe was repeatedly hospitalized, and her medical record during her stays there. Also tapped anew was Florence Chadwick, athlete par excellence, to whom George turned for comfort upon Babe's death. Finally, Sigrid Hill, Babe's childhood friend who lived with the Didriksen family, was eager to resurrect memories not requested before.

Most important, Betty Dodd, Babe's mate of several years, discussed and reflected upon her bond with Babe and the psychodynamics and tensions existing among the two women and George Zaharias as they cohabitated. Dodd had been interviewed many times before, but recognition of her intimate and life-sustaining bond with Babe allowed a richer portrayal of their relationship than earlier "buddy," "sidekick," or "caretaker" versions allowed. Ironically, her death in July 1993 prevents her from reading this account and receiving whatever public response might follow.[11]

Once the center of inquiry became the historical context of women's sports, gender, homophobia, and culturally constructed sex-role expectations, new insights emerged. Betty Hicks, golf peer and author, for example, offered new interpretations of old events. The same is so for Gene Sarazen, who reminisced about his 1935 golf exhibition tour with Didrikson.

Significantly, the death of George Zaharias in 1986 (before this project was far enough along to allow an interview with him) further expedited new tellings of old tales. Many interviewees volunteered that his death had freed them from a sense of loyalty to portray the Zaharias marriage as he had always done so—idyllically. Bertha Bowen of Dallas, Babe's surrogate mother and life-long friend, and Dodd repeatedly noted their increased comfort with being more revealing, knowing George could not be upset or turn on them in anger.

All of these narratives provided more factual material than was already known. They helped corroborate or contradict the facts of Babe's life as she told them. And yet these accounts at times echoed the legend alongside the life. As rewarding as oral histories are, they are also limited, for the speakers, too, choose to create a representation of the subject's life that is in keeping with their own set of truths or silences. Babe was the charismatic, willful, and at times bullying leader of many in her life. The unwillingness of those interviewed to reveal and portray her flaws and inclinations may be due to their loyalty to her self-crafted image. Their own desire to portray harmony, "normalcy," or clarity of vision may also obscure her travails and dilemmas. This necessitates constant "filtering" on the biographer's part. The legend-building aspects of oral histories need to be constantly weighed and analyzed for continuities, choices, pain, silences, voices, and the articulation of legitimate identity.[12]

This writing of Babe's life history is, first and foremost, grounded in feminist theory, because I have focused on society's view of gender during her time and the role of gender in her life. As several scholars have noted, "whether she has accepted the norms or defied them, a woman's life can never be written taking gender for granted."[13] I have discussed the "unthinkable" in her life: the causes of her anger and powerlessness, her lack of control, and the startling possibility that for several years she did not make a man the center of her life. "The constraints of acceptable discussion" have been transcended. Through understanding the silences she chose and the voices she allowed herself, we can understand the processes of cultural domination and social construction as they worked against her articulating and building a personal identity.[14]

To the extent that Babe remains an enigma, she would no doubt be pleased. That the revelation of her frailties and fears would anger her, I have no doubt. That her legacy is strong enough to survive anything that a pen can create, I also have no doubt.

Women's Place in Sports Competition: An Ambivalent Cultural Legacy

What helped force Didrikson into some of her silences was women's place in sports. As she rose to prominence in the 1930s, debate and controversy continued to surround women's sports and their participants at both the organizational and personal level. Women athletes' physiological limits and culturally constructed notions of "appropriate" sports dominated dialogue, rules, organizational hierarchy, and the thoughts of women athletes.

In 1922, the Amateur Athletic Union (AAU) took control of women's competitive sports in the United States and allowed white women to enter track meets at local, regional, and national levels. Although some of the local AAU membership had to be forced to include women, membership still expanded during the following five years. In 1923 amateur play for women came under the direction of the Women's Division of the National Amateur Athletic Federation (WDNAAF). Formed in 1922 by representatives from the National Collegiate Athletic Association, U.S. Lawn Tennis Association, and Girl Scouts and Boy Scouts of America, the WDNAAF had a major effect on girls' and women's amateur sports. The umbrella group's inspiration stemmed from the poor physical condition of young people at this time, which was discovered during the draft for World War I. Lou Henry Hoover, a spearhead in the movement and the wife of the president, decided that to improve their physical condition, both men and women should be allowed to participate in sports but in separate activities with different goals. Underlying her plan was the premise "that all girls and women should have the opportunity to engage in sports, but that no girl or woman should be singled out to receive special attention or training."[15]

Female physical educators involved in the WDNAAF agreed that women should participate in sports and also opposed championship competition for women; this approach was carried over into the high schools and colleges as well. Competition, they believed, was exploitation. They protested "that women were being pushed beyond themselves physically and emotionally to satisfy crowds." The damages that would follow this unnatural strain were gruesome to consider. Sure to follow were "nervous instability, premature pelvic ossification, narrowed vaginas, difficult deliveries, heart strain, and spinsterhood." These, they intoned, were "the high prices women would pay for being serious contenders."[16]

Thus the WDNAAF wanted to develop women's participation in sports, but consistently strived to "protect" women from competition.[17] The WDNAAF's conservative policies, begun in 1923, were a direct result of Hoover's investigative committee, which recommended an end to competitive team sports for girls, playing before crowds, and scheduling girls' games as part of doubleheaders with boys' games. These practices, she claimed, jeopardized young women's reproductive health and modest demeanor and should be "stopped in the name of decency." After this ban, women's high school and intercollegiate sports became tame and uncompetitive affairs, degenerating into "playdays" and "sportsdays" devoid of the excitement of fiercely fought competitive sports.[18]

This move to suppress competitive sports for women in the 1920s grew out of a long-standing opposition to the well-organized sports teams available to collegiate women since the 1890s in track, basketball, archery, baseball, volleyball, field hockey, rowing, bowling, swimming, exercise, and golf. In colleges, physical activity had long been recognized by many for its positive contribution to the physical well-being of the (supposedly) fragile woman. The pro-women's sports arguments of the 1920s sounded strikingly similar to those given in the 1870s that argued in favor of sports for middle-class girls.[19]

In fact, one women's sports historian has argued that three distinct approaches governed the three principal sports organizations of this period. The WDNAAF, a female-run organization, was opposed to competitive individualism for middle-class girls and young women. Members believed it would harm their nervous systems, encourage rowdiness, and lead to injury and exploitation. Jumping events in particular were thought to injure the pelvic organs. These physical educators believed that although girls should never compete with boys or pursue individual fulfillment, through playdays and statistical comparisons after the meets, women trained "through physical education would be ready to perform their social duties." The AAU, unlike the WDNAAF, endorsed and promoted competitive amateurism for women.[20]

At the other extreme of sports philosophies were the industrial sports leagues, which were highly competitive, offered monetary rewards, and promoted individual stars. These leagues relied on male ex-athletes as coaches and referees and stressed winning. The industrial leagues grew out of the ideology of welfare capitalism, which approached labor relations paternalistically. By offering extras such as sports programs, picnics, and paid holidays, owners hoped to induce loyalty and productivity in their workers. The services and amenities they provided were a direct attempt to thwart union activism and labor radicalism. The sports leagues helped companies' images, which were important factors in determining the outcomes of strikes or labor disruptions. The programs also boosted worker morale, fostered a cooperative spirit amongst workers, and promoted efficiency and harmony within the workplace. Sports relieved the monotony of work and lessened accidents, they argued. As one historian commented, "In the 1920s, American welfare capitalism appears to have been a curious combination of profit-seeking and humanistic concerns."[21]

Social Class and Women's Sports

Had Babe, born to a working-class, East Texan, Norwegian family, not consciously tried to transcend her social class and region, she would have gone untouched by middle-class Anglo norms of behavior. But in her view, her ascendant popularity necessitated the adoption of both middle-class behavioral norms and gender ideals.

In the mid- to late 1800s, while exercise for boys was gaining acceptance, middle- and upper-class girls of European descent were barred from it. Their exclusion was based on two rationales. First, medical experts echoed and promulgated societal beliefs that physical exertion would damage the girls' ability to bear healthy children. Second, popularly held cultural norms proscribed "unladylike" behavior, including robust exercise and sports, as immodest. These notions of modesty and frailty were class-based ideologies. The physical toil of immigrant working-class and black slave women was given little thought, while the slight exertion of upper- and middle-class women was considered jeopardizing to their health and their morals. Between 1880 and 1910 a dramatic shift occurred: "Women changed . . . from the 'swooning damsel' to the swimming, bicycling, healthy modern sportswoman." In fact, women did not change, but ideals of womanhood did.[22]

When the first generation of college women began its schooling, there was serious concern that either too-intense study or too-intense exercise would impair the young women's child-bearing abilities and have deleterious effects on their sexuality. Required physical education and health classes were one way the first women's colleges responded to the debate and made it acceptable for women to attend college at all. As early as 1862 Vassar College included academic instruction in anatomy, hygiene, and physiology as part of the curriculum. Similarly, Smith College required lectures in physiology and hygiene and regular exercise classes under the direction of an educated "lady physician." By the 1880s college women appeared to be thriving under this regime. By the 1890s most women's schools increased their efforts toward physical education to include gyms and special sports programs.[23]

By the 1890s women themselves were showing they preferred organized sports over anatomy lessons and unstructured exercise. Women's physical education programs reflected these changes; in 1891 basketball was introduced. It was followed in 1893 with volleyball and in 1897 with field hockey. By 1900, competitive sports instruction was an integral part of many physical education programs (versus emphasis on health and beauty), and women joined team sports in unprecedented numbers.[24]

In the 1890s bicycling became a national craze as middle- and upper-class girls moved out of the parlor and into the sunshine. Yet even this necessitated cautions. An 1896 advertisement in *Ladies Home Journal* for "The Duplex Safety Saddle" reassured prospective buyers that there would be "no pressure on sensitive parts of the body. . . . Endorsed by Physicians as the ideal saddle for women. It is broad and short; easy to mount and dismount." Later, bloomers, pantaloons first introduced at midcentury by ardent health reformers, gained quick popularity. These "bifurcated skirts" allowed greater freedom of movement and facilitated a dramatic overhaul of women's clothing. Aided by the new ideal of the "sporty, companionate wife" and less cumbersome clothing, women with some leisure time and varying amounts of money participated in golf, tennis, skeet shooting, ice skating, basketball, and running by the thousands.[25]

After this, unprecedented opportunities opened up for women in sports, but they still met with obstacles. The modern Olympic Games were over-whelmingly hostile toward female athletes. When reestablishing the games, Pierre de Coubertin, president of the International Olympic Committee (IOC), proclaimed them "the solemn and periodic exaltation of male ath-leticism with internationalism as a base, loyalty as a means, art for its set-ting and female applause a reward." Coubertin, no friend to female athletes, once called women's sports "against the laws of nature."[26]

Yet women desired to compete. Women made unofficial appearances in several sports at the 1900 and 1904 Olympiads, and their participation was retroactively rewarded with partial legitimacy. Thus unofficial gold medals were won by women in golf, archery, and tennis. Yet following the 1904 games, both golf and tennis were closed to women. James E. Sullivan, chair of the United States Olympic Committee (USOC) and executive secretary of the AAU, opposed women competitors. He barred women swimmers from registering with the AAU. Without that official sanction, they could not compete in the Olympics. The IOC voted on women's participation, and while the decisions were never publicized, only Coubertin of France and Sullivan of the United States voted against allowing women to compete.[27]

Grim opportunities persisted. In 1908, only tennis, archery, and figure skating were open to women, and three exhibition events, swimming, div-ing, and gymnastics, were added. All of these were considered "ladylike ac-tivities and aesthetically pleasing." Hence, the British Olympic Committee said in 1908 that the women "gave most attractive displays" at the London games that year.[28]

Social class and ethnic biases produced great resistance to women track and field athletes and their competitions. After the IOC voted against includ-ing women's track and field at the 1920 games, the Federation Sportive Fem-inine Internationale (FSFI) was formed to organize an international wom-en's track and field contest. In 1922 the first meet, dubbed "The First Women's Olympic Games," was held in Paris. Women athletes from seven countries, U.S. track and field competitors among them, attended the Paris games. This move to hold an independent women's games reflected years of frustration. Yet ongoing friction between the FSFI and ruling bodies in U.S. sports disadvantaged U.S. athletes. Babe and sprinter Stella Walsh, for example, had their pre-Olympic world track records rejected by the FSFI because they were not made at Olympic distances.[29]

As the FSFI gained power, more private men's sporting clubs began to include women's competitions. Thus the International Amateur Athletic Federation (IAAF), track's ruling body, considered sanctioning women's sports. In 1926 the FSFI agreed to give up its control over women's sports in exchange for a recommendation by the IAAF to the IOC to include women's events in the next Olympiad.[30]

In spite of their regular competition in fifteen events, the IAAF recommended to the IOC that women compete in only five track and field events. Thus, five women participated in five events at the 1928 games in Amsterdam despite objections from Coubertin and Pope Pius IX. World records were set, but when two poorly trained contestants collapsed at the finish line of the 800-meter race, the IOC instantly banned women from this "distance" event. They called it "hazardous to a lady's health." The ruling held for thirty-two years.[31]

In 1929 the WDNAAF proclaimed its disapproval of women's participation in Olympic competition. Female physical educators also spoke out against this "new" level of competition. Despite this, American women competed in the 1932 Olympics in track and field in seven events, but by a special rule, each woman could compete in no more than three events.[32]

Because women's events were not well represented in the Olympics, the FSFI continued its Women's World Games until 1936. When the FSFI disbanded that year, only six Olympic sports were open to women: track and field, swimming, fencing, gymnastics, yachting, and figure skating. Ironically, field hockey and basketball, two of the most popular team sports for women, were denied entry longer than any other team sport because they were deemed inappropriate and unfeminine. Although men's field hockey was admitted in 1908, women's field hockey wasn't sanctioned until 1984; women's basketball did not gain entry until 1976. Clearly team sports were seen as undesirable for women as were the individual "unfeminine" sports. Team sports, it was believed, fostered "perverse competitiveness." However, through dogged determination, women gradually entered Olympic competition. They struggled "against the views of the sports establishments, public opinion, the biases of sports reporters, and the personal conditioning which demanded conformity to existing social models of femininity."[33]

Other developments also strengthened women's sports. *Sportswoman*, a monthly magazine published at Bryn Mawr and devoted to upper middle-class college and club women who loved sports, flourished from 1925 to 1936. It endorsed non-profit, medically supervised competition played by less competitive and more restrictive rules. It preferred intramurals or schooldays over championship play, downplayed Olympic coverage, was opposed to professionalism and scholastic "semiprofessionalism," and spoke out against "spectator-oriented basketball programs and tournaments." Well-crafted articles penned by athletes, physical educators, and officials— replete with photographs of technical fine points and competitive events— focused on lacrosse, field hockey, swimming, skating, and track and field. The magazine served as the prime communicative mechanism for burgeoning women's sports organizations and enthusiasts.[34]

Women's sports also benefited from a positive, albeit qualified, shift in cultural opinion demonstrated in contemporary magazines and newspapers. A 1923 writer in *Ladies Home Journal* insisted that "physiological necessity . . . decidedly stands in the way of [women's] unrestricted physical achievement." Menstruating women were impaired, so women's teams needed more members at all times. Yet, in the same article the "ideal girl" in 1927 was described as "'one who is active, graceful, skillful in at least one sport, but at the same time a girl who is mentally alert and socially attractive, who does not make her athletic ability her chief hobby.'"[35]

The subject was suddenly open for wider discussion. Articles were written about women's skills in the "manly" sports. "Finding there was nothing that 'unsexed' them in these sports," a 1914 *New York Times* article noted, women who had participated in sports secretly "now indulged in [them] openly and under the direction of brothers, sweethearts and even professional trainers." In this atmosphere "the spirit of success in competition has been fully aroused." In 1922 Walter Camp reviewed women's sports for the *Woman's Home Companion* and noted their "positive physical and psychological advantages." Camp argued that girls and women ought to increase their involvement in sports since their household duties had lightened. He claimed that the emotion women had formerly expended as energy in housework could find expression in sports. Some experts even took a progressive stance. Dr. Celia Duel Mosher compared the body strength of men and women and concluded that there were no innate sex differences. What differences did exist between these gender-mixed, physically active people "resulted from cultural limitations, such as restrictive clothing, poor eating habits, and inadequate training."[36]

Other experts and lay commentators clashed over the right and safe way for girls to exercise and compete. In 1926 one writer presented the views espoused by physical education teachers at a recent conference, "most of whom were women who disapproved of interschool competition." These included Payson Smith, Massachusetts state commissioner of education, Elizabeth Quinlan of Boston Teacher's College, and Florence Sommers, assistant state supervisor of physical education. Their opposition, the author noted, was invariably based on the "bad physiological and emotional effects" arguments. The girls' basketball leagues came under particular attack from the physical educators. Quinlan invoked stories of "girls, egged on by the taunts of the howling, cheering crowds in gymnasiums, losing their temper and swearing at the opponents. . . . The girls [were] imbued with a fanatic enthusiasm . . . [and] a 'win-at-any-cost' spirit." In this atmosphere, Quinlan warned, they would fail "to gain any of the recreational benefits from the game." The results could be quite horrid, she intoned. She knew of "girls fainting during and after the games and emotionally upset for days afterward." The author of the article rejected these views and decried the limitations they imposed on women: "The movement now on foot to restrict and abolish, or denature sport for girls is a part of the enslavement from which women have suffered through the ages." Ultimately, the author predicted, this blunted approach to women's sports would fail, although "it may gain sufficient present vogue to cheat a generation of girls of the contact with the world which is their right."[37]

Overt opposition came from anticipated sources. Medical experts, among them Dr. Frederick Rand Rogers of the New York State Education Department, gave ironclad "scientific proof" that women should not compete in sports due to physical differences. "Olympics for Girls?" (1929) decried the "costs in terms of impaired health, physical beauty, and social attractiveness" for women competitors. Discrediting those who disagreed with him, Rogers said, "It is almost futile to argue this point with either feminists, many of whom violate nature themselves," or with psychologists, whose techniques are "too crude to discover emotional and mental sex differences." Similarly, a widely circulated article argued that women were naturally less competitive, less strong, had less rapid muscle reflexes, and less endurance. The author concluded that a woman's greater development of her abdominal organs suited her for motherhood, not athletics, and "she justly belongs to the weaker sex." Her greatest power lay in her tears. An unlikely critic was Dr. Margaret Mead, herself a professional woman living a nontraditional life. Mead's studies showed that games and sports sometimes served as direct substitutes for childrearing and hence were of dubious value, perhaps even of disservice to women. Negative opinions like this, voiced as they were by women who were experts on women, had an adverse effect on public opinion and women who wanted to compete.[38]

The posture assumed by women's sports organizations created and reflected this ambivalence. The WDNAAF opposed all fiercely competitive sports "on the grounds that they tend to encourage spectatorism instead of participation, and that they produce 'experts' instead of inviting all to play." It formulated "women's rules" in an attempt to "eradicate physical danger and untoward behavior" including physical intimacy, which may have reflected a growing concern with lesbianism within sports. Specifically, women's range of movement was limited through strictly demarcated zones of play; trespass over your shortened area of play meant a foul. Struggles over ball possession were also highly regulated and fouls resulted from vocal exchanges. Women needed exercise and enjoyment from sport, not grueling challenge and physical and emotional exhaustion, the WDNAAF argued successfully. Despite the steady rise in competitive team sports for college women in basketball, track and field, and field hockey between 1892 and 1901, by 1930 the number of colleges sponsoring varsity competition for women dropped from 22 percent to 12 percent of the total.[39]

The WDNAAF suffered because of this cultural ambivalence toward sports. Although it had 444 organizational members in 1932 and women controlled nearly all the decision-making positions, it had "minimal prestige" and power. Similarly, the United States Field Hockey Association and Women's International Bowling Congress carried little weight in the sports world, and in the AAU women were removed from power in committees governing women's sports. Although they arguably gained ground with the public at large, women athletes and their female overseers did not gain ground or status with their male peers.[40]

The Rise of the Female Sports Hero

Although individual competition for women was suspect, some athletes, depending on their sports and appearance, could garner accolades and a warm public reception. Thus, despite efforts to limit the growth of women's sports, female sports heroes emerged in the 1920s. Several superstars preceded Didrikson. Sonja Henie won gold medals in figure skating at three consecutive Olympics beginning in 1928. Her grace and curvaceous feminine demeanor, according to one historian, "transformed the sport with her dancelike movements." She also enjoyed a successful career in Hollywood feature films.[41]

Greater investment in women's sports by individuals, cities, and corporations gave immigrant and working-class women greater opportunities to participate. Because working-class and immigrant women could not afford to finance their own careers before this time, this was the first opportunity for many athletes from these groups to train and compete. "Ethnic women—immigrants and the daughters of immigrants—figured prominently in this group." A study of these women and their public images, accomplishments, socioeconomic status, and money-making capabilities revealed that "traditional moral standards seem to have mattered more in the public image of female athletes than of male athletes." As the historian Susan Cahn pointed out, by participating these athletes "articulated competing philosophies of sport and competing concepts of athletic womanhood." Faced with the contrast between the ideal woman and the ideal athlete, journalists and promoters bowed to these "traditional moral standards" by first and foremost explicating women athletes' femininity even while touting their athletic ability. As a result, athletic excellence and muscular bodies remained profoundly masculine domains while women were required to remain profoundly feminine or face the consequences. Thus "media campaigns and organizational policies worked to suppress lesbianism and to marginalize athletes who didn't conform to dominant standards of femininity."[42]

Conversely, after 1945 historians of male athletes began arguing that nonconformity, identified by entertainment value, personality, and packaging, fueled the value of individual male athletes as commodities. "Gorgeous George" Wagner, a wrestler in the 1940s, went so far as to bend gender dictates in the ring. Lavishly clothed in satin, silks, and an ermine jockstrap, his "pseudo-pswish" was denounced by sports reporters but his masculinity was not questioned. He did owe "part of his success to America's fascination with homosexuality." His image, replete with permed hair held by gold-plated and sequined Georgie pins, discredited wrestling but not his gender identity; because he was a man he personified athletic masculinity. Similarly, "Babe Ruth, despite his sexual exploits and problems with syphilis, suffered no apparent loss of public respect."[43]

As the outstanding female athletes' individual athletic achievements were hailed as victories for all women, they simultaneously challenged gender boundaries. They stilled naysayers who scorned women's ability to conquer physical tests and contradicted notions of women's membership in the "weaker sex." In short, they helped redefine womanhood, femininity, and female capabilities. They introduced and embodied critiques of appropriate behavior, appearance, and female nature. As one historian argued, "Their physical prowess challenged standard notions of feminine capacities. They, more than any other group of women, carried on the struggle for recognition and respect in an historical period that held out the promise of greater equality between the sexes." They also proved that top-notch women athletes had few money-making opportunities in their sports once they turned professional. Star male athletes, conversely, "could make a comfortable living from their skills for a long period of their adult lives."[44]

Despite these limitations, several women athletes garnered loyal followings. Helen Wills's tennis play was covered throughout the 1920s in the *New York Times*. She also penned stories for the *Saturday Evening Post* and *Ladies Home Journal*. Her fashionable appearance and trend setting earned her the nickname "Queen Helen." Not economically dependent on her sport, Wills was not hounded by earning a living through it. Glenna Collett was often described as an "amazing" golfer and one of the "Golden People in the Golden Decade of Sport." Gertrude Ederle also shared celebrity superstar status with the others. In August 1926 she became the first American woman to swim the English Channel. After her channel swim, her image changed to that of a "modern and fashionable flapper" and a modern consumer. Most notable and adored was Amelia Earhart. She was the first woman to fly the Atlantic alone, the first person to make the crossing by air more than once, and the first pilot to solo from Honolulu to the American mainland. Earhart rivaled Babe for headlines until her disappearance in March 1937.[45]

In the mid- and late twenties Babe had three predecessors in track and field who claimed headlines and the lion's share of stardom: Lillian Copeland, Jean Shiley, and Stella Walsh. In a May 1932 *Collier's* article focusing on upcoming Olympic track and field hopefuls, Walsh took center stage, there was some attention paid to Betty Robinson (1928 Olympic gold medalist in the 100 meters), but there was no mention of Babe. Babe competed against Shiley and Walsh, who increased their own fame by beating her. Walsh, considered by many the best track athlete ever, won thirty-five national titles in sprints, broad jump, discus, and baseball throw. Rumors still abound that Walsh was later "found out to be a man." If she was indeed a genetic male, it would make Babe's defeat of her all the more phenomenal. While these three lacked nothing in talent, they did not, ultimately, approximate Babe's press coverage, charisma, or popularity. Babe's fame dwarfed them all.[46]

Women's Place in Sports Competition

During this time the social classes had differing perspectives on the respectability of women and sports. Upper-class women "found an escape from the ennui, the convention, and the confinement of life in the leisure class." Their social and economic status shielded them from ridicule. Middle-class women in college, meanwhile, legitimized physical education and eventually sports competition because both protected them from physical deterioration during study. Working-class female athletes were judged by a more lenient set of standards although they too had clearly demarcated lines they were not to transgress.[47]

All of these athletic women were stigmatized by male physicians who defined them as "inverts," then the medical term for lesbians. The inverts expressed, "if not verbally, then through their actions, a strong dissatisfaction with traditional definitions of feminine social roles. In the eyes of male doctors, this social deviance inevitably led to sexual deviance."[48] Physical traits, including muscularity, small breasts and hips, short hair, coarse facial features, occasionally noticeable facial hair, a low voice, and a masculine confidence and energy in movements were all "indications" of lesbianism. A study of Babe Didrikson gives us further insight into these cultural frictions. Working-class, ethnic, southern, and masculinist, her presence exacerbated these charges of abnormality. Neither Babe nor her cultural context could risk expanding a definition of womanhood to include the alternatives presented by her. Rather, she became the personification of all that was to be feared.

Indeed, Babe's emergence on the local and national scenes during her adolescence occurred in an era generally cautious, and at times hostile, to women's athleticism. Adolescent girls, it was believed in the twenties and thirties, were entering a period of critical psychological development. Their "heterosexual adjustment" entailed prioritizing being attractive to men, protecting themselves from men when necessary, and abandoning "male" achievements such as "schoolwork, athletic competition, and rough play." These girls, experts claimed, ought to be training for heterosexual relations and popularity, not competing in sports.[49]

The middle-class ideals to which Babe ultimately aspired conflicted with gender roles in Babe's Norwegian, working-class, Texan subculture, where tomboyishness was still widely accepted at least until one reached adolescence. When her accomplishments became national news, she found herself deemed inappropriate by ideals different from her own region's and ethnic group's norms. To complicate matters, even her own culture viewed her as extreme. Although many working-class adolescent girls confronted enforced obedience and conformity imposed by parents and cultural dictates by participating in sports, the types of sports Babe pursued were deemed especially problematic because they were unfeminine. Running, jumping, and throwing did not compare favorably with sports that emphasized grace and feminine attire, such as swimming, tennis, and golf. Peggy Kirk Bell, an outstanding golfer and peer of Babe's learned this distinction. Speaking of choices for women in that era, and the acceptability of certain sports over others, she said, "Sports were not in yet. . . . Girls in sports were tomboys and a little weird they thought. Women were supposed to stay home and cook. . . . A woman did nothing but teach school, [be a] nurse or a secretary. . . . Women were housekeepers. My father wouldn't allow me to work." Her sports efforts were curtailed and patterned because of these beliefs: "When I got into golf he financed it all because he thought it was respectable. I wanted to go play softball and he said girls don't do that."[50]

To further complicate matters, Babe excelled at the shot put, the javelin, and the high jump, sports that many physicians and educators "believed interfered with successful pregnancy . . . by supposedly making the chest inflexible." Culturally constructed ideals of womanhood dictated mothering and childrearing as the goals of every "normal" woman. Pursuit of athletics revealed both deviant goals and deviant "use" of the female body. Further, competition and personal goals were also deemed inappropriate and foreign objectives for girls and women. Thus, the woman athlete was often viewed as psychologically and physiologically abnormal.[51]

Two groups of experts wrote on tomboyish athletic behavior in the early decades of the twentieth-century: those schooled in physical fitness, and those in behavioral sciences. Generally, both sets of experts cautioned against sports for girls.[52]

Amram Scheinfeld's *Men and Women* (1943) came closest to typifying ideals during the 1930s. Women "were clearly inferior to men in all physical regards, such as strength and endurance." He echoed the views of medical experts when he counseled against athletic competition lest it impair women's ability to bear children. As one historian characterized Scheinfeld's views: "Female athletic excellence was possible, but only if the woman risked being considered a freak." Behavioral scientists who focused on tomboyism linked it to lesbianism. Some experts said tomboyism endangered the girls' erotic development; one claimed tomboyism was "rare" in heterosexual female development. Despite later research demonstrating that tomboyism was a completely functional behavior, the die had been cast: tomboys, the experts agreed, inhabited a grey area that was not quite female, not quite normal.[53]

A convincing case has recently been made that prior to the 1930s, the mannish female athlete, rather than suffering the social stigma of lesbianism, often had to endure the stigma of associations with prostitution, aggressive heterosexuality, and reproductive malfunction. This heterosexual deviance also entailed her "seeming sexual inaccessibility to men. The frequent use of the term 'Amazon' in pejorative labelling of female athletes in this period suggests not only fear of strong and aggressive heterosexual women, but also a fear that the female athlete's sexuality might be inaccessible to men: autonomous, autoerotic or even nonexistent, and therefore not subject to change."[54]

In this cultural context Babe's childish tomboyishness earned her unique status among her peers. She experienced admiration, ridicule, and self-imposed ostracism because she was an extreme example of tomboyishness even within her own group. As a young girl, she'd learned the tag of tomboy could wound; as a young woman it was a label she tried to flee. Recalling sportswriters' near-obsession with her tomboyishness and gender-crossing, she said, "Their idea is that I used to be all tomboy, with none of the usual girls' interests, and then all of a sudden I switched over to being feminine. Well, with almost any woman athlete, you seem to get that tomboy talk." Babe was also aware that the type of sport a woman played affected her perceived femininity and gender identity. That tomboy talk "happens especially with girls who play things that aren't generally considered women's sports, like basketball and baseball, the way I did." The stigma associated with participating in track, basketball, and baseball for girls and women in particular rang with social class and racial biases. As non-elite sports requiring little special equipment or facilities, they were mainly pursued by working-class and ethnic and minority women and shunned by the Anglo middle class.[55]

The Emergence of Sports Media amidst Consumer Culture

Babe, the hustler, knew where the power lay. She was savvy enough to know that the press could—and must—be manipulated to her benefit. As Bubba recalled, "They called her a sports writer's dream because she always had time for them. . . . She never rejected anyone who wanted to interview her. She was wise. She knew that they could make her or break her. . . . She knew that, and she liked it."[56] What she liked most was the opportunity to promote herself to reporters who would then magnify her to the nation.

Babe's self-aggrandizement was patterned, in part, on the press's own tactics. One chronicler noted that "nowhere in America was there a sport page that simply told what happened; all dealt in the purplest hyperbole and glorification of athletes." Newspapers, sports journalists noted, "printed a daily paean to this super race of sportsmen. . . . The dispensing of on-the-spot immortality was common, and most sportswriters engaged in the constant building and gilding of supermyths."[57]

It is true that reporters in this era helped create larger-than-life characters. Babe's ascendancy coincided with a burgeoning of various media (radio, movies, improved newspapers, special sporting sheets, telegraphs, telephones) that fueled public interest in sports. By the 1920s sports pages were a standard feature in all major daily newspapers. Increasingly, they appealed to "many Americans (especially men) [who] turned first to the sports pages where they found clear-cut triumphs and defeats, continuity, and orderliness."[58]

A new generation of sportswriters emerged who waxed effusive about society's heroes. Some "converted the sporting experience into poetry; only poetry, they believed, could reduce the wonders of sports to human comprehension." Grantland Rice, Babe's ally and friend, was the best of this genre. He literally wrote poetic verse singing the praises of athletes and inspiring competitions. By the 1920s, Rice's popularity notwithstanding, sportswriters reconceptualized their trade as constructing interpretive narratives of events. They used colorful verbiage, showered athletes with nicknames, and indulged in dramatic prose. Best known in this new school were men who dramatically affected Babe's life and fortunes, including Paul Gallico, Damon Runyon, Ring Lardner, and Westbrook Pegler. Radio brought sports fans in intimate contact with competition, and radio announcers, like sportswriters, became personalities in their own right.[59]

The explosion of sports media coincided with the emergence of modern consumer culture from 1890 to 1920. Improvements in transportation, in-home conveniences, and places of amusement offered an alternative set of aspirations to that of "work, thrift, or self-restraint." Self-indulgence, play for play's sake, escapist amusements, and less rigid social mores fueled the popularity of amusement parks, dance halls, sporting events, saloons (for men), vaudeville, circuses, carnivals, and movie theaters.[60] Leisure pursuits varied by social class in rowdiness and freedom of expression. Sports in pre–World War II America "was a pastime, diversion, leisure, recreation, play-fun. In sports people found relief from the real things of the world and their own lives—wars, unemployment, social conflict, politics, religion, work, and family." Fueled by television, mass culture, wrestling, boxing, and roller derby reached greater numbers of viewers than ever before. "For a decade, boxing was the most popular show on television."[61]

Thus Babe's fame and ensuing press scrutiny developed while vibrant sports media personalities were forging their own identities within a consumer culture. Her relationship with these cultural interpreters was symbiotic, problematic, yet ultimately self-serving. The athlete needed the scribe as much as the scribe needed the athlete. In Babe's case, however, it was often not a harmonious bond.

The press and "historians" crafted an image of Babe replete with hyperbole. For example, one chronicler claimed that when Babe began working for Employers Casualty, she "reportedly sold ten insurance polices her first day." A nifty feat for a secretary who had nothing to do with sales. And in another newspaper article one of Babe's "legitimate" accomplishments was typing "86 words per minute." Babe, in *This Life I've Led*, chuckled when recalling the coverage of her collecting Olympic souvenirs: "A story got in the paper that the 'wonder girl' had been climbing up eight-story buildings to get herself some Olympic flags."[62]

Yet, Babe was at all times the other hand sculpting the form. She co-created myths of her own difference. She *liked* to shock people; deviance was transformed into defiance. Both resulted in dollars. A New York reporter once said to Babe, "I'm told you also swim, shoot, ride, row, box, and play tennis, golf, basketball, football, polo and billiards. Is there anything at all you don't play?" "Yeah," the Texas Babe replied, "dolls." In another interview she told Frank G. Menke with the *Dallas Daily Times Herald* that any qualms about competing against boys and men were stilled because "I figured no matter how tough they were they couldn't be any more so than my brother Louis when he began pumping leather into my face and body." Oh sure, he dropped her a few times during these slug fests but she bounced up and "we would be at it again." But this daring nonconformity in the early 1930s cost Babe dearly.[63]

Unfortunately, Babe believed the press was her ally. In her era this was usually a correct assumption because sportswriters shielded athletes' indiscretions, shortcomings, and personal lives from public knowledge. Heavy drinking, marital infidelity, sexual preferences, temper tantrums, foul language, and interracial relationships were considered personal matters beyond public scrutiny. This makes these sportswriter's innuendos about Babe's physique—and jabs taken against her manners—all the more surprising. Possibly "indiscretions" by male athletes were still considered normal. Yet because Babe's behavior broke all molds, she lost that layer of protection. She persisted in portraying and even believing in their allegiance, despite their cruel scrutiny that tormented her. This view only strengthened as the years went by. Thus she often played to the press, putting on a certain outfit for a photo, dancing an impromptu jig, or hurdling a wall on the way back into the golf clubhouse. "The reporters and photographers always have been about the best friends I've got," she said. Other athletes complained about the press, but "not me. When those boys want a story, I know they're working on a job, and if I can make their job easier for them, I'm going to do it." Twenty-five years as a columnist's subject spurred Babe to make just one proviso: "If it's a nice story, and a clean story, then I'm going to help them all I can." In 1930–32, the "nice, clean" stories had an ugly counterpart.[64]

Ideals of Womanhood

In addition to pursuing "inappropriate" sports, Babe was also limited by her appearance and style. The criticisms and innuendos were relentless. She was deemed unfeminine and worse—freakish. Babe realized that further success depended upon rejecting working-class norms, ethnic norms, and boy-girl behaviors and recasting herself to conform to acceptable middle-class notions of femininity. She was caught in the midst of conflicting and rapidly changing notions of ideal womanhood. Between 1915 and 1930, catastrophic worldwide events and broad cultural shifts led to growing participation by women in the economy and politics, yet the dominant ideology asked them to remain housewives.

In these decades, the ideal of female beauty underwent major changes. In the twenties and thirties, "a youthful appearance became fashionable for the American woman—and an 'athletic' image, or at least one of fitness and health . . . which made action itself a sort of fashion." Women's fashions changed to reflect this ideal. In fact one historian claims there was a "strong public acceptance of women sports figures [and] the most prominent women in the United States in the 1920s and 1930s were sportswomen." On the one hand health and physical fitness were to be used to increase one's heterosexual attractiveness. Overdevelopment of female physicality and psychological competitiveness, on the other hand, rendered a woman heterosexually inaccessible. The degree to which a woman approximated male norms and appearance determined her unacceptability. "Sporty-compassionate" women were tolerated and even praised while masculinist women were rejected and ridiculed. The degree—really the fierceness—of an athlete's pursuit deemed her "ideal" or "freakish."[65]

Concurrently, the modern commercial beauty culture developed, replete with the Rubinstein, Revlon, and Arden cosmetic empires and the first Miss America pageant. For women athletes this meant facing the contradiction between developing the body in what was seen as an unfeminine fashion and adorning the body like a "real" woman. If she was shapely but not muscular, sporting but not overly competitive, heterosexual and participating in a "beautiful" sport—then and only then did she fulfill the ideal.[66]

Female athletes, naturally, were affected by these contradictions. They either adopted an apologetic attitude, offering "proofs" of their femininity, or they struggled with their identities as the criticisms and innuendos were sure to follow. Thus, one researcher commented, "many girls and women who participate in sports lack complete and uninhibited joy in their competitive and play experiences because of the conflict it creates between their need to play and their concept of themselves as girls and women." As a girl and a young woman, Babe straddled and at times intentionally crossed over into Amazonian territory.[67]

As Amazon, as athlete, as tomboy, as hustler, Babe constructed, molded, and amplified her identity. At war with the media, with culture, and ultimately with herself, Babe struggled with her image, trying always to stay in the limelight and in people's hearts. Her life stories, those she created and those others created for her, reflect the intersections of women's sports, public scrutiny, sex-role and heterosexual expectations, gender, marketing, and ambition. Babe used them all, was used by them all, but ultimately rose above them all to remain an enigma, to emerge a star.

CHAPTER ONE

The Texas Tomboy:
Not Nobody's Ordinary Girl

B abe's athletic prowess made her noteworthy to local Texans even as a child. This marvel, christened Mildred Ella Didriksen, was born June 26, 1911. Immediately a point of controversy and contention surfaces. The official Texas historical marker at the entrance to her grave in Beaumont says she was born in 1914, but her gravestone, only yards away, reads 1911. On her 1932 Olympics application she wrote 1913. She claimed 1914 in *This Life I've Led*. By her early twenties Babe was stating her birth year as 1913. By her midforties, she was claiming 1915. On a visa application she declared the date 1919. The Jefferson County courthouse in Beaumont has no birth certificate, but a baptismal certificate lists the date as 1911. Her two surviving siblings both state 1911. Didrikson didn't deceive merely to shave off those few nebulous years that demarcate early middle age. Rather, Babe thought youthfulness would render her athletic accomplishments all the more dazzling. If a twenty-year-old excelling at the Olympics in 1932 was heralded, then an eighteen-year-old—or better yet a seventeen-year-old—might be worshipped. Despite her chronological sleight of hand, she was, unquestionably, born June 26, 1911.[1]

Babe's parents, like so many others at the turn of the century, emigrated to the United States with hopes of improving their lot. Babe, tellingly, fiddled with her surname. Though born "Didriksen" she spelled her name "Didrikson." It was apparently recorded incorrectly on her school records, and Babe chose never to rectify the error. She was quoted once as saying, "I didn't want people to think I was a Swede." Perhaps she was proud of being Norwegian or maybe she simply wanted to deny her Scandinavian heritage altogether. A less analytical explanation was provided by family members and friends who said Babe liked the mistake and "it was just another trait of Babe to be or do something that was different." After Hannah and Ole Didriksen married in Oslo, Norway, one of his voyages on an oil tanker took him to Port Arthur, Texas, on the Gulf of Mexico. Smitten by the area, he resolved to bring his young family there. He lived and worked in Port Arthur for three years, 1905–8, satisfying immigration requirements proving he could support his family. The young couple saved and in 1908 Hannah joined him with their three children, Dora, Esther Nancy, and Ole. They completed their family in East Texas. Four more were born in a matter of a few short years: Lillie and Louis (twins), Mildred Ella, and Bubba (Arthur).[2]

The children's paternal grandfather was a cabinetmaker in Oslo. Their father later gave up his life on the seas to refinish furniture and build cabinets. The senior Ole was not above spinning fabulous yarns for his rapt audience of seven. He told his children he left home and made his first voyage at the age of nine. In her autobiography Babe's enthusiasm for his tales had not dimmed at all. "He'd describe one trip where they got stranded on an island, and kept themselves alive by eating monkeys and things." In another saga, "his ship broke up in a storm and he clung to a mast rope by one hand for hours, holding another guy up with his other hand." Babe's glee when recalling these tales is palpable. "What a bang we used to get out of his stories. . . . We'd huddle around him and listen like mad. . . . It could all be true. Things like that happened to these old seafarers." In his own circle, Babe's father was also something of a hustler. He'd traveled the globe eking out a living in a tough male subculture. His footloose and roguish early life no doubt influenced Babe, who mimicked not only his eclectic path of earning a living but also his ample embellishments of his adventures. Ole's storytelling was a carefully honed and greatly appreciated ethnic skill. And family storytelling was a cherished tradition. Storytelling prowess often surpassed book knowledge. Playing to your listener with vivid and graphic detail gave you control at "tongue's end." Babe learned very young that if the impact of the tale exceeded its veracity, little was compromised; you'd satisfied yourself and your listeners. This lesson she applied liberally to her own accomplishments.[3]

Babe's mother, Hannah Marie Olson, was the daughter of a shoemaker in Bergen, Norway. She stood about 5 feet 4 inches and was, by all accounts, graced with the natural ease of an athlete in her daily movements. Hannah had a considerable reputation as a fine skier and ice skater in her native land. As the telling and the retelling of this occurred, she was called in some accounts "a champion in her native Norway." Though she never competed officially, and her talents were only known locally, it was fitting that the mother of Babe Didrikson be a champion—and so the story was written and told. Hannah never did share her husband's enthusiasm for the humid, oil refining town whose industrial odors blanketed the dirt streets, but it became home.

The Didriksens' experience in America was largely atypical for Norwegian immigrants. They did not move to an ethnic enclave, nor did they manifest the widely documented Norwegian disdain for assimilation.[4] As a result, they contradicted several key ethnic patterns: the tendency to engage in agriculture; the retention of clothing indigenous to Scandinavia; the reliance on religion, the church, and mutual aid societies; the access to the numerous church-sponsored summer schools; and the participation in a vibrant and reinforcing visitation network among kin and Norwegian friends. In fact religion played no role in Babe's upbringing. Neither her autobiography nor her siblings' oral histories mention religious observance as a familial mainstay. Only upon her repeated hospitalizations in her mid-forties did Babe begin to tap religion as a source of strength, support, and continuity. The Didriksens' religiously nonobservant household may well have been due to the parents' desire to "Americanize."

Babe's father, in particular, appears to have rejected his cultural roots in significant ways. His exposure to America as a sailor was not atypical but his decision to build a home in southeast Texas, where there was no Norwegian community to help his family psychologically or materially, was unusual. As early as the 1870s Scandinavian sailors formed a "River View Scandinavian Union" and helped the greater New York Scandinavian population burgeon to nearly 42,000 in Brooklyn alone in 1930. Staten Island also had a large colony when shipbuilding got underway in the 1880s. The American flag that Ole proudly displayed on national holidays from their rooftop was also unusual for Norwegian Americans. "'I'm Norwegian,'" he used to say, 'but nobody's a prouder American than I am.'" It's likely that her father's attempts at rapid assimilation greatly affected Babe's soft-peddling denial of her own ethnic background. Babe also copied Ole's unwillingness to seek security in ethnically familiar regions and pursuits.[5]

The Didriksen home was also uncharacteristically emotional for a Norwegian-American family. Babe once called her parents "sweetly strict," a reference, no doubt, to the gentle blend of discipline and amusement that greeted Babe's shenanigans. In a rare instance of emotional revelation in *This Life I've Led,* Babe said, "We all just loved Momma, and Poppa too. We were forever hugging them and all that. I'd go lie in bed with Momma when I was little. She'd say *Min Babe*. My best girl." As the seven Didriksen children matured, the bond intensified. For Babe her family became a pillar of certainty in a world where she was not always accepted or understood. "Some families don't show their love for each other," Babe realized. "Ours always did. Momma and Poppa lived on for their kids, and they had that love from their kids all their lives."[6]

And yet, despite their isolation and conscious detachment from Norwegian ways and community, the Didriksens did maintain many important ethnic characteristics. Babe's favorite poem reads: "Ten thousand Swedes ran through the weeds, pursued by one Norwegian."[7] She did feel ethnic pride and the desire to beat other Scandinavian peoples. Her family did observe certain cultural holidays; they were, like many other Norwegians, industrious, patient, honest, strong, stubborn, frugal, and proud; they enjoyed alcohol and tobacco; they desired to improve themselves and their place in the world; they integrated English into Norwegian with their own speech pattern and were ridiculed for it; they were rejected by propertied, upper-class "Yankees"; they did not observe strict rules of etiquette; and they retained Norwegian eating habits—although Babe's fondness for Swedish meatballs was dwarfed by her love of onion sandwiches and strawberry sodas.[8]

As a result, the Didriksen home retained the character of Norway, especially since it was built by Ole to resemble a ship and was crafted with materials and skill from his homeland, despite its burgeoning American inhabitants. Lillie, one of the twins and Babe's favorite sibling and tireless chum, remembered that the children spoke Norwegian and "understood nearly everything our father and mother used to say in their native language." Their parents spoke Norwegian when they wanted privacy in front of the children, unaware that the brood could decipher their dialogue. The two tongues were used interchangeably in their Port Arthur home. "Mama used both languages so much that she got to the place where she would talk in English and think she was using Norwegian and in Norwegian when she thought she was talking English." This delighted Lillie and the others who "used to have a lot of fun out of her about it." As an adult the hustler Babe also talked two languages where appropriate: streetwise Texas talk and mainstream ladylike talk.

Whether using Norwegian or English, the Didriksen children "picked up a colorful vocabulary of profanity when they were tiny kids." Lillie said her father "was a sailor and he swore as unconsciously as he breathed." No harm was ever meant by it, and their neighbors in the gritty working-class oil refining environs of Port Arthur "were the same way, and we thought nothing of our language until we got older." This accounts in large part for Babe's struggle to tone down her "colorful" language as she became an increasingly popular—and quotable—personality. As an adult Lillie reassured an interviewer that "Babe doesn't use profanity promiscuously as many women do."[9] Others close to Babe also commented on her lack, or minimal use, of profanity. These disclaimers ring with a recognition that she had at one time spoken coarsely and still could redden some listeners' ears. In fact, swearing, like smoking, was typical of women in her poor, southern subculture.[10] Had she remained within her working-class East Texas cultural context and not become a national figure, Babe's dialect in all its varied hues might have gone unchecked.

From the time she was born, Mildred Ella was called "Baby" and continued to be called that even after the birth of her younger brother. As Babe tells it: "They were still calling me 'Baby' when I was in school, until Momma said I was getting too old for a nickname like that. Then they switched to my regular name, Mildred or Millie." Bubba and Louis, however, claimed "Baby" or "Babe" stuck. Bubba recalled, "My mother used to call her Baden, which expressed in broken American Norwegian is Babe, baby, and that's where she picked up the name." Babe, of course, had a different story. She claimed "the 'Babe' came later, when I began hitting home runs in ball games. Babe Ruth was the big hero then, and the kids said, "She's a regular Babe Ruth. We'll call her Babe." In truth, the media concocted the Babe Ruth connection, and it stuck as the correct derivation in the public's mind. In fact nicknames were common in the Norwegian community, and unusual ones often distinguished people.[11]

In 1914, when Babe was still a toddler, the family moved seventeen miles inland to Beaumont after a hurricane ravaged their Port Arthur surroundings. Here, Arthur Storm "Bubba" Didriksen was born and they bought their second residence—a house on Doucette Street in the south end. Doucette Street was in the seedy part of town near the Magnolia Oil Refinery, railroad tracks, and tanker cars, a "junkyard of odors pouring out of pipes and chimneys." In 1915, Ole earned about $200 per month when he was employed. Although this was a hefty wage for the period it was nonetheless stretched thin supporting seven children, so Hannah took laundry into the home. Ole added onto the house as need dictated, and one of Babe's standing chores was swabbing the external porch that ran the length and girth of the house—a chore she readily abandoned should anything more interesting present itself. But on those occasions when she tended to it, Babe strapped brushes to her feet and "skated" the floor clean. To Babe, any game was preferable to mundane work. Her athletic excellence eventually freed her from the woman's lot of endless housecleaning and service to others.[12]

Beaumont itself in 1910–30 was a bustling shipping port. A city of 40,422 by 1920, its population had increased 100 percent since 1910. It billed itself as "The Nation's Greatest Inland Harbor" and boasted modern wharves, docks, freight terminals, railway lines, and warehousing and distribution capabilities. As the geographic center of the lumber, rice, and oil refining industries of the region, Beaumont's economic prospects looked bright. Pending more transportation and mechanization, the 1921–22 *Beaumont City Directory* predicted boons in the grain, cotton, sulfur, rice oil, coal, and coke sectors of the economy. By 1929 the population had ballooned to nearly 68,000, of which 25 percent were black and only 5 percent foreign born. Many residents enjoyed modern conveniences since there were 10,800 telephones in operation and one-third of the streets were paved. Numerous parks, 45 churches, 2 newspapers, 10 hotels, 4 railroads, 9 theaters, 3 hospitals, and 23 schools, which were segregated, completed civic life. Jobs were plentiful and unemployment was low, although of the 6,400 workers only 400 of them were women. By 1929 even the city admitted that it needed to draw industries that would provide work for women. Plentiful work led to plentiful leisure time, and Beaumont became a sports-loving community. The city was home to the Exporters, a Class A Texas League baseball team, which had a new park for the 1929 season. Summer swims and pleasure drives were favorites given the town's distance from the Gulf. People were encouraged to hunt and fish amid Beaumont's plentiful streams, lakes, woods, and marshes.[13]

Despite a bright future triggered by the discovery of more oil at the nearby Spindletop field, the twenties were a dark period for Beaumont. Between 1922 and 1924 the Ku Klux Klan controlled the town. Boasting 4.5 million members nationwide, the group claimed to stand for "traditional values, particularly law and order," yet it really sought to impose its morals on others by a well-organized system of vigilante justice. The Beaumont Klan tarred and feathered a local physician who had been indicted, but not tried, for abortion. After he left town lashings and pistol whippings directed against suspected "abortionists, bootleggers, and other violators of the Klan's moral code" followed. After months of violence, the Klan began to contribute to charities to mend its tarnished image.[14]

Opposition to the Klan grew and it sharply divided the community. The publisher and editor of the *Beaumont Enterprise* were criticized by Klan supporters for their opposition. The Rotary Club condemned the Klan, but a similar resolution failed to pass at the Kiwanis Club. The mayor, an attorney, and a judge tried to purge the Klan from government office, but not surprisingly no one admitted membership. In 1922 a citizens' committee tried to remove suspected Klan member and Jefferson County Sheriff Tom Garner. The plan failed, and in the 1922 primaries the Klan swept the election.

Until 1926 the Klan's membership grew "virtually unchecked." During Garner's trial 801 new members were recruited and 10,000 attended a rally for him at Magnolia Park. In 1922, 30,000 assembled to hear the national founder of the Klan speak at Fair Park and 50,000 watched the local Klan's first parade. When a staunch anti-Klan judge was replaced by a pro-Klan judge, the path was cleared for a sweep of the 1924 local elections. The state Klan waned by 1925, but locally it remained strong until the late 1920s.

Amidst this violence and hatred, blacks, the largest minority and undeniably the most disenfranchised, kept a low profile. A local chapter of the National Association for the Advancement of Colored People had opened in 1918 but remained quiet. In 1924, in the midst of Klan power, the chapter disbanded, not to be reconstituted until 1930. "Although rigid segregation was somewhat tempered with paternalism, the position of blacks in Beaumont remained basically unchanged from Reconstruction to the late 1950s." Most blacks worked as laborers or domestic help for white bosses, but the black community had created its own social and economic structure that included restaurants, groceries, recreational areas, labor unions, and neighborhoods.[15]

Inducements to keep one's "difference" quiet were profound in this Klan-dominated era. Likely this contributed to the Didriksens' insistence that they were Americans first. Other allegiances seemed to lead to only hostile responses. Babe seemingly absorbed the rhetoric of difference from her town by at times reiterating racist and anti-Semitic sentiments. By seeing herself as separate from and better than blacks and Jews, Babe, like many other immigrants, sought to minimize her own differences and benefit from dominant cultural beliefs and trends.

Babe and the Masculinist Model

Babe quickly earned the dubious appellation of "the worst kid on Doucette." It was partly unearned, ever-loyal sister Lillie protested. Whenever a window was broken by an errant baseball, Babe got the blame (many were, however, her doing). Her brother Ole both admired Babe and knew whom he was up against. "Boy, that Babe was a cutter when she was a kid. I was much older than Babe but she gave me lots of trouble. And she could hold her own." Her biggest chums, according to Ole, were Lillie, Bubba,

and Louis, "and they were always busy doing something." Ole also underscored Babe's fleeting relationship with housework. She would do it, he
recollected, if she was "watched like a hawk." She wasn't one who liked
predictable domesticity. Ole "never remember[ed] Babe playing dolls. She
was just too active to settle down and always wanted to be running, jumping or throwing something."[16]

To corral his children's boundless energy Ole Senior built a rustic gymnasium in the backyard. The wooden barbells and pull-up bars compensated
for the movie money he was unable to grant at the children's request and
offered them an opportunity for physical fitness. Several Didriksen children
reveled in the hours spent in the backyard gym. Babe adored it. "In the ga-
rage he had this weight lifting device. It was an old broomstick with a flatiron
at each end." The girls were not discouraged from using it but "he put it there
for the boys," Babe knew, "so they could strengthen their muscles. But . . .
Lillie and I would get in there and work out with it too." Their parents, in
keeping with the Norwegian tradition of unabashedly competitive mixed-
sex sports, allowed the girls to use the equipment as well. Bubba put it thus:
"They encouraged us to be the best in everything we attempted to do. . . . We
just did our own little thing and whatever we wanted to participate in we
did."[17]

Gender roles in the Didriksen household thus overlapped considerably,
which may have given Babe the impetus to break out of her role as a woman later. Babe actually personified the stereotypical Norwegian "masculine
imperative," as one scholar labeled it. This value system, attributed exclusively to men, is "made up of courage, selfishness, physical strength, self-
discipline, endurance, self-sufficiency, cunning, unscrupulousness and competitiveness." Held high were "craggy independence, toughness, cool
resourcefulness, and resolute self-discipline." Her fierce competitiveness and
aggression, even as a very young child, in the roughest and most daring
games embodied the precise attributes assigned to the ideal man's physical
and psychological makeup.[18]

Norwegian-American children in the 1930s held sex-stereotyped expectations for girls and women. They were considered more afraid to take risks,
act boldly, and make fools of themselves. Further, girls expected to give up
more easily and be more dependable, awkward, dependent, obedient, easily confused, rational, careful, and nervous. Men were thought to "maintain
'their masculine selves largely through exercise and sports'" while women
manifested their admiration of these traits by choosing male mates who
embodied them.[19]

Also like Norwegian-American men, Babe distanced herself from her ethnic role too. Adopting the misspelling of her name may have been the first sign of her reluctance to acknowledge her ancestry. But one scholar has noted that this is a typical reaction among lower-class immigrants and especially among those seeking to imitate American ways. In Babe's case, her parents' choice to identify minimally as Norwegians, Hannah's work doing laundry for more well-to-do neighbors, Babe's early work opportunities, and her desire to transcend poverty fueled her distancing from her ethnic past.[20]

Babe defied the ethnic mainstream again in her choice of sport—this time due to circumstance. Although skiing, yachting, skating, and riflery were the preferred sports of Norwegian Americans, winter sports were hardly an option on the Gulf of Mexico. Her pursuit of individual events also contradicted the ethnic tendency to "avoid personal head-to-head competition. . . . They prefer victories over human limitations and natural impediments; they race against the impersonal clock, jump against the meter, and pit themselves against harsh natural conditions to demonstrate the bravery, toughness, and endurance that the masculine imperative demands." Babe's love of beating her opponents one-on-one was her creation.[21]

Babe was further influenced by her southern, poor-white subculture, which regarded women quite differently than did the upper crust of the South. Unsupervised outdoor play, physical games, bawdy humor, and physical exhibitionism were considered acceptable because they enticed the less restrained, less self-controlled members of the working class.[22] Ensnared in work environments that left little chance for personal improvement, self-expression, or individual excellence, working-class people looked to self-generated arenas for excitement and personal distinction. Leisure hours were filled with "drinking, fighting, gambling, playing sports, attending the theatre . . . and promenading in distinctive dress." These behaviors contradicted middle-class ideals of moderation, economic diligence, and self-restraint. Gamblers in particular (Babe was one) enjoyed "the thrill of the moment, thereby mocking middle-class ideals of thrift and progress."[23]

This rough behavior by both men and women instigated a working-class cult of masculinity that permeated well into the twentieth century. Able-bodiedness and muscularity increasingly distinguished "manly" virile men in contradiction to the "sloth and ease" embodied in "feminized" men who didn't use their muscles to make their livings. By the 1880s–1890s, being a man in the working-class subculture "meant being not womanly. . . . 'Sissy,' 'molly-coddle' and pussy-foot now became popular terms of derision." Fears of effeminate men and domineering women emerged.[24]

These ideals were male-defined, yet Babe internalized them as her own. Hallmarks of maleness, "toughness, ferocity, prowess, and honor," informed her development and decision-making. Like the boxer in the ring, being "manly" was defined as "not how responsible or upright an individual was but by his sensitivity to insult, his coolness in the face of danger, and his ability to give and take punishment." This streetwise creed guided Babe's actions and choices. She was not alone among poor girls who fistfought their way to a protected, if lonely, status among their peers. In this cultural context, cussing and smoking were symbols of roughness and readiness. Babe, like other girls in these settings, embraced these behaviors as badges of courage.[25]

Other girls did not approximate Babe's ferocity or androgyny, however, as schoolmates' and teachers' oral histories and photos in the high school yearbook reveal. She was an anomaly. Her self-confidence and "masculinist" value system benefited from her parents' approval of her physicality and their equal inability (or unwillingness) to tame her spirit and check her rock-'em-sock-'em behavior. It also stemmed from regional and social class tolerance for "tougher" women. Yet the degree to which she internalized these masculine ideals was singular and shocking.

Babe roamed the streets untethered. The street was her playground. The children's games she played were unbridled—at times dangerous. A favorite Halloween trick, which Babe admitted masterminding one year, was soaping the trolley tracks on Doucette Street, thus making the streetcars slide and halt. The ringleader mounted the car's back and disjointed the trolley pole from its wire, forcing the conductor to reconnect it. On one such jaunt, Babe slipped in the mud and was nearly crushed under the streetcar.[26]

Not Nobody's Ordinary Girl

Despite cultural constraints, Babe's physical self-confidence was palpable. Little wonder since her father proudly claimed her raw athleticism came from him, and she was the undisputed "first pick" of every neighborhood game: baseball, marbles, races, jumping, and throwing. As Lillie never tired of saying, "She was the best at *everything* we did." Her favorite, roller skating, kept the two of them "all *over* the streets, always gone from the house." Hannah had her patience tested more than once by her fearless daughters. "We knew when it was supper time, all right," Lillie fondly recalled, "but we never paid no attention to nothin' else. Momma, she was always callin' and *callin'* to get us home."[27]

Babe was not an easy child to raise or to discipline, a task which typically fell to Hannah, because there was a sweet, predictable simplicity in her misbehaving. A case in point: Hannah made Babe a brand new dress that she promptly tore and dirtied on the playground. Angered, Hannah sprinted after Babe when she saw the damage. But Hannah had recently sprained her ankle getting off the street car and when Babe saw her "trying to run on that ankle [she] said, 'Momma, don't run. I'll wait for you.'" A tender moment followed. She came up to Babe, ready to spank her. But, Babe told lovingly, "Then she looked at me and began to laugh. She said, 'I can't whip you.'"[28]

Sigrid Hill told a similar tale. Like the Didriksens, Sigrid's family was Norwegian and had moved from Port Arthur to Beaumont. When Sigrid's mother died, Hannah took Sigrid into the Didriksen family to raise until adulthood. Hannah's love for Babe was tremendous, Sigrid recalled, as was her frustration with her. When Babe's behavior was especially troublesome, "Mrs. Didriksen would say I don't know where I got that 'ting'—couldn't say 'thing' so she'd say, I don't know where I got that 'ting,'" referring to her rambunctious daughter. Sigrid was often sent to round up Babe from some athletic field. Babe often convinced her to stall Hannah's pursuit and cool her mother's ire. When Babe, denied supper as punishment for her absenteeism, asked Sigrid to raid the pantry for her, Sigrid dutifully tiptoed downstairs to feed her recalcitrant bedmate.[29]

Family members always knew where to find Babe when she vanished for hours while sent on a simple errand: the schoolyard or wherever there was a contest in progress. One such occasion was the day Lillie graduated from grade school. Hannah sent Babe to the store near the Magnolia Refinery, ten blocks from the house, for ground beef. En route home, meat in hand, Babe felt that magnetic pull to a baseball game. Sigrid, sent to bring home the "missing" Babe, found her behind the school playing baseball with the boys. Sigrid recalled, "The groceries were sitting on the ground. So she says, 'You take it and go home with it.' And I said, 'You're gonna catch hell.' She was something else." An hour later "along came Momma down the street looking for me," Babe recalled. A dog was devouring the last of the meat Babe had on the ground. True to prediction, when Babe finally returned home, Hannah closed herself and Babe in the bathroom and Babe got "a good lickin' and she [Hannah] said that's for what you did." "Poor Momma!" Babe empathized in her autobiography. She realized how troublesome she had been. This incident, according to Babe, was a turning point. "I felt real bad about the way I'd let her down on a night when she had so much to do." From then on Babe resolved she was going to do everything she could to ease Hannah's life; she honored this resolution throughout her adult years.[30]

Courting trouble was Babe's prime activity in her youth. To be Babe's friend, even as a child, meant to follow or be left behind and miss the action. Lillie knew this well. Some of Babe's and Lillie's games invited danger. Babe coaxed them to jump off of a moving freight train. "It started goin faster 'n' faster 'n' *faster*," Lillie recalled. Babe hollered to Lillie to jump off, but the older sister was frozen with fear. Undaunted, Babe "had to get back up on the car and push me off. Then she fell off, too." Scared and "skinned up," Lillie proudly reported, "we never got hurt no worse than that."[31]

Lillie was then and throughout her life Babe's biggest fan. They were an interesting contrast: Babe, angular, dark haired, lean, and a natural leader; Lillie, blonde, feminine, and a willing follower. Babe claimed "Lillie was a tomboy too in them days" but she may have been alone in that opinion. Schoolteachers and classmates almost always referred to Lillie as "the feminine one." Louis and Bubba attributed Lillie's shadowing of Babe to her sheer devotion to her sister, not her devotion to competition and winning. For Lillie, playing the games came with the territory of loving Babe. She enjoyed the contests too, of course, but they were not her life's blood. What made Lillie tick was Babe's companionship and unleashed spirit.

Throughout her life, Lillie never tired of telling stories about her famous sister. One of her favorites stemmed from 1925, when Babe was fourteen. A neighbor across the street, Christine McCandless, traveled with a Ringling circus troupe. Hannah was persuaded to let the two inseparables go to California and stay with McCandless while the circus performers trained for the coming season. Their mama "thought Babe might develop into a good trapeze artist from the things she had seen Babe do around the place when playing." The girls liked circus life just fine and "Babe learned to hang by her toes, turn flips in the air and walk the tight rope without the umbrella." They also used a balancing bar. At Christmas Hannah sent for them. It is unclear what nixed Babe's fledgling circus career, but the talent and will were there. Years later Lillie's only memento of the adventure was a photo of Babe, Christine, and herself atop "The Biggest Elephant in the World."[32]

Beaumont School Years: Charmer, Rebel, Ruffian, Practical Joker

Babe, as an adolescent, tasted the full measure of bittersweet responses that her talents, behavior, appearance, and personal style elicited. Neighbors, elementary, junior, and senior high classmates, and teachers and principals offered a portrait of Babe that is at once endearing, engaging, extraordinary, and, paradoxically, alienating. As a child Babe was good, loyal to her family, humorous, and disarmingly appealing. Unfortunately, she became famous for relentlessly teasing others, shirking her responsibilities so that she could play sports, being excessively self-confident and even brazen, and being "a pest who was mean at times."

Emma Andress, a Doucette Street resident as a child, recalled decades later, "Babe was known as a little tartar and the neighborhood pest. She was mean in the way that kids are when they get into mischief." She was honest, though, and took responsibility for any wrongdoing. But the meanness wasn't what irked Emma the most. Babe's verbal zingers kept Emma off balance and were used at the least opportune moment. Emma "never knew what she was going to say. She usually said anything that came into her head, and sometimes it was pretty embarrassing." This included unsolicited remarks to Emma's beaus as they called for her.[33]

In her years in Beaumont's Magnolia Elementary School her distinctive personality traits and abilities emerged and were honed. Her sports versatility and acumen were first noticed when Babe was in second grade after she "won the marble championship against boys and girls much older than she." But it was her relentless mischievous streak that was most captivating. Effie Piland, Magnolia's principal from 1919 to 1924, recalled, "One day I heard the kids outside yelling for me. I went outside and there was Mildred, sitting on top of the flag pole. She had climbed to the top and I told her to come down." Piland also notes Babe's exceptional love of sports and her ability and desire to beat the boys at their own games. "I remember she could out-play anyone in marbles and out-play them in baseball. She could out-do all the boys."[34] Reagan Baker, constable of Jefferson County, had known Babe since childhood when his family owned an ice house. Like the other kids, Babe would ask for small pieces of ice. Yet, "if we didn't let her have it, she sure turned loose on us." "Yup," he concluded, "that was the baddest little youngun!" Babe also used her quick tongue to charm Ruby Gage, in charge of physical education and playground activities at Magnolia Elementary. She shared vivid and agreeable memories of the young Babe: "She was witty and in a teasing manner, liked to catch the teachers off guard."[35]

As Babe moved up into David Crockett Junior High her competitiveness toward boys and her general lack of interest in girls' games and friendships heightened. In 1933 she told a reporter from the North American Newspaper Alliance, "As far back as I can remember I played with boys rather than girls. . . . The girls did not play games that interested me. I preferred baseball, football, foot-racing and jumping, with the boys, to hop-scotch and jacks and dolls, which were about the only things girls did. . . . I guess the habit of playing with boys made me too rough for the girls' games. Anyway, I found them too tame."[36] She was popular with many, although she was, clearly, a ruffian whom some of her schoolmates feared and avoided. This dichotomous reaction to Babe intensified as she grew older; she evoked strong emotions—from adoration to active dislike.

Babe's behavior did, at times, also elicit scorn from her young peers. She was a street-tough youngster and willingly used her fists to back up her opinions. In 1923, when she was twelve years old, one of the boys at school, "a boy much older and larger than Babe," made a remark she didn't care for "and without any comment or hesitation Babe knocked him squarely to the floor." Incidents such as these facilitated the principal's decision to exempt Babe from the usual rules and to allow her to compete in boys' games.[37]

E. W. Jackson, David Crockett Junior High principal during Babe's years there, asserted that "she was one of the best liked students in the school." Indeed, she was friendly toward many until they wronged her. One female classmate remembered, "One time Babe came down the hall where I was . . . and just by way of a friendly greeting she slapped me on the shoulder. Her 'gentle' slap nearly floored me and sent me staggering half the length of the hall."[38] Two other former teammates reiterated Babe's good humor and her unpredictable roughness. Edwina Lockhart said, "We all liked Babe. She was so good humored. We were afraid of her though. She would go around hitting us on the arms with her knuckles to make our muscles knot up into 'frogs.'" It wasn't only the girls who watched out for Babe. John Lockhart remembered the boys in junior high were a little afraid of Babe too. "If we didn't do as she wanted us to she'd chase us down and sit on us until we promised to play by her rules." But the boys, unlike the girls, tasted sweet revenge—if only fleetingly. Babe's homeroom teacher vividly recounted, "The boys in my room continually teased Mildred, thumped and hit her when going through the halls, but she had a way of getting even out on the grounds. She would step on their heels and kick them. They didn't make anything off Mildred." Occasionally Babe engaged in fisticuffs with girls with an inevitable victorious outcome. One day Babe came to school waving two five-dollar bills she had won in a wrestling match against another girl.[39]

By the time she reached Beaumont High School Babe's character was formed and became accentuated. She was friendly, rowdy, enjoyed practical jokes, shunned girls' games and girls' friendships, yet was blessed with raw talent and virtuoso skill in widely diverse sports that took the school by storm. Babe won a swimming match sponsored by the YWCA. A schoolmate who caddied for Babe at the nine-hole municipal golf course recalled, "Nobody had to teach Babe how to hit a golf ball. She was a natural. She had great confidence. She believed she could do anything—and she could."[40]

At Beaumont High Babe was on both the golf and tennis teams, although in later years she claimed she was a golf neophyte until 1932. Babe appears in the yearbook, *Pine Burr of 1929,* along with six other women in the team photo. Babe seems quite self-assured there, hands clasped behind her back, in a loose-fitting white dress with her straight bangs and straight lips. She and Lois Blanchette also had little trouble winning the doubles crown in tennis, which made them eligible for the state meet.[41]

Babe rose to nonsport challenges as well. On one such occasion, "Red" Reynolds, halfback on the Royal Purple football team, challenged her to a boxing match in a boys' gym class. "Hit me as hard as you can, you can't hurt me," Reynolds taunted. Roger Reese witnessed the showdown: "The Babe took him at his word, looked him over and swung." "The next thing I knew," Reynolds admitted, "I was lying on the gym floor and they were pouring water on me to clear the bells and birdies out of my head. That gal really gave me a K.O."[42]

Babe's fights in senior high, though, were not always confined to the gym. One school morning "Babe came in. Her knuckles were skinned and we asked her what was wrong. 'Oh, I passed a bunch of Negro kids on my way to school and one of them cussed me and I had to clean up the whole gang' Babe answered." Thelma Hughes, a former teammate acknowledged that "she really did hate blacks in those days. I think she went out of her way to antagonize them, and truly, to hurt them."[43]

With her ruffian streak firmly entrenched, Babe's reputation for verbal victories increased. Reagan Baker, a former schoolmate, vividly reconstructed her verbal skills: "You couldn't win an argument with Babe. She'd sure tell you off. She was the boss around these parts . . . the rough and tumble type." She did have her defenders. One classmate "didn't think Babe was a tough girl. She wasn't. She was just sure of herself and could do everything in athletics well and wasn't bashful about telling you about it." Even teachers were on the receiving end of Babe's sharp—although not necessarily unkind—tongue. Babe's cooking instructor said, "She used to call me 'Little Sugar' in and out of class and I would get after her, telling her the principal would come by and catch her some day and scold us both. Babe would grin at me and say, 'All right, Little Sugar, I won't call you that,' and in two minutes she would be at it again."[44]

She also began her basketball career on the all-white Beaumont High team. Beatrice Lytle, Babe's physical education instructor, "started Babe on her basketball career and taught her shooting style, fitness and fundamentals." The team photo from 1928 shows twelve short-haired teenagers wearing baggy V-neck tops proclaiming "Royal Purple." Babe, standing in the front row with hands clasped behind her back, has a squinting smile. It was the first year "girl athletes were out of bloomers, and this was appreciated by girls and boys alike."[45]

And for a fleeting moment it seemed as if she might actually be allowed to kick for the boys' football team. Another coach, Lilburn "Bubba" Dimmit, also laid claim to tutoring her. Dimmit got her "on the right trail. He devoted much time to Babe and took time out from his many duties to instruct Babe." Coach Dimmit had "planned to suit her up and have her kick points after touchdown. But the high school biggies frowned on the idea and it never came to pass though Babe was anxious for the chance." Lytle and Dimmit led the way among those claiming "credit due" for Babe's tutelage and accomplishments. There has never been a shortage of people doing so; to be in Babe's "inner circle," however tangentially, meant everlasting fame.[46]

Straddling Fences: The Texas Tomboy

In her teens Babe did not fit tidily into any one clique. In her high school yearbooks from 1928 to 1930, Babe appears in athletic team photos as "a squinty, pugnacious kid with straight hair and severe bangs, dressed in a formless cotton frock, sagging socks, flat shoes. She never wore jewelry, abhorred makeup, and didn't own a pair of silk stockings or a girdle."[47] In short Babe stood apart from the fashionable teenagers with their curled hair, flattering skirts and blouses, and coquettish mannerisms. These young women were middle-class daughters of white-collar managers, industrialists, and shippers whose family fortunes had boomed during Beaumont's "golden era." This group of young women who adopted the dominant ideals of femininity personified distinct gendered behavioral ideals determined by social class. They were in synch with national ideals but at odds with local, ethnic, working-class norms. The athletic students were more in Babe's league. Yet even compared to them Babe was more muscularly developed and the plainest dresser.

Ruth Scurlock, a teacher at Beaumont High, remembered that "Babe's excellence at sports made her unacceptable to other girls. And these frothy girls, in her eyes, were simply not useful. Babe was bucking society even then." In fact Babe disdained the socially elite clique of teenagers who comprised the Kackler Klub, the number one female social club at the school.

Babe's biographers are even blunter. "Babe's behavior was an aberration in those times." She rejected the other girls and was rejected by them.[48]

Babe was a tomboy. A self-avowed tomboy writing in a women's sports magazine correctly summarized the mixed power of the appellation. "The girl who displays 'boyish behavior' loses the name 'girl' and becomes something else. The word can be an insult or a badge worn proudly." The age of the tomboy has a lot to do with the label's positive or negative connotations. Prepubescent girls are granted "a special exemption from staying clean and staying still, which is what girls are supposed to do." But this foray into male turf is fleeting, and "her temporary visa to male territory . . . gets stamped 'cancelled' at the age of 12 or 13." If a girl persists with "unfeminine" behaviors and appearances, she becomes a curiosity. Lillie Didriksen, for example, made the "appropriate" transition into adult femininity. Babe, for many years, did not. In fact, descriptions of Babe often read like chronicles of a third sex. Sigrid Hill said of Babe, "She should have been a boy. . . . Lots of people thought she was a boy, but she wasn't. She was a girl. She was tough." Hill realized Babe "crossed over" gender boundaries and fit neither category.[49]

Statements describing Babe in her late teens resound with even greater confusion—and condemnation. In a reporter's depiction of these accounts both her physical appearance and her character are scrutinized. She was a "thin, muscular girl with a body like a Texas cowpuncher, an unfeminine looking, hard-bitten creature with nothing on her mind but setting athletic records." She was not, he assured, "a freakish looking character . . . [but a] normal, healthy, boyish-looking girl." Despite her "normalcy," crowds followed her not to see her win or lose, but just "to see the Babe." There was a "strangeness and mystery about her" that fascinated the curious public. Not only her body elicited curiosity, but her character did too. She displayed "all of the human emotions, friendliness, humor, egoism, envy, hope, dislike, despair, tearful grief and joy." Babe, ever-mindful of this painfully public speculative scrutiny, "went out of her way to be a crowd pleaser," he wrote, to present herself as a "well adjusted friendly woman."[50]

In what became a familiar narrative, those who knew Babe intentionally resurrected examples of her "typical femininity" to fight against this tomboy image. The listener is reassured that despite Babe's athleticism and coarseness she was indeed "all girl." A few of these narratives sound slightly combative—as if the speaker is correcting or arguing against previous unkind accounts or insults hurled. Demonstrably, an interviewee's first recollections often stress the appropriateness of Babe's appearance. "She came to school each day spotlessly clean," one respondent told the *Beaumont Journal's* sports editor in 1970. "She wore skirts and blouses, mostly white blouses, but very clean and fresh." At times, carefully constructed recollections of Babe's feminine pursuits turn unexpectedly midstream, like a story by Babe's home economics teacher: "I remember Babe made a little blue dress with long sleeves, and after she had finished it and got her grade on it she whacked the sleeves off nearly to the shoulder because they got in her way and she couldn't be bothered with them." Interestingly, Babe's sewing skills received considerable press throughout her life. When she was ill in 1953, a news story on her highlighted: "When at Beaumont High Babe made a dress in home economics class and it was entered in the South Texas State Fair. It won first place." In later years Babe transferred the victory to the Texas State Fair—many times larger than the South Texas Fair. Although they provided good press, her domestic skills were not foremost in her mind. "Contrary to general opinion, she could keep house well and she could cook and sew . . . the only trouble was that if she thought of something she wanted to do more she would go off and leave what she had started in the house."[51]

Thus tomboyism could be temporarily tolerated in Babe because she was still all girl and "normal" physiological and psychosocial development would cause its end. Dating, interest in boys, and marriage were all further "proofs" of the tomboy's normalcy. Babe, in fact, elaborated on these precise topics when discussing her adolescence in her autobiography. Babe's tomboyishness, which lasted until her late twenties, elicited concern, unkindnesses, speculation, and curiosity.

To the larger public, her tomboyishness was compounded by her rowdiness. Her East Texas, working-class ways were thought boisterous and ostentatious by some. "Exuberance and physical display," one historian notes, "were far more the province of the poor, the immigrant, the working-class woman." For members of the middle and upper social classes, "the tendency towards display itself was often taken as a mark of moral corruption." Manners, therefore, were a key sign of morality, and "the manner of one's sport and athletic practice also assumed a moral intonation."[52]

Despite her rowdiness and crude manners, she had a captivating physicality to some. Her physical education teacher remarked on "how her muscles flowed when she walked. She had a nerve-muscle co-ordination that is very, very rare." Babe was the only one in her many years of instruction with that special coordination. She was taut, quick, and strong and she looked it.[53]

Thus Babe straddled several fences. She competed with the boys, in fact was welcomed into their games, but was teased and ridiculed by them. She was a pesty student, but an engaging one. And she was supposed to be friends with the girls but couldn't stand them. As Hearn, her classmate, noted, "Babe didn't particularly like PE classes. She didn't like the daily routine and games with girls. She wanted to be playing with boys and did most of the time when she could 'escape' [assigned tasks]." Hers was a spirit-to-be-reckoned-with for her teachers. Whether climbing flag poles as a ten-year-old or "scampering up in the steel rafters high above the floor" of the gymnasium, Babe needed "handling." A classmate vividly remembered Babe's rafter walk while the gym was being decorated for a carnival: "She had to be threatened before she came down." In an even less endearing stunt her former cooking instructor cringed when telling of the day a large rat appeared in class. Everyone "fled shrieking to high places." Babe, alone and unafraid, herded the rat into a corner and claimed she captured it in a box. "She finally announced that the beast was gone, then as soon as everyone was back on the floor she maneuvered the rat out of a corner where she had [it] corralled and started the panic all over again." This was of dubious amusement, no doubt, to those in the room. Babe thought it riotous.[54]

This love of pranks was another residual ethnic influence, although one usually practiced by boys. Chroniclers of Norwegian Americans record gunpowder put in fathers' tobacco, wheels removed from farm wagons, blackberries popped underfoot in the classroom, and lights turned out during a particularly droll school reunion speech. These practical jokes were often expressions of affection among people disinclined to express emotions directly.[55]

Yet as irritating and taxing as her shenanigans were, there was also something eminently endearing about her. Beaumonters stress her friendliness and humor, despite her uncouthness. Mrs. Whitaker, known to Babe as "Little Sugar," was impressed by Babe's loyalty and persevering friendship. Babe visited her repeatedly when she returned to Beaumont as an adult. And when Whitaker was hurt in an automobile accident, she said, "Babe came to see me, and wrote to me several times to see how I was getting along."[56] The same young woman that threw punches also warmed hearts.

Because she was a hybrid, because she was boisterous, she was often alone. She was isolated from girls because of her athleticism and tomboyishness, so she sought companionship with boys. Yet despite admiring her, they teased her. At times her daring-do was too much for them, too, and she'd end up companionless. Still, she unabashedly befriended students who were snubbed by others; she stood by those who didn't "fit." She knew the pain of not belonging, though she did not speak of it.[57]

She didn't fit into an academic niche either. Interviewees claim Babe was an average student, yet private correspondence, laced with misspellings and grammatical errors, challenges this claim. Math gave her trouble, but she never failed a subject. Of her elementary and junior high record her former principal said, "I'd say she had a creditable record and she passed." He changed the subject rapidly and spoke enthusiastically about her personal impact: "Her deportment was more outstanding. I remember her as I'm sure do all of her teachers as being very congenial and cooperative."[58]

Clearly, cultivating her intellect was not Babe's forte. No one recalled Babe reading magazines or books or more than glancing at newspapers, which was quite typical behavior for women of her poor southern background. She did, however, read press coverage of herself. Ruth Scurlock, quick witted and blunt, quipped, "I have no doubt that Babe had the best IQ of anyone in the Didriksen family, but I don't think in her whole life she ever read a book unless it had the rules of some game in it." Betty Dodd, too, attested that Babe did not read for pleasure. She "might look at a magazine," but really, "she just liked to be with the people she liked and do fun things."[59]

"My Goal Was to Be the Greatest Athlete That Ever Lived"

More than anything, however, Babe wanted to compete. This rowdy, endearing, and relentlessly energetic spitfire, even as a teenager, possessed a remarkably clear vision of her goal: "I knew exactly what I wanted to be when I grew up. My goal was to be the greatest athlete that ever lived." The goal originated when her father read the children newspaper coverage of the 1928 Olympics in Amsterdam, and Babe was enthralled with the star athletes. Babe quickly resolved that she would be in the next Olympics. True, she had raw talent, but she had no coaching, training program, or top-level competition behind her. She told Lillie, and a few others, "It sounded like the greatest thing in the world to me."[60]

Babe and Lillie shared big hopes for the Olympics. Despite obvious differences in their abilities, Babe decided that "Lillie was going to be a runner and I was going to be a hurdler and jumper." To this end they practiced endlessly. Babe hurdled the seven hedges in the yards along their Doucette block between their house and the corner grocery. One hedge, higher than the others, impeded her course. "I couldn't get over it," she said. "That sort of messed up my practicing." She approached the homeowner and asked "if he'd mind cutting his hedge down to where the rest of them were, and he did it." Told by an adult Babe, this anecdote minimizes her brassiness. As

Bubba told it, Babe was even far bolder than that. "Those hedges were so tall they were over her head . . . and she just went along and talked to the neighbors, which was about four or five houses before you reached the store, and asked them if they wouldn't mind cutting their hedges lower." This boldness and willingness to make her presence felt and desires known were qualities that later in life endeared Babe to her fans. These traits also aggravated critics who perceived her extreme self-confidence and razzle-dazzle as arrogance.[61]

Hedges trimmed, they'd tear down Doucette Street. Babe hurdled hedges using her unusual style adapted to the bushes; she crooked her left knee, which enabled her to clear the two-foot width of the bushes and escape unscratched. She kept this style throughout her track career, despite later pressure to use the more orthodox straight-leg position. Lillie raced alongside her on the pavement. In the heat of competition Lillie mustered her share of determination. Babe tried fervently to beat her to the finish (despite the obvious burden of adding hurdling to their equidistant course). But Babe admitted admiringly, "I didn't beat her very often, though, because she had too much fight in her to want to lose. Lillie was a competitor." Coming from Babe, this is high praise, hard earned.[62]

Babe's competitive spirit was spurred on by more than just a love of winning. Babe's intense love for her parents was a prime motivator in her drive to succeed. Babe's family life, through age nineteen when she left home to pursue a semiprofessional basketball career, was her haven from adventure, uncertainty, and turmoil: it empowered her. Her autobiography is laden with comfortable domestic references to night-time storytelling by her father, Halloween trick-or-treating, cookies made, meals shared, poppa's daily breakfast offering of oatmeal, his bringing Hannah coffee in bed every morning, parental tempers slow to boil and quick to cool, Hannah's rosebushes damaged by errant baseballs that earned only a slight rebuke, and numerous evenings making music, when Babe's love of harmonica playing bloomed. The other source of motivation was her impassioned vow to escape poverty. Hannah and Ole were poor but too proud to accept charity. Betty Hicks, a golfer in the 1950s and a sports author, distinctly recalled a conversation with Babe that pinpointed the origin of her relentless drive to win. Her motivation, according to Hicks, was "the streets of Port Arthur." She once said to Hicks, "'I can remember them hamburger days. Where I go now I gotta have mink.'" The poverty the Didriksens had known in Port Arthur was duplicated in Beaumont. Raymond Alford, a childhood friend of Babe's, said, "We went barefoot all the time. Some of us never did have shoes. Everyone was poor. We weren't collecting any relief checks, but we were poor." Babe, too, was perpetually barefoot except at school and on Sundays.[63]

In her autobiography Babe recounted small disappointments triggered by poverty: cheap shoes bought for her, infrequent money for the four youngest children to go to a movie, and her father's inability to buy her a harmonica, which she eventually bought for herself with her own money. In addition, she made numerous references to poverty, borderline making-do, lean meals, odd jobs taken up, and scrimping. "There were times when things were plenty tough," she admitted, and the toughest period was "when I was still a little kid. For several years there Poppa couldn't get work regularly. He had to go back to sea now and again when he couldn't find any jobs in Beaumont. And Momma took in washing. The $200 a month cabinet maker's income was wildly unpredictable." Those were grim days of uncertainty and Babe remembered, "All of us pitched in and helped her, so she wouldn't wear herself out. Little as I was, I'd wear my knuckles down scrubbing on that wash board."[64]

During the worst of times, the Didriksens needed the generosity of Sigrid Hill's mother, who supplied them with meals several times a week. Despite their hardships, Hannah counseled against all charity; to accept these meals was permissible because "we'd all sit down and eat together. It was a sociable occasion among friends. But nobody could give us food or clothing." They were poor, fiercely proud, and, however haltingly, self-sufficient. Yet this aid was acceptable, as it demonstrated "a sense of kinship and a feeling of mutual responsibility" with other Norwegian settlers.[65]

"Except for that one bad spell, we always had plenty to eat." Babe's optimism here is contradicted many times by her own telling of her life story. She described Hannah's struggle to provide: "Momma had to go in a lot for things like soup that were inexpensive, but filling and nourishing." Dora, the oldest child, was already working and contributing six dollars a week for her room and board. Feeding the family of nine cost sixteen or seventeen dollars per week—a sum that boggled Babe's young mind as she and Lillie pulled the loaded wagon home from the grocery.[66]

Babe added her efforts to the family coffers as a youngster. She'd be paid ten cents for brushing Sigrid's mother's hair—an honorable way, all agreed, for Babe to "earn" a dime. At twelve she took her first after-school job at a fig-packing plant, which paid thirty cents an hour. Her job was to peel the bad spots off the figs as they came her way, clean them, and toss them back in the trough. The acid made her hands quite sore since she could not afford the rubber gloves workers were advised to wear. Better wages at the nearby potato gunnysack factory lured her away. Paid a penny a piece for each constructed sack, Babe dazzled her employer by earning about sixty-eight cents an hour; her output surpassed that of all other workers. And, true to form, she'd slip out of work to play sports "and then I'd work overtime and everything to make up for it." These early jobs, no doubt, inspired her to rise above a future of similar employment. Babe kept a nickel or a dime of her earnings and put the rest in Hannah's sugar bowl. Babe urged her mother to use the money on little things for herself, not on groceries or necessities. "But she never did." Babe recalled in 1955, "She saved it all for me, and when the time came that I needed something, she'd have the money right there." Through Hannah's example, Babe was familiar with self-sacrifice and generosity and tried to do all she could for her parents when she had the chance.[67]

Through all of these hardships she became a survivor and learned to do whatever was necessary to get what she wanted. In her adolescent and teenage years Babe's fierce competitiveness, self-congratulatory bravado, and love of her family and sports solidified. She knew that with her family's love, warmth, and acceptance she could do anything. Family, friends, local reporters, and Beaumonters witnessed the first ripple of excitement about Babe's abilities in what would become a tidal wave. Everyone applauded her sports talents. She was as exceptional as they said. Babe soaked the accolades in through her pores. She was born to be a star.

CHAPTER TWO

One Golden Cyclone:
The Rise to Prominence

Babe blossomed into greatness during her cocky and confident late teens. She was, as Bill Scurlock, a sportswriter and her friend, wrote, "flamboyant, down-to-earth, apparently gruff at times, perhaps, but considerate, humorous, friendly, warm-hearted and generous." Thanks, in part, to "Tiny" Scurlock, who interviewed her old chums, Doucette Street neighbors, school officials, and siblings, articles about Babe appeared regularly in the *Beaumont Journal* and her fame grew. After she became high scorer on the basketball team her junior year, Scurlock charted Babe's even more impressive feats during her senior year.[1]

In 1930, Melvin J. McCombs, the coach of the Employers Casualty Insurance Company women's semiprofessional basketball team in Dallas, saw the articles and traveled to East Texas to watch her play. His company had begun an employee athletic program in 1924 because athletes were found to be more efficient, reliable, and accurate in their work than nonathletes. After seeing Babe play McCombs offered her a position in the company upon her graduation in June and a chance to join the Golden Cyclones basketball team. Ruth Scurlock recalled the Beaumont team's excitement over the offer. "But after the game, up in our rooms in the Rice Hotel, Babe didn't seem to be thinking about the offer," she said. "She was too busy leaning out the window trying to see how many people she could spit at and hit on the head when they walked below on the sidewalk." Babe accepted the offer and the deal was considered closed. But "about two weeks later," McCombs wrote, "she informed me that she had made arrangements with the high school authorities to retire from school at that time" and re-

turn in June to get her diploma. She asked to begin work immediately because "the financial circumstances of her people demanded that she secure
employment somewhere."[2]

Babe told McCombs that she wanted to be an athlete, but she knew how
to type and take shorthand as well. She thought she couldn't make a living
in sports, except perhaps in physical education, so the merger of basketball
and secretarial skills seemed an ideal solution. To razzle-dazzle readers of
her life, Babe always interjected at this point that she had won a gold medal
in school for hitting the best speed on the typewriter. "I think it was eighty-
six words a minute. I practiced by typing out 'The Story of My Life.' I was
only fourteen or fifteen, and that story ran 42,000 words!" In fact, she learned
to type while at Employers Casualty and no evidence exists to support her
claim of expert and world-record-pace typing. In fact, some nonathlete
employees complained of the players' work performances. Babe's father gave
his approval to her move to Dallas, and Hannah, despite her reservations,
eventually consented. No doubt the appearance of Mrs. Henry Wood, the
"team mother" and chaperon, reassured Hannah. Babe, in the dress she'd
won a prize for, traveled with her father to Dallas. She had $3.49 in her pock-
et—the change from the money her new employer had given her for a train
ticket.[3]

Babe's clerical duties at Employers Casualty involved "tabulating and typing detailed statements of losses." Her efficiency, McCombs claimed, was on
par with that of her co-workers. Then again, he was known to spin yarns of
clerical skill for his players. Some evidence suggests that his prime motivation was not to provide his company with better employees. McCombs's
program personified the highly competitive athletic system detested by the
ruling body of the WDNAAF. He recruited athletes to join his company,
hired young women for their athletic ability alone, gave them clerical positions, encouraged some to quit high school to join the team, abandoned the
demure bloomer outfit, and did not encourage those less skilled to play. Mc-
Combs rebuffed these criticisms. Sure, he hired women for their athletic
talents alone, but he did not fire them if they underachieved at work or did
not make the team. Also, only two of his one hundred recruits failed to meet
the company's job criteria.[4]

Babe's athletic duties included competing on the Cyclone basketball,
baseball, and track and field teams (competing in running, broad jump, 80-
meter hurdles, javelin, and shot put) with exceptional athletes. The wom-
en's team had eight All-American basketball players on its roster, while track
team members held nine out of eleven southern track and field records and

two world track records. As Babe excelled amongst these stars, McCombs and Babe became mutual admirers. Yet, in an interview with the *Dallas Dispatch* McCombs revealed their relationship was not always trouble-free: "Babe Didrikson was the easiest girl to coach and the hardest to handle of all athletes I have had in the past 15 years."[5]

The Employers Casualty team participated in a Texas-wide network of company-sponsored women's basketball teams that flourished in the 1920s and 1930s, the national heyday of the sport's popularity and profitability. Semiprofessional basketball in Texas, the state most receptive to the sport, drew highly competitive players from school leagues, recreation and industrial leagues, college teams, and Sunday school leagues. By 1920 the AAU had relaxed its 1910 policy barring sanctioned women's play and listed 962 Texas women who had applied for permission to play in tournaments. Colleges in Oklahoma, Arkansas, and Texas recruited non-college-bound women with promises of housing stipends, tuition assistance, and financial aid. The player/employees took these positions because they offered job training with a reputable company, extended opportunities to play ball, and better salaries. One ECC employee saw her wages increase from $36 to $65 per month when she joined the company's team. Companies such as Franklin Motor Car, Sunoco Oil, and Piggly Wiggly Groceries sponsored local teams as an advertising tactic to gain national recognition. These teams played league competition and awaited AAU-sponsored state, regional, and national tournaments.[6]

By 1930 Dallas newspapers covered forty-eight women's teams, both college and semiprofessional, and offered literally no negative reactions to the athletes' competitiveness or physicality. In fact, women's basketball was the most popular spectator sport in the Dallas area until the 1950s. Press coverage of women's basketball usually dominated the North Texas sports pages from January through March in 1927–33. Thus, the athletes, and Babe in particular, lived in an insulated and approving milieu.[7]

The industrial league was dominated first by the Sunoco Oil Company Oilers, who won the national championship in 1928, 1929, and 1930. No doubt McCombs's aggressive recruitment of Babe sought to salve the wound of his team's one-point loss to the Oilers in 1929. But the Employers Casualty Company (ECC) team soon eclipsed Sunoco's popularity, thanks largely to the power of the team, McCombs's considerable promotional skills, and former professional pitcher Danny Lynch's contributions as coach, business manager, chaperon, trainer, and mascot.[8]

The Cyclones' dominance was total for five years. The team won 36 tournament championships and 361 individual medals. While playing over forty games per season, ECC averaged thirty-eight points per game but their competitors averaged only eleven. They held a national record by scoring ninety-seven points in tournament play and once held an opponent to four points. They routinely drew 1,000–4,000 spectators for home games. Regional and tournament play swelled the crowds to 3,500–5,000. Games were also carried live on the radio, thus expanding the teams' and players' fame and notoriety throughout the region.[9]

The Women's National Basketball League, to which ECC belonged, consisted of forty-five teams by 1933. In later years it was limited to thirty-two teams. It was under the auspices of the women's branch of the AAU. Teams were "sponsored by businesses, wealthy individuals, and civic organizations." A few had church names. The first All-American team was selected in 1929, one year before Babe began play. Babe was selected for the All-American team for 1930–32, highlighted by her tournament play in 1931 when she scored 106 points in five games while leading her team to the national championship. Both Scurlock and Paxton claim she scored 210 points in five games at the AAU tournament in Wichita in 1930, which seems unlikely given the team average of only 38 points per game. Scurlock boasted in his other releases that she scored 195 points in Dallas over six games and had a one-game high of 130 points. Yet he qualified these "statistics" to the editor of *Coronet Magazine* with, "Most of the information I'm sending I know is true. . . . Some of the quotes you'll find are contradictory, but as you know stories on the famous grow and grow with the years."[10]

And as her fame grew opportunities most uncommon for a young woman of the era emerged for Babe. She earned an excellent income playing a team sport in its only available venue. She also moved several hundred miles away from home and parental influence and attained economic independence while doing so. She earned $75 per month, sent $45 of that home, and spent $5 a month for a room and virtually nothing on clothes. This left a nineteen-year-old, chaperoned only by a woman overseeing more than a dozen teenagers, with $25 a month to call her own. Such a sum imbued Babe with a sense of power and of her own "marketable worth" and even greater self-confidence. It was fertile ground in which to nurture a hustler.

Babe—brash, unpolished, and immensely talented—burst into this complex and controversial national women's sports scene. She was not particularly enamored of the sports heroes who preceded her and she was naive to many of the simmering complex organizational distinctions. Ironically, the politics of amateurism would come to play an insidious role in her life. She

was at once equipped by sheer talent and ill-equipped by historical circumstance and her lack of sophistication to handle the excitement and controversy that swirled around her. She was also slightly taken aback by her physically intimidating bunch of teammates. "I'd never seen so many large
girls—large feet, and large hands." Babe reminisced. "They were really
husky."[11]

As a nineteen-year-old Babe was unrestrained and unaffected by cultural conceptions of "proper" athletics. She hurled herself into this new level
of competition and outshone everyone else. She wore number seven, the
same number she'd worn in high school, and made her uniform over to fit
skin tight. McCombs, a P. T. Barnum showman himself, approved. He
changed the team's "baggy woolen bloomers, long stocking, and flapping
middy blouses" to "blue and white shorts and sleeveless blouses." He caused
controversy, created publicity for his team, and upped attendance from 1,000
to 4,000 per game. Crowds came to see the display of women's bodies, and
in Babe's third year the team shed the woolen shorts for bright orange pant-
ies. This caused "a sensation."[12]

In fact, the ECC outfits smashed traditional boundaries of women's sports
uniforms. At the turn of the century, women were expected to wear their full
petticoats and long dresses while participating in sports until divided skirts
and bloomers became more acceptable. In 1900 women played in ankle-
length skirts rather than bloomers. In 1926 the *New York Times* carried a
front-page story listing the dress code for French female athletes set out by
the Women's Sports Federation (WSFF). Previously, French women donned
"trunks and sleeveless tunics for their track and field competition, but now
they were forbidden by the morality committee of the WSFF to wear them."
The new regulations also required dark colors and brassieres. Prominent
American physical educators endorsed these standards. Yet, these conservative requirements went unheeded by the competitors. In the 1932 national
track and field meet, Babe "wore short track pants, sleeveless blouse, and no
stockings."[13]

Babe played in her first ECC basketball game, donned in her sleek uniform, against the Sun Oil Company team. The Oilers had heard about Babe
and hoped to put her in her place. Babe, unruffled, excelled nonetheless and
was the game's high scorer. This snowballed, years later, into the autobio-
graphical claim "I got four or five points more than the whole Sun Oiler's
team did." Hyperbole aside, her play was sterling. By the end of the tournament she was chosen for the All-American team.[14]

Babe loved the press coverage given her. She drank it in. Of the tournament coverage she said, "My picture was in the center, blown up way big. There were just little head shots of the others. Man, I just loved that! It was the first big publicity I'd ever had. I cut it out and sent it home to Momma. She always saved my clippings." Sports pages usually featured Babe in head-lines such as "Babe Didrikson Is Star of Cyclones Game" and "Beaumont Girl Plays Tonight in Cage Meet." Babe was truly delighted when a big cartoon of her face entitled "Mighty Mildred" dominated the coverage.[15] Babe's unabashed egocentrism caused two biographers to comment that while Babe was the best, the fame, money, and praise did nothing to smooth her jagged edges. "It was a heavy burden for an unsophisticated, uneducated young woman to carry and Babe did not do it very well. She became more arro-gant, more self-centered, than before."[16]

This unfriendly appraisal of Babe's character is harsh, but not undeserved. It correctly reveals the abrasiveness her competitors knew too well. A case in point: upon arriving at ECC Babe announced to the Cyclones' star for-ward that she wanted her position and intended to get it. True to form, she did. Yet she also had friends and certainly admirers among her ECC team-mates. Autographed photos inscribed to Babe by Cyclone teammates con-firm this. Notations ranged from the cool "To Babe: *The Best*" to the affec-tionate "Love to My Speedy Running Mate" to the adoring "Passionately yours" to the worshipping "To the *Great God Babe*," while another was teas-ingly playful: "To My 'Low-life' Girl-Friend-'Babe.'" Strained relationships perhaps, but emotionally powerful.[17]

After the AAU tournament she went back and finished up at Beaumont High. Her high school principal remarked "that the mark on her school records that merely said 'withdrew, Feb. 14, 1930' should be now revised to say, 'Left school to be world's greatest athlete.'"[18]

After basketball, Babe competed on other ECC teams. In softball Babe was a power hitter, and in one herculean outing Babe claims to have hit "some-thing like thirteen home runs in one double-header." Granted, the women weren't very good fielders, but she "was fast enough to get around the bases before they could throw it back in." Although this home-run extravaganza is an unsubstantiated claim, her exceptional talent makes it believable. She also played doubles tennis and shone in exhibitions of springboard and plat-form diving. This ECC diving team was called "Mildred Didrikson and Her Employers Casualty Girls."[19] Babe's proficiency in this sports potpourri was equalled only by her effusive cockiness. "I won diving events in swimming meets," she said, "and I honestly think I could have qualified for the Olym-pic swimming team if I had concentrated on it." The ECC female athletes also gave golf lessons at the Dallas Country Club and, in the summer, competed in track and field.[20]

McCombs, aware of Babe's boredom once basketball season ended, introduced her to track and field. Babe announced she would try all of the events "because I thought I could do it." McCombs taught her how to time her steps approaching the long jump, the high jump, and the eight hurdles in the 80-meter event. Thus coached, the rest was Babe's doing. She regimented herself to a grueling and relentless routine. She often ran well into the dark hours and pushed herself beyond physical comfort. "I really worked hard at that track and field. I trained and trained and trained." She was that way in every sport she took up. Her successes resulted from raw talent coupled with relentless training sessions. After dinner she'd lace up her tennis shoes and run in her neighborhood, the Oak Cliff section of Dallas: "They had a hill on Haines Street that went down to a lake. I'd run all the way down there, and then I'd jog all the way back up. I'd jog my legs real high, and work my arms high, to get them in shape. Of course, they were already about as hard as they could be, but I thought they had to be better." Her practice sessions at Lakeside Park lasted until 9:00–9:30 P.M.[21]

McCombs was well aware of her rigorous routines. In fact, he said, "Her only fault, as I have found it, is that she unconsciously and unknowingly overtrains." This is a curious comment from a coach who set the high jump cross bar—during training sessions—at 5 feet 3 inches—the women's world record at the time—and rewarded successful jumps with chocolate sodas. Nevertheless, he worried about "Babe's juvenility and nervous energy [which] oft times work to her disadvantage." She tended to brood over coming events, and even when not training on the field she was obsessed with competitions to come. If not continually cautioned, he intoned, "she loses the spark that has carried her like a sweeping meteor to the very pinnacle of success."[22]

This same obsessive desire to excel at any cost prompted Babe to practice golf, which she was just learning, until her hands bled and blistered. She would hit 1,000–1,500 balls for eight to ten hours per day. Lillie, who lived with Babe at that time, had clear and disturbing memories of her sister's unwillingness to recognize any physical limits. "She'd hit and hit the balls until she had to put tape over her hands." It would be dark and Lillie would "*beg* Babe to go in, but she'd say, 'no, I got to hit just a few more.'" Gene Sarazen said of Babe's practice regimens in the mid-1930s, "I only know of one golfer who practiced more than Babe and that was Ben Hogan."[23]

Babe's singularly fierce determination to win overrode all else. At an AAU track and field meet against the Boswell Dairy team of Fort Worth in June 1930 held at Ownby Stadium at Southern Methodist University, Babe stepped on a broken bottle at the bathhouse before practice. As she wrote Tiny Scurlock, "and of course I would step on the biggest piece and I went to the Doctor 2 times and he gouged around and made it so sore. but boy did I jump, and throw that Ball & Javelin put that shot." Press coverage of this meet also marveled at Babe's U.S. record in the high jump (5 feet 1½ inches), her first in the shot put (37 feet 1 inch), her first in the baseball throw (264 feet 16 inches), and her first in the javelin (118 feet 7 inches) given her injury. Babe's team won the meet, 78 to 46, with Babe scoring 28 points. One paper headlined "Didrikson High Point Scorer When Cyclones Capture A.A.U. Crown" and commented, "Didrikson, star performer of the E.C.C., lived up to expectations by shattering mark(s)." With an off-handedness that could only come from one as self-assured as Babe, she added a postscript to her letter to Tiny: "Oh Yeah! right after the Track Season I'm gonna train for the Olympic in 1932 on the Broad Jump."[24]

Piling Up the Golds

Within days of arriving in Dallas Babe began an active correspondence with Tiny Scurlock. Each had something to offer the other. Babe wanted Tiny to be her manager and in exchange she would feed him her Dallas-based news with strict instructions to write her up as often as possible in her hometown region. Tiny, aware that he had a meteor in his pocket, willingly complied.

The contract between Tiny and Babe, formally ready to sign in September 1931, was to have been a three-year deal. Tiny was obliged to look after Babe's welfare. The contract notes that because of Babe's skill and bright future, "there will be offers or tenders of money in such forms as vaudeville contracts, contracts with motion picture concerns, contracts for various kinds of public appearances, endorsements of an advertising nature, etc." He was to protect her amateur standing in athletics until she decided to become a professional. He was to handle all feature stories about Babe. In return, Tiny would receive 25 percent of all of Babe's monies "except what she is receiving in the form of wages or salary."[25] The brief two-page contract was certified by a notary public in Jefferson County Texas.

Babe, at the tender age of nineteen, already showed signs of being a masterful self-promoter. In later years she perfected this. No doubt she would have made an outstanding sports agent for others, but she was her only commodity. In fact her hustler attitude led her to become a fairly unpleasant character. Determined to outshine teammates and opponents and dominate press coverage of her team's successes, she became a controversial, often unlikable, self-involved young woman. Her correspondence with Scurlock highlights this.

It also reveals her poor writing and language skills. Numerous misspellings and grammatical errors belie her claim that she was an above average student in high school and give her principal's cryptic comment that she was an "adequate" student new validity. Her letters, replete with colloquialisms, demonstrate her working-class, East Texas roots. Her speech was not contrived, it was colorful. In later years she'd work to transform both her coarse speech and her unpleasant image, but in these letters it is pure Babe.

In one of her earliest notes to Tiny she penned, "I was one of six girls from—America to go to Germany next August 1930 and Tiny Mr. Bingham President of the National A.A.U. and all of the officials said that I had a berth on the Olympic team in 1932 without a doubt." Babe shared her hopes with Tiny. The magnitude of her goals are juxtaposed against her simple language. As she wrote him in May 1930, days after the Southern Methodist University track meet, "Boy Tiny if I hadn't sat down on that last broad jump I could have broken the world's record just like taking candy from a baby, But next Saturday the 31th and I am gonna break a record in every thing that I go out for." Her expectations reflected recent successes: "Last Saturday I entered four things and won first in all four."[26]

At times she sent him write-ups that appeared in out-of-town newspapers covering the track meets. Such was the case when she wrote, "Just got back from Shreveport from the Southern track meet Well that makes the 13th gold medal that I have gotten. Made me a bracelet out of the first one that I got. and I got 3 from the Southern Meet. All gold and no silver. I am sending you a write up from the times."[27]

Babe's goals were perfectionist, striking, and unrelenting. In her letters to Tiny we don't see a young athlete striving solely for steady improvement or personal bests. We see a woman with a consuming hunger attacking—and determined to conquer—world records. In May 1930 she was frustrated by her failure to set a world's record in the broad jump. In early June she was plotting how to fortify her stash of thirteen gold medals. After the Shreveport meet she wrote Tiny, "I am gonna enter the tennis, swimming and every other kind of meets over here and over there. get full of medals. You know like ants." After a few chatty lines she closed with, "Well Tiny I have got to go out to the track field at S.M.U. and brush up for the Texas and the National meet." Her motivation? "So that I can Break a few worlds records."[28]

She and Tiny also had a running dialogue about monetary opportunities. Although Tiny's letters are not available, his efforts to secure her endorsements and better pay are evident from her side of the correspondence. Yet he seems singularly uninformed about the complexities and quirks of maintaining A.A.U. amateur status. Babe responded to him in June 1930 with, "Tiny about that Fleshmens Yeast [endorsement] won't that Make me professional Well I don't want to get that way right away." Babe, the hustler, emerges as a sharp scout for her own interests. In May, she wrote one of her lengthiest notes to Scurlock outlining a letter she'd received from the Kansas City Life Insurance Company that invited her to play for their team. "Girls are paid $80.00 per month to start, also are given free medical attention," she wrote. Another boon was "a cafeteria operated in the building for employes only and is not run for profit. All this is a saving and makes it possible to live even cheaper." But it was the per-game system of monetary rewards that appealed to Babe the most. "$25.00 per victory in regular games, $50.00 per victory in city tournament games, $100.00 per victory in national games, with an additional $100.00 for winning of local league cup, $100.00 additional for winning of city championship," and an additional—proportionate—bonus if they won the national tournament. "This bonus," she knew "does not make a player a professional as it has been approved by the head of the Western A.A.U."[29] She concluded with the usual instructions for him to save all papers for her scrapbook. Significantly, Babe's restless discontent about pay surfaces a mere three months after she began competing for Employers Casualty at a salary heftier than many heads of households earned.

Much of this discontent stemmed from her economic hardships growing up and her desire to care for her parents as they had cared for her. Her victories and success often translated into gifts sent home to her family. Victory and prosperity became enmeshed. She sent home generous gifts that put her into debt and increased her desire for more money. She sent home $45 of her $75 pay. Ruth Scurlock felt Babe tried to reciprocate when she was barely able. Of the Didriksens, Ruth said when interviewed, "Babe's family was really on their uppers all the time. They always had their hands out to her—even in those years in Dallas when she was a child making a pittance pay. She was under a lot of pressure all the time. She never had as much money as they thought she did, but they wanted her to give, give, give." Babe's gifts later increased in size and value. In 1933 she bought her father a De Soto. She bought a radio on credit for her parents that cost almost an entire month's salary. She then bought a wicker bedroom set for her mother that she'd bargained down from $100 to $80. She bought her father new clothes and took her mother shopping and purchased eight new dresses for her. For Mother's Day, Babe, still in her teens, bought her mother a refrigerator and a stove. She arranged for the store to deliver them and secretly surprise Hannah. She paid this purchase off on credit.[30]

Hannah's joy at receiving these gifts was palpable. "She was so overwhelmed she started to cry," Babe recalled twenty-five years later. "She came over and began hugging me. 'Min Babe,' she kept saying 'You did it! My best girl!' "[31] Hence Babe redoubled her efforts to ease her parents' burdens. She managed to spare them the brunt of the difficulties most experienced during the depression while continuously alleviating their earlier poverty.

The symbiosis of victory and money seemed natural and desirable to Babe. She said of her constant gift-giving, often far beyond her means, "Whenever I got extra money, one of the things it always meant to me was that now I'd be able to do more for mother and dad." She was not shy in her quest for money. She once chastised Fred Corcoran, her business agent from the late 1940s through her death in 1956 (loud enough for others to hear), after he'd suggested she play golf for charity: "You get me the jobs that pay. I'll take care of the charities."[32]

She was the consummate hustler. In fact Babe excelled at parlaying her fame into dollars. She boldly suggested, then accepted, a horse, jewelry, dinners, clothing, entertainment, and other items given in exchange for a photo taken with a store owner, her presence at a restaurant, or simply for the pleasure of having met her.

She was, in the fullest sense of the word, a survivor. She did what had to be done to earn the money she wanted. She was the primary family breadwinner, an ominously burdensome role for a young, working-class, depression-era woman.[33]

Because of the pressure to help her family her dissatisfaction with her wages escalated in the months ahead. In April 1931, her affection for Tiny had grown, as had her determination to get more money from McCombs. "Why hello old top, how in the heck are you getting along. Now this is the time that I need a manager," she wrote. She lamented that she wanted a job that paid at least $125 a month, but was constrained by the "twelve month rule," which prohibited an athlete whose team played in the national tournament from changing clubs for one year following tournament play. Frustrated by this technicality, Babe displayed cunning, business savvy, and, possibly, questionable ethics when she asked Tiny to write a trumped-up letter to her designed to unnerve ECC. She asked Tiny to send a letter telling her about a "keen proposition" he had found for her "and kina stretch it see, cause when I show it to him [McCombs] he will raise my pay to about what you say in that offer. This is just to make them break loose and pay me a little more dough." Babe knew the trickery involved—it prompted her to tell Scurlock to keep their scheme secret. Yet she felt justified. Her evaluation of her own worth is unswerving: "I am the ony prospect of him winning the National and he knows that, plenty of teams want me but can't get me on account of the 12 month rule, the only way out is to turn professional and that will make them cherp up and pay me what they ought to."[34]

Scurlock declined the chicanery. The next letter from Babe, a month later, includes write-ups from two Dallas papers, the *Dallas Journal* and the *Dallas Dispatch,* which carried her stories regularly. Babe recommended that Tiny subscribe directly to them so that he could run the stories in Beaumont. She signed her letters "Your friend, Babe" by 1931 and occasionally asked that he give her regards to his family and questioned, "How do you like my typing? eh." In October 1931 she related an advertisement soliciting "Girl Athletes" in Ohio, and declared, "Heck Tiny if I get me another letter from Wichita, Kans. I'm Gonna take it."[35]

In November Babe learned that it violated AAU amateur standing to have a manager "unless it was a team manager and so I guess we'll have to tear up that contract, don't mind do you?" Besides, she wrote disgruntledly, "it won't do any good to have a manager—anyway I'm gonna quit soon and go to school and be a gym teacher some where in California right after then done got it all arranged"[36] Thus the articulate business contract between Tiny and Babe, signed September 15, 1931, was never implemented. Babe was on her own.

A month and a half later Babe's frustration with McCombs's unwillingness to renegotiate her pay was at the breaking point. "Well, Heck it seems as though I'm gonna have to go somewhere else, they think I'm just putting them on up here and know I wont go, but I'm gonna show 'em." She staunchly believed she was worth at least fifty dollars more per month. There was a poignant urgency to her despair. She felt her playing days were limited—a rare admission of vulnerability for Babe. "I goto make something on my athletic ability now or never—I'm not gonna be good always you know." Things had deteriorated considerably between Babe and McCombs. She had "shut down" her basketball skills as a form of protest. He, in return, benched her. She remained strong-willed and angered and alienated teammates and management. "I don't care whether I play basket ball anymore or not I'm sitting on the bench most of the game now because I won't try to play ball."[37]

There are at least two interpretations of this series of events. Earlier biographers lash out at Babe, saying "she had become a prima donna: petulant, unreasonable. If the years with Employers Casualty had sharpened her athletic skills, they had also put some jagged edges on her personality." In a separate incident, she left Employers Casualty because McCombs refused to give her an extra week's vacation for her sterling performances. This was reported as "Babe quit her job, storming out in a tantrum," an interpretation that trivializes her motivation and rationale. They also ridicule her exacting concern with her press coverage: "Babe was so full of herself in these months. . . . Her 'scrape book' of newspaper clippings was attended with the same ecstatic care as another girl might handle love letters from a particularly exciting beau." The inference is clear: Babe's aggressiveness was unfeminine and her exclusive focus on sports unnatural for a female. In short, her desire to be taken seriously as an athlete through hefty paychecks rendered her pushy, self-centered, and unseemly. It's doubtful this analysis would be applied to a male athlete in similar circumstances; his actions might be interpreted as savvy business moves. This is not to argue that Babe was faultless. She was abrasive and egocentric, traits that do not foster good team play. Hence, after her Golden Cyclone basketball days she always chose to compete in individual events and sports.[38]

Yet, a case can be made that Babe deserved more than her teammates did. Her accomplishments in 1930 and 1931 were phenomenal and unparalleled: she was a two-time All-American basketball player and won the 80-meter hurdles in 12 seconds at the AAU-sanctioned event (1931)—a record that held up for eighteen years. At the national AAU meet in 1930 she set an unofficial world record of 18 feet 8½ inches before being bested by Stella Walsh, in the same meet, by half an inch. In 1931 Babe won the women's national AAU championship with a broad jump of 17 feet 11¾ inches; this record stood for six years. In the baseball throw she won the AAU championship in 1930 and 1931. Her 1931 effort in Jersey City set a world record at 296 feet. Babe said of her performance in the broad jump and baseball throw in 1931, "It was my medal hunting in this meet that started the sportswriter's keys clattering." In 1930 at the national AAU meet in Dallas she won the javelin with a throw of 133 feet 6 inches—an AAU and a U.S. record. This mark was also unofficially considered a world record because before 1932 women's records were kept less formally.[39]

Friction amongst Babe and her teammates, the second thorn in her side, revolved around her self-interested, antithetical approach to basketball and track and field—both considered "team" sports.[40] She was more interested in her own excellence, fame, popularity, and pay than in collective glory. After being in Dallas only one month she wrote Tiny, "I have a whole lots of fans now." But it's likely her teammates were not among them. Wichita, where Babe considered relocating, appealed in part because her teammates "are just like they were in Beaumont High School Jealous and more so because they are all here and trying to beat me. But they can't do it."[41]

Her teammates had ample reason to be jealous: her talents and persona dwarfed any victories they gained. And special favors were accorded "The Babe" from the minute to the significant. Early in her career, when the basketball team members resided in Oak Cliffs, they all ate together. At times they also ate at the drug store lunch counter. "The guy at the soda fountain would never charge me for my coke," Babe recalled. "He'd say, 'How about another one, champ?' That made me feel good, because I wasn't any champ then."[42]

Former Golden Cyclone teammates, overshadowed by Babe for years, did not mince words when describing her egocentrism. One said, "She was not a team player, definitely not. Babe was out for fame. There were lots of players on the Cyclones more popular than Babe was. But she got to be famous. And that's what she wanted." Another AAU teammate stated, Babe "was out for Babe, honey, just Babe. . . . She was not a team player, definitely not. Babe, she was out for fame." Thus hustling lost Babe friendship and respect, but gained her special status, notoriety, and eventually the wealth she coveted.[43]

What especially infuriated her competitors was her bragging and claims of superiority. Most distressing to them was her ability to deliver on her seemingly impossible predictions. She successfully created myths of herself that diverted all attention to her. Describing the 1930 Dallas AAU meet to a reporter, she claimed she saw a javelin lying on the ground. "What do you do with this thing? I picked it up and somebody showed me how to grab it. I just rared back like one of those Texas steers and let her go." And then the deceptions that so frustrated teammates who knew the truth: "The first time I threw it I broke the world's record. I threw it 129 feet 10 inches. I was sixteen years old." The fact is, Babe had zealously practiced the javelin for several months, set an AAU-U.S. record with a throw of 133 feet 6 inches, and was nineteen years old. Rhetoric and reality had become so scrambled that Babe, in this instance, undercut the length of the actual toss. But far more common were the exaggerations that at once built her up and minimized others. In the same aptly titled article, "I Blow My Own Horn" (1936), Babe claimed she was "discovered" by McCombs when he'd been scouting another athlete. But her play so impressed him that he immediately offered her a spot on the team at $90 a month. What Babe accomplished in her rendition of this incident was twofold: by exaggerating the quickness of the offer she'd added excitement and tension to the McCombs deal; and by exaggerating her pay from the actual $75 to the fictional $90 she outearned, hence was more valuable than, her teammates. As elsewhere, she gained notoriety but lost respect and trust.[44]

Thus myth begat myth. Lawrence Lader, a columnist for *Coronet,* wrote, "The Babe picks up a new sport as if she had been playing it all her life. Five minutes after stepping onto a bowling alley she was scoring 170." The fact is she devoted herself to bowling: she worked at it tirelessly and became quite good after grueling practice sessions. There was no instant 170 success. But no matter, people believed there was.

In 1932 she predicted her solo victory at the National Track and Field Championships—and delivered. During a team trip to a Los Angeles amusement park several of the women unsuccessfully shot at moving ducks. True to form "Babe grabbed the rifle and announced: 'Ah'll show you some shooting.' Then she proceeded to knock over 24 out of 24." As time went on, this feat became enshrined as her "expert marksmanship." Yet another sport conquered.[45]

Babe, much to her detractors' dismay, did predict and deliver. This was never more true than in her performance at the 1932 national AAU championship in Evanston, Illinois. This meet, where Babe was the one-woman team for Employers Casualty, doubled as the tryouts for the 1932 Olympics. To the 250 outstanding athletes assembled in Evanston, Babe announced, "Ah'm gonna lick you single-handed."[46]

The next two hours propelled Babe into unparalleled glory and national fame. It's a mind-boggling scene to contemplate. As the announcer called out the names of each competing team, they ran out onto the field to the applause of the crowd. When Babe's team was called, "she ran onto the field all alone, waving her arms wildly, carried along by the roar of the crowd." Toward the end of her days Babe called this one of the most thrilling moments of her life. The thrill was mixed with fear, however. The night before the meet she couldn't sleep because of stomach pains so severe that "when I put my hand on it [stomach], the hand would just bounce up and down." Mrs. Wood, team chaperon, called the hotel doctor. Diagnosis: her excitement was affecting the nerve center in her diaphragm. This became familiar to Babe, who read this pain as a signal that she was "really ready" to compete. Conquering her anxiety, she changed her clothes in the car on the way to the stadium.[47]

Her challenge seemed literally insurmountable. She was pitted against two hundred women on teams with as many as twenty members. She entered eight of the ten events, all but the 50- and 220-yard dashes. She ran from one event to another; and on a few occasions the judges delayed starting so that she could catch her breath. Officials also gave her extra minutes to rest between events. "Babe's special treatment," according to one chronicler, "made other competitors fighting mad. Babe made them madder by going around the infield bragging and hollering, 'I'm going to win everything I enter.' "[48]

Despite her hurrying, excitedness, possible fatigue, and abrasiveness, she won six events. She set an AAU and a U.S. record by a throw in the shot put of 39 feet 6¼ inches. Her performance of 272 feet 2 inches in the baseball throw earned a world record. She captured the javelin throw with 139 feet 3 inches, better than her own recognized world record of 133 feet 5½ inches set in 1930. In the 80-meter hurdles she won one heat in 11.9 seconds, which was one-tenth of a second better than her previous world record. She went on to win the event with a time of 12.1 seconds. She tied Jean Shiley for first place in the high jump with 5 feet 3/16 inch, an AAU record. She won the broad jump with 17 feet 6 inches. Although she usually did not compete in the discus, she managed to capture fourth place. She didn't make the finals in the 100-yard dash, missing third place in her heat by a step. Babe won six gold medals and broke four world records "in the space of three hours in a single afternoon." She earned thirty points. The second place team, Illinois Athletic Club, had twenty-two points.[49]

The press, then the nation, went wild. The *Dallas Morning News* headline crowed, "Didrikson, Unaided, Wins National Track Championship: Babe Lands Thirty Points to Outclass Nation's Best Feminine Teams." George Kirksy, a United Press reporter, called it "the most amazing series of performances ever accomplished by any individual, male or female, in track and field history." Babe, always taking pulse of her fame, knew this was a turning point. "This is when that stuff about me being a 'super athlete' and a 'wonder girl' started up," she recalled.[50] And this "stuff" was just fine with her. Other journalists openly marveled at her. Arthur Daley mused that "implausible is the adjective which best befits the Babe. As far as sports is concerned she had the golden touch of Midas." An editorial from the *Chicago Tribune* was no less effusive. "Babe Didrikson of Dallas, Texas, nineteen year old marvel, has started out to win the Olympic games single handed. Beginning with the javelin throw Babe is hard to believe even when she proves it." Again, the editorial spouted incredulity at her excellence and her diversity: "She is a bowler, baseball player and basketball player. She is a sprinter, hurdler, high and broad jumper and shot putter. She does the 100 yards in 11 seconds, can put the eight-pound shot over 37 feet and throw a baseball 296 feet."[51] And another paper, debunking the notion of "the weaker sex," warned, "Gangway! Here comes a real woman athlete. With the speed and grace of an antelope." Babe announced her intentions to all who would listen and those who labored to avoid her; she planned to win all her events in the upcoming Los Angeles Olympics. Her time had come.[52]

The 1932 Olympic Games: Where All the Hedge-Hopping Paid Off

Babe described herself as a supple and lithe "18-year-old kid" (though she was twenty-one) who "didn't need any rest in those days." After her impressive performance friends took Babe and Mrs. Wood out dancing until 3:00 A.M. to celebrate. Next morning it was business as usual for Babe, who worked out "to make sure my muscles didn't tighten up or anything." Mrs. Wood took the trophies to Chicago and Babe went on to Los Angeles with the Olympic team. Babe jogged the length of the train, hurdled over her teammates in the aisles, and exercised while the other athletes "watched the scenery and played cards and gabbed."[53] This anecdote, however, had a darker, unapplaudable side that Babe did not tell. Evelyn Hall, her Olympic high jump competitor and teammate, said, "Babe kept running through the train, shrieking and yanking pillows out from under your head if you were sleeping." She further alienated her teammates by announcing to the press, "I came out here to beat everybody in sight and that's just what I'm going to do. Sure, I can do anything." She told Paul Zimmerman of Los Angeles, "I'm going to win the high jump Sunday and set a world's record. I don't know who my chief opponents are and anyway, it wouldn't make any difference. I hope they are good. . . . I plan to keep on setting records."[54]

This braggadocio did not alienate sportswriters. The *New York Times* said of her, "The Babe is no boaster and no braggart. She tells you simply what she can do, and then she does it." This reporter, stumped in finding something she could not do, asked about sewing. Babe bragged about her prize-winning dress and cooking skills. "'I've never played dolls though," Babe admitted proudly. "'When I was a little girl I'd rather play with my dad's hammer or hatchet than fool with dolls." This retort was picked up by the wire service and reprinted nationwide.[55]

On the way to Los Angeles, the team stopped in Denver. In her autobiography Babe recounted her youthful wonder at the effects of the altitude on her workouts; she became quickly winded. She also discussed how in later years, when Denver became her home, "I found out that the altitude made a difference in the kitchen, too." In what would become a familiar pattern, Babe interspliced recollections of track and field days with later, "feminine days." At times these juxtapositions are glaring non sequiturs. But the intent works: the reader's attention is diverted from track to her later, more "appropriate" pursuits. Thus in the midst of retelling her Olympic travel she continued with: "On a lot of dishes you couldn't go by the cooking times the ordinary recipe book called for, you had to make adjustments for the thinner air." Without so much as a pause she continued, "From Denver we went straight on to Los Angeles, and settled down there for regular workouts."[56]

Babe failed to mention one travel event that was seared in her teammates' memories. Babe, at the station stop in Albuquerque, New Mexico, took a Western Union bike and while riding it yelled at the top of her lungs: "Did you ever hear of Babe Didrikson? If you haven't you will! You wiiilllll!!" Hall recalls that "she was exactly like Muhammad Ali even then. Such a braggart."[57] Her teammates were embarrassed and angered at her unabashed self-promotion. It was the first of many clashes Babe would have with the other women. This irked Hall especially: "Babe was pretty cocky. Everyone was doing things for her. If she wanted a drink of water, someone got it for her. She seemed to have managers; her teammates waited on her." Babe was an antihero in these years. She exhibited few of the attributes expected of a champion. She was selfish, loud, and annoying. Self-promotion at any cost was her goal regardless of fallout. Here, the hustler role worked to limit her appeal.[58]

Babe's Olympic visa, issued to her on January 25, 1932, listed her name as "Mildred Didrikson" and her birthdate as June 26, 1913. Her photo shows an angular-jawed, serious-looking, straight-lipped young woman with eyes cast upward. She's wearing a snug-fitting stocking cap that covers virtually all of her hair; she is androgynous and determined.[59]

At the opening ceremonies, a sun-drenched, white-shirted, straw-hatted crowd of 105,000 welcomed 2,000 athletes from 39 countries. The U.S. team had 357 men and 43 women; 85 specialized in track and field. In grandiose fashion, 5,000 doves of peace were let loose as the Olympic flame was lit. All of the women on the U.S. team wore dresses, stockings, and white shoes they'd been "issued" by the Olympic Committee. For Babe, "I believe that was about the first time I'd ever worn a pair of stockings in my life; I was used to anklets and socks. And as for those shoes, they were really hurting my feet." Later she claimed, with mischievous delight, that during the long

ceremonial speeches she slipped the shoes off. This action was soon duplicated by most of the other women. Also, at the Chapman Park Hotel, the
women's quarters, she tried to teach Mexican fencer Eugenia Escudero how
to say "okay, baby" in English. She was a cut-up to the core.[60]

A drama of another sort was brewing while the games got under way.
Bubba Didriksen had left Texas riding a freight train aimed for Los Angeles
to see his sister compete. Bubba had been given $2.50 and a parental bless-
ing to make the trek by rail. The trip west took Bubba and a group of rag-
tag boys with whom he traveled several days longer than expected. The press,
following his journey, reported him lost. Recalled Jackie, Bubba's wife, "His
mother didn't know where he was, Babe didn't know where he was. The news
had these headlines that he'd been lost. [Babe] knew he was on his way out
there but that's all. . . . She was worried that he'd really been lost." The *Beaumont Journal* followed Bubba's whereabouts: "Arthur . . . [has not] been
heard from . . . since he started for Los Angeles two weeks ago to see his big
sister sweep her Olympic events. 'Bubba' started out on the highway route
to the far-western metropolis, but Babe in a letter home said that she had
not seen him."[61]

Slowed but undaunted, Bubba finally arrived at the Ambassador Hotel
in Los Angeles. His clothes filthy from the train ride, he and his chums saun-
tered into the new hotel, inquired after Babe, and learned she was out. "I
thought well, I would just sit down in those chairs there where they had those
doilies on the chairs—and well my feet never did hit the chair before somebody had me and told me that I couldn't wait in there." So he and the rest
of the disheveled pack waited down on a nearby street corner for Babe's
return. An hour later, when Babe's bus pulled up, Bubba told his pals to wait
for him elsewhere. Bubba's excitement while telling this moment was palpable. "She came on down and I met her," he said. "And she said, 'Where the
hell have you been? I've been lookin' for you for seven days.'" Bubba had the
thrill of watching her compete, as did their sisters Nancy and Dora. Bubba
stayed three weeks and chose to return to East Texas via freight train, "with
the boys," despite Hannah's urgings that he fly.[62]

Babe shattered records in her events and was the undisputed star of the
women's games. She set a new world and Olympic record in the javelin with
a throw of 143 feet 4 inches. The German women, thought to be the best,
were also-rans. Babe's first toss was the winning one. She'd been unable to
warm up because there wasn't room enough "without hitting someone."
"When my first turn came," she recalled, "I was aiming to throw the javelin
right over that flag. I drew back, then came forward and let fly." As she "let

the spear go" her hand slipped off the cord on the handle. It didn't arch the way it usually did; instead, it "went out there like a catcher's peg from home plate to second base. It looked like it was going to go right through the flag. The awkward toss tore cartilage in her right shoulder. She kept this to herself, completed her two other throws, and was aware that "people thought I wasn't trying because the throws weren't much good."[63]

Her second win was the 80-meter hurdles. She set another world and Olympic record of 11.7 seconds by beating her old time set in Evanston at the AAU meet. This victory, Babe quipped, was "the payoff on all the hedge-hopping." Betty Hicks, who saw Babe run the Olympic hurdles, classified her as "a superb, natural athlete. Unrefined I would say. Her form was pure raw talent. She ran the hurdles like she was jumping the hedge row in Beaumont." Babe beat Evelyn Hall of Chicago, an Olympic teammate, by a hair. "If it was horse racing," Babe said, "you'd say I won by a nose." It was a controversial win and a bitter pill for Hall to swallow.[64]

In fact, the loss embittered Hall even fifty years later. In a 1988 interview with the *Los Angeles Times,* Hall, then seventy-eight, remembered the race against Babe in fine detail. Hall said their wool racing clothes were "just short of miserable. . . . Some of us cried, they were so uncomfortable." Adding to her discomfort was pre-race nervousness and the fact that someone else dug her starting hole. At the finish, she and Babe crossed together. When they crossed the finish line, Babe yelled to Evelyn, "Well, I won again," digging Hall about their two earlier races against each other in Los Angeles. Hall's friends, she recalled, "were standing by Tunnel 6 with their hands up, cheering, and giving me the No. 1 sign with their fingers. They thought I had won. I thought I had won." Babe's comment clearly changed Hall's thinking for a second. "I shook my head and held up two fingers to them," she said. "Later, I learned that at that very moment a couple of judges were looking at me. It's possible they made their judgement from this gesture of mine. . . . I was heartbroken."[65] Looking at a photo of the finish fifty-six years after the race she said, "See where my leg is in this picture?" It was a statement more than a question. "I thought I won because [Didrikson] threw her arms out, while I breasted the tape." After considerable official debate Babe was declared the winner thirty minutes later despite Hall's claim that her neck bore the welt from hitting the tape.[66]

Another close race later that day prompted officials to review tapes of this race taken by an electric-eye camera. According to Hall, the Olympic officials then "declared the least I had done was tied." Officials also hinted that if the two runners had been from different countries a protest would have been filed, but since it was between teammates "a protest was denied."[67] Hall believes to this day that she won the race. In fact, Babe told her competitors that the officials were stupid: "All you have to do to win if it's close is throw up your arm just before the finish." Hall believes she was denied the medal because "Babe had so *much* publicity, it was impossible to rule against her." Hall's disappointment remains unabated. "I have always been taught right is right, and I felt, and still feel, that I was every bit the champion. My foot was over first, and I broke the tape first."[68]

"A Thorn to Women of the American Team"

For the women on the American team, this conflict over the 80-meter hurdles was much more than a question of who'd won the race. Feelings of hostility toward Babe had been on the rise since her Albuquerque bellowing. Jean Shiley, team captain, said, "I had to room with her in Denver because no one else would. Then as time went on I realized she certainly did have a big mouth." Shiley's portrayal didn't get any rosier when she added, "She would horn in every two minutes. If someone said they rode a kayak down from Alaska in three days, Babe would have done it better."[69]

Babe's desire to constantly be center stage infuriated her teammates. Shiley stated flatly, she "had no social graces whatsoever." In Colorado, a radio interviewer talked individually with each team member. After Babe's turn, "she kept horning in on the other interviews." The radio host ignored her but Babe, determined, "stood there and played her harmonica to call attention to herself; the noise drowned out the other girls' answers, of course." These antics came to haunt Babe. Dodd acknowledged that one reason Babe never spoke of her Olympic days in her adult years was because "she did a lot of practical joking when she was in the Olympics and the other girls didn't care too much for that."[70]

In fact, even Shiley's captaincy evolved from division and strife on the Olympic team when Babe, Lillian Copeland, and Shiley were nominated for team captain. Lillian withdrew so there would be no chance of Babe winning due to a three-way split in the voting. "If Babe had won," Shiley recalled, "the team would have been simply torn apart." Team sentiments were against Babe and were so high that her biographers editorialized, "Throughout the games, Babe Didrikson was to remain a thorn to women of the American team and they came to detest her."[71]

Shiley and Babe had an even greater drama and personal rivalry afoot. In the running high jump—Babe's third and final Olympic event—they'd been one another's arch rival for years. The Olympic match-up between the two became a focal point for the team's animosity toward Didrikson. Evelyn Hall said, "We were all actually praying for Jean Shiley to win. We were very high strung and we put a lot of pressure on Jean to beat this obnoxious girl." Other jumpers pressured Shiley to turn Babe in for fouling during her jumps. The point of controversy was Babe's style. She used the Western Roll, which was an acceptable jumping technique that had never been in contention until the Olympics.[72]

Shiley, intimidated by Babe, "couldn't turn her in for [fouling]. I knew she'd clobber me—with her mouth—if I caused her to lose by claiming a foul." They tied with a jump of 5 feet 5¼ inches. But, because of her style, the officials ruled Babe "dove" over the bar head first instead of clearing it with her feet first. As a result of her illegal jump, they awarded Shiley the gold and Babe the silver. Symbolic of the jump's controversy, Babe's medal was literally half gold and half silver—the only such medal in Olympic history. After the officials ruled, "Babe left the field very, very, angry." Shiley remembered that "the other girls on the team were delighted, like children at Christmas because I had beaten Babe. I was under terrible pressure, you know, because they had spent the last two days in my room saying, 'We couldn't beat her Jean, *you've* just got to beat her, cut her down to size.' Oh, it was a nightmare."[73]

Others too reveled in Babe's failure to win her third predicted gold medal. Betty Hardesty, writing in the *Sportswoman*, also crowed with delight. The entire tone of her article was "Babe can be stopped! Rah!" Shiley's hometown Philadelphians, Hardesty wrote, had their hopes fulfilled when she "returned to them a world champion high jumper, an Olympic record holder . . . a celebrity." Hardesty was joyful that Shiley "proved to the most skeptical that she would not be beaten, for not even Babe Didrikson, the Texas wonder and self-styled 'one-woman' track team, could outjump her." Jean "not only equalled the accepted world record but she bettered it by 2⅛ inches!"[74]

Hardesty was less effusive about Babe's accomplishments: "But Babe Didrikson, Texas' pride and joy, who had finished in a tie with Jean in the Olympic trials in Chicago was equally inspired," she wrote. Already she'd won two golds, setting world marks in each. "In addition, she had announced to her public that she would return to her native state with three Olympic victories—meaning that the high jump would be her third." The author's glee at Babe's "failure" is palpable. "Both cleared 5 feet 5 inches. But, with an opportunity to become the only triple winner in the Olympics, Babe

Didrikson found her last jump ruled out as a 'dive' and Jean Shiley cleared at 5 feet 5¼ inches to win the event."[75] Apparently Babe's reputation for cockiness preceded her. It gained her critics beyond her teammates. Her predictions, and her often infuriating ability to actualize them, irked and angered competitors. The press reveled in Babe's razzle-dazzle but athletes and many sports fans decried her poor taste. "Dethroning" Babe became a contest within a contest; for Shiley (and others to follow) there was winning the event, achieving a personal best—and then there was beating Babe.

Shiley's win remained a controversial decision. Members of the press corps rallied to Babe's defense. Grantland Rice, sportswriter and early, avid, and loyal idolater of Babe's, covered the event. Babe remembered "he talked to me right afterwards, and said he thought I'd been given a bad deal. So did some of the other writers." Though it didn't remove the sting of the judge's decision, "that made me feel a little better about winding up in second place."[76] To cheer her, Rice invited her to play golf. This consolatory match, ironically, was a turning point for Babe.

Two golds, two controversial calls, one gold-silver medal, and much animosity and publicity later, Babe emerged from the 1932 Olympics the undisputed star of the games. She was the epitome of a "golden cyclone," blessed, yet constantly enmeshed in turmoil.

Building the Pedestal

Babe rivaled and exceeded the headlines male Olympians received. She alone broke world records "while the men gained recognition only for breaking Olympic records." The *New York Times* named her "America's Girl Star of the Olympics," while the Metropolitan Newspaper Feature Service dubbed her "the outstanding personality of the Xth Olympiad." One piece called her "Iron-Woman" after she won the 80-meter hurdles, and another lamented, "when one looks over the athletic records of Miss Mildred Didrikson . . . one cannot help regretting that there is no all-around event for women athletes similar to the decathlon and pentathlon for men." And, based on her 1932 performance, chronicles of Olympic history feature Babe as that game's premiere Olympian. She is invariably described in glowing terms as "one of the best all-around sports women of all time." Based on her performance, the Associated Press voted her Female Athlete of the Year for 1932. Babe garnered 77 of 199 votes.[77]

The press exalted Babe. They dubbed her "The Amazing Amazon," "Belting Babe," "The Terrific Tomboy," The "Texas Tornado," and "Whatta-Gal

Didrikson." *Literary Digest's* column on Babe called her "The World-Beating Girl Viking of Texas." It's a flattering title, and unique, because it alone attributed her herculean achievements to "the Viking capacity for berserk rage in battle." "Only a Slim, Sunburned Girl" the line under her portrait read: "But, Oh, What Dynamite!"[78]

Striking in its absence was any mention of Babe's ethnic heritage in the Norwegian-American press following the 1932 Olympics. She is also glaringly absent from general accounts of Norwegian-American athletes, which include Molla Bjurstedt Mallory (tennis), Knute Rockne (football coach), Sonja Henie (ice skater), "Snowshoe Thompson" (America's first skiing mail carrier, 1830s–1850s in the Sierra Mountains), and Ragnar Omtvedt (ski jumper). Babe's omission is likely due to her own detachment from her ethnic heritage and her public image that contradicted Norwegian gender norms.[79]

The national press helped build Babe's pedestal. She was ideal copy: always willing to talk and full of folksy one-liners that were often risque, charismatic, and unpredictable. What attracted the press corps to Babe was her dazzling athleticism. What endeared her to them was her wit and warmth.

Headlines of her Olympic feats waxed effusive: "Babe Gets Praise on Coast: Is Called Greatest Woman Athlete of the World," "Babe Breaks Records Easier Than Dishes," "Babe, Heralded like Lindbergh or Big Dirigible Akron, Planes into Texas in Sailor Pants Carrying Three Javelins," and "World Famous Babe Is Given Tumultuous Dallas Welcome Amid Ticker Tape Showers: Tells of Having Picture Taken with Clark Gable." Babe became "Our Babe" to the press, and praise ran rampant in coast-to-coast headlines like "Three Medals for Babe World's Greatest Woman Athlete." The text below the headlines was sheer adoration. Tiny Scurlock, still Babe's unofficial public relations agency, declared her "the greatest competitive athlete of either sex since the human race began." In later years he added to his assertion that she was "a super-performer in 20 sports."[80]

In fact Babe's and the press's affinity for one another began before and during the games. Los Angeles papers revealed minutiae about athletes doing their laundry in hotel sinks. Amidst droll copy like this, Babe's retort when questioned about her "beauty diet" was big news—and entertaining. "I eat anything I want," she said, "except very greasy foods and gravy. I just pass the gravy. That's just hot grease anyway, with some flour or water in it."[81] This down-home frankness quickly placed her in a separate category with reporters and fans. Amidst glamorous Hollywood stars who packed the arena and a bevy of "lovely competitors," Babe offered an antidote to predictability and slickness.

And Babe served as a working-class hero. She was unpretentious and her humble roots, which became widely known, were perfect stuff for folks reeling from the depression to identify with. A couple of cases demonstrate the appeal of her simple wit and her ability to outsmart others, both decided and admired survival techniques in an era of unemployment, despair, and homelessness. Babe shrugged off the fancy talk that attributed her excellence to "hand and eye coordination," saying, "That sure is a powerful lot of language to use about a girl from Texas. . . . I know . . . I can run and I jump and I can toss things and when they gun or tell me to get busy I just say to myself, 'Well, kid, here's where you've got to win another.'" A reporter asked Babe after the Dallas parade why she was traveling with three javelins. She grinned and answered, "'Well, I got even with somebody. I took one discus out there and somebody hooked [stole] it, so I swung onto these three javelins. I come out ahead, don't you all think?'" Remarks like these reaffirmed her street-smart ways and survival instincts and kept reporters' pens poised.[82]

Dallas and Beaumont built the pedestal even higher by honoring her as a conquering hero. A full-page ad in the *Dallas Journal* proclaimed, "Welcome Home, Babe!" The "World's Greatest Woman Athlete," their "Illustrious Daughter," returned "with laurels reaped from the world's great field." The glowing tribute was signed by firms and individuals and carried sketches of Babe and her exploits. The *Dallas Dispatch* called her the "reigning queen" and a "most unusual woman." She arrived in Dallas in a privately chartered American Airways transport escorted by fifteen United States Army planes, all paid for by Employers Casualty.[83] Headlines capture the frenzied festivities: "Stupendous Welcome for Babe Didrikson," "Olympic Champion Flies Home for Great Tribute," "Thousands Line Dallas Streets, Acclaim Babe," "Five Hundred Sports Fans Honor Babe at Country Club Luncheon," "Wonder Girl," "Thousands Cheer Babe Didrikson in Mammoth Home-Coming Demonstration," and "Whole City Pays Honor to Heroine of Olympic Games." Her teammates, meanwhile, drifted back into everyday life: Shiley took the bus home to Philadelphia (it was cheaper than the train) and Hall drove home to Chicago in a car that was repossessed shortly thereafter.[84]

Babe, conversely, received only royal treatment and all the perks of stardom. In Dallas she was interviewed immediately upon descending from the plane by radio station WFAA and "ushered into the presence of high Dallas city dignitaries who will accord her an official welcome." For her glorious return home she was dressed in "blue sailor pants, blue gob cap and cute little blue-striped white blouse. She carried a javelin in her hand." She received a testimonial from the Citizenship of Dallas, signed and presented by the mayor, "in grateful appreciation of [her] accomplishments" at the Olympics. The Dallas Advertising League gave her a similar award saying, "Now that Babe has another Gold Medal, she's trying to find some place where she can hang it up." She was greeted with a ticker-tape shower as part of a "monster parade" through the business section while the Dallas Police Department Band played "Hail to the Chief." Her parents and Lillie joined Babe in the chief's red limousine, draped with roses. Her three relatives, dirty from a trying car trip hampered by two flat tires from Beaumont, were mildly self-conscious, but since Babe was oblivious, their concern disappeared. "Big shots was all lookin' at us country folks," Lillie recalled, "but we didn't care. Babe didn't care. We had our parade right thru Dallas—confetti fallin' on the cars and everythin'."[85]

After the parade, Babe was honored at a luncheon at the Adolphus Hotel. When called to the microphone after praise was heaped upon her, Babe's speech "was a gem for brevity." "I'm tickled to be back home," she said, and sat down. Hannah, overcome with excitement and sentiment, took a linen napkin from the hotel as a souvenir. When she left the hotel, "she was ashamed—it was a big white napkin," Lillie recalled. She was so embarrassed she wanted to return it, "but they said Miz Didriksen, keep it, you keep it for a memento." She kept it, and Lillie remembered how Hannah treasured it. "She took it home and washed it and ironed it and she kept it folded up in a drawer till the day she died."[86]

Stories like this made the papers and furthered Babe's popularity. Most subsequent stories make family love and loyalty critical ingredients, portraying Babe as the ideal daughter and the Didriksens, hardships aside, as the ideal family. "The Didrikson family is extremely proud of Babe," one post-Olympic release noted, "and from morning until night nothing but Babe's accomplishments are discussed. . . . Mrs. Didrikson thinks there is no one like her daughter and believes that Babe can win anything she enters." In fact, her economic hardships, unpretentious ways, and family loyalty accounted for a significant part of her appeal. She was a working-class hero that every commoner could embrace. She made good and even managed to pay off her parents' mortgage. This part of her image benefited Babe, and she came to use it to help transform the unseemly hustler into the popular hero.[87]

In Beaumont her reception was equally stupendous. On August 16, 1932, the *Beaumont Journal*'s front page headline read: "Crowds Cheer 'Babe' in Welcome Parade: City Turns Out to Pay Girl Honor." A photo of Babe, family, ever-present chaperon, and local dignitaries dominates the front page.

The reporter who wrote the seven-column story that appeared that same day went to great lengths—early in her story—to describe Babe's appearance and attire. "She was wearing a white pique jumper dress with a most feminine little dotted swiss blouse." Soft moccasins with socks and a hat, "tipped rakishly back on her head," completed the outfit. As for Babe's appearance, "she is neither big, brawny or Amazon-ish. In fact, one marvels the more, looking at her wiry little figure, that such latent strength lies in the slenderness of her." Her burnt brown hair, "cropped boyishly," was disheveled, and a long lock kept trailing into her eyes. This attention to physical detail became the literary norm; Babe's appearance was virtually always discussed before any mention of her athleticism. These descriptions were written for a curious— and a concerned—public.[88]

The "conquering daughter," as the *Beaumont Journal* reporter called her, sat on the high seat of the fire chief's car, "decidedly at ease, affably nonchalant, and quite in command of the situation." The car, bedecked with a blanket of roses "made by a special committee from the Women's club" carried Babe. In fact the whole town participated in the event. The celebration was the idea of the Kiwanis Club, and other groups, including the Girl Reserves, Scouts, and Babe's former teammates, all joined in. Despite all the fuss and fanfare, Babe didn't appear cocky, but "she is simply very sure of Babe Didrikson." "The girl is human—disarmingly, bigheartedly, admirably human." Another lavish luncheon followed, this one at the Edson Hotel, with Babe's parents and her brother Ole and his wife in attendance.[89]

Babe was showered with accolades. She was given the key to the city and an engraved certificate of merit from the citizens of Beaumont signed by the major, the superintendent of schools, and the Kiwanis Club president. The Kiwanis, Rotary, and Lion's Club presidents all presided at the luncheon, where she was presented with a silver cup from her former teammates with the inscription, "We knew her when."

Speakers included M. L. Lefler, who presented her with the city keys; E. C. McDonald, Beaumont high school principal; Bill Scurlock, sportswriter; and Lil Dimmitt, Beaumont High's coach. Each in turn sang her praises. Dimmitt declared there wasn't a coach in the country who could teach Babe anything "she did not naturally know [because] she had a perfect coordination of mind and body." Dimmitt, who'd been in Los Angeles with Babe, said she was the most popular athlete in the games "and that in one afternoon, she autographed 5000 score cards." This hyperbole bothered no one. Scurlock, ever ready to coronate Babe, said she is the "same swell kid she used to be." Tiny apparently was a main mover and shaker behind the grandiose events. On August 25 Babe wrote him a thank-you note typed on Employers Casualty letterhead. "Thanks, Tiny for the party in Beaumont," she wrote. "I realize that it took lots of your time and lots of hard work to put that over in the way it was handled, and I know that you had much to do with that." "P.S.," she closed, "Don't forget to send me that scrapbook."[90]

The day's events were a high point in community cooperation for Beaumont. "Never before has a celebration been planned in Beaumont on so elaborate lines for any one person" as had this one for Babe. Babe was a rallying point for these people as well as for those elsewhere in Texas. Her larger-than-life accomplishments, her self-congratulatory bravado, predictions, and boastings all were synonymous with Texas's own larger-than-life self and national image. The *Amarillo Globe*'s cartoon perched Babe atop the globe and noted proudly, "The eyes of the whole world are upon you." And another paper wrote, " 'Babe' is about the most self-assured young person who ever came out of Texas—which is saying considerable. . . . She is one of those astounding marvels who happens once in history."[91]

Spurred on by the press, Babe Didrikson's talents and personality exploded on the national scene. With painstaking calculation, within one week of her Olympic victories and amidst the tumultuous fanfare and celebrating that followed, Babe secured her own legal emancipation through a court order. Unprotected by Tiny, unable to hire another manager, and fiscally aware that the iron was hot and right for striking, Babe secured "the legal right to transact her own business affairs" at the age of nineteen. As the *New York Times* reported on August 30, 1932, "The Olympic champion said several opportunities had been offered her, through which she could benefit financially." She saw her age as a disability to remove "in order that she could sign contracts, or handle other legal matters, if she choose."[92] If America was ready for Babe, Babe was ready for America.

CHAPTER THREE

A Sportswriter's Dream:
Beautiful Sports, Manly
Sports, and Muscle Molls

When Babe Didrikson garnered national attention in 1932, the country was in the midst of a social and cultural upheaval. General opinion opposed married women working, even in female-dominated occupations. Yet 22 percent of all workers were female and 11.7 percent of these were married. By 1940 over 25 percent of workers were women and 15.3 percent of these were married. Although most women were employed in domestic service or clerical and sales positions, considered "traditional" occupations for women, they faced hostile public opinion. Most Americans believed that male breadwinners deserved priority over all women workers. Women, conversely, were idealized as domestic, nurturing, full-time companions for their husbands.

These expectations of motherhood and home conflicted with the real economic need to work during the Great Depression. Because the male head of household was "supposed" to be the sole breadwinner, bills were introduced in twenty-six states to prohibit married women from working. In fact, the employment of women was viewed by many as "reprehensible." The Economy Act of 1933 declared that two members of the same family could not both be employed by the federal government. Workers were forced to resign. Seventy-five percent of them were women. Part of the impetus behind this legislation lay in changing attitudes about appropriate behavior for women. As Katharine Hepburn and Joan Crawford demonstrated on the screen, a strong and assertive woman ought to willingly give up her career for the man she loves. As the depression wore on, women's job opportunities dwindled when men began taking jobs in teaching and other occupations considered traditionally female.[1]

As one historian maintains, despite the gains of the twenties—the vote and greater job opportunities—life for many women really did not change much even by the thirties. Women were still discriminated against at home and at work. The media, she argues, created the illusion of an improved status for women by focusing on the image of the sportswoman as an ideal and especially by singling out star athletes.[2]

Women did participate in high school, college, semiprofessional, and league sports in greater numbers than ever before, yet chroniclers of the 1900–1930 era largely fail to make social class distinctions when discussing sports popularity. Although by the 1870s women participated in baseball, wrestling, boxing, ballooning, and gymnastics, the majority of these athletes came from the working class. Wrestling, circa 1870, was a "titillating spectator sport performed by women in music halls and theaters." Boxing between women also enjoyed only a brief heyday. Richard J. Fox, editor and proprietor of the *Police Gazette,* a sports magazine that was flourishing in the 1880s, did much to promote female pugilists. He staged the matches, awarded the prizes, and published the results, all to boost his circulation and draw attention to himself. Although evidence suggests he never took female fighting seriously, "he did crown the woman champion of New York, a powerful Amazon named Alice Jennings, who had a great left hook."[3]

Although boxing and wrestling enjoyed short-lived popularity, other equally physical pursuits followed; soccer, shooting, skiing, gymnastics, muscle-building, bowling, and roller skating dominated indoor activity during the 1880s. Roller skating continued as a favorite street sport among immigrant and working-class girls into the 1920s. Horseback riding, swimming, and footraces were among girls' and women's favorite country pastimes. Shooting in particular was popularized by Annie Oakley's expertise in the 1880s. In her stage appearances, her corsetted waist, tight dark stockings, short dress, and leather boots cast a fetching—and daring—image. Oakley shot holes in playing cards with such proficiency that a free ticket, generally punctured with holes (so it wouldn't be tallied with the receipts), a pass on the house, or anything free became known as an "Annie Oakley." Trap shooting, one of the sports in which women were on par with men, began around 1916 and attracted sharp-shooting women from all social classes.[4]

Working-class girls and women also popularized skate sailing and yachting, ski jumping, downhill skiing (which got its greatest boost after the 1932 Winter Games held in Lake Placid), snowshoeing, archery, mountain climbing, curling, stag hunting on skis, bobsledding, and tobogganing, which were special favorites in many Scandinavian countries. Ice skating, spurred to even greater popularity by Sonja Henie's first Olympic crown in 1928 at age fourteen, had been a favorite for years among working-class youth who frequented local ponds.[5]

Without stuffy parlors to enclose them and without any of the economic accoutrements to circumscribe their social behavior, "exuberance and physical display were far more the province of the poor, the immigrant, the working-class woman." Middle-class Americans were appalled, indeed threatened, "with the unbridling of instincts for bodily display [which] were thought to lead to such evils as prostitution."[6] The popularity of the physical oddity shows of P. T. Barnum among the working class, which shocked many middle- and upper middle-class Victorians, proved the working-class's appreciation of physical display. Similarly, dance halls and amusement parks, a favorite destination from 1890 through the 1920s, provided ample opportunity for young working-class women to cavort and frolic with abandon. These places were viewed as morally suspect by middle- and upper-class Americans and some ethnic working-class parents but were considered great fun by young working-class women.[7]

In short, working-class and middle-class girls and young women were judged according to different standards. Many working-class girls (like boys) spent the bulk of their days outdoors, away from parental supervision, playing in sex-mixed groups. Sports that required little or no equipment, such as running and swimming, were pursued at will, with or without parental approval, by working-class girls. Middle- and upper-class girls, in contrast, were expected to behave with decorum since their social status and marriageability were largely dependent upon their perceived femininity, refinement, and domestic skills.

Thus the explosive popularity of sports for girls and women from 1890 to 1930 really applied only to members of the middle and upper classes; working-class girls and women were already active players. When a social observer commented in 1894 that "outdoor recreation and the spirit of sport had transcended the former image of American womanhood," he was describing ideals of genteel middle- and upper-class womanhood. Middle- and upper-class women gained greater opportunity to participate in sports at college. Foot racing, for example, done in floor-length skirts, was common by the early 1900s. Collegiate play, however, was characterized by heavy attention to rules and proper etiquette—features less accentuated in street play. Women's athletic clubs also pandered to sports enthusiasm by the middle and upper classes. The Chicago Women's Athletic Club, founded in 1903, boasted seven hundred wealthy members who "participated in activities such as fancy dancing, aesthetic calisthenics, fencing, basketball, bowling, gymnastics, track and field events, water polo, and swimming in the club's luxurious pool." Even traditionally working-class pastimes like bowling became more tightly organized. The Women's International Bowling Congress was "established in 1916 for the sole purpose of fostering women's athletics."[8]

Here again Babe defied norms. Unmarried, self-supporting, and earning big money, she implicitly rejected the economically dependent status expected of women. Babe experienced virtually none of the austerity and sacrifice that ruled most depression-era women. True, her own economic fortunes followed an alarmingly predictable boon-bust cycle, but she always had her Employers Casualty income. That alone was three times as much as the yearly average income of an American man and six times that of a woman.[9]

Friends, Foes, and Friendly Foes: Sportswriters Respond to a Shifting Cultural Context

To ensure her income, Didrikson pursued the press relentlessly and often pandered to it at her own expense.[10] To ensure attention, she supplemented her accomplishments, dramatic and frequent as they were, with self-aggrandizing mythmaking. Her father's penchant for storytelling, coupled with Texas's tall-tale tradition, helped her create an irresistible verbal style.

For example, after her Olympic victories she was asked by a reporter when she had first become aware of her exceptional coordination. "Babe told a story of teasing an old farm bull, then jumping onto a fire engine to outwit him."[11] An unlikely feat given her upbringing in an industrialized oil city, yet a tantalizing Texas tall tale.

Another curious myth Babe fostered was that of her physical invincibility. In numerous interviews she claimed she'd had an injury-free childhood. Yet in *This Life I've Led* she tells of slipping while scrubbing the floor. I "slit my knee wide open sliding around like that."[12] In later years, she continued to disavow any physical frailties or accidents. This was done, no doubt, to complement the "otherworldliness" of her physical prowess.

She also lied about her size. When in the Olympics, she claimed, "I wasn't much over five feet tall, and weighed only 105 pounds."[13] In fact, she approximated her full adult stature: 5 feet 5 inches and 130 to 140 pounds. Like age myths, size underestimations were employed to accentuate her feats. In minimizing her size, Babe was perhaps also attempting to heighten her femininity. By 1955, petite stature might well have appealed to Babe more than her own "lithe, muscular, sinewy" nineteen-year-old body.

Another example of myth-building is the much contested date of her first game of golf. In 1955 she claimed in the *Saturday Evening Post* that until Grantland Rice invited her to play following the Olympics, she had never golfed before.[14] In fact, Babe had played regularly at the Beaumont course during her high school days and was shown in the 1929 high school yearbook as a member of the golf team.

Her self-aggrandizing, however, was truthful at times. In 1932, just after she had set a new world's record for the 80-meter hurdles and had won the broad jump and baseball throw in Dallas, a reporter wrote that she had boasted that "one big university offered her a four-year scholarship if she'd matriculate there in time to represent the school in the Olympics." In fact the University of Southern California had offered her a scholarship so she could represent it at the games. She declined, fearful it would jeopardize her amateur standing. This opportunity has been ignored by many journalists because it was believed to be another Didrikson ruse.[15]

Members of the press fed on her tales and made up a few of their own. Tiny Scurlock led the way among sportswriters enshrining Babe. As he wrote, "Our 'Babe Didrikson' file is jampacked with stories and pictures and we have collaborated on several yarns on the Babe that hit national slickies." Theirs was a mutual promotion. Sure, he admitted, "some of her exploits might have been glamorized over the years . . . but most of the stories are right smack on the nose." Tiny's claims of veracity were undermined by Frank G. Menke, who dug through Babe's clippings in search of the true statistics. Few wanted the mundane information; most preferred the lavish praise. Tiny's assertion that Babe won 634 events, may be, by his own admission, "slightly inaccurate." Unhindered by exactitudes, copy like this enthroned her: "She is just the athletic marvel of this age," Tiny wrote (again, and again, and again). "There is only one Babe."[16]

A sportswriter and devotee like Tiny was useful for much more than reporting scores and times because he reaffirmed her normalcy. Particularly in the twenties and thirties, when controversy swelled around Babe's gender identity, Tiny, who at one time had called her a "muscular gal with the litheness of a Texas cowpuncher" wrote, "Feminine? decidedly so. She can cook, sew, and is a neat housekeeper when she stays around home long enough." She was also a splendid dancer, Scurlock claimed, liked and knew flowers, and could play the harmonica and tunes by ear on the piano.[17]

Other press coverage had the same power. The author of a July 1932 *New York Times* article entitled "Miss Didrikson Buys First Hat for Trip to U.S. Title Games" managed to fill three paragraphs describing her purchase. It was a pink hat, Babe's first bought under the prodding auspices of Mrs. Wood. Her sports accomplishments were mentioned only in the final sentence. The point was clear: Babe had done something appropriately feminine that at least momentarily superseded her Amazonian persona.[18]

Grantland Rice, Didrikson's ardent admirer, supported women's participation in sports and used Babe in his arguments. In the twenties he wrote of "the accomplishments of the great female stars in track and field, tennis, golf, and swimming." Like others of his era he was "intrigued [with] . . . how close women were to the athletic accomplishments of men." He suggested that the disparity in women's and men's athletic performances was attributable to a less competitive experience for women.[19]

Rice blew Babe's horn as a female athlete who proved detractors wrong. In a July "Sportlight" column he proclaimed her "the most remarkable athlete of the entire [Olympic] lot [who] doesn't happen to be a member of the male species." Her versatility and stamina ("more than a battleship") impressed him immeasurably. From afar, he appraised her as "lean, wiry, and strong-looking without an ounce of surplus flesh. She wears no bulging muscles to her wars. She has hands that are hard and strong with the grip of steel." In *Collier's* in 1932 he used Babe as an example of why women should be allowed to participate in Olympic competition. He decried critics who claimed "women don't show to advantage on the track or in the field. . . . Maybe, too, these critics overlooked Babe Didrikson. But Grantland Rice did not. She belongs to the future—women's future in sports."[20]

After their first meeting Rice became smitten with Babe. He was not alone among sportswriters in his response. He thought her clever, limitlessly talented, fun, witty, and excellent company, and his stories about her reflected this. He had vociferously proclaimed she'd been cheated of the third gold medal against Shiley. He admitted once trying to conjure realms in which Babe didn't excel. "Frankly," he wrote, "I failed. But I was certain, one day, I had the stopper. 'How is your sewing?' I asked. 'I frequently make my own clothes,' she replied. 'And if it interests you, I'm a pretty good cook.'" Rice, further enamored of her after these latest revelations, editorialized, "I forgot to ask how her archery was. I knew it was excellent."[21]

Rice recalled their first round of golf together, along with Paul Gallico,

Westbrook Pegler, and Braven Dyer, a prizefight manager, with admiration: "The Babe was then a tallish, slender young kid of 17. In legs, arms and body she was constructed like a champion. She had powerful hands, legs like a halfback and, above all, complete confidence in herself." In her physique he saw the makings of a champion—"not in track and field where she already had proved her gold medal rating—but in golf, a sport where a gal might compete with men on their own terms." "If Miss Didrikson would take up golf seriously," he wrote, "there is no doubt in my mind but what she would be a world beater in a short time." He returned repeatedly to her form, which he saw as structurally ideal: "In my mind she had all the physical attributes . . . wonderful legs, slender enough but strong . . . long muscled arms . . . nice height and above all, a pair of fine strong hands and wrists." He stated emphatically, "You are looking at the most flawless section of muscle harmony, of complete mental and physical coordination the world of sport has ever known."[22]

Rice mistakenly believed their golf game together was Babe's first and marveled that she drove the ball farther than the men on the first hole and shot "around 100." Only years later did Babe confess to her previous experience and also that after their match had been scheduled she got a quick lesson from Olin Dutra, the club pro. Rice, paired with Babe against Gallico, Pegler, and Dyer, recalled that Babe's clever trickery and will to win emerged even in that informal contest. On the seventeenth hole it was all even, and Gallico "drove the green." Babe whispered, "Don't worry, Grant, I'll handle this." She turned to Gallico and said, "Paul, I'll race you to the green." Rice delighted in the recollection. "Paul," Rice wrote, "takes no challenge from any woman and few men." Babe outran him easily, but tauntingly, staying two feet ahead of him "like Rusty the electric rabbit at a dog track." When they reached the green, Gallico collapsed. "When it came his time to putt, Paul four-putted. We won the hole and the match." Rice, immensely entertained, was delighted when Babe became known as "Grant's girl." It was all right with him. She, meanwhile, nicknamed him "Granny."[23]

Rice has been accused by one historian of being the leading "ladler of syrup" regarding Babe. At times he praised her to the point of incredulity. As he wrote in "The Other Babe and Women in Sports," "the two girls who did most to turn the world spotlight on their sex—with the possible exception of Cleopatra—were Eleanor Sears [tennis player] and Babe Didrikson Zaharias." His characterization of the two near-Cleopatras, however, was believable: "a Boston society girl and a solid Texas miss." Unlike many of his male colleagues, Rice preferred women in "manly games." He glowingly described Sears's "smashing game" and Babe as a golfer who could "punch her shots."[24]

Another sportswriter in the ilk of Scurlock and Rice was Herb Grassis, a sportswriter for the *Chicago Daily Sun* and *Esquire* magazine when he met Babe in the mid-1930s. He said she was "always good copy, easy to interview, liked to showboat and was attractive and pleasant." She "had the ideal stroke, a swinging hit" and revolutionized the game of golf, according to Grassis, who later became president of the Golf Writer's Association.[25]

Other sportswriters were not so charitable with Babe or other women athletes of the time. These writers did not welcome women athletes on the national scene and held their competitive play in contempt. John R. Tunis argued in "Women and the Sport Business" that women's sports had adopted the evils inherent in men's sports, "where winning and financial gain were the only concerns." He, like other critics, attributed these changes to women's "new position in society."[26]

Westbrook Pegler took a far more hostile position in a syndicated piece in 1933 entitled "That Didrikson Babe Is a Sissy: And, According to Mr. Pegler, It Seems She Can Sew." This article, attempting humor, succeeds in ridicule, generates laughs at Babe's expense, and fosters a "freakish" perception of her. Ironically, the author liked and admired her and hoped to demonstrate her "well-roundedness" in this piece. Pegler used Babe's own definition of girls' games, sports, and domestic interests as "sissy." "She is a sissy and I can prove it," he wrote. "I can prove that she sews for one thing." About sewing, Pegler recounted her prize-winning dress and asked what her prize was: a flask? suspenders? shaving brush? No. "She got a beautiful hand embroidered pin cushion. Yoo-hoo, sissy, how are you getting along with your ruching? Did you even hear of Jack Dempsey or Babe Ruth sewing or ruching?" She's a sissy, too, because "she makes the beds and does the marketing." While affirming her "normalcy," Pegler speculated on the outcome of a match between Babe and a known boxer in a fifteen-round fight. "Name me one good boy she ever licked," he challenged. His sarcasm permeates the piece. He wanted her to be both traditionally feminine and athletically invincible, but the possibility of the latter repulsed him.

But it was her touting of their golf scores—in which she emerged the rightful winner—that provided the final straw. Humorously he wrote that the next time he sees her "I am going to walk up to Miss Didrikson and pop her right square on the nose. Then I am going to kick her a couple. Then I am going to chase her right out of town, publicly."[27] What's so striking is the gender slippage in his treatment of her. At times he affirms her femaleness, yet in the next sentence uses male images and language to challenge her and feign violence toward her. In fact, he doesn't know what she is—he bullies her literally and figuratively as if to punish her for her difference. It's a disturbing example of the cruelty and insensitivity that greeted Babe in many instances.

Paul Gallico, however, articulated the most extreme contempt for Babe and for other athletes as well. After his defeat to Didrikson at golf, he expressed his displeasure in print at will. His first salvo, "The Texas Babe," appeared in 1932 in *Vanity Fair*, where he labeled her a "Muscle Moll." This was merely part of his larger disdain for female athletes who fit the masculine stereotype. His copy was often cruel in making his point. In "Women in Sports Should Look Beautiful," a *Reader's Digest* article condensed from *Vogue* (1936), he said that women looked beautiful in only eight of the twenty-five sports they generally participated in. Ball games were no good—they made women perspire. "The acceptable included archery, shooting, fishing, riding, flying, and skating because women moved gracefully, if at all, and wore 'some pretty cute costumes.'" Curiously, golf doesn't meet with Gallico's approval. "Golf was never meant for women. . . . If you are a gentleman reader, [think back] to some of the instructions given you by your professional as to what to do with your whatsit and your whosit when you swing. A girl just can't do those things and still be a lady."[28]

Gallico was not alone in his suggestion that women should play only "beautiful" sports. People subscribing to this viewpoint argued that women participating in these sports were normal and healthy; no harm had been done to them by their athleticism. Gallico surely approved of a September 1940 *Life* magazine article entitled "Beautiful Skeeter: Pat Laursen Is National Champion," which followed up on an earlier *Time* piece declaring Laursen the world's most beautiful athlete. *Life*'s reporter dubs her a good shooter from a rich family. The remainder of the two-page spread pictures her physique alongside running commentary. There's a full-body profile of her shooting a rifle, a series of three pictures of her legs while she shoots, a full-body swimsuit pose, a back view of her curly hair and her winning patches sewn on her jacket, and a close-up of her in a short tennis outfit. Commentary also focuses on her physical assets, not her sports acumen. A photo of her holding a rifle in resting position is captioned "Glasses, used for shooting, handicap her beauty but improve her aim. They also protect her eyes from flying pieces of pigeon. Here she is holding a twelve-gauge Winchester repeater." Another caption debates the significance of the engagement ring she's wearing.[29]

Others echoed support for "feminine" sports and feminine sports stars. Ethel McGary, the assistant director of Life Saving Service at the New York chapter of the American Red Cross, wrote in favor of competitive swimming for women in a 1931 issue of the *Sportswoman*. Her rationale? Of the sixty women who participated in the last three Olympic Games, "investigation shows that about 20 are married, others are engaged in business, professions or college. All report no harm from their swimming activities."[30]

McCombs, Babe's Employers Casualty coach, hurled himself into the debate on female athletes' femininity in an interview with *Collier's* in 1936. Of course they make fine marriage partners, he argued, he himself married Ruth Almand, a Golden Cyclone. Sports don't "unfit them or weaken them for marriage and motherhood. It's positive bunk. . . . I don't know a finer group than those of the former Cyclones who have set up homes for themselves." The rules of fair play, he asserted, were also "the rules for successful homemaking."[31]

Echoing these thinly veiled concerns with social and sexual normalcy was a 1939 *Life* magazine photo spread on the national women's swimming championships. In two photographs swimmers comb their hair and put on lipstick while juggling a mirror. One swimmer is shown posed in a racing start, but none of the eleven photos show a swimmer in the water. The message was clear: female athletes must constantly prove their normalcy. Even women in the "beautiful sports" were suspect. But for women in the "manly sports," speculation knew no bounds. Gallico was eager and, he believed, qualified to thus testify.[32]

Within this charged cultural context, labeling Babe a muscle moll was like damning her, not simply teasing her as other writers have trivialized it. He later regretted the weight and implications of his words and rescinded his earlier aspersions. In "Frisking for Sex," Gallico gave a brief history of sex testing and women Olympians. He rakishly recalls that in 1932 "the accepted method of determining that a lady was indeed a girl—less clinical and more delightful [than physician's certification]—was to date her and take her out." There "was an absolute swarm of lovelies competing that year," and, he asserted, "even if Babe Didrikson was rawhidey and hoydenish, no one challenged her on matching the requirements of a regulation girl." Gallico, of course, did just that. This piece, written twenty years later amidst Babe's repeated hospitalizations, was more an attempt to save face than an apology.[33]

She did not struggle alone with these misogynist sentiments. Among all women "muscles, strength, strain, sweat and dirt were offensive and unfeminine," according to some journalists. Musculature specifically was thought to be particularly damaging to women's real calling: motherhood. As Dr. Donald Laird wrote in "Why Aren't More Women Athletes?" (1936): "What woman needs—and has—is a good system of involuntary muscles . . . for simple household tasks. . . . She has ample development for a multitude of light office and factory work." "But men," he cautioned, "should keep her away from the heavier tasks, both out of chivalry and good sense." Other medical experts in the midthirties were equally vehemently opposed to "Amazon athletes." Their contentions, explained in the misleadingly entitled "Emancipation of Women," were simple: "that excess exercise is more harmful to women than men" and "that nothing can be good for a girl's body which renders her less capable of motherhood."[34]

In fact, the muscle moll label came dangerously close to the mythic mannish lesbian. Richard von Krafft-Ebing, a turn-of-the-century psychological and sexual theorist, asserted that "not only was the most degenerate lesbian the most masculine, but any gender-crossing or aspiration to male privilege was probably a symptom of lesbianism." Didrikson dressed and acted like a man with enough frequency that she became suspect—if not defined—as lesbian because "her behavior or dress (and usually both) manifested elements designated as exclusively masculine." The cross-gender figure that she embodied had "become the public symbol of the new social/ sexual category 'lesbian.'"[35] Her physique, her trousers and plain shirts, her short-cropped hair, and her sheer competence in the male realm of competitive sports presented an intimidating image to a culture recently attuned to the medical definitions of female homosexuality. According to Krafft-Ebing, lesbians "desired male privileges and power as ardently, perhaps more ardently than they sexually desired women." Also called a true invert, this creature, neither man nor woman, constituted a "third sex" or "trapped soul." Krafft-Ebing, Havelock Ellis, and Sigmund Freud delineated the derangements of this new type. She was "between genders and thus illegitimate." What these sexual theorists failed to consider was the "gleeful skepticism" toward gender categories, access to male privilege, and rebellion against the male order that the mythic mannish woman enjoyed. Sportswriters and social commentators spent ink on all of these fears as they met its embodiment in Babe.[36]

Living with Difference

As her biographers noted, Babe was "seen by many reporters and members of the public as a freak. She was insulted, ignored, laughed at. . . . She was an aberration, in her way, a living put-down to all things feminine." Her high school days barely behind her, Babe "was bucking society even then," as Ruth Scurlock said. But suddenly she was in a national arena with cameras rolling and pens poised where "just being herself" was tantamount to gender heresy. Once she gained national prominence she lost the flexibility she had had in her working-class town because she was judged by middle-class ideals, which increasingly circumscribed her image. She abhorred the accoutrements of femininity (clothes, makeup, flirtation) and could not conform. "She really had no other choice," Scurlock believed. And while Babe spoke of the toll of her nonconformity to no one, "it must have been painfully difficult at times." Babe, significantly, never spoke in later years of these innuendos about her androgyny. In fact she refused to discuss her track and field days at all, saying, "My sports career began with golf." Denial of this magnitude hints at immense distress and severe personal pain. Just as Babe kept her silence so did her family members, athletic peers, and allies. Even thirty-five years after her death only a couple of people dared discuss this aspect of Babe's life. [37]

Her sexual identity provided a constant tension in press coverage between 1931 and 1938. Surrounding her Olympic victories, sports copy dissected her physique and features, often painting a fascinating creature who was not quite female. For example, one story comforted the reader that "she is not a freakish looking character . . . [but] a normal, healthy, boyish looking girl." Another account in 1932 said, "She likes to fight. Her voice is deep, her remarks virulent and pointed. She has few close girl friends and isn't much interested in boys." Babe was keenly aware of how these portrayals cast her outside the female gender. The latter interview closed with Babe saying, "I know I'm not pretty but I do try to be graceful."[38]

One reporter, stammering and blushing, croaked out the question, "do you-er-find that binding undergarments-er-what I means is . . ." Babe, always to the point, asked, "Are you trying to ask me if I wear girdles, brassieres and the rest of that junk?" "Y-y-y-es," sputtered the reporter in sudden relief. "The answer is no," she snapped. "What do you think I am, a sissy?" This "sissy" comment came to haunt Babe. Because the term was usually used as a pejorative levied at effeminate men, Babe's use of it further muddied her gender identity in the public eye.[39]

Speculation about Babe's sexuality escalated when she returned to Dallas to continue competing for Employers Casualty Company in the fall of 1932. As she prepared for the next basketball season, Babe claimed the Illinois Women's Athletic Club, the team that had come in second to her solo first place finish at the national track and field meet, offered her $300 a month to join it. In a bidding war that Babe had hoped for all along, Homer R. Mitchell, the president of ECC, raised her salary from $75 to $300 a month.[40]

At this time Babe was aware of the rumors about her personal life, according to Betty Jameson, a friend and golf peer of Babe's in the 1940s and 1950s. During her track and field days "some people even questioned her being, you know—she looked—she wore her hair a little short and she was so strong and did all these things—and they would say well she never lost her tomboyishness." Babe later told Peggy Kirk Bell, a dear personal friend, that she was glad she'd gotten into golf because it had quieted "that talk." Bell told Jameson, "She knew what people said about her at one time, about being mannish, but she really outlived that. . . . That was in her track and field days." So badly did Babe want to shed this chapter of her life, Dodd recalled, that she kept her Olympic track and field medals stuffed in a coffee can on the kitchen counter, not displayed openly alongside the golf trophies.[41]

Although she was pained by her androgyny in her later years, in the 1930s Babe embraced her oddity status. In fact, she often separated herself even further from other female athletes, a group already on the social fringe. For example, after the Olympics Babe told reporters that she wasn't nervous before running a race. "Why should I be that way?" she cracked. "I'm only running against girls." In an ironic twist, Babe cast herself in a separate category from female track athletes. To her thinking, her separate status spoke to her superior skills. To the public's ear, her comments easily reinforced her freakish status.[42]

Because of this attitude she was often judged harshly. To her biographers she "began to act more mannish, more hard-boiled. Her features were lean and bony, and her hair was cut in a stark bob that could scarcely be less complimentary." To these authors, "she seemed to glory in a coarse demeanor which implied that if she could not be feminine and pretty, then she would be as absolutely *un*feminine and *un*pretty as possible."[43]

One could interpret this as willful, almost acidic arrogance, as these biographers do. Yet a more likely—and more sensitive—interpretation is this: Babe felt alien among women, as Ruth Scurlock said. She was also a foreigner to male privileges and norms. Thus stranded, she developed a set of survival skills that helped her excel in a large family, a tough neighborhood, and international athletic competition. Through her midtwenties, being different worked for Babe. She gained attention, status, money, and their accompanying privileges: parental approval, fame, self-esteem, self-determination, and a complex gender identity. The press helped her attain these things. She recognized that. Although she never became psychologically independent of the press and public attention, in the 1930s she was, fleetingly, able to function without their full approval.

The press helped Babe gain notoriety in these few years. Texas physical education teachers, themselves squeezed between cultural tolerance for girls' and women's athletics and their own personal fears of innuendo and accusations of abnormality, used Babe to prove a point. They "posted signs on school bulletin boards reading: 'DON'T BE A MUSCLE MOLL.'" "Muscle moll" had become code for unfeminine, rough, and unacceptable. Dr. Belle Mead Holm, dean of the women's physical education department at Lamar University in Beaumont, said of her youth, "My mother used to cry when I played softball. She'd say, 'I just don't want to you grow up to be like Babe Didrikson.'"[44]

Holm, a native Texan, speculated on how things might have gone for Babe "if there had been fashions to make her look attractive." "The Babe and the bob," Holm recalled, "it was bad business, men didn't know how to cut women's hair in those days." While short hair was the rage in big cities, it was also accompanied by an undeniably flirtatious and sexual demeanor. Babe had the hair, but not the behavior to go with it. What Babe "violated," as Holm correctly knew, was "proper" female aspirations. "A girl was taught from babyhood," Holm said, "that she must always be presentable in order to be marketable."[45]

Babe was anything but a "marketable" female at that time. Sportswriters zeroed in on this. Pegler wrote, "Few girls deliberately assume the disadvantage that the Babe imposed on herself in refusing to paint on a new mouth and arched brows." What's critical to note is that Babe did not want to be marketable, she did not want to conform, she did not want to fit in quietly to sex roles as they existed. Not then.[46]

Paul Gallico epitomized columnists obsessed with Babe's lack of femininity. She was, he wrote, "a lean, spare girl of medium height, made apparently of rawhide, with taffy colored hair, green eyes and a prominent Adam's apple." Her hair was "cut short like a boy" and she had "a faint down on her upper lip." His description of her behavior capped off this alien creature: she was "brash, truculent and cocky." And Betty Hicks paid Babe a backhanded compliment that echoed Gallico: "The image remains vivid of the geometric, bosomless, narrow-thin Texan with the hacked-off hair, skimming the low hurdles to an 80-meter world record. I had dreamed adolescent dreams of being a star athlete; now I saw what a woman athlete had to be."[47]

In "Texas Babe," penned in October 1932 and run in *Vanity Fair* just two months after his much ballyhooed afternoon with Babe on the links, Galli-co was obsessed with Babe's oddity. He compares his curiosity about her with his attraction for the bearded lady and the albino girl at the circus sideshow. After their golf game, "Nobody knew whether to invite the Babe into the men's locker room for a bath and a drink, or whether to say—'Well, good-bye kid, see you later.' " She went off with some women folk, but "the strange, nineteen-year-old girl-boy child would have been right at home there." Gallico's is a bipolar love-hate, admiration-disdain account of Babe. He used the word "boy" over a dozen times in describing her, yet crowed, "She can do anything" athletically. The same characteristics that made her "not-quite-female" also made her a champion. It apparently did not occur to Gallico that she could be both a woman and a champion.

He painted her as comic in their golf match in her pink dress and hat perched on the crown of her head. He wasn't alone in his speculations about Babe, he told his national readership. "Everybody in Los Angeles was talk-ing about the Babe. Was she all boy? Or had she any feminine traits?" She roughhoused with men she barely knew but bought undeniably women's shoes on a Dallas shopping trip. An enigma.

Gallico pitied Babe, whom he called "a very paragon of Muscle Molls. But not a very happy girl I judge," because she was not pretty and "cannot com-pete with other girls in the very ancient and honored sport of mantrapping." She used no cosmetics in her quest for competing rights with other wom-en, "but she competes with girls, fiercely and hungrily, at everything else." She was closed out of the inner circle of good-looking female athletes be-cause she was always competing for the wrong prize. As her peers chattered away in a clique, Gallico concluded, "The greatest woman athlete in the world stood on the outside, looking on."[48]

While others echoed Gallico's sentiments, few rivaled his acidity. In "Hon-ey," a short story printed in *Vanity Fair* in the spring of 1933, Gallico rid-dled Babe with accusations of being neither male nor female and discussed, but dismissed, her lesbianism. It's fiction, yet a huge, full-body shot of Di-drikson, titled "Tough Babe," dominates the page opposite the story. It's a handsome, strong, self-confident twenty-year-old, with elbows resting on spread knees, who's smiling at the reader. Gallico despised all three of these attributes (although he was bewitched by her strength) and attacks each in turn.

The story would be libelous if it were not a story about "Honey Hadwell." But for those too dense to see through the charade, Gallico inserts "Babe Fredikson," another female athlete. Gallico's fictional Babe is first assailed for her looks. When Honey appeared at the Olympic Games in Los Angeles, she "had the most beautiful body that anyone ever saw on a woman because it happened to be a boy's body . . . and the two little buttons she wore for breasts" did not hit her in the chin as she hurdled (a common problem for the other girls, we're told by Gallico). "Her chassis," Gallico informs the reader, "was strictly utilitarian."[49]

Here, Gallico disembodies Honey's face and head from her impressive, albeit boyish, body. Thinly veiled sexual imagery permeates his text: "Her face," he begins ruthlessly, "is something else again." It is hard, as hard and tough as Honey is. "Her mouth was just a pale slit." She is pale because she shuns rouge as sissy, her term for all that is frivolously feminine. "She had a hawk's beak for a nose and a pair of cold eyes."

Gallico builds a thin plot around Honey and her uncategorizable physique and gender. He strikes a nerve here; she does not "belong" with women or men. Perhaps she is lesbian, he speculates. In the Olympic village she "danced a lot with one of the girls because the men rarely asked her." The dance partner "wanted to be her sweetheart," but Honey overhears her female suitor referred to "as a Lez." And though "Honey had never heard the term before, her instincts made the small hairs at the nape of her neck bristle." Honey abruptly rejects her suitor. Gallico, convinced that Honey is neither quite female nor male, thus dismisses lesbianism. Gallico has a second reason: he needs his hero to have a heterosexual encounter so he can determine her success at that as well.

Honey overhears "real" women gossiping, who ridicule her drawling speech, her swearing, and her unattractiveness to men. They also mock Honey's attempts at femininity, roaring at the backless swimsuit she has shown them. Honey, hearing all through the walls, rips and shreds the suit as she tears it from her body. Her outsider status among women is now secured.

Unfeminine, not-even-female Honey floors one and all when big Mike Suss, the Polish javelin thrower who is as gloriously all man as she is perplexingly "other," attaches himself to her at several consecutive nightly dances. The young women swoon with furrowed brows. Why did he choose Honey? They never danced; "mostly they just stood on the fringe." Gallico's decision to disallow Babe any real heterosocial contact reasserts her third sex status. The female in-fighting is ugly in its stereotypical predictability. Jocasta, a high diver, complains to the others, why did he pick "that dried-up tough-as-nails-little-bitch?"

It seems that Suss was practicing javelin throws with Honey, and once he'd smashed the world record by ten feet, he stopped paying her any attention. He'd used her to learn her javelin skills, much to the delight of the other athletes, one of whom muses, "All's fair in love and sport!"

The story closes with Honey's self-hatred in full swing. "The sobs tore her boy's breast. . . . She lay on her face on her bed, like any girl, and cried miserably and seemingly without end. . . . She clawed at herself," crying, "Sissy! Sissy! Sissy! Sissy! Cry baby!" And to literally punish herself for her inability to catch and keep a man "she punched at her chin with her own right hand and hurt herself."

The very next day Honey Hadwell breaks the javelin record. Alone in her room she touches "the steel tip of her spear with a horny finger" and ends this dreadful piece of fiction by saying, "Ah throwed it right through his black heart." The message is clear: Honey traded athletic excellence for any semblance of a personal life. She is a freak to one and all—the bearded lady, the albino girl.[50]

Gallico, who many believed was Babe's personal friend, "wrote about her as a member of a breed of 'women who made possible deliciously frank and biological discussions in the newspapers as to whether this or that woman athlete should be addressed as Miss, Mrs., Mr. or It.'" Although in retrospect this may have fostered some meaningful reinterpretations of sexuality, it did so in the cruelest possible fashion that left Babe bearing the pain of it.[51]

In retrospect even Gallico admitted his painful barbs at Babe were excessive. She bore "all the jokes that were made about her—mostly having to do with her prowess and masculinity—many of which were on the borderline," he wrote. In a self-reflective moment Gallico confessed, "I wrote about her in this vein in those days, . . . we were free and easy in our prose and columns then, . . . and I am afraid that we often wrote as though the subjects were blind, or could not read, or would never see our articles, or had no sensibilities." He comforted his conscience by maintaining that Babe never "seemed to be angry with [him] for thus publicly prying into her being" or reprimanded him for "discussing the possibility of [her] case of suppressed femininity." Perhaps she "was too polite to say so, or shy of the power of the press." Gallico speculated that "while Mildred's exterior might be thorny and callused (circa 1932) [she had] a deep-seated desire for the very frilly things she so mocked."[52]

Gallico, even years later, underestimated the virulence of his prose labeling Babe as someone somewhere between man and woman. Members of the "intermediate sex," as one historian argued, had "shed their primary identity as women before the world they inhabited accepted the legitimacy of androgyny." In turn they received "public condemnation, social ostracism, and legal censorship." Lacking real economic or political power to legitimize their difference, they failed. Little wonder that Gallico's and others' prose wounded Babe deeply and helped precipitate her fierce public rejection of all things "masculine."[53]

Sex Testing and Women Athletes

Babe's personal circumstances were compounded, no doubt, by widespread speculation about the chromosomal and gender identity of women track and field athletes in general. Hostility toward women track athletes and their feared abnormality permeated all levels. In 1936 at the Berlin Olympics, Avery Brundage, the U.S. Olympic Committee president, remarked, "I am fed up to the ears with women as track and field competitors. Their charms sink to less than zero." Brundage's sentiments were shared by many. According to one sportswriter, "What male does not want girls to be sweetly feminine, and nice and sweet and frilly?" He then attacked one sprinter, nicknamed the "Galloping Ace," as "a big, lanky, flat-chested girl with as much sex appeal as grandmother's old sewing machine." Like Brundage, the sportswriter concluded that her success was due to her masculinity and "beauty and success in girls' track and field sports don't go together so well."[54]

Unfortunately, the only defense against such virulence was to prove one's femininity rather than decry the attacker's limited worldview. Thus Roxy Atkins, adoringly referred to as "the most beautiful competitor" and thus beyond reproach, "challenged the 'masculine' label, emphasizing that 'innuendoes' concerning the 'Galloping Ace' were false, and citing numerous examples of sportswomen who were attractive, feminine and 'gilt-edged securities in the marriage market.'" This strategy did not work in all instances, as the name-calling continued. In the 1936 Olympics, Helen Stephens, an American sprinter, was described derisively as a "bobbed-haired, flat-chested, boyishly built winner." And these were the kinder cuts.[55]

Rumors abounded in the 1930s "that several of the outstanding performances in the women's track and field competitions had been contributed, not by females, but by males," according to a sports historian. A few highly touted cases fueled these suspicions. Some female athletes were male and others were pseudohermaphrodites according to contemporaries who relied on visual inspections, the athletes' confessions, or their own surety. Middle European countries, American logic declared, "in their zeal to have winning teams," encouraged or recruited these individuals. Suspicion of one athlete led the genders of all to be impugned, and since such cases were nearly impossible to prove or disprove, a charge was tantamount to assumed guilt.[56]

In many instances it is difficult, if not impossible, to separate truth from fiction. Stella Walsh of Poland, credited by many as being "the greatest woman track athlete of all time," is still believed by some to have been a man. Her skill at events such as the broad jump, discus, basketball throw, and sprints led her to thirty-five national championships between 1930 and 1951 and made her one of Babe's prime competitors. Their rivalry climaxed in 1930–31. At the AAU nationals in 1930, Walsh set three world records; Babe set two records but lost to Walsh in the long jump. In that same year Walsh appeared in the Women's Olympics in Prague and won the 60-, 100-, and 200-meter dashes. The two met again in 1931. This time Babe won three events to Walsh's one. Speculation about Walsh's chromosomal makeup remains just that: speculation. There were no tests, and rumors were founded upon visual impressions. Yet even some athletes who competed against Walsh still maintain she was a man.[57]

This debate deeply affected Babe's perceived normalcy. If Walsh was male, as many believed, and Didrikson proved to be the superior athlete, what did this mean about Babe? To some it meant she dwelled in or bordered on third sex status; rumors abounded that she took estrogen to "qualify" as female. As Bertha Bowen recalled, while on the golf tour, "when Babe was first coming out, and was a little husky there was always whispering going on. . . . You have to cope with it [the talk] when you get it."[58]

Little wonder, then, that Babe began to transform her gender identity between 1932 and 1936. Several years after she was dubbed a muscle moll, she was still openly refuting the charge. In "I Blow My Own Horn" Babe adamantly reaffirmed her "normalcy" in an attempt to hush rumors. She did this by pointing to ways in which she was heterosexual and feminine. First, she cautioned the reader not to think her unfeminine because "when I was little I would rather play with my Dad's hammer or hatchet than dolls." Here she scolded the reporter, "Don't put that down as proof that I'm not feminine. I like to sew and knit, and I can cook pretty good, too. One of the first dresses I designed and made won the first prize at the Texas State Fair." She further claimed that her love of dancing exceeded her love of golf. And though when "the boys shuffle up to dance with me they look kind of doubtful [because] they think I'm a Muscle Moll and they wonder if I'm goin' to hit their feet like I hit those tee shots," she surprised them with her smooth footwork.

As for the frequent and annoying inquiries about marriage? People, she said, "are always asking me 'Are you going to get married, Babe?' and it gets my goat. They seem to think I'm a strange, unnatural being summed up in the words 'Muscle Moll', and the idea seems to be that Muscle Molls are not people." Babe reassured her fans and doubters that "I look forward to having a home and children just like anybody else, maybe more than some." As deftly as she'd tinker with a sprint's time or the length of a javelin toss, Babe created this bit of "fact": "Only I can't get married for a while yet. My contract won't let me, and I've got a three-year contract." This was followed quickly by a statement that approximates the truth. "I wanted to be independent first before I got married."[59]

We can see the evolution of her persona through this question. In 1931 she said that she wouldn't pick out a husband because "a girl can't get ahead that way." She was wearing a diamond and snapped, "Bought it myself. It was a diamond I wanted, not a man." To Babe, her professional sports career meant money and money meant freedom, "doing the things I want to do when I want to." One year later an article entitled "Babe Sure She Will Marry" finds Babe sounding more certain, less adamant about independence, and siding with mainstream middle-class gender-appropriate values. "Of course I am going to marry . . . and there is plenty of time, after I have had a year or two of touring the country. I haven't picked out my future husband—and so far as I know, no one has picked me out." Annoyed, Babe continued, "Another question that disturbs me is: 'Babe, are you going to have children?' Every normal woman looks forward to having children, and I don't think I am much different from most women. At least I know I like children, and expect to have some of my own."[60]

Later this speculation about gender escalated. In 1957, Dora Ratjen, a German world record holder in the high jump in 1938, "admitted . . . that his name had always been Hermann." Similarly Lea Caurla and Claire Bressolles, 1946 European track and field medal winners, "later appeared as Leon and Pierre." And in 1964 Sim Kin Dan of North Korea, who set records in the women's 400- and 800-meter events that year, "was soon thereafter recognized by an elderly South Korean gentleman as the son he had lost during World War II."[61]

This string of revelations plus rumors about other "questionable" women athletes prompted the International Amateur Athletic Foundation in 1966 to force women track and field athletes at the championships in Budapest "to prove their femaleness before their events by parading nude in front of a panel of three women gynecologists." Outraged by this "invasion of privacy, 234 participated and passed with flying female colors." Yet several prominent Eastern European athletes failed to show up, causing speculation in *Time* and *Life* magazines. *Sports Illustrated,* however, questioned the ethics of the examination.[62]

In fact, succumbing to cultural pressures, women athletes themselves often decried musculature in female competitors. Also in 1966 the female chair of the Women's Board of the U.S. Olympic Development Committee, referring to the bulky physiques of competitors, said, "To most of the women in the U.S. and to many women of other nations, the shot put and discus throw are forms of competition that are generally unacceptable to the feminine image." Reliable chromosomal testing to determine gender came thirty-four years after Didrikson's Olympic appearance. But the rumblings and suspicions were ever present in 1932 and Babe was the primary target.[63]

CHAPTER FOUR

Trials, Triumphs, and Sideshow Trickery

I n 1932–33 Babe was marginally successful at exploiting her deviance. Yet double-edged appeal, bragging, and gender slippage rendered her an enigmatic character to many. After the Olympics she ran afoul of the AAU, which devoted itself to reducing her competitive chances. Her antihero status had begun to backfire. Yet she continued to mold the characterization of herself as an Amazonian renegade. A patchwork existence of one-on-one exhibitions and sideshows gained her notoriety, but it also exacerbated her appearance as "other," an outsider status that haunted her for years.

On February 1, 1933, a Dodge automobile ad appeared in the *Chicago Daily Times* that pictured Babe hurdling with the caption "Dodge 6 is a real champion. Claims she owns one, her second Dodge. The Stuff That Makes Real Champions—Babe Didrikson." The southern branch of the AAU acted swiftly, decisively, and disastrously: it declared her a professional. Although Babe claimed she did not receive any money for the ad and wired the AAU, "I positively did not give anyone authority to use my name or picture in any advertising matter," she was instantly disqualified from rejoining the Golden Cyclones or entering future AAU track meets. The Dallas Dodge dealer wrote the AAU, as did the advertising agency involved. Both swore to her innocence. It is difficult to determine Babe's complicity or motives in this matter, however. She did deny any firm endorsement of the ad and she did know product endorsement and compensation equaled professional status. Yet did she try to hustle Chrysler and the public? She may have privately given her approval of the ad in return for later compensation. That the dealership as well as the agency echoed her every word could speak to their savvy that Didrikson as an ally would become an asset.[1]

This incident served to highlight the contradictions in women's amateur sports at the time. According to a 1928 article in the *Sportswoman,* AAU rules of amateurism varied from sport to sport. U.S. Lawn Tennis Association amateurs could accept full expenses while touring, whereas amateur golfers "are even required to pay fees for entering some of the tournaments." Her conclusion applied perfectly to Babe's predicament: "the standard of play is being lowered so that our best players are often excluded through sometimes inadvertent acts." Deemed a professional by the AAU, Didrikson was barred from amateur competition in other sports for one year.[2]

Babe realized that the AAU's decision was not designed to deny her participation on the ECC team but was really a move to exclude her from the ranks of women's amateur golf, where the only extant competitive tournaments existed. Golf, then a sport of the monied and leisured elite, abhorred the likes of Babe Didrikson. As a columnist for *Coronet* wrote, "In retrospect, it seems clear that the AAU was determined to eliminate 'muscle molls' from its ranks. No official ever put it that bluntly, of course, but the decision was called 'for the best interest of the game.'" During an interview with a reporter, Babe was even blunter. She'd been suspended, she said, "Because they didn't want me to beat the rich dames." Babe declared the charge against her "all 'a bunch of hooey.' " A photo in *This Life I've Led* portrays Babe looking on forlornly while the Cyclones play.[3]

In December, once word of her "endorsement" spread, the *New York Times,* which had given little play to her 1932 AAU and Olympic shinings, ran eighteen stories on the controversy. Babe later admitted to buying a car from the Dodge dealership the previous year and allowing them to photograph her at that time. Steadfastly claiming her innocence, a representative of ECC committed the company to fight for Babe's reinstatement as an amateur. Moreover, its support of Babe garnered the company favorable press. This battle took on the overtones of class warfare; Babe was the persecuted working woman "who we shouldn't expect to match wits with fast-thinking men in the business world." Her plight was compared with that of other shunned athletes, including Jim Thorpe.[4]

The AAU officially suspended her on December 14 and then handed jurisdiction over to the Southern Association of the Amateur Athletic Union for a final ruling. Much was at stake in this decision. Babe was a candidate for the James E. Sullivan Memorial Medal, presented by the AAU to the all-around athlete of 1932. The balloting, due to close on December 27, could not include Babe if she was disqualified prior to that date. Although she had received a stunning blow, Babe did not crumble under its impact. She issued a concise and unapologetic statement: "I have already said and now repeat, that I did not receive a single penny or any other consideration or advantage of any kind in exchange for the opinion I expressed about an automobile."[5]

Despite her disclaimers, Babe was suspended from amateur competition until she produced a photocopy of the unsigned release alleged to have been sent by the auto firm to its advertiser in New York. Babe responded immediately with "I will do everything that I can to be reinstated in the A.A.U. and I don't want to turn professional. I have only played three years of basketball and I'm not ready to quit as an amateur." The following day the auto dealer produced evidence that Babe had not authorized the ad as an endorsement.[6]

Yet, despite these reassurances, the southern branch of the AAU continued the suspension of Babe's amateur status. It wanted her to further explain a telegram from the Dallas car dealer to the New York ad agency mentioning Babe's endorsement. This request—and further delay—snapped Babe's patience. In a bold move she asked the AAU to explain its tolerance and authorization of other amateur athletes' photos used in ads. Babe's team had done its homework. It cited the case of a Miss Waterman of the Illinois Women's Athletic Club, which was similar enough to Babe's that the company believed it contradicted the AAU's present ruling against Didrikson. The AAU denied the allegation.[7]

This was both a terribly stressful and empowering period for Babe. On December 21 the *Times* reported that Babe had resigned from ECC. Babe went home to Beaumont and the very next day she told the press she was resigning from the AAU. She wired the secretary of the southern branch of the AAU "with her kindest regards" to that effect. Babe had had it. Infuriated by the AAU's slow and irrational decision-making, she resigned even though her case was still under review pending examination of the original telegram. True to Babe's larger-than-life visions and skills, she predicted she would "do some film work" and swim the English Channel and Hellespont, after circumnavigating Manhattan Island to warm up. Ironically, the AAU exonerated Babe of all charges only a few hours after her resignation.[8]

Babe's resignation was probably prompted by a combination of three concerns: fear of losing the impending ruling, the hope of better prospects, and anger over the AAU actions. She was angry and insulted. And she'd had time to think during that month. Now was the time to cash in on her name. Now she was famous, now people would pay to see her. Unfortunately, as so many outstanding athletes have painfully learned, being a headliner on the athletic field does not necessarily translate into an income. Babe explained that "the pressure got pretty heavy on me during the fall of 1932. People kept telling me how I could get rich if I turned professional. That big-money talk," the adult Babe granted, "sounds nice when you're just a kid whose family has never had very much."[9]

The press shadowed Babe for several days following her decision to turn professional; as a result, she got her licks in against the AAU. She complained about the maze of AAU rules with a mix of naivete and well-timed blows. "Not until last weekend," she told reporters in St. Louis, "did I realize what a terrifying business it is to maintain one's self as a member in good standing in the AAU. . . . Being an athlete and being a member of the AAU are two quite different things. I'm not sure which is the more difficult." There are some 350 pages of dos and don'ts, Babe said, "And I'd rather try to smash another world's record" than memorize them.[10]

Babe was pleased that she'd taken a potentially devastating blow and turned it to her advantage, while managing to make the almighty AAU look foolish in the process. The AAU responded by banning her from amateur competition in any sport for one year because of her professional status. Avery Brundage, national president of the AAU, expressed his disgust with the controversy. "You know," he mused in Chicago, "the ancient Greeks kept women out of their athletic games. They wouldn't even let them on the sidelines. I'm not so sure but they were right."[11]

Didrikson then launched a farewell salvo at AAU officials: they "'bungled' in suspending me in the first place." Thus, she explained, she declined to accept the reinstatement and "made a few playful, and I think justified comments, on the length [of] the rule book." Her closing remark was by far the feistiest: "If the A.A.U. will permit me, I am doing my best to attend to my own affairs. . . . It would make everything so much more pleasant for everyone if they should elect or could be induced to do likewise." This articulate retort—which capped the whole affair—was, no doubt, crafted with help from her supporters.[12]

At age twenty-one, legally emancipated from her parents, and cut loose from the controlling hands of the AAU and ECC, Babe began her professional career. She undertook a series of stunts, sideshows, one-on-ones, and endorsements. She quickly signed on with the Chrysler Motor Company to tout the very model that had gotten her expelled, explaining that the company felt "sorry about what happened, and they wanted to make it up to me." Babe went to Detroit with her sister Nancy as chaperone and was put up in a suite of rooms in the Book Cadillac Hotel. She was introduced to Chrysler executives including the president, K. T. Keller. "And they were real nice," Babe commented, obviously tickled with the attention, respect, and opportunity that lay ahead. She signed autographs at the Dodge booth at the Detroit Auto Show, talked to people, and played the harmonica to attract the crowd. She must have been an advertiser's dream—a self-contained one-woman show.[13]

Chrysler then helped couple George T. Emerson, of the Ruthrauff and Ryan advertising agency, with Babe. At no cost to Babe, he got her a contract as a live RKO stage performer. She got top billing in a stage show at the Palace Theater in Chicago with Fifi D'Orsay and Bob Murphy and His Collegians. Her name stood four feet high in lights, and she got the star's dressing room. Babe's segment was an eighteen-minute act. She'd never done theatrical performing before, and on the first day when she pulled up and saw the crowd lined up and down the block, she panicked—momentarily—but she soon took to the stage.

After a performer named George Libbey opened Didrikson's segment with an imitation of Eddie Cantor, Babe made her grand entrance: "I'd come down the aisle wearing a real cute panama hat and a green swagger coat and high-heeled spectators." She and Libbey swapped a few lines, then Babe sang a parody of "I'm Fit as a Fiddle and Ready for Love." The lyrics seem dull given the electricity Babe generated: "I'm fit as a fiddle and ready to go. / I could jump over the moon up above. / I'm fit as a fiddle and ready to go." The next stanza seems painfully ironic given the turmoil Babe had known in her twenty-one years: "I haven't a worry and haven't a care. / I feel like a feather floating on air. / I'm fit as a fiddle and ready to go."[14]

After her song, Babe literally shed her feminine attire and "transformed" herself into an athlete. She shed her high heels for track shoes and removed her coat to reveal a red, white, and blue jacket and shorts of silk satin. In a caricature of her great talent she ran on a treadmill in front of a black velvet backdrop while a huge clock timed her. Another woman, on a similar treadmill, ran alongside her. At the end of the bit, Babe surged briefly ahead to "break the tape and go on to win." She also skimmed hurdles, drove imitation golf balls, and played her harmonica. Her tunes included "When Irish Eyes Are Smiling" "Begin the Beguine," and "Jackass Blues."

The critic for the *Chicago Tribune*, Clark Rodenbach, praised the show. "Friday afternoon was the 'Babe's' first time behind footlights," he wrote, "and the girl from the Lone Star State took the hurdle as gallantly as she ever did on the track." He complimented her stage presence and her obvious athleticism and noted that "Mildred ends her turn by playing a harmonica with no mean skill." In her autobiography Babe fondly recalled the ovations she received. One critic insinuated that it wasn't really she who was singing, so she sang without a mike to prove her authenticity. The crowd loved it. In another show, she glanced at a sign beside the stage indicating the act's name. Libbey asked her what she was looking at. "Oh, I'm just looking to see who the hell's on." The crowd roared, and the ad-lib was incorporated into every show thereafter.[15]

During that week in Chicago she did four or five shows daily. She was booked in advance for Brooklyn and New York City, she claimed, "at something like" $2,500 a month. But despite the promise of wealth, Babe felt cramped and hemmed in. She complained to her sister Nancy that all her time was spent in the hotel or the theater. They talked it over. Babe recalled saying, "I don't want the money if I have to make it this way." So after only one week in show business, she canceled her advance bookings. Years later she marveled at her own cavalier action, walking away from "easy money." And, as always, she needed money. "If I'd known what tough financial times I was going to face," she reasoned, "I'd probably have thought twice about passing up the money." But she had decided. As she put it crisply to Nancy, "I want to live my life outdoors." And, she added, "I want to play golf."[16]

Although she was a harmonica-playing stage entertainer for only one week, Babe got publicity mileage out of it to last her entire lifetime. Virtually any piece written about her from 1933 onward lists this as yet another realm in which she excelled, at $2,500 per month. As a myth-builder, it was one of the better week's investments she could have made. But for Didrikson to realize her goal of playing golf she would have to traverse a singularly unusual, and self-constructed, path.

"She's Capable of Winning Everything but the Kentucky Derby": Stunts and Sideshows

So, in the summer of 1933 Babe set about earning her living her way. She lined up a series of stunts designed to beat men at their own games. Here, victory was not assured, but the contest itself was sufficiently bizarre. In one-on-ones against exceptional male athletes she was able to showboat her talent and prove, once and for all, that she was in a league of her own: a "girl athlete" who could take on—and beat—any athlete. By playing like a man Babe violated feminine and heterosexual ideals.

As early as January 1933 Babe plotted her first contest. Although the publicity and anticipation far outweighed the results, this ploy proved successful at generating coverage whenever other opportunities were scarce. She and sister Nancy, lodging at the Hotel Biltmore in New York City, were biding time until various deals were clinched. First, Babe planned a trip to McGovern's gym, where she hoped to meet George Herman "Babe" Ruth. "I'd love to be able to spar a bit with him," was her eager remark. "I never met the Babe, but, gee, I'd like to put the gloves on with him for a while. I hope they have a punching bag over there. Boy, how I can punch that bag!"

As if this wasn't news enough, Didrikson let loose with a string of quotable quotes, tall tales, and self-aggrandizing myths. In the space of two newspaper columns she claimed no woman "rivals me very closely as an athlete." As for which sport she did best, "I do everything best." And as she stretched her arms two feet apart, showing by how far she'd beaten her nearest rival in the Olympic hurdles, she cockily said, "I guess no one will ever touch that record. No sir, they will never touch that one. I could have done even better except I was left at the start." Here the reporter comments drily, "This surprised the interviewer, since motion pictures reveal that 'this much' was only an inch or two." She never did meet Ruth in the ring, but it hardly mattered. Her interview ran nationally and snippets were quoted for decades.

But it was her responses to questions about women and womanhood that were the most shocking. Babe remarked that she hated "those darn old women reporters" for constantly asking her about marriage. A reporter asked if Babe was interested in coaching girls. "Shucks, I wouldn't want to coach girls. I would rather train boys. They develop more rapidly and are easier to handle." And when asked if she thought, as Brundage's infamous remarks implied, that women's athletics should be curtailed, she answered, "Curtailed? It's all right for them, but they shouldn't overdo it." Here Babe found three ways to separate herself from other women: marriage was rejected, female athletes were underdeveloped, and she was in a class of her own. Yet, cultural attitudes that stressed moderate participation had begun to seep in.[17]

In New York she starred in two exhibition matches in diverse sports. First she faced Ruth McGinnis, a professional, in billiards. Tiny Scurlock later claimed that Babe had parlayed this match into a cross-country billiards tour. Then she played basketball one night with the Brooklyn Yankees against the Long Island Ducklings. Her team won 19-16. She was presented a duck—replete with ribbon—as a gift and tried housing it in her hotel bathtub. She soon sent it on to Beaumont to her folks.[18]

But after these outings her opportunities dwindled. With a bankroll of $1,800 that she felt would cover her for three years, she returned to Beaumont determined to devote herself to golf. She practiced tirelessly during the months that followed, often under the tutelage of male pros. By sum-

mer's end, however, Babe's funds were depleted and she returned to ECC as
a publicist. "There must have been four or five times when I had to come
back to them" she recalled, "and always there was a job for me at $300 a
month."[19]

Babe's luck plummeted in the fall of 1933. Her car struck and killed an
elderly man coming out of his driveway in a station wagon. This incident
received virtually no press at the time. In her autobiography, Babe only expressed her gratitude to ECC for paying her auto insurance premium and
noted cryptically, "They paid the damages." Ruth Scurlock confirmed that
Didrikson "loved to drive very fast." Although "there was some litigation over
it," Scurlock recalled, "Babe had good lawyers and she got out of it all right."
Like other such incidents, because it didn't fit with Babe's image, it was simply silenced.[20]

Also in the fall of 1933 Didrikson's father fell ill. Flat broke, the family
took him to John Sealy Hospital in Galveston, a charity university teaching hospital. All went well with Ole's respiratory-related surgery, but while
he recuperated he was out of work for some time. So, Babe felt, "It was up
to me to earn some money. I wanted to make more than the $300 a month
at Employers Casualty if I could." She accepted an offer from a promoter,
Ray Doan of Muscatine, Iowa, to tour with a basketball team he'd name
"Babe Didrikson's All-Americans." The team included one or two other
women, including Jackie Mitchell, who at times pitched to male pros in
staged baseball contests. The *Post Dispatch* pronounced Babe "wiry and
physically hard," while Mitchell "wore masculine clothes but was especially
feminine." One player who tried to befriend Babe said, "When Babe was
with us I never saw her take a drink. She wasn't masculine looking, didn't
talk like a man either."[21]

This atypical collection of athletes traveled to different cities, always
matching up against local men's teams and always garnering headlines. In
Akron, Ohio, in a contest against the Firestone Nonskids, prepublicity
press crowed, "If only half the things they say about Babe Didrikson is true,
she will undoubtedly be acclaimed by Akronites as the most unusual bit
of femininity ever to appear here." Other cities found her equally good
copy. One reporter asked Didrikson if she liked the pro tour. Babe responded that she liked the money. "Once more," the reporter wrote, "we raise
our hats to one that has the courage of her convictions." When asked if she
was married, Babe used sleight of hand: "She kidded me at first and said
she was married and had two children, but then finally admitted that she
was still unmarried."[22]

The team drew decent crowds, and Babe later admitted that while "we weren't worldbeaters . . . we had a pretty fair bunch of basketball players." When basketball season ended in the spring of 1934, her promoter, Doan, booked her to appear with the House of David all-male, all-bearded baseball team after she had pitched in exhibition games against minor and major league teams. The House of David played nationally and drew good crowds; with the addition of Babe, it drew excellent crowds. The *New York Evening Post* headline exclaimed, "Famous Woman Athlete Pitches for Whisker Team." Babe received a salary of somewhere between $1,000 and $1,500 per month. Other teammates got between $300 and $500 per month. In 1934, with 11 million of 52 million workers unemployed and women garment workers earning $2.39 a week in New York sweatshops, Babe was doing just fine.[23]

That summer the team's travel schedule was exhausting. They played over two hundred games from Fort Lauderdale, Florida, to Coeur d'Alene, Idaho. At one stop Babe was hyped as "donkey woman." "Yoicks! The Babe Rides to Hounds" pictures her in a baseball uniform perched on a donkey and holding the reins. In this contest, base paths were "run" on donkey back. Alongside these sideshow photos were always startlingly incongruous "feminine" images. One such pictured Babe in a full-length skirt and blouse, with a bow at her throat and purse tucked daintily under her arm. These feminine poses offer a striking contrast to the House of David tour press copy, which proclaimed that Babe did everything like a man in an athletic way. "To begin with, she possesses a physique that the average high school or college male would envy. . . . One forgets that he is watching a girl, for there isn't the slightest semblance of anything feminine in her actions. She [does everything] with the same naturalness of a man."[24]

The *Detroit Evening Times* captured the paradox perfectly. Accompanying "'Babe' Didrikson, World's Greatest Girl Athlete, Just a Real Girl" are three photos: Babe in an evening gown, in boxing trunks hunched to jab, and in a long dress with heels and purse. Granted, it "is a strange study in contrasts. A peacock could not be prouder than 'Babe' when she donned her first evening gown. . . . She does not look like the world's foremost woman athlete. But a left jab and right cross are part of her repertoire and she is perfectly at home in the gymnasium or on the field." The juxtaposition of primping debutante and socking powerhouse inspired the subhead "Babe No 'Muscle Moll' in Evening Gown." At first, Babe told her interviewer, she resisted the gown. "Aw, I don't want to get all dolled up like a sissy," she said. But the Detroit reporter convinced her that gowns were necessary in her line of work. "Now she really enjoys getting 'all dolled up' despite the feeble pro-tests she makes when reporters quiz her." Pandering to such is-she-or-isn't-she shady journalism gained Babe press coverage but reinforced her status as "other."[25]

Despite her crucial publicity role, Babe shared little of the camaraderie that often accompanies team play because contemporary mores, which she bowed to this time, forbade her from traveling with the team. She had the schedule of games and would drive herself, alone, to the ballparks. She pitched the first inning or two and then left. Leroy Olive, a House of David teammate, said that "Babe wasn't really all that good a pitcher, so we'd have her pitch one or two innings, but we'd fix it so the other teams wouldn't score against her." Olive didn't clarify how this was "fixed." But he did say, "She could hit pretty good though." At Logan Park in Chicago before a packed house of eight thousand, Babe hit a long line drive she legged into a home run. It was the only run scored in the game.[26]

Such theatrical plays were Didrikson's hallmarks. She lived to excite the crowd. Grover Cleveland Alexander, a former member of the Philadelphia Phillies who pitched with the House of David, said, "With a crowd Babe, she'd really put out, but if there was no crowd, she wasn't worth a damn. And the bigger the crowd, the bigger Babe's performance." "Give me a big city," she said at this time. "There are more people to please, more places to go. I wouldn't be afraid even in New York City."[27]

During one House of David game on Staten Island, New York, Sigrid Hill went to see the team. When Babe entered the park, Sigrid reminisced, "lo and behold she went out into the park and everybody gave her a big hand." Sigrid sent word to Babe down on the field that she was in attendance. Babe summoned her down to the field level, and "she said to the lady that sat next to her 'this lady and my mother were very close.'" Each time Babe emerged onto the field, Sigrid remembered, she was cheered anew.[28]

It was during one such game that Babe let loose with one of her bawdiest and most quoted lines. "I didn't wear a beard," Babe remarked in her auto-biography, but one day a woman spectator leaned over the rail and called out to her, "Where are your whiskers?" Babe called back, "I'm sitting on 'em sister, just like you are!" This saucy retort was picked up by reporters in at-tendance and given wide play in sports columns across the country. Spoken in 1934, the same year the Catholic hierarchy formed the "Legion of Decen-cy" to clean up the sexual content of movies, Babe managed to offend the conservative middle-class moralists and entertain the working-class crowd.[29]

Babe understood her role with the team: "I was an extra attraction to help them draw the crowds—I was the only girl." Her singularity triggered some speculation that a romance might be afoot. Walter Winchell hinted in his column that Babe and one of her bearded teammates might be sweethearts. This annoyed Babe terrifically, but she answered coyly when she wrote Tiny Scurlock on September 22, 1934, on Majestic Hotel stationary: "I got a letter from home and also a clipping which I will enclose about it being said from Walter Wentchels column that I was married or going to be—Well, he may be right, but I'm not saying a thing. I may be married, but if so it isn't to one of the Wisker boys—I've garenteed you that." Babe's inference that she might be romantically involved is, by all sources, a fabrication. She probably fueled this rumor in hopes of silencing other, uncomplimentary, scuttlebutt. And it kept her name in the news.[30]

To increase her visibility and her income, Babe set up one-on-one pitching outings against big leaguers. Her first was against Jimmy Foxx and his Philadelphia Athletics. Her "team" would be Dizzy Dean and Paul Dean of the St. Louis Cardinals. The Athletics loaded the bases on hits, "not walks," Babe pointed out. "I always had pretty good control . . . but I couldn't seem to throw the ball past these major-leaguers." The next batter lined into a double play and no one scored. That brought up Foxx, a premier hitter and a future Hall of Famer. Paul Dean, Babe's outfielder, positioned himself deep on the edge of an orange grove. With the crack of Foxx's bat, Dean faded back into the trees and emerged shortly "holding up his glove for everyone to see. There was a baseball and about five oranges in it. That's how we made the third out." Babe commented drily, "And that was enough pitching for me that day."[31]

The papers went wild and reported that Babe Didrikson got Jimmy Foxx out with the bases loaded (there was one on, but "loaded bases" makes for more excitement). Retrospectively, Babe knew she'd gained a dubious notoriety. In a rare self-reflective moment she said of this contest, "Sometimes, in those early barnstorming days I wasn't sure if people were laughing with or at me. Jimmy Foxx might have been thinking, 'Go home, girl, and jerk sodas . . .' but he was considerate." This outing and a workout with the Ray Doan Baseball School pupils prompted Burleigh Grimes of the Cardinal hurling staff to say, "Babe Didrikson would be one of the best prospects in baseball if she were a boy."[32]

In 1933, Grantland Rice's Sportlight film company made a moving picture of Babe participating in twelve sports. Rice admits that "perhaps the sequences of her playing football with Ray Morrison's Southern Methodist team were gagged a little." As she zigzagged down the field "they'd keep diving for me and just miss me. . . . And they had me tackle a fellow." Shown at high speed, it looked like the real thing. Babe played replete with tapered pants, shoulder pads, helmet, and a convincing kicking and passing style. Photos of this staged event were reprinted for years and tellingly used as part of the before-and-after late 1930s article "What a Babe: Babe Is a Lady Now."[33]

Another staged photo session featured Babe in her basketball uniform supposedly sparring with Bill "Baby" Stribling, the younger brother of Young Stribling, a heavyweight contender. "The more the story was told, the wilder it got," Babe said. "Some versions had me do everything but knock him out." An autographed photo from the session only escalates the drama. Babe looms over a sprawled boxer on the floor with Stribling's inscription, "May You Have Everything At Your Feet Babe. Baby Stribling." Press lore exaggerated her boxing prowess until she had even sparred with Jack Dempsey. Red Gibson, a sportswriter, recalled asking her about her clash with Dempsey. She demonstrated her pugilistic skills while they were riding in an elevator. "She decided to show me how she boxed him," he wrote in the *Dallas Morning News.* "Bam! Bam! Whap! Thank God we were only going to the third floor—that took just long enough for a TKO." These stunts were a regular part of Babe's life through the 1930s.[34]

Ironically, "Didrikson's versatility probably had its roots in the lack of opportunities for women in sport." Male athletes could specialize in one sport with aspirations of turning professional in it. But Babe, proficient in two sports that had no pro ranks for women, "moved from sport to sport as opportunities presented themselves to her. [She] plied her trade by taking limited engagements in everything." In the spring of 1934, Babe pitched a few innings for Cleveland in an exhibition game against the New Orleans Pelicans.[35] That same spring, for $200 per game, she pitched an inning or two for the St. Louis Cardinals against the Boston Red Sox. Bucky Harris, the Boston manager, said of her, "She can handle that old apple with some of the boys." One New York sportswriter, awed and nonplussed by Babe's diversity, quipped that she ought to swim the English Channel. "What could be a better conditioner for a golf tournament?" He also suggested she race horses and wrestle the best men.[36]

It was a patchwork existence, traveling across the country, splicing together $200 here, $500 there. At times it was lonely and exhausting, but it was profitable. In September 1934 Babe wrote Tiny Scurlock from St. Louis. She clarified for him that her golf lessons started October 8 and, contrary to rumor, she was not married. But the real surprise of the letter comes in the postscript. "I said I would not come home again unless I'd made about or not less than $10.000, well I'm ready to come . . . I'm really doing it." Despite her nomadic life, replete with controversies, Babe Didrikson was—temporarily—well off.[37]

"No Coquette Ever Stole Second Base"

Years later as Babe retreated from her aggressive past and embraced her feminine future, she vehemently denied that she'd ever played football or boxed save for these staged photo sessions. She said in 1955 as she retreated from her rough-and-tumble past, "I've always drawn the line at certain things. I never played football, although it's been printed hundreds of times that football was one of my sports."[38]

One incident was impossible to deny. During a basketball game between the Cyclones and Oklahoma Presbyterian College, Babe sank a last-minute field goal that would have tied the game if "Runt" Ramsay, the referee, had counted it as two points. Instead, he awarded only one point according to the rules of girls' basketball at the time. In a flash, Babe swung at him and landed a punch. Ramsay laughed it off, but Babe was devastated. She wrote him several times during the winter, apologizing. She said, then and for years afterward, that it was one incident she would always regret. Babe had violated her own standards of fair play by punching the referee. But she also reaffirmed her physical and psychological difference. Her reaction was automatic but inexplicable by traditional female standards.[39]

A similar incident occurred years later. At a party, a 250-pound man, standing 6 feet 4 inches, boasted that no woman could throw him. Laughing, "the Babe reached out and a second later he was sprawled on the floor." Once on his back Babe pinned him to the floor. Again she'd responded with unbridled instinct and strength. She deeply regretted this incident also; she felt ashamed. She did not mention either one in her autobiography, although interviews and press coverage confirm both.[40]

As Babe began to redefine herself in more traditional terms and retreat into femininity, she tried desperately to shed her past. But her past had made an indelible impression. As one author noted, "No coquette ever stole second base, no shy maid ever flirted through a 100-yard dash." Her fame, ironically, cast her as an antihero that no denials could undo. Sports fans and sportswriters believed her capable of anything. As one sportswriter quipped, "She's capable of winning everything but the Kentucky Derby." Unbelievably, Babe once considered doing just that—footracing against a horse. "I almost agreed to [the] stunt," she said, "But I didn't do it." As she strived for acceptance in the 1950s as an unquestioned female, she editorialized, "I knew that wasn't really the right kind of performance for a girl to be putting on." Indeed. But between 1932 and 1934, both she and her promoters had thought it a dandy idea. They had sculpted a creature who was well-nigh impossible to deconstruct.[41]

Painful Transitions:
From Amateur Amazon to
Professional Lady Golfer

I n 1933–34 Babe Didrikson had two immense problems: earning a
living and living down her image. Her career, made up of one-on-
ones and a smorgasbord of exhibitions, was floundering. In retrospect Babe said, "These years . . . were a mixed-up time for me. My
name had meant a lot right after the Olympic Games, but it had sort
of been going down since then." She was not alone in this perception. A reporter for the *Chicago Sunday Times* wrote, "Few sporting figures ever thud-
ded [from the headlines] with the ravishing rapidity that la Didrikson did."[1]

Even her unimpeachable sports accomplishments were being sullied in
the press. In 1935 Joe Williams, a columnist with the *New York World-Tele-
gram,* revived a line of denigration that had begun in 1932 by sportswriter
Charles E. Parker.[2] Parker, perceptibly annoyed that Babe would "cash in"
on her Olympic fame once the AAU banned her from amateur competition,
wrote, "Misogynists are breathing easier today [because] so much had been
written during the last year of Miss Didrikson's prowess that the poor misogynists thought the only way to combat it was to go into training and prove
she was wrong." Fortunately misogynists were saved from this fate because
Parker thought to really "compare her achievements with those of the opposite sex."

What spurred Parker's investigations was Babe's unabashed claim that she
could do as well as a man in any sport. Parker, after hours of research, was
delighted to learn that "Miss Didrikson has yet to come within speaking

distance of even the schoolboy records, let alone the real champions." Tables and charts followed "for the benefit of his fellow misogynists," reassuring them they needn't bother with diets or muscle-building exercises in order to compete with Babe. Her claims were false; men remained superior. Parker's glee not only denigrated her sports accomplishments but also exemplified the ire and dislike that Babe, and what she represented, elicited from certain members of the press and the general public. Parker and his ilk found Babe's achievements and her self-congratulatory style obnoxious— and threatening.[3]

Further, her participation in track and field kept her inextricably linked to the ugly muscle moll tag and more jabs by the press. Babe had already designed a solution: abandon track and field in favor of golf. This sport offered her only realistic hope of greater stardom. When Helen Jacobs, the tennis champion, was voted Female Athlete of the Year by the Associated Press in 1933, a brief wire story said, "Due to the relatively limited sphere of noteworthy feminine competition, the voting was confined almost entirely to those engaging in tennis, golf and swimming." In addition, golf promised a way up in social standing. Golf, then an upper-crust, refined, ladylike pursuit, entailed no unseemly sweating, no muscle moll accusations, no ridiculing press hovering in the wings. In fact, tennis, which offered some of the reassurances of golf plus more of the physicality she was famous for, had attracted Babe momentarily. But a shoulder injury, resulting from torn ligaments during her Olympic javelin toss, prevented her from getting off a powerful overhand serve.[4]

In addition, Babe had seen a Bobby Jones golf exhibition shortly after her House of David tour. Jones, due to play at the Houston Country Club, had become Babe's idol. She traveled from Dallas to watch him, and though the match was shortened by rain, she distinctly recalled that "seeing Jones sort of fired up my own golf ambitions." She chose golf deliberately as a sport to gain money, fame, and an escape. She studied both golf and femininity rigorously. Success in either depended upon the other.[5]

Most of all Didrikson needed "social polish" to ease her entry into the country club circuit. The watchful press underscored and exaggerated every subtle shift in Babe's image. Gallico, her "friendly foe," wrote that as Babe's game smoothed out, "she would raise hell with the average competing ladies by her wholly masculine aggressiveness and pugnacity." He concluded his familiar blend of compliments and barbs with, "Knowing Babe as I do, I can well imagine her swaggering down to her ball, saying 'Reckon Ah'll have to sink this-a one." Later, as "the rough-and-tumble tomboy disappeared, the press took notice of the new Babe's silk hats and red finger nail polish." Babe gradually adopted traditional female standards of beauty, demonstrating her social graces by applying fingernail polish, styling her hair, and using cosmetics. She knew that her fame would not continue unless she became unquestionably female.[6]

Ironically, women athletes, who challenged traditional notions of femininity with their physicality and competitiveness, were also "among the most prominent women in the United States" aside from film stars. They led the way in promoting freer dress for women by popularizing sportswear. Clearly women's feats of "masculine character" captured the popular imagination in the twenties and thirties. Their physical endurance, bravery, and considerable money-making capabilities held a carnival-like fascination. The praise bestowed on Gertrude Ederle after her 1928 swim of the English Channel, Sonja Henie's successful film career resulting from her 1932 gold medal Olympic skating performance, and swimmers Eleanor Holm's and Esther Williams's popularity all testify to this. One historian includes Babe in this list of athletic national treasures, calling her "a golfer and all-around athlete, [who] was nationally beloved." True. But not until she metamorphosed from third-sex status into unquestionable femininity.[7]

Adopting femininity meant abandoning her past. Babe Didrikson's working-class, Scandinavian background provided her with pride in her athleticism but kept her out of middle-class norms. Despite the rise of the sportswoman spurred on by working-class athleticism, middle-class anecdotes, editorials, cartoons, and magazine stories still disparaged women in sports. Thus, Didrikson was caught between personal confidence and public ridicule. Middle-class ideals deemed her uncouth for her working-class notions of unaffected physicality and unfeminine for her inappropriate behavior. Even working-class standards were taxed given her vulgar speech, mannish look and aspirations, and noncompliance with the female domestic and maternal roles. By taking up golf, she took a large step toward erasing the perceived stigma of her working-class background by distancing herself from it and her ethnic origins. She went even farther by studying the rules and etiquette of femininity as doggedly as she conquered the intricacies of golf.[8]

Women's magazines of the 1930s, directed at a consumer-oriented, literate, largely middle-class readership, provide ample insight into the traditional values associated with womanhood to which Babe aspired—at least in her public moments. The ideal woman, according to *Ladies Home Journal* and *Vogue,* was an attractive, traditionally feminine mother, domestically competent, with a clean, well-decorated home and a healthy and happy family.

Although she placed some emphasis on career and education, she had greater talents in cooking and budgeting. Uppermost was that she keep her husband happy. Article titles including "Our Marriage Comes First" and "Everything to Make Him Happy" leave little doubt that the ideal woman sacrificed herself for her mate: his dreams became hers, his tastes her pleasure to fulfill.[9]

Women's major concerns should be with their relationships and their appearances. *Ladies Home Journal* articles in the winter of 1935 urged college women "to be a lady and dress the part [and] act civilized" to secure a husband. A March article, "What Does He See in Her?" states unequivocally that the American woman "is rather pleased with the picture of herself pouting prettily on a pedestal." "Helplessness," the author notes, "is another of those fascinating tricks that knock a suitor all of a heap; he yearns to protect his delicate little flower." An advertisement in the same issue exhorts the woman reader, "Today your lipstick must match your nail polish."[10]

Indeed, the importance of fashion and makeup surfaces in every issue. An ad in the April 1933 issue cautions a woman to "accent her natural coloring" and end "that painted look!" Beware of "'B.O.' fatal to romance!" another ad roars. Girdles to slim bulging hips figure prominently. The imperative that one's nail polish match one's toenails is discussed in a 1937 *Harper's Bazaar* piece, while soft wavy hair is a must "Dictated by Fashion" according to an April *Ladies Home Journal* photograph's caption.[11]

Fashion, however, began promoting the image of the sportswoman, which served to undercut the ideal, feminine woman. *Vogue* in May 1932 pictured four thin, slinky women in "silk sport dresses" and white gloves posing with tennis rackets and golf clubs. The June issue advertised "Sportocasins For Smart Women." These shoes were "not only the most comfortable but also the most practical of all active sports wear." Saraka, a laxative promising it was "the modern way to keep intestinal muscles strong and active!" pictured a female golfer, smiling widely, smashing a ball from atop a spoonful of the crunchy, dissolvable granules. And a 1937 *Harper's Bazaar* fashion layout featured Alice Marble, the tennis champion, modeling her sport's latest fashions. The text accompanying the photos exclaims, "Our national champion, who astonished all Wimbledon with her dynamic volleys, generally wears *dresses.*" Yet another attitude coexisted with this favorable one toward women's sports. Women were belittled in their activities through articles such as "Setting Up in Bed," which suggested that women imitate babies' movements as a means of exercise.[12]

Mass-market magazines aimed at both sexes also began covering women's sports more regularly and thoroughly in the 1930s. *Collier's* in its May

1932 issue discussed the history of the Olympics and women's involvement in them. *Literary Digest* in the same year detailed the proceedings at the British Ladies Championship and the U.S. Women's National Lawn Tennis Championship. In fact, the *Digest*'s coverage of Helen Jacobs's victory over Carolyn Babcock was extensive, detailed, and carried two familiar-sounding references to femininity. Babcock was described by Francis Wallace as "twenty, a bronzed little thing with black hair . . . [though] throughout the week her boyish face had never relaxed from its grim lines as she fought her way to the final." But as her defeat neared, "Carolyn's mask fell off. She smiled . . . the smile of a beaten somewhat bewildered little girl, a pretty girl with white teeth where the firm line of her mouth had been." This fleeting reference to her appearance and boyishness, albeit redeemed by her girlishness, underscores the scrutiny all female athletes were under, though none to a degree equalling Babe's. The second page of text on the match is interrupted by a photo of a curvaceous woman diver: "Not a Legless Wonder—Just Dorothy Poynton Upside Down." "Her shapely legs," the caption coos, "are trailing safely behind, and her champion dives are still a high-light of Post-Olympic discussion."[13]

Curiously, despite the growing popularity, albeit qualified, of female athletes, few articles focused on women and sports. Not one female sports figure endorsed a single product or appeared in an advertisement in *Ladies Home Journal* or *Vogue* between 1933 and 1950. *Harper's Bazaar* carried just the Marble ad during those eighteen years. Rather, the unquestionably feminine stars of Hollywood's silver screen—Jean Harlow, Greta Garbo, Rosalind Russell, Rita Hayworth, and Barbara Stanwyck—were paid to promote products ranging from clothes to makeup to detergent. Even swimsuits, obviously sports apparel, were modeled by the actress Anita Page, not an athlete. In contrast, male athletes at the top of their games were endorsing "manly" products: tobacco, automobiles, and sporting goods. The only feasible explanation for this disparity is that because they were athletes, these women were not deemed appropriate for endorsing "feminine" products, and because they were women, these athletes were not deemed appropriate for endorsing "masculine" products. This ambivalence toward female athletes' excellence permeated the culture.[14]

On the Road Again

In this economically unprofitable milieu for women athletes, Babe set her business mind calculating the possible dollars if she did exhibitions with the male pros. This tack provided three opportunities: cash, print coverage, and tutoring. Bill Nary, a golf pro who played with Babe on several occasions, remarked, "there was a touch of resentment as most of [her] exhibition matches were with the men stars, such as Gene Sarazen and Sam Snead, etc." But this was Babe's strategy to generate large galleries, which she learned from her House of David tour. As Nary said, "The galleries were huge because they wanted to compare Babe's distances to the men stars of that era."[15]

By turning to staged golf matches, Babe used a familiar strategy to generate income and fame. In fact, she'd been challenging men to golf games informally on and off for a couple of years before she turned her talents to the pros. "I always liked to play golf with men and boys," she said. "In fact, people advised me to do it. I was told that it would be better competition for me." In the summer of 1932 she approached Frank Craven, actor and playwright, and suggested a game. He hesitated and Babe said, " 'If that doesn't suit, we'll try boxing or wrestling.' 'No we won't,' he retorted, 'you've already broken my right hand just being introduced.' " Babe, always the quickest wit, snapped back, " 'Well, then I'll play dolls with you.' " Craven, understandably, was stopped cold without a rebuttal of any sort. She often approached potential golf rivals in this manner and secured the desired match.[16]

In 1933 Babe told a reporter for the North American Newspaper Alliance that golf offered her a welcome challenge. "Most things come natural to me," she said, "and golf was the first that ever gave me much trouble." Thus Babe "determined to learn to play and kept plugging away at the ball." Babe constructed numerous tales about her start in golf. In a couple of renditions Babe initially scorned the game. She went to El Tivoli Golf Club with some friends, played five holes with borrowed clubs, and declared it silly. In another version, McCombs took her to watch him hit a few balls, trying to plant the idea of becoming a golfer in her mind. She said "something about how silly I thought it was for people to hit a little white ball and then chase it."[17]

But her favorite account was that she had stopped in at the Beverly Hills Golf Course in Dallas to watch folks at the driving range and been struck by the trouble most people had hitting the ball. "I had never paid much attention to golf," she claimed, but watching these folks she thought, "I could do a lot better than any of them." She went in, got equipped, and missed her first swing. By day's end she "happened to hit a couple right and they went about two hundred yards." In one version she hit the ball so far that "the little Scotsman who ran the driving range came running up to us. He was shouting." Then "Lefty" Stockhouse, clubhouse pro, showed her how to hold her club and improve her stance and swing. Shortly, her drives were 225-250 yards. Sure she missed on occasion, "But when I did connect," she stated, "they would fly." Watching those balls "that sailed down there for 200 yards [sure] was a sweet feeling."[18]

Thus smitten with the sport, she soon bought a set of clubs. Her first score, over 100, was due largely to poor putting. She won nearly all the driving contests she entered at El Tivoli Golf Club, and this furnished her with balls given as prizes with which to practice. After three or four rounds, the story goes, she broke 100, and "Boy was I thrilled," she said. After three or four more rounds, she broke 90, then 80. "If I ever get a chance to practice regularly and get some professional to work with me," she told an enthralled reporter for *American Magazine,* "I think I could break 80 regularly."[19]

Beatrice Lytle, who swore she taught Babe to play golf in high school around 1927, said, "Those stories about her driving the ball two hundred and fifty yards the first time she swung a club or about shooting in the nineties her first round—they are just not true. She could out drive me after a while, it is true, but she never did beat me on the Beaumont course."[20]

Another nifty fluke that became enshrined was an episode from her first golf tournament. Babe predicted she would shoot 77. This was "a bit of bombast," the reporter interjected, "which she airily characterized as 'Texas talk.'" "So the gal from Texas shot a 77. It was a freak, of course, and she did not linger long in the match play rounds that followed." On occasion Babe did predict her scores; on even rarer occasions she was right. That this happened one in several dozen times dissuaded no one. What people remembered were the astounding instances when performance and prediction coincided.[21]

Just as when she'd calmly announced her intention to win the Olympics and become the world's greatest athlete as an early teen, Babe declared in July 1933, "I have enough money to last me three years and I intend to win the women's amateur golf championship before these three years—and my bankroll, are gone." To this end Babe packed up all her belongings and moved to Santa Monica, California, to live with her married sister. She paid her parents' way out so that they could join them for a time.[22]

Babe turned her ferocious will and immense raw prowess to golf. She approached it with the same intensity that made her unparalleled in track and field. Babe's golf aspirations were greatly enhanced by her tenacious practice sessions. Stan Kertes, pro and mentor, noted Babe's inexhaustible determination. Kertes said she would practice for hours, going through almost 1,500 balls every day. She would get on the practice tee "at 9 in the morning . . . and often stay there till the place closed at midnight." "For eight months," Kertes continued, "she hit ball after ball until her hands began to bleed, and I had to make her wear gloves and finally beg her to stop and rest." Gene Sarazen, her touring partner in 1935, noted similarly, "After we'd play 18 holes she'd practice for hours more."[23] Her practice sessions were deservedly legendary. Thus she "would practice 12-16 hours per day on weekends. During the work week she practiced mornings from 5:30–8:30 before going to work. Lunch hours were spent . . . chipping balls onto a leather chair in her boss' office. After work she took lessons for an hour and practiced until dark." "I'd hit golf balls until my hands were bloody and sore," she explained again and again. "Then I'd have tape all over my hands and blood all over the tape." This was one instance where no amount of hyperbole exceeded fact. "The price for perfection was high," one sportswriter wrote, "but she paid it willingly."[24]

Babe utilized the tutelage of any willing male pro—especially if it was free. As her funds were depleted, she gratefully accepted generous offers of free lessons. In 1933, the folklore goes, she strolled up to Stanley Kertes and said, "I want to be the greatest woman golfer in the world." In *This Life I've Led* Babe claimed she was introduced to him by Lou Nash, a golfer friend, in Los Angeles. In Babe's version, Kertes complimented Babe's drive and said she should take lessons to learn the fundamentals. Babe replied, "Yeah, but it costs too much money." He said, "I'll teach you free."[25]

Whichever version is correct, their bond was instantaneous and built on mutual respect. He bought her a set of clubs at the driving-range shop, began her lessons the very day they met, and treated her to several more buckets of golf balls and supper. He invited her back the next day and for days after that. "It went on like that day after day," she said. They'd only been playing together a week when he smashed an especially long drive. Babe slammed her ball thirty yards farther. "Right then," Kertes recalled, "I knew she had the makings of a champion."[26]

Babe took lessons from Kertes throughout the spring and summer of 1933 and blossomed under his tutelage. "But eventually my money did run out," she said, "and I knew I couldn't keep on taking up all Stan's time with free lessons." Babe recalled him as "a great teacher of golf" and she returned to him over the years for impromptu lessons whenever she had the chance. With Babe's bankroll exhausted by summer's end, Ole and Hannah returned to Beaumont. Babe went back to Dallas, where she rejoined ECC as a publicist for $300 per month.[27]

Yet she continually improved her golf game, partly through the help of pros. When Babe met Gene Sarazen in 1933, he was on top of the golf world. In 1922 he'd won the U.S. Open and PGA championship, in 1932 the British and U.S. National Opens, in 1923 and 1933 the PGA championship once again, and in 1935 the Masters. Not surprisingly, there are several different versions of their meeting. Sarazen recalled that Grantland Rice and Paul Gallico had asked him to take her out on a tour, to which he agreed. It was a one-month tour, and Babe's manager booked the matches for them. To dispel any rumors of impropriety, Mary Sarazen, Gene's wife, traveled with the two of them as a chaperon. In her autobiography Babe claimed the P. Goldsmith Sons sporting goods company sent her on the tour with Sarazen. In a 1936 article with *American Magazine* Babe told her interviewer that she'd gone to see the U.S. Open and had played a few pick-up holes against female and male golfers. "There's where Gene Sarazen saw me," she said, "So he asked about a tour this year. It sounded good to me."[28]

Sarazen knew there was a great curiosity factor about Babe. "People wanted to come out and see this freak from Texas who could play golf, tennis and beat everyone swimming up and down the pool," he said. Sarazen was rather amazed by her too. While he thought both Joyce Wethered and Glenna Collett were better all-around golfers than Babe, he noted her "natural swing," her ability as a "long hitter," and her power: "She was strong as an ox." She was "physically perfectly built, a real specimen, although not the prettiest face I've seen." She wore slacks, uncommon for the times, but never shorts.[29]

Babe made the most of her time with Sarazen. She asked him countless questions. "If I was gong to be the best, I wanted to learn from the best. And he was the best in championship golf at that time. In between matches," Babe recalled, "he would get out and work with me." For his part, Sarazen was glad to help. She learned by watching and "she had the natural ability at golf, all right: She had the rhythm, it was just as if she was throwing the javelin. She was very intense and wanted to learn." He, too, was struck by her phenomenal work habits. After playing a full eighteen holes she'd practice for hours more.[30]

While Sarazen praised her practice habits, he was critical of her propensity to seek out new teaching pros whenever her game needed fine tuning. Bill Nary recalled many instances of Babe seeking lessons from pros at every opportunity. Two years before she died Babe approached Sarazen for just such a lesson; he refused because there'd been too many people giving her advice on her game. In Sarazen's view, this confused her and muted her own style of play.

Babe is likely to have had a second motive for these teaching sessions. Haunted by her waning fame, these lessons got the local press out and her picture back in the papers. As the caption under a picture of her with Chicago golf pro Bob McDonald noted, "On Upswing Again: Queen of athletic femininity two years ago, a virtual nobody now, Babe Didrikson follows the club's upswing for an anticipated comeback in golf." On other occasions, she'd inform the local press when she'd be on the green—in case they wanted to watch her. Eda Squire, thus informed, wrote in 1934, "To watch the 'Babe' hurl a baseball so that it breaks sharply away from the batter is thrilling, but to see her sock a golf ball for a 300-yard drive down the fairway makes the eyes blink." Squire complimented Babe's "free, natural swing" and noted with surprise, "She is not as large as I expected, and although slim hipped and of medium height, has powerful forearms."[31]

During her month of touring with Sarazen Babe delighted in the press's coverage of their rivalry—even better if they focused exclusively on her. She had a reserve of quick one-liners. Once when Gene announced he'd play a five-iron, Babe called out, "I'll play the seven." Sarazen, not one for hot-dogging, admitted "the galleries like her very much, like Lee Trevino." The *Washington Post* wrote of their repartee, "All afternoon she took a gentle riding from her partner, who constantly ribbed her as she went along, especially on the tees. Always she set him back, either with a side-splitting return, or a great shot when it was least expected." The columnist noted the weaknesses in her game (putting, approach shots, slicing), but unabashedly swooned over her drives: "She socks hard, and at least three times she outdrove her men opponents, including Sarazen himself."[32]

A Real Gallery Pleaser

In the summer of 1935 Babe Didrikson relearned two important lessons: how to get the press on your side and keep your name in print and how to turn a buck. During her tour with Sarazen Babe reveled in both. One reporter chronicled, "She would pile on her thickest honey-pie East Texas drawl and call out to the galleries: 'Heah, you all! You-all come closah mohaw, 'cuz you-all've heerda Waltah Hagen and you-all heerda Bobbuh Jeeones, but today, folks, you-all ah lookin' at th' veruh best of 'em all—yoahs truleh, li'l ol' Babe Didrikson.'" In moments like these she became a caricature of herself. She also learned to poke fun at her less-than-feminine physical features. Explaining her formula for success she said she had determination. "And my jaw helps plenty, too. It's more like a Texas Ranger's jaw than anything else.

And those rangers were hot when the going was tough." The galleries loved it.[33]

In fact, Babe said of herself, jokingly, in 1935, "The biggest weakness in my game has is that I have too much fun with the galleries. I give the gallery a run for its money." Her favorite quips included, "Well can we *play* now?" after the announcer gave long-winded introductions to Gene and her, and the ever-popular one-liner that followed a number of shots sliced over to the right, "Well, there must be a bottle of Scotch over there in those bushes." She occasionally spoke of her desire to "be in the Men's Open and all of the women's opens I can get in." But unsettling and controversial comments such as these were gradually being overshadowed by her charismatic effect on the crowds.

She was a charmer. She used the crowds to bolster her own game and increase their enjoyment. "Sometimes," she said, "when I connect with one clean and pretty and it goes streaking down the fairway making a white line in the air like a piece of string, I turn to the gallery and say 'How'm I doin?'" The crowd would roar its appreciation. And Babe, for that moment, was on top of the world. She'd pulled them all into her game—they'd become part of her action. And she loved it.[34]

Babe's familiar fascination and obsession with money reemerged during her tour with Sarazen. A *Sports Illustrated* article claimed Babe was paid $150 per match. In *This Life I've Led* Babe put her take at $500 each. And in "I Blow My Own Horn" Babe told her interviewer, "My share of the tour with him comes to $600 up to $1,000 a week. Sometimes we give half the gate to charity funds." Sarazen was struck by Babe's insistence on being paid in $1 bills. "I'd go to write her a check and she'd say, 'No Squire, make it in one dollar bills.' Then she'd stack them up and mail them to her bank in Beaumont."[35]

Also while playing with Sarazen, Babe received an offer from the P. Goldsmith Sons sporting goods company to play with their clubs and balls, which would carry her name. Babe agreed, and she and Sarazen played against Joyce Wethered and her partner before Babe had practiced with her new clubs. This cavalier approach bothered Sarazen, who said, "She couldn't hit the ball at all, we were trounced. She would do anything for a buck, it was like a trout going for a shrimp." To Gene's chagrin, Babe wasn't upset about losing the game. "Squire," she said, "I got me some do-re-mi." Then she laughed and said, "Watch me from now on, boy."[36]

Babe was economically flush again after her stint with Sarazen and had "a really good bankroll." She'd played about eighteen matches for between $250 and $500 each and by her own recollection "was still getting my $2500 a year from the sporting-goods company, and they were giving me all the golf supplies I needed free." Little wonder that by summer's end Babe confidently said, "That Gene made a golfer out of me. Now I'm on the right track." But mastering her golf game and the crowd was only half of her problem.[37]

The name-calling returned anew in April 1935 at the Texas State Women's Golf Championship at the River Oaks Country Club in Houston. When she entered the event, Peggy Chandler, a Texas Women's Golf Association member announced, "We really don't need any truck drivers' daughters in our tournament." And several women, insinuating that Babe was too masculine to compete against, withdrew from a pre-tournament driving contest. Babe responded by clowning. She feigned exaggerated femininity, taking intentionally ludicrous, "girlish" swings at her balls. Except one. She stopped clowning long enough to rocket one ball 250 yards. She won.[38]

In true Hollywood fashion, Babe obliterated her first three challengers in the tournament to vindicate herself against their unkindnesses. She also whipped her semifinal opponent on a rainy eighteenth hole "with a 20-foot putt that spurted water across the green." Her opponent in the finals was none other than the openly hostile Chandler, a bona fide Texas society miss "who had snubbed Babe and was one of the more feminine and well-dressed golfers on the women's circuit." Paul Gallico, ever-present and always ready with his barbs, wrote, " 'The Texas Babe seems to be working out a life long vendetta on sissy girls.' "[39]

A photo taken that day is a study in contrasts. Both women are wearing short-sleeve knit jerseys and long skirts that stop several inches above their bobby socks and two-tone golf shoes. But it's the way they don them that's so strikingly different. Chandler, hand perched confidently on her hip, looks trim, neat, and self-assured. Babe looks uncomfortable in her skirt. She is noticeably rumpled beside her smooth opponent. Her socks lie in a crumpled heap about her ankles. Her hair, pulled off her face (and noticeably longer than its most severe cut), is held back by a headband. It looks uncombed. She's squinting, standing stiffly, while Chandler, posing for photographers, with her perfect smile and white straw hat, gracefully holds Babe's arm.

They went head-to-head for thirty-six holes, much to the delight of the gallery. Chandler, up by three after twenty-six holes, saw Babe rally to even the score at the thirtieth hole. On the thirty-fourth the drama escalated: Chandler reached the green on the third shot (on the par 5) and a birdie seemed inevitable. Babe teed off with a powerful—but wild—250-yard smash that landed in a ditch. Her second shot skidded over and past the green, stopping in a rut holding an inch of rainwater. Unbelievably, Babe's third shot found the cup for an eagle 3. It was an astounding rally. The women played the thirty-fifth hole to a draw and Babe captured the thirty-sixth hole to win the match. Unexpectedly, the gallery erupted with cheers and applause. As one paper crowed, "Staging a sensational finish, the irrepressible Babe Didrikson Saturday rudely upset the polite circles of women's golf in Texas by defeating the veteran Mrs. Dan Chandler of Dallas two up to take the State title. . . . The tom-boy girl took up golf only two years ago. She went out on the green and found it 'fun to sock 'em and see how far they would go.'" *Newsweek* succinctly entitled its lengthy coverage of her victory "'Best at Everything' Babe Garners Another Trophy."[40]

It was a fantastic victory for Babe. She had earned respect as a bona fide golfer and overcome the emotional upset of pre-tournament name-calling. As she would do with so many other painful episodes, Babe whitewashed the whole ugly affair with Chandler. A bland caption beside their photo obscures the tumult of the tournament in her autobiography: "Just before the final of the Texas State Tourney in 1935. That's Peggy Chandler, a swell girl. I won it for my first golf victory. The title was sweet."[41]

In what must have seemed like a nightmarish rerun, shortly afterward the United States Golf Association (USGA) banned her from amateur competition. When Babe registered for the women's southern championship to be held in Louisville, at the request of Mrs. Willard Sullivan of Ashland, Virginia, secretary of the Women's Southern Golf Association, "the U.S.G.A. amateur status committee investigated Miss Didrikson's activities as a professional in other sports—baseball, basketball and billiards." The amateur status committee, headed by Archie M. Reid, advised the southern association to reject her entry. He simultaneously announced that Babe was ineligible to compete for the 1935 national championship.[42]

The USGA ruling was apparently based upon a precedent set nine years before. Mary K. Browne, a former national tennis champion, was barred from amateur golf for three years after she had toured the country with Suzanne Lenglen playing professional tennis. But when Reid told the press the ruling was made in "the best interest of the game" and in keeping with the USGA's policy, he refused to specify the grounds on which she had been dismissed. Didrikson had been barred from competing as an amateur for only one year, but Reid did admit that "the rule contains much elasticity." The implication was that he, like Chandler, wanted no truck drivers' daughters to play in his tournaments.[43]

Babe's East Texas friends galvanized into action on her behalf. Ben S. Woodhead, president of the Beaumont Country Club, which Babe had represented in her golf play, petitioned the USGA to give her a full hearing. Woodhead was "confident" Didrikson could answer any accusations. Other members of the Beaumont Country Club as well as members of the Texas Professional Golf Association spoke out against the USGA ruling: " 'Bad mistake,' 'big joke,' and 'dirty deal' and harsher words came from Dallas." They sensed a personal—perhaps regional—rejection under way, even though it was a Dallas socialite's disdain that had triggered the maelstrom.[44]

Babe, in a distinct reversal of form, at first responded mildly, almost meekly. McCombs, speaking for Babe out of Dallas, said she did not know what her next step would be. He reported that Babe had sent a message to the association asking for a ruling on her status because "she does not want to force herself upon an organization which might not want her." Later Babe lamented, "How can they call me a professional when I've been competing only a few months?" Her professional career in other sports, she claimed, "ended nearly a year ago." Yet Babe spoke with none of the rancor and flippancy she'd directed at the AAU during her earlier ousting. Golf was her future, and golf's officialdom needed kid-glove handling. "What the U.S.G.A. says, goes," she conceded, "and there's nothing I can do about it." At this time, Babe was unsure if her disbarment would be for one or three years, so holding her tongue was, decidedly, in her best interest. She said she would shun pro sports and ask for reinstatement as soon as possible.[45]

By June 1935 the die was cast: she was banned for three years. Babe then announced she would join the ranks of pro golfers. She sealed her decision with a new contract with P. Goldsmith Sons sporting goods company. She was paid $2,500 per year to promote their supplies and play exhibition golf. Still, in a surprisingly diplomatic move, Babe refused to criticize the USGA. In fact, she praised it, "for sticking to its rules." "Of course, I was disappointed when they told me I couldn't compete as an amateur," she said, "but I admire them for barring me too. They were big enough to adhere to their rules."[46]

From Rowdy Miss to Poor Texas Gal

The USGA ban allowed Babe to bring her desire for money and press together with her changing image of herself. During this period she learned better how to use the press and stop its use of her. Despite the constant tension between who was manipulating who, Didrikson steadily gained control of the image she molded. She reaffirmed her new relationship with golf. "I'm very happy," she said. She believed golf to be a women's game because it was "a game of coordination, rhythm and grace. Women have this to a much higher degree than men, as dancing shows." Here, Babe intentionally linked golf, femininity, and herself—a triumvirate she came to tout regularly. In her first professional tournament, the Western Open held in Chicago in June 1935, the "old Babe's" aggressive self-confidence shone through despite her attempts to appear more feminine. She told one reporter, "They may as well wrap up the cup and give it to me now for I'm going to take it." She also told a *Time* reporter, "Good golf is not a male monopoly. My own case proves it."[47]

Given this slippage in her portrayal of herself, the old comparisons between Babe's body and strength and those of men were not yet extinguished. A *New York Times* article closed with the claim that "her powerful shoulders and athletic coordination [would have her] out drive three-fourths of the men professionals in golf." Her golf scores and drive lengths then follow. But the emphasis had shifted. First, there was a note of sympathy toward her. "The girl wonder from Texas" was, after all, "rebuffed in her effort to gain an amateur standing" and was thus forced to "market her 260 yard drives and personality on the fairways" by turning pro. Babe was the underdog, done in by bureaucratic red tape and worthy of sympathy. And second, she was softer around the edges, less coarse with the press, and less masculine in appearance. In a word, her inching toward "proper" female behavior seemed already to be reaping rewards.[48]

It's hard to say if she could have transformed herself completely if she had not met Bertha Bowen. Betty Hicks credited Bowen with "feminizing the Babe Didrikson of 1932 Olympic fame. [It was] a task comparable to carving a new face on Mt. Rushmore." Photos of Didrikson from this period show a confident, strong, handsome young woman, comfortable with her body and exuding grace and self-esteem. But her huge gallery of observers was not completely comfortable despite the cheers. It's possible Babe's drive to succeed, impeded by negative press, would have forced a self-guided feminization; she wanted fame, fortune, and acceptance that badly. But meeting Bertha Bowen in the fall of 1935 expedited matters considerably.[49]

In October Babe turned to Bertha and her husband R. L. Bowen for help and guidance with her new career and her new image. R. L. was president of an electric light and power company, Community Public Service, and Bertha was a member of the group that managed women's golf in Texas. Didrikson turned to the Bowens specifically because Bertha had previously made sure Babe's entry to the River Oaks Tournament went through with no trouble and because of Bertha's connection with the Fort Worth Invitational amateur competition. Bertha promoted golf to further amateur play, not a popular stance at the country club. She managed the three-day stroke tournament, which allowed amateurs to qualify for the Curtis and Walker Cup Teams.[50]

Bertha, in particular, was horrified at the treatment Babe had received from the USGA. Babe called and said "she didn't mind what had happened to her, but she just wanted to play in the Southern so much and in other amateur tournaments to improve her golf." At Bertha's invitation, Babe headed for Bertha's home with Kate Anderson, a basketball teammate. "My husband was out of town," Bertha recalled, "and I just didn't know what to do except to call our best women's promoter, whose husband was an attorney." Bea Thompson, the friend Bertha phoned, "was a great promoter of young golfers," one of whom was Aneila Goldthwaite, who became the Curtis Cup Team captain in 1952. In fact, Thompson had played on the cup team once herself and had won many tournaments. She too was appalled at Babe's treatment. Bertha's rage at the ruling was palpable. She understood the true basis of Babe's exclusion: "I was just furious at those people who had been so cutting to her. The fact that she was poor and had no clothes did not mean she had to be ruled a professional."[51]

Bertha and Thompson plotted to transform the Fort Worth Invitational into the Texas Women's Open. Instead of head-to-head competition, the winner would be determined by the lowest total score and play would be open to both amateurs and professionals. The new tournament "started us getting Betsy Rawls and all the prominent amateurs. Peggy Kirk Bell and Patty Berg and all those girls that didn't have anywhere to play either. . . . We just gave small prizes and it developed." Babe stayed with the Bowens during the tournament, which was only the second in the country to welcome professionals. Although she fared poorly in it, the tournament was created, in a real sense, for her.[52]

Instead, Babe developed an intimate bond with the Bowens, who'd lost a son in 1930. Babe doubled as surrogate daughter and friend to the couple. Although the tournament lasted only three days, Babe and another golfer, Helen Dettweiler, stayed three weeks. It was an instantaneous and mutual bond. The Bowens had a pool room, "and my husband loved pool, so did Babe, and we had a boat, a small boat at Eagle Mountain Lake and she adored fishing. We had so many wonderful things in common." R. L. and Babe competed at every game imaginable, whereas Bertha was "more likely to attend to their appetites."[53]

Press coverage, Babe's narratives, and interviews with her family and golf peers tell an unequivocal story of love and devotion between Babe and the Bowens. Bertha and Babe's friendship was pivotal to both of them. Betty Hicks and Betty Jameson, another golfer, count Bertha as one of Babe's closest friends. Bubba and Jackie Didriksen emphasized the Bowens' parental role toward Babe. "They really took Babe under their wings. They were good to her." And Thelma Didriksen thought Babe's relationship with Bertha was secondary only to her own. Of the Bowens Babe said, they've "always been like a godmother and godfather to me." Babe accepted Bertha's tutelage because she sought refuge from public condemnation and because Bertha's affection for her was overriding. Bertha's was a friendly, loving influence, not a critical one.[54]

Babe, Bertha recalls, "was eager to be proper." She was moving in different social circles now, but not infrequently her streetwise East Texas roots shone through. She'd be behaving just fine, Bertha said, "and then I could hear sometimes her talking to men or somebody who liked off-color stories. That was another side of her. She was very careful, discreet about it, you know, but I could tell she liked what you'd call a good story." Yet charges of tomboyishness—and more—exacerbated by critical media attention "never entered our minds. She seemed at ease with any and everybody. If she didn't like them, she could be pretty cool, but that would be about it." Evidence from the era, though, belies this account. Both the print media and Babe's own recollections give primary responsibility to Bertha for the metamorphosis.[55]

"She was so poor it was pitiful," Bertha said of Babe in 1935. Despite the tens of thousands of dollars Babe had earned little of it was spent on herself. Rather her parents and siblings benefited. "One night [during the Western Open] we were invited to a formal party and we asked Babe to come along. She hemmed and hawed because she didn't have any clothes." Bertha got her an evening dress and when Babe took a look at it she said, " 'I'm not going to wear that naked thing.' We had to chase her all over the house before we could get the dress on her. We finally cornered her in the kitchen and forced her into it." Determination, mixed with fun, marked Bertha's campaign to feminize Babe.[56]

Other reports chronicle that Bertha took Babe to "Neiman-Marcus for seven hundred dollars worth of new clothes, advised her on a more feminine hairdo, and applied subtle makeup; but try as she might, she could never get Babe to play golf in a girdle." Once, Bertha did succeed in squeezing Babe into a girdle. This was a particularly sensitive issue as far as the Texas Women's Golf Association leadership was concerned. They'd pressured Bertha "that Babe really must wear a girdle when she played golf." Bertha recalled with mirth the scene that followed on the fateful day Babe wore the girdle. She played a round and returned to the Bowen house "in a frenzy." "I heard the car come screeching in the driveway," Bertha said, "and Babe came tearing into the house. She was yelling, 'Goddam! I'm chokin' to death!' As far as I know, she never put on a girdle again."[57]

Bertha and R. L. Bowen appreciated the unpolished Babe, too. Bertha noted Babe's eating preferences when they met: pork and beans, onion sandwiches, strawberry sodas, and banana chewy candy. She was the funniest person they knew and Bertha testified, "We'd rather be with her than almost anybody, my husband and I." The three went dozens of times to the Bowens' cabin up in Bayfield, Colorado. Babe loved the outdoors and although she loved to fish, "she wouldn't even eat a bird or quail, let alone hunt one." Babe adored stream fishing and as Bertha recalled, "we were always making a bet or something. Competition always came in. . . . We'd meet at noon and everybody'd put up $10 and whoever got the most or the biggest [fish] would get the money."[58]

One day, Babe took off by herself. Bertha and R. L. were sure they'd beaten her with their large catch. They were tickled because "that was really something to ever beat Babe at anything." They were gleeful as they awaited her return, but it was short-lived. "Well here she comes in with her hip boots on and all her paraphernalia and willow branch with the biggest trout you can imagine—and it *don't even grow* in that river!" To this day "we don't know where she got 'em. And that's the truth. We figured she must have met a hatchery truck somehow and bought them or made a deal with the truck driver." These were golden days for Bertha, R. L., and Babe.

The Bowens also knew, and modulated, Babe's wild side. They owned a private plane, and R. L. would take Babe up flying. He was a conservative flyer and "she always wanted to learn everything you did. He'd be teaching her the quiet, nice way to fly." But Babe, ever-ready for the new and exciting, would say, "I don't want to do that. I want to do nip-ups, not straight flying." R. L. let her take the controls of the plane, "but he wouldn't put up with any foolishness."[59]

Years later when Babe and Betty Dodd became inseparable, Babe jokingly acknowledged Bertha's feminizing influence on her. Bertha came home one day to find Babe giving Betty a permanent. "She kept screaming at her: 'Sit still! Bertha made a lady out of me and I'm gonna do the same thing to you!'" In fact, Bertha kept an eye on Babe's dress and appearance throughout the forties and fifties. Betty Hicks remembered, "One day we played an exhibition in Fort Worth and [Babe] borrowed a dress from Bertha Bowen which was not exactly suited for golf, but she was so proud of that flowered dress."[60]

Casual observers as well as hawkish followers noticed the transformation. Gallico was stunned—and pleased. "I hardly knew Babe Didrikson when I saw her," he said. "Hair frizzed and she had a neat little wave in it, parted and prettily combed, a touch of rouge on her cheeks and red on her lips." "The tomboy," he said with obvious relief, "had suddenly grown up." Gallico quotes Babe as saying to him—in his own version of a Texas drawl—"'Ah got tired of being a tomboy, so Ah quit, Ah'm a business woman golfer now, so Ah guess Ah hyev to look th' part!'" Another columnist, Henry McLemore, announced bluntly "that her sleeping beauty had been at last awakened."[61]

Babe, wizened from years of press criticism, enlisted their pens in announcing her "crossover" into womanhood. Where better to start than with the acidic Gallico. He wrote in *Esquire* the details of an encounter they'd had during this time that was often quoted as proof positive of Babe's change. They met at a golf tournament in Ohio, when Babe "was older, less hoydenish, and her hair had a wave in it." They sat on a bench talking "and shyly, with infinite femininity she confessed, 'I got 'em,' and lifted the edge of her tweed golf skirt to disclose the silk-and-lace undergarment beneath. Then she opened her handbag and let me peer at the usual female equipment of lipstick and compact, eye shadow and lace handkerchief. She had gone all the way and was delighted with it." So was Gallico.[62]

In her autobiography Babe acknowledged that these years were a turning point in cultural opinion of her. She claimed, "Some writers have said that around this time, a big change took place in me. Their idea is that I used to be all tomboy, with none of the usual girls' interests, and then all of a sudden I switched over to being feminine." Babe claimed this was wrong. And here she began recreating her past as it would best serve her in the present. This strategy contrasted radically with her offhand honesty in earlier interviews in which she talked straightforwardly and told the truth with little concern for its reception, but also created myths with little concern for the truth.[63]

As she told Frank Menke, then sports editor for the International News Service, in Los Angeles in 1932, "I am what I happen to be today because I had 3 brothers who were plenty rough, and I lived in a neighborhood in Beaumont, Texas, where the neighbor boys weren't any nicer to little girls than my brothers were to me." Boys "always would slam-bang me around." At first she didn't respond, "and then I didn't see any reason why I shouldn't. . . . I made a pretty good job of it after I learned boxing in 1929." She was good enough to deck her "brother Louis onto the floor once in a while," but he responded with "pumping leather into my face and body . . . and [we stood] "there slugging it out, each trying to flatten the other." In 1932 Babe gloried in her tough and aggressive posture with boys. She recommended it for other girls. Her athletic success "proves that if a girl wants to get herself a few championships and some trophies the way to do it is to be a tomboy like I was, taking the banging that the boys would hand out and then do some banging on your own."[64]

Two years later in 1934, she effectively rewrote her personal history. She emphasized her romantic contact with boys, not their fisticuffs. She'd had boyfriends as a late teen back in Beaumont, she claimed, a statement negated by dozens of testimonials. She did admit, though, that at fourteen, "I didn't have any boy friends then. . . . I was too busy learning to dribble and pass and shoot baskets." That was the cutoff age, apparently, for tomboyish behavior. She also claimed Dallas-based beaus. "I had dates and boyfriends from the time when I was working in Dallas," she told reporters. "For a while there were two that were fighting each other." She went with one for several years who wanted to wed her, but she wasn't interested. "I was too busy working on my sports career."[65]

Babe consciously created a heterosexual past for herself and made certain it was a nonthreatening heterosexual past replete with adolescent savvy of gender boundaries. In her autobiography she advised—then cautioned—aspiring girl athletes: "I am afraid that the only real first class advice I can give is get toughened up playing the boys' games, but DON'T GET TOUGH. There's a lot of difference there." Babe's emphasis on heterosexual ideals dovetailed with cultural expectations and norms. That she was personally "late" in adopting these norms likely accounts for the enthusiasm with which she embraced them.[66]

The press heaved a collective sigh of relief at this feminizing process. It's as if once this shadow was lifted, her march to greatness could proceed unhampered. Herb Simmons, writing for the *Chicago Sunday Times* in 1934, wrote that she was "a little more feminine, a little more amiable than she was [in 1932]. Shaking her tousled brown hair out of her eyes—incidentally, brown hair girlishly bobbed, grown out of brown hair boyishly cropped—" the "Texas tommie" ceased her practice shots long enough to tell Simmons of her love of golf. "La belle Babe," to Simmons's eye, had "the rhythm of a ballet girl and the power of a ballroom bouncer." In *"Whatta-Gal,"* the authors editorially interject that at this time "obviously, a more womanly new woman was in the making. The fiercely sheared bob was gone and the vendetta against femininity was at an end." Later they compare a photo from the Olympics and a photo from her golfing days. The caption comments, "The metamorphosis from the tough young Texan known as Muscle Moll to a vibrant, graceful woman who dominated golf . . . required enormous courage [and] almost superhuman athletic talent." Babe's successful ascension to femininity is hailed as an applaudable accomplishment, not the tumultuous, contrived, and limiting self-molding that it really was. Portrayed as a win-win situation, the toll taken on self-esteem, individuality, and difference is ignored. Even many years after her transformation, it remained standard fare for interviewers to spend as much time describing her physicality as her sports accomplishments. In so doing, they reassured themselves and their readers of Babe's acceptability.[67]

Hence Pete Martin's *Saturday Evening Post* article, "Babe Didrikson Takes Off Her Mask" (1947), repeated all the old innuendos—and a few flat-out insults. He devoted much time and space to observations like "Babe is no longer button-breasted." Babe's bust measurement, originally "born halfway between masculine flats and angles and the rubber curves of femininity" had become 40 inches. Jane Russell, "Hollywood's leading sweater filler," had a bust of only 38½ inches. Martin continued with Babe's waist and hip measurements and body weight. A few paragraphs later he comfortably asserted, "There is little resemblance to the so-called 'muscle moll' of yesteryear." Her arms resembled those "of any normally healthy woman, although her legs are still impressive columns of flesh and sinew." As if in an extended search for "proofs" of Babe's normalcy, Martin, like Gallico, detailed her feminine accoutrements: lipstick, perfume, fingernail polish, and classy clothes.[68]

There's a striking consistency to press portrayals both before and after her so-called feminization. Most authors dwell on her physicality, both positive and negative, and many are incapable of discussing Babe without ritually denouncing her gender-crossed past. Nonetheless, the period 1935–37 was a turning point for Babe. Although the shadow of doubt lingered, she came out of the darkest hours of scrutiny and name-calling. Through golf, an unimpeachably ladylike sport, and active self-feminization, she had begun to transcend her past and get on with her future.

CHAPTER SIX

Romance

Thus it was perfect timing when Babe was teamed with George Zaharias at the Los Angeles Open in January 1938. Her match tour with Sarazen complete, her bankroll exhausted, she gladly looked for new opportunities to make money. By her own admission, she "didn't have any business" being in the Los Angeles Open. It was one of the regular tournaments on the men's circuit, "but there was no rule that said a woman couldn't play in it." Although Babe knew she wouldn't be able to beat the top men pros, she was still trying to establish herself as the greatest woman golfer.[1]

Babe was teamed with two other dubious entrants: C. Pardee Erdman, a Presbyterian minister who was a professor of religion at Occidental College in Los Angeles, and George Zaharias, a professional wrestler known as the Crying Greek from Cripple Creek. He'd entered the Los Angeles Open on a whim and a dare from his buddies after he'd broken 80 "and put down five bucks." The golfing trio was a gag pulled by a local sports promoter. "But it was no gag," Babe told Laurence Lader of *Coronet* magazine in 1948. "It was love at first sight."[2]

Babe's feminization was well under way. She'd already constructed an appropriate heterosocial past for herself, and the press was primed to become her ally. Even Paul Gallico had satisfied himself that she was "struggling like a chrysalis to emerge from a cocoon." "The transition from the man-girl who hated sissies," he wrote, "to a feminine woman, confident of herself" had taken place. Babe nurtured this feminized image of herself at every turn. A photo in *This Life I've Led* shows George and Babe smiling at each other on the golf course. The caption reads: "I'd had several boy friends as a youngster, but when I met George Zaharias at the '38 Los Angeles Open, I knew this was IT."[3]

Their meeting and their courtship were the stuff reporters dream of. They were both media hounds. Both knew how to clown to have the cameras and the pens point in their direction. And they got right to it. "What an introduction George and I had!" Babe reminisced. "One minute we were saying hello, and the next minute photographers were crowding around and calling for him to put wrestling holds on me. He put his arms around me, pretending to apply neck holds and stuff. And I didn't mind at all." Typewriters and flashbulbs exploded with the news.[4]

George had his own version of the events. Told one year after her death, the tale makes George look like a model husband and Babe a fragile dependent wife. George was initially annoyed by his pairing with Didrikson. "Well, I knew she was good, for a girl, but I had figured I would be paired for that first round with some of the big pros, Hagen maybe, to draw a crowd. I was always crowd-conscious. . . . [I learned] I was paired with a girl and, hell, I didn't want to go out there with a girl, no matter what girl." At his friends' urging, George overcame his reticence and teed off at 11:00 A.M. "I saw her," he said. "When we shook hands, a big thrill went through me. In a minute, I had my arms around her, showing her wrestling holds for the press photographers. There were cameras all around us and it seemed to me there was electricity all around us. I couldn't get my eyes filled up with her. It was wonderful."[5]

Reassured that they were, indeed, the photographers' focus, George watched Babe on "the sixth or seventh hole, and she was walking ahead of me down the fairway and she looked back over her shoulder, like girls do, and she said, 'What are you looking at?' and I said, 'I'm looking at you. You're my kind of girl.' That was when she said 'You're my kind of guy.' She shot an 82 that day and I beat her by one stroke." George's account of Babe's flirtation lends added legitimacy to her newly realized femininity. A later story claimed that photographers requested that George put his arm around Babe, which he did with a huge smile. This spicy tale has George asking, " 'Am I holding you too close?' Babe replied, 'No. You may stay there all my life.' "[6]

Babe was twenty-seven when they met, although she claims she was twenty-three. George, twenty-nine, weighed 235 and was described by Babe as "husky and black-haired and handsome." Zaharias, born Theodore Vetoyanis in 1908, was the son of Gus and Demitra Vetoyanis, immigrants from Tripolis, Greece. Zaharias was a world-class wrestler from 1932 to 1938 with credentials impressive enough to have him inducted into the Hellenic Hall of Fame for Greek Athletes in 1982.[7]

Gus initially worked in a steel mill in Colorado, but soon settled on a farm outside Pueblo with his family. George worked on the farm and in the mills, which, Babe noted, "must have helped to develop those tremendous muscles of his." As a teen he moved to Oklahoma City to learn the hat-cleaning business while living with an uncle. He did his share of shoe shining, too. George, like Babe, knew what it meant to scratch out a living. In fact, their similar backgrounds meant that initially, at least, their worldviews, aspirations, and some social graces were similar too.

"Then the wrestling bug bit him," Babe recalled. And while he "had a hard time breaking in, . . . he finally became a real attraction." When they met in 1938, George had already built his parents a new home, set up two brothers-in-law in business, and paid for the educations of his two younger brothers, Chris and Tom. Like Babe, George showed generosity toward his family. In the black-and-white world of feigned wrestling personas, George found success as the Crying Greek from Cripple Creek, "the big bad villain that everybody hated." He was also billed as Gorgeous George Zaharias, the Colorado Crooner, the Pueblo Pouter, and the Meanest Man.[8]

Pro wrestling, called by one columnist "a rough-house ballet form of improvisational comedy," did require fine athletes. "These lumbering behemoths can flash with agility," this keen eye noted. "They are not so much gladiators of camp as movie stars who do their own stunts." Wrestling, a type of vaudeville performance art, made George Zaharias to the ring what Babe was to the green: camera-ready, self-promoting, flamboyant, exaggeratedly physical, and eminently watchable. George had crafted a ring persona.[9] Harry Brundridge wrote of him in 1932, "Zaharias [is] known to the fans only as a scowling, growling demon whose every action in the ring is greeted with hisses." "The fans hate me," George admitted, "but pay money to see me wrestle, probably in the hope I'll get my neck broken." He was a honed villain with "an incredible assortment of whines and grunts, whinnyings and groans which would put a herd of bird and animal imitators to shame." Zaharias practiced facial grimacing a la Frankenstein's monster and Dracula in the mirror and "abandoned approved rassling formula for such quaint routines as sticking his thumb in his opponents' eyes and kicking them in the head while prone."[10] A Cleveland reporter documented the usually hostile reception of George's antics. He was razzed and fans "gave him the 'bird,'" when he uses elbows and sometimes fists upon the anatomies of opponents." Like Babe, George used predictions of imminent victories to heighten fans' expectations and reporters' interest.[11]

George's ring personas, and the ethnic rivalries they fueled, gave controlled expression to social conflicts and "offered cathartic, albeit temporary resolution of deep social problems." He and other wrestlers and boxers exemplified the independence lacking in the lives of most working men and women. His work "embodied a distinctly working-class version of the American dream, providing models of upward mobility within bounds acceptable to the street culture." In short, he "shaped violence into art."[12]

He was a caricature of manliness: tough, ferocious, powerful, defensive of his honor, sensitive to insult, cool in the face of danger, able to take punishment. His exaggerated manliness contrasted favorably with Babe's attempted womanliness. He softened her image, she heightened his. Zaharias and Didrikson were both hustlers. They were working-class sports entertainers who reflected certain mainstream sensibilities: individualism, the will to succeed, and materialism. The two performers had found one another. There was more than a little of each in the other. Both knew that a well-executed show, be it in the ring or other arena, "was a performance, a pageant, a ritual."[13]

George, like Babe, was endearing to the casual observer in these early years of their union. He was "the kind of guy you felt like giving a big cookie to," one writer commented. He was "a big shambling bear with cauliflowered ears." Another wrote that he "has an attractive personality. He is friendly and his boisterous good humor and booming laughter are contagious. . . . [He's a] clever story teller, easy to interview, and speaks first-class English." He was also strong as an ox, well-proportioned, and immediately attentive to Babe.[14]

After their first round of golf at the Los Angeles Open was over, George invited Babe and Erdman for refreshments. As she was parting George called out, "I'll be seeing you tomorrow." She was looking forward to a second round. After the second day, George invited her back to his apartment, which he shared with his brothers. Babe phoned Lillie and Hannah, who were living with her at the time, and told them she was going out to dinner. They each took their own car. When Babe took a wrong turn, Zaharias noticed and caught her. As the oft-repeated anecdote went, he asked her, "Are you trying to run away from me?" When she assured him she wasn't, they headed on to the apartment. While George cooked steaks for dinner, the Zaharias brothers took turns demonstrating wrestling holds on Babe. "George was watching pretty close to see that they didn't get rough with me. Which they didn't of course." After the steak dinner they went out dancing. Babe went home first to change and George went there to pick her up. He met Hannah and Lillic, and Babe noted, "Momma liked him straight off." She also gave her approval to their dancing, saying, "Well, that's fine. He's a nice man."[15]

"For many years until the Babe met and married her big, hearty, and adoring wrestler husband, George Zaharias," Gallico wrote, "she was a pathetic and solitary figure, neither one thing nor another in the average, normal world of ordinary men or women or even, for that matter, of athletes." But George's "manliness," evidenced in his exaggerated physical form and prowess, reaffirmed Babe's femininity. Beside him she was assured of unquestionable normalcy. In what became an oft-repeated one-liner, Babe said of George, "I always said I could fall in love with a man strong enough to outdrive me."[16]

George called Babe "Romance." Their affection for each other grew, but their careers often pulled them in opposite directions. Once, when Hannah, Lillie, and Babe were going to visit sister Dora in Phoenix on their way to Beaumont, Babe dropped her kin in Phoenix and turned around to go back and be with George. He wasn't at his apartment, but he'd left a note saying, "Romance, I'm in San Francisco." George's brother Chris drove her to San Francisco, all 460 miles, through the night. When they got to the St. Marks Hotel where the wrestlers were staying, Chris and Babe went up and pounded on George's door. "He came out and said, 'Come here, Romance,'" Babe recalled. "He gave me a big kiss. And then I wasn't lonesome anymore." After that they tried to arrange their schedules to be near one another.[17]

The Western Women's Open was held in Colorado Springs in June that year, not far from where George's folks lived in Pueblo. George had arranged wrestling matches in the area, and during a mutually free afternoon Babe met his parents. "His mother didn't speak too much English," she recalled, "but she and I got along fine just the same." George's parents probably triggered warm thoughts of her own mother and father: immigrants, unfamiliar with English, protected and provided for by their successful child.[18]

Babe was in love. And in a rare moment of noncompetitiveness she said of her elimination in the semifinal round of the tournament: "But that particular summer, losing a golf match didn't seem to matter as much to me as it ordinarily did." Her transition to womanhood seemed complete. Ruth Scurlock, keen eyed and quick tongued, noted that "Babe seemed to love to play 'the little woman,' to have someone there to protect her and defend her. It was a role she had never played before." And Zaharias loved to play the "big buck" in his role as leading man. Of their meeting in 1938 he told *Look* magazine: "She was like a little deer, like a little fawn, scared of the world. When I put my arms around her, I felt her tremble. There was a flutter through her whole body, like she felt afraid and insecure. Then, she quieted down, and I felt that if I could keep my arms around her, I could make her strong."[19]

They announced their engagement in St. Louis on July 22, 1938. Babe told a St. Louis paper, "We're very much in love." In this piece George is dubbed "Kid Cupid" who "Stole Our Babe's Heart." Her family was happy and excited for her. In addition, "there was a silent but heart felt cry of joy among her women conferees when Babe Didrikson announced that she was going steady and would be married." Although they were aware that her grandstanding style and toughie mannerisms were "good show biz" for her, "still, it was something of a relief for them to observe the change in Babe's looks and her obvious feminine dress." It deflected speculation about the inclinations of all women athletes.[20]

They kept postponing the wedding hoping to have both families present. Plus, their appearances kept them running in opposite directions. "What with this commitment and that," Babe recalled, "we never could seem to work out a date for the wedding." In December they found themselves in St. Louis together, and by Babe's account George "got real stern with me." He said, " 'We're going to get married this week or call the deal off.' She shook like a leaf, and then she quieted down as though she had complete trust in me and everything was going to be all right."[21]

"We had been happy and we were not under any pressure," George recalled, "but I wanted her to be mine, and I told her so. And she said, 'If that's the way you want it, we'll do it.'" With this George began a tradition of making decisions and presenting ultimatums to which Babe usually complied. Thus, Babe said, " 'It's a deal. Let's go!' " The much-anticipated event was conducted, rather innocuously, in the home of Tom Packs, a wrestling promoter, on January 3, 1938, by Judge A. G. Jannopoulo. Leo Durocher was George's best man, and Leo's former wife, Grace, stood up for Babe. How difficult it must have been not to share the occasion with Hannah, Lillie, and the rest of her family. But George was emphatic that they wait no longer, and his will ruled. It was, Babe noted quietly, "A very nice affair." And while they'd stilled their hectic schedules for the ceremony itself there was no time for a honeymoon.[22]

Polka Dot Dresses and Rolling Pins

After marriage Babe and George settled in Los Angeles in a rented duplex with a yard. George reminisced, "Right away she was a housewife. She bought furniture—big overstuffed chairs I could sit in." She was the perfect wife, "thinking of me all the time." Zaharias boasted, "I was a big money-maker in those days, as loaded as a kid could be loaded, and I had saved my money." Although unconcerned about finances, Babe made the curtains herself and used her skills to furnish and decorate their home. The press loved their union. It was perpetually portrayed as ideal, even in unabashedly corny prose such as this: "She was married to one man in her life, George Zaharias, and they lived happily ever after." Harry Paxton wrote in the preface to *This Life I've Led,* "There was an easy oneness that existed between Babe and her husband George." The harmonious image was zealously guarded by Babe and perpetuated by the press.[23]

Yet evidence suggests that Babe's actual relationship with George had already struck discord this early in their marriage. George's will ruled supreme, and he was overbearing at times. He was always hustling for Babe's fame, which occasionally exceeded her own comfort. Further, Babe had clearly tired of her nomadic existence by 1938. By all accounts she wanted a more settled life, but he continuously pushed her to travel and grab a few bucks wherever possible. This often meant lengthy separations. Finally, through her marriage she lost the power to make autonomous decisions affecting her life. Likely this both burdened and relieved her. She gained companionship, but lost control.

Positively, it is clear there was a deep affection, and passion, between them. They were more alike than not in their early married years. Babe, who had rarely been protected, now surrendered to her forceful mate and kept their disputes private. Newspaper stories about them crowed unequivocally positive reports like "It is nice to hear news of Mr. and Mrs. Zaharias, a couple who have, to my mind, achieved the pinnacle in married harmony." Westbrook Pegler wrote that George "was so affectionate and tender that he made the pair of them conspicuous in a world which took special note of mutual devotion because it was so rare." Will Grimsley reported in 1942 on their new home in the fashionable suburbs of Denver, where they relocated to be near George's promotional activities, which "contained an eight-foot square bed, an idea of Babe's." Here, the mention of the huge bed for its two larger-than-life dwellers hints at superhuman sex. And Babe didn't mind that innuendo one bit. A friend told her biographers that Babe claimed her sex life with George was "red hot." And she didn't mind the public knowing it either. Once, in the 1940s, Babe was attending a cocktail party with a group of reporters and editors in Los Angeles. One editor who did not know her well approached her rather tentatively and spoke in serious tones: "Tell me, Mrs. Zaharias, of all the records you've broken and all the events you've won, what was the single most thrilling experience of your life." Without a pause Babe replied, "The 'first night I slept with George.'"[24]

Here, Babe echoed a hallmark middle-class ideal of the era: companionate marriage. Companionate marriage emphasized emotional compatibility and good and fulfilling sex with wives as eager partners. Significantly, this culturally accepted emphasis on heterosexual expression emerged alongside increasing disdain for homosexuality. Thus Babe managed to align herself with newly espoused heterosexual ideals, simultaneously distancing herself from suspicion of homosexuality.[25]

The press and its eager reading public loved stories and photos of Babe doing traditionally feminine things. Babe, as always, co-created images of herself. In her autobiography she actually paused in her narrative to give her mother's recipe for Norwegian meatballs and to explain how she had modified it for George's Greek tastes. Over the years Babe posed many times for an adoring public while doing life's daily chores; one biographer included a photograph of Babe and George grocery shopping. Babe also posed, aproned, with rolling pin in hand in her kitchen. But she clutched it as one would a javelin, upright at the center, as if she was ready to hurl it. She appears in *This Life I've Led* laying bricks while adorned with earrings, hosiery, white shoes, pearls, dress, and coat. The message is clear if overdone. Babe enjoys womanly pursuits, yet is still enough of a "character" to master a manly skill like bricklaying.[26]

Despite their shared domesticity, they had yet to go on a honeymoon. In her autobiography she spun a warm yarn of George's spontaneity and thoughtfulness. "One morning in April of 1939, George suddenly says out of a clear sky, 'Honey, get yourself packed up. We're going on a trip.'" Babe guessed their destination as Florida, but George wouldn't tell. They went to Hawaii for three weeks and rented a place where they could keep house. "We loafed around the beach," Babe reminisced, "and I tried out recipes for Hawaiian dishes and everything." Babe, according to this version of the tale, thought George had forgotten about her desire to go to Australia. But to her delight, "he'd been working out arrangements. He'd lined up some wrestling matches for himself, and a lot of golf exhibitions for me."[27]

George remembered his sixteen sellout matches as the point of the trip. Ever-conscious of press coverage and fan devotion, he continued, "And there were pieces in the paper about us, and a lot of people wanted her to play golf there, exhibitions and such." Hesitant to admit he was behind it all, Zaharias claimed the choice was Babe's. "They offered us all kinds of deals. I didn't want it much but she liked the idea, so we booked two or three exhibitions a week for her. Babe, who desired a less public and work-oriented honeymoon, was told to fulfill her booked schedule. This was the beginning of

George's management of her career. He said, "I was sweetheart, husband, manager, adviser." But for him, he added nostalgically, "they weren't jobs. It was a chance for me to be with the greatest girl in the world." Even to her dying day, Babe chose to portray George's thoughtfulness, husbandly leadership, and tenderness in a way befitting a happily married woman.[28]

So she went to Australia and fulfilled her bookings. Archie Keene, the golf promoter, gave them a "little bitty English car" for traveling that George could barely squeeze into. An Australian cartoonist drew them stuck in the mud with George sitting in the car and Babe at the back pushing it out. Her powers were legendary even continents away but not yet proven. So Babe played on big and little courses in major cities as well as in the back country. She played in Sydney, Perth, and Bath but was repeatedly rained out in Melbourne. The prime minister complimented her on her game and her "watchability." George handpicked a gallery of writers to witness her smashing drives in Victoria. Jack Dillo, an Australian golf writer, became an instant fan of Babe's: "What this magnificent specimen of athletic womanhood showed us certainly was impressive." He ranked her above all other women golfers he'd ever seen and was awed by her drives of 230, 245, and 250 yards on the first three holes. "In bunkers," he wrote, "her class was that of Sarazen." Her game on the greens was good, "but not overly impressive." "If Miss Didrikson tightens up her short game," he concluded, "she may get a place among the best male professionals in golf."[29]

This staged spectacular assured Babe of bigger galleries, ample press coverage, and impeccable hospitality wherever she played. After one particularly grueling 125-mile ride to get to a nine-hole course in the back country, Babe was initially put off by the course's poor condition and the "barn" of a clubhouse. But when she realized eight or ten women were scurrying around decorating the rafters and setting up homemade cakes, cookies, and teas, Babe's heart warmed. One family had driven their horse 120 miles to see her exhibition round. The community had actually reopened the closed course just for her display and groomed it the best they could. That day, Babe said, "sticks in my mind more than any of the others, because it was so unexpected and they'd gone to so much trouble over it." The international star still had the heart of a small-town girl. She recognized and understood fans' devotion to their hero and she was duly moved.[30]

She also came within one shot of beating Charley Conners, Australian PGA champion, whom she played at the Yarra Country Club. They competed under men's rules, "driving from the back tees and everything." It was a dazzling display of golf for Babe, who reveled in the memory. Playing her second shot on the par 5 last hole, "I hit the best four-iron of my life. The ball sailed high over a clump of trees and went on the green right up to the pin." She closed with an eagle 3 that gave her a 72 for the round. Conners shot a 71. This sterling match prompted one columnist to write that her one-shot loss to Conners made it "too bad she can't play Patty Berg and the other top-notch amateurs."[31]

Babe's whirlwind tour of Australia was a brilliant career maneuver for her and for George. At George's behest, she relied on competitions against men and public displays of her prowess to generate income, fans, notoriety, and prospects. When they left Australia after several months she had accomplished a tremendous amount: she had kept her name and skills in the limelight and introduced George to the world as her husband and business partner. A stopover in Auckland illustrates how they worked together. While they loosened up on the course early one morning "nobody was there. But before we had played more than three or four holes, there must have been six or seven thousand people. They just wanted to see her." His estimations of the crowd size seem grossly inflated, a nostalgic merger of fantasy and fact, but the point is clear: Babe was an excellent drawing card. Together they made a team of self-promoters that P. T. Barnum would have admired.[32]

Three Years of Grace

Although Didrikson was sky-high with elation from her overseas successes, her spirits fell when they returned home in the fall of 1939. Once again, Babe credited her spouse with the brainstorm that turned things around: "George began to do some heavy thinking about my golf future. It was something that had worried me, too." Babe's intentionally passive attitude rings untrue from a dynamo who'd managed to mock-box the middleweight champ, pitch for the St. Louis Cardinals, and punt for Southern Methodist University—all by her own clever design. But as Ruth Scurlock had said, she enjoyed playing "the little woman."[33]

Her frustration was palpable: "Here I'd been practicing all the time, and developed this fine golf game, and about all I could do was play exhibition matches. I wasn't getting a chance to show whether I was the best woman's player, because I was barred from practically all the women's tournaments as a professional." Years before Babe had admitted, "I'm going along doing the best I can carving out a living with a 14-ounce driver and a wisecrack or two." It's clear through her lament that the sustenance derived from wisecracks had grown thin.[34]

Because of George's success in wrestling and his good business investments, Babe didn't have to continue to work as a professional so that she could support her family. He supported her and her totally dependent family for three years. Said Babe, "George could see that what I really wanted in golf was to compete and win championships. So he set out to see if we could get my amateur standing back." In a 1973 article, Zaharias confirmed this rendition of his leadership role. "I had a great career of my own," he told his interviewer. "I found myself dedicating myself to her and letting her do what she wanted." Their mutual admiration rings true when he says, "I'd put her on a pedestal up high and doggone it, she'd put me just a little higher."[35]

George's wrestling career had come to a halt around 1939. He'd been hurt wrestling a couple of times and, he recalled, "she started getting headaches, worrying about me." He decided to retire from wrestling and become a sports promoter. Because of the war, business was bad, but Babe buoyed George at every turn. "She kept saying to me to keep going, everything would work out. She helped every way she could. When there was a big house sometimes and I didn't have enough ticket sellers, she would open a booth herself and sell tickets." Ultimately, George had considerable success as a wrestling promoter. He was granted a license by the California athletic commissioner to conduct matches at Olympic auditorium in Los Angeles and went on to promote championship matches.[36]

George also turned his promotional talents Babe's way. The USGA ruled that she could not apply for reinstatement as an amateur until she had been a professional for five years, and even after that she would have to sit out a three-year grace period. I knew "that wouldn't be easy," she understated, "but I was willing to go through with it. I was ready to do whatever it took to get me eligible for all those golf tournaments."[37]

She needed and secured four letters of endorsement from prominent golf amateurs. She submitted her application in January 1940, several months before the deadline. In a personal note to Joe Dey, the USGA's executive secretary, she reassured him, "I'd much rather be competing for the fun of the game than just playing for money. . . . What I really loved was the sport itself." "The USGA," Babe recalled, "agreed to restore my amateur standing if I went through the three-year waiting period. I settled down to sweat it out. I dropped all my professional contracts and appearances, and when I entered the occasional open tournaments that I was eligible for, I told them to count me out on any prize money."[38]

In 1940 Babe threw her immense skill and equal passion into the Western Women's Open held in Milwaukee and the Texas Women's Open at Fort

Worth. In the former she beat Mrs. Russell Mann on the Wisconsinite's home course; in the latter she overcame Betty Hicks to win the match by one stroke. "This gave me a 'little slam' of my two major 1940 tournaments," she wrote. "I could hardly wait for my amateur standing to return, so I could begin going after all the top championships."[39]

Meanwhile, Babe was frustrated with no outlet for her athleticism and competitive spirit. To pick up the slack, offer a focus, and provide challenge and stimuli, Babe took up tennis wholeheartedly. Her shoulder no longer impeded her serve, so no physical limitations stood in the way. George arranged for lessons from Eleanor "Teach" Tennant at the Beverly Hills Tennis Club. Tennant catered to many of the top women players from Alice Marble to Little Mo Connolly.

"I went all out on my tennis," Babe reminisced, "just the way I had in the past on basketball and track and golf." During her tutelage and training with Tennant, "I played as many as sixteen and seventeen practice sets in a day. There was hardly a day when I didn't wear holes in my socks, and I ran the soles off one pair of tennis shoes after another." Even George, himself a taskmaster when it came to Babe's training, thought she "was going at it too hard." While running a custom tailor shop in Beverly Hills a short distance from the tennis club, he would stop by more than six times a day to watch Babe work out and he'd tell her to take a little rest. "Rest?" she'd retort. "I've got another set to play." George expressed his displeasure to Babe and Tennant, but the two women closed ranks and trained as they pleased.[40]

Within months Babe could beat Tennant. Then she practiced against some of Hollywood's leading male film stars with considerable tennis skill: Paul Lukas, John Garfield, and Peter Lorre. She soon could beat them. Next she played Mary Arnold and Louise Brough, two of the leading women players in the game. Because of their compatibility on the court, Brough and Didrikson considered entering the national doubles as partners some year. Babe delighted in her practice doubles match victory with Brough over Pauline Betz and Margaret DuPont, both of whom went on to win the national singles championship several times.

At last Tennant announced that Babe was ready for tournament play. In the fall of 1941 she filed to enter the Pacific Southwest Tennis Tournament, the last major tournament of the year on the American circuit. She was barred from the competition, even though she had never played the game before. Tennis rules stipulated that once you've been a professional in any sport, you are considered a professional in tennis too. "That possibility hadn't occurred to me at all," Babe lamented. Apparently it hadn't dawned on Tennant either. Familiarity with rule books was not Babe's forte. She almost deliberately ignored them. Babe only excelled at things she chose to focus on. Peripheral concerns, like rules, disinterested her. She was a race horse with blinders. Often her detachment from the technicalities of her sports came back to haunt her.[41]

That ended tennis. For Babe, without the trophy the hunt lost all appeal. "Once I knew that I could never compete in tournaments, that took the fun out of tennis for me. It's not enough for me just to play a game," she said in a classic understatement. "I have to be able to try for championships. So I quit tennis cold. I still have my rackets," she said years later, "but I haven't touched one from that day to this."[42]

What next? George had been considering buying a bowling alley, so they had looked at dozens of prospects. They never did buy an alley, "but naturally," Babe recalled, "it wasn't long before I decided to take a whack at this game myself." Predictably, she underplayed her previous experience with the game, although this was her first serious try at it. "Once more her obsession for perfection took over," two chroniclers noted, "and she spent hours every night in bowling alleys." She took lessons from several pros and "learned to throw a straight power house ball that thundered down the alley like an express freight train. Later she switched to a sharp, swift hook."[43]

She was able to contend as an amateur in bowling with ample competition. The press pounced on her latest sport, with writers picking her to win seasonal average competitions and bowling tournaments. Said one, "Here's a good tip to the wire service. A gal who has bowled only 28 games is a very good bet to win the women's international bowling tournament which opens here in May. She rolled 143 her first game, 200 her fifth, has averaged 182 for the 28 games. Her name? Babe Didrikson Zaharias." Another journalist wrote, "Tenpins titans are hereby warned that . . . Babe . . . has begun to frequent bowling alleys." The greatest woman athlete "and perhaps the greatest all-around muscle machine of both sexes . . . has boomed the ball down the planks in only 100 games thus far. But already she's scored a 268 and regularly hits 200." Said Babe with disarming humility, "I think I'm doing pretty good for the short time I've been bowling. I took it up because George likes it and now I find it's swell fun, too." With an average of over 170 on the King's Jewelry team of the Southern California Major League, she was its anchor woman. She bowled on several different teams in different leagues in the Los Angeles area. No wonder more than one writer called her "one of the best women bowlers in Southern California." In 1941–42, with her considerable help, her team was league champion in the Sunset Bowling Center. One columnist noted, "Everything seems to come natural to Babe."[44]

Hurling twelve-pound balls down a slick runway and watching passive pins careen and scatter must have been a comforting sensation for Babe. She may have fantasized that she was smashing down all the arbitrary rules of sports amateurism that were thorns in her side. George worried that bowling might overstrengthen her right arm and lead to her hooking golf shots, but that fear never materialized. It's quite likely that bowling did more for her competitive edge and psychological equilibrium than it has ever received credit for. It was a focus that Babe clung to while trying to keep her golf game sharp.

As empowering as her bowling stint was, it still was only an interlude. She wanted golf. Babe entered and won the Women's Open in San Francisco in 1941, but she normally had to content herself with several practice rounds per week. During one such round she shot a course record 64 at the Brentwood Country Club. Another highlight was winning an alternate shot tournament at Inglewood with Sam Snead. In this tournament the two took turns hitting the ball over eighteen holes for a record 68.

Just because Babe couldn't compete as an amateur, she didn't fade from the limelight. In her exhibition matches Babe was at her stage entertainer best. Paired with Bing Crosby and Bob Hope, she gave the crowds riotous afternoons. Hope's favorite line, one she was flattered by, was "There's only one thing wrong about Babe and myself. I hit the ball like a girl and she hits it like a man." The crowd would howl, Babe would "play the stooge" for Hope, and their antics would pick up steam. Hope, ever the comedian, would pound the tee on hands and knees after one of Babe's thunderous drives. He made self-deprecating wisecracks as he putted all around the green. Crosby, the more serious golfer, would join in on the fun and games by exaggeratedly consoling Hope. As if this carnival wasn't enough, Babe loved to tell of the time Hope, Crosby, Patty Berg, and she played an exhibition at the San Gabriel Country Club. Berg and Babe won. "Yes," wrote one reporter, "these two long-swatting gals played from scratch and gave the likeable, anything-for-a-laugh pair from Hollywood a going over, but the match goes down as worth a guffaw a stroke—strokes, it might be added, were plentiful." But the victory was not Babe's favorite part of the story. On one of the holes Babe's ball hit a woman's hand. "They tell me it knocked a diamond out of the ring on her finger." The unlikely drama of it tickled Babe.[45]

Once the United States entered World War II, even celebrity golf tournaments became fewer and farther between. Babe began playing in these scant tournaments to benefit armed service charities, which kept Babe in the papers and rubbing elbows with the cream of the sports world and Hollywood's elite. In addition to Bing Crosby and Bob Hope, she played with Mickey Rooney, Johnny Weismuller, John Montague, Sylvia Annenberg, and Babe Ruth. Babe loved to refer to Ruth and herself as "The Big Babe" and the "little Babe."

Another pet wartime project of Babe's was community involvement in Denver. In 1943, Denver juvenile court judge Philip B. Gilliam appointed her a probation officer and recreation consultant. He thought Babe would be a hero to the children of the city. "Babe accepted her job without salary with great spirit and spent hours teaching children in detention and orphan homes to play ball, swim, and golf." Babe doesn't mention this in her autobiography, but she is pictured receiving the key to the city.[46]

But whenever possible, Didrikson leapt at chances to play with Byron Nelson, who was "at the top of the heap" during the war years, and Ben Hogan, who was on the rise. In an amateur-woman-pro tournament in Long Beach she played with Bill Nary and George. Nary, forty years later, still sparkled when recalling her talent, charisma, and joy in the game.[47]

By this time, George had become her twenty-four-hour-a-day manager. Although he had willingly given up his own sports career to manage Babe, in later years he obviously had second thoughts about his second-class fame. R. L. Bowen recalled that "when Babe was at her zenith, George used to beg her to come stand with him on street corners in Tampa. Poor George, he just wanted to be seen with her." This portrait of George seeking recognition, vicariously lingering, literally, on the fringe of Babe's life, forewarned of stresses and conflicts the Zahariases would face.

R. L. tagged George the businessman "a real wheeler dealer. He had a walrus hide, he was *real* thick skinned. He wasn't welcome everywhere he went, but George was real restless and he went where he wanted to go." He plunged into investments and promoted deals. In the late thirties and early forties he was making about $100,000 per year. Some ventures were failures, some were successes. The Beverly Hills clothing shop was good, the source of finery for Charlie Chaplin and Damon Runyon, among others; his cigar store in Denver was also successful; yet the San Diego Gunners, a pro football team in the Pacific Coast American League, never paid off. In 1947 he was promoting weekly wrestling matches in Denver. Despite his other business ventures, Babe remained his first priority.[48]

George inspired Babe. He pushed her, he worked her, he supported her. As soon as the decision had been made to regain her amateur standing, "We got up a program," he reminisced. "I told her she would win every tournament." As was often the case, George's praise of Babe echoed with a curious mix of husbandly admiration and entrepreneurial glitz. "Nobody ever could play golf like her, right up to her last game. . . . She could hardly do anything wrong, and if she did, she would work until she made it right." George's praise and promotion of her at times were embarrassingly effusive, at times almost heart-breaking: "I knew her better than anybody else ever knew her, and I can say she was perfect in everything she did. She was the best."[49]

But despite the seeming partnership of their marriage and Babe's history of financial competence and cleverness, George controlled all the financial decisions, especially in the early years. Two years before meeting George Babe told an interviewer, "I figure I'm about two years ahead of myself on this business of making the future safe for Babe Didrikson." She'd bought some annuity bonds, and "I play the stock market a little bit. But not *too* much. I'm not going to be broke when I'm through." At this point Babe could justifiably boast, "I'm putting my nieces and nephews through school. And my Dad doesn't have to work anymore." Babe's faith in herself is palpable here, although she went through money as quickly as she earned it.[50]

Immediately after her marriage, however, Babe surrendered this aspect of her independence to George and sung his entrepreneurial praises at every turn. Babe said flat out, "George is the business head of the family." In a complete lie Babe told Will Grimsley of the Associated Press that although her earnings averaged $100,000 per year, George, wealthy in his own right, refused to touch the money. "He makes me keep my earnings myself," Babe said. "Besides every day he deposits a $100 defense bond in my name." In truth, both Babe and George used her money, George controlled it, and no evidence exists that he made daily deposits in her name, let alone deposits totaling $36,500 per year. Babe once again aligned safely with cultural norms. Wage-earning married career women elicited cultural hostility and fueled the debate about damaged domestic harmony and "rights" to wages. Babe's money-making capacity placed her in the minority, since by 1940 only 29.6 percent of all married women were in the labor force; even fewer approximated her earning potential. Her ability to be financially independent of a man made her atypical. She sought to minimize this difference by letting George "own" her labor—a widely used practice between husbands and wives of that era. Babe, at least on the surface, didn't mind. She emoted, "I don't think I've ever been happier in my life. From their marriage in 1938 until 1943, Babe and George functioned as one. They both spoke in the royal "we" more often than not.[51]

In 1945, Babe's reentry into top-level women's competitive golf began with a thirty-six-hole charity match pitting her against Clara Callender, the California State women's champion, at the Desert Golf Club in Palm Springs. Callender scored two 72s, while Babe walloped a 70 and a 67, which broke a course record. After this dazzling win, Babe and Callender met again a week or two later in the Midwinter Women's Golf Championship at the Los Angeles Country Club. In the two head-to-head championship rounds, Babe beat Callender. One particularly sweet victory was the Western Women's Open in 1944. She won the finals by five strokes against Dorothy Germain. This was the same tournament she had won as a pro in 1940.

Years after her victories, Babe could still remember which holes she had won, where she had shot well. In fact, *This Life I've Led* is peppered with painstaking recountings of drives, putts, course idiosyncracies, iron selections, and greens' slopes. It's telling that Babe recalled each tournament, each hole, each maneuver, with such slow-motion mind's-eye replay. It speaks to her love of golf, eye for technical excellence, and thirst for competition. What's striking about Babe's chronicle are the choices she made about what not to talk about in her autobiography while reliving every round of competitive golf in all its minutest detail.

She did tell one family-oriented story in detail. In June 1945, Babe defended her Western Women's Open title in Indianapolis. George called after she'd won her quarter-final match to say that Hannah had been rushed to the hospital. A diabetic, she'd had a heart attack. Babe's priority was clear: she wanted to return to her failing mother's bedside. But George and her sister persuaded her otherwise. "Your momma wants you to finish the tournament," George said, and Nancy concurred. Besides, wartime priorities made it impossible for a civilian to get a seat on a plane or train. In what looms as singular proof of Babe's ability to concentrate under any circumstances she continued to play—and won. Recalling the tumultuous emotions of fear, anxiety, loss, and competition, Babe said, "So I went through with my semi-final match against Mrs. Marge Becker. A lot of times I'd have to step away and wipe my eyes before I could putt, but I won, four and two."[52]

Nancy called with the news of Hannah's death the night Babe won her semifinal match. "I've got to get back," Babe said, but Nancy reassured her, "You go ahead and win that tournament. That's the way momma would want it." Again Babe tried to get out of Indianapolis, again she was unable. In a touching scene, Peggy Kirk Bell recounted how Babe invited her and Marge Row to dinner the night her mother died. "We went to her room and Babe just sat there and played her harmonica," Peggy recalled. "We didn't really know her and didn't know what to say. She played for hours. She didn't speak, she just played on and on."[53]

"When I went out for the finals the next day against Dorothy Germain, the same girl I'd played before, I was really inspired," Babe recalled. "I felt I was playing for Momma. Dorothy was shooting good golf, but I won that match, four and two." At five o'clock the next morning Babe got a seat aboard a plane bound for the West Coast. But she was bumped several times for priority passengers and laid over several times until another seat opened up while her family, already assembled, waited for her.[54]

Babe was more openly emotional about Hannah's death than she had ever been about anything else in her life. Even her father's death two years earlier, from cancer, rates only an addendum to Babe's grief over Hannah's death. "It just broke me up when I got the word . . . that my mother was critically ill in the hospital. I'd always been so close to Momma." Of her quarter-final match she said, "I sure didn't have my heart in it, but somehow I played well enough to win." In another gargantuan understatement, Babe said, "Well, I never could cry too easy when I was a kid." But that changed, momentarily at least, when Babe saw Hannah. "When I saw Momma that day in 1945, I really broke down. The others just left me alone in the chapel to cry it out." She'd lost her momma who'd chased her on a bad ankle to punish her—a woman she loved so much she'd stopped to let her catch her. She'd lost the friend who kept her newspaper clippings for safe keeping. She'd lost her biggest admirer who was overjoyed by the gifts she received. She'd lost the fan who thought she had hung the moon while everyone else whispered and speculated about "that boy-girl Didrikson." With both her mother and father gone, that left George as her sole supporter, advisor, and fan.[55]

Gender Roles in 1938–48

The 1938–48 period found Babe unusually in synch with cultural trends. Most women were married, and the necessity for female war workers had lessened the stigma of older or married women working. Still, with the changing roles, many people participated in the "conflict between traditional ideas about woman's place and the increasing reality of female involvement in activities outside the home." As a result, most women still worked in sex-segregated fields doing menial jobs for inadequate pay. During the war women were encouraged unabashedly to work in war plants. Beyond economic necessity, this became a patriotic duty, albeit a temporary one. Despite articles for young working couples entitled "Hints to the Office Wife's Husband" and "Two Cooks Are Better Than One," most efforts at equality were vastly overshadowed by an increasing emphasis on a new, limited notion of desirable womanhood.[56]

Following the war men replaced women in the plants and again were expected to support their families. With nowhere to go, women were unceremoniously pushed into a new "cult of domesticity" that stressed skillful homemaking and selfless mothering. The tension between ever-increasing numbers of women working outside the home and the feminine, self-sacrificing role prescribed for them led to anger and discrimination.[57]

Babe was directly affected by sex segregation and discrimination in her work. Professional sports were a male-dominated arena, so her choices were severely limited. Sex discrimination placed a ceiling on possible advancement from an amateur to a professional. Instead of having the steady income a career in professional sports would have provided, she was forced to take a series of temporary jobs. Further, like other women, she was treated as a sexual commodity and continuously evaluated for her attractiveness and accessibility. By remaining a working woman even after her marriage, she retained her outsider status as she shirked her "real" responsibilities in the home. As one historian noted, "The woman who did pursue a career in a male-dominated field traveled a largely uncharted course and violated the most deeply held conceptions of her proper role."[58]

The rules for women were clear in the 1940s and loudly proclaimed in the media: be feminine, find and keep a man, and conform your will to his desires. Failure to do so meant risking personal despair, charges of abnormality, and societal disruption. Women were still encouraged to participate in sports, but only to remain slim, not to become athletes. Dieting for women appeared as a frequent theme beginning with a February 1941 *Ladies Home Journal* piece. The starkly entitled "Nice People Don't Eat" disdained hefty women.

Women were increasingly urged to catch and keep men. "Not with My Heart," "Men Like Red," and "When Is It Love?" provided three fictionalized portrayals of women battling for male attentions. This message permeated fiction aimed at teens, too. In "Nobody Loves a Phi Beta," two girls competing for the same boy were cautioned in the lead paragraph: "When two smart girls are after the same boy, one of them has to be smart enough to play dumb." Even Eleanor Roosevelt, who personified the strong, independent woman, held these traditional views of women. She counseled a distraught defense worker to comply with her husband's desire to have a baby immediately, despite her own misgivings. "Since you married him," Roosevelt wrote, "I should think a baby was something you both should want. Every woman can hold a job, but not every woman can have a baby." The message is clear: the husband's will ought to rule supreme at all times.[59]

In fact, despite wartime job opportunities, the acceptable parameters of women's, and men's, self-expression were narrowing, as if to counterbalance their expanding work roles. Dr. Leslie B. Hohman of the Johns Hopkins Medical School counseled in "As the Twig Is Bent: Girlish Boys and Boyish Girls" (1941) that "it is unwise for parents to encourage too much masculinity in a daughter or smile upon too much femininity in a son. Self-expression is desirable, but [it] . . . will lessen the chances for happy adjustment, [and] in such instances it ought to be curbed."[60]

In fact, women who deviated from these norms were deemed sexually and psychologically abnormal in "Men Have Lost Their Women," a 1944 *Ladies Home Journal* article by Dr. Marynia F. Farnham and Ferdinand Lundberg. The authors decried feminists' rivalry with men and preoccupation with sexuality, which proved that "all the militant feminists suffered from acute psychological disturbances." According to these experts, the healthy woman's "full acceptance of her sexuality requires, among other things, that she look forward to motherhood" and a good relationship rests on "a fundamental and deep-rooted womanliness and manliness." They asserted that the sexes have distinct psychologies. Hence their claim that "only a man could give birth to the Ninth Symphony" seems bizarrely feasible alongside their monolithic argument that "only with the final attainment of motherhood is any sort of reality reached for women." According to these authors, competition with men in economic, sexual, political, and public spheres would lead women to lose the men in their lives, which was the ultimate tragedy for men, women, society, and social order.[61]

In response to these cultural pressures, Babe began chiseling her married status in cultural granite. After she described to Paxton her California Women's Open victory over Callender, she didn't skip a beat in saying: "And all the while I was enjoying being Mrs. George Zaharias. That's what I've been ever since we were married, whether I was keeping house or playing in a golf tournament. I've always competed as Mrs. Zaharias, not Babe Didrikson. We're a team."[62]

They were also a team, quite consciously, in creating the image of an appealing, feminine Babe to the public and the press. This effort was so deliberate and incessant that it took on the aspect of a campaign. Why they felt such a need is a matter of speculation. One sport sociologist noted that "even marriage would not necessarily establish suitable sex-role identification for the woman athlete. In 'Babe' Didrikson's case, the problem may have been complicated by marriage . . . to a 'fringe' sports entertainer, George Zaharias. It was a moot point how much respectability Didrikson could win from a marital match with 'The Weeping Greek,' who played a cowardly villain in the ring." As the author concluded, "Didrikson's manner and tone as well as her actual accomplishments in sport continued to moot her gender identification." Another author, writing on women, sports, and sexuality, rightly observed that "the femininity of women who play traditionally male sports is suspect unless they make deliberate efforts to meet male-defined standards of attractiveness and to assert their heterosexual orientation." In Babe's case, her abandonment of masculine sports and the adoption of lady-like attire did not signal her undisputed entry into appropriate femininity. That "failure" was a function of individual will, social class, and athletic prowess.[63]

Thus Babe, George, the media, and the public continued to battle about her gender identity. In 1947 Babe so desired to shed her past that she asked Pete Martin, who was doing a story on her for the *Saturday Evening Post*, to call her Mildred. "She is no longer given to unseemly braggadocio, but married life hasn't made her a shrinking violet, and as a part of her anti-Babe campaign she suggested that I call this article 'Marvelous Mildred!' " Despite Babe's objection, Martin entitled his article "Babe Didrikson Takes Off Her Mask." Babe would always be Babe. Her style had obviously softened, though, as Martin noted. Seven years later, Quentin Reynolds's *Reader's Digest* story on Babe proclaimed her "confident," not "cocky."[64]

Part of this new style involved playing down herself and playing up George. She effusively praised him and glorified their union to dozens of reporters. She told one interviewer, "Everything I do, I do for George. He's the only thing I've got on my mind. I'd give up golf if he couldn't be with me. You can't tell a husband how much you love him after he's dead."[65]

Once Babe had affirmed her feminine persona, reporters inevitably went on to affirm her feminine appearance. Pete Martin, like others Babe spoke with, quickly learned the parameters of acceptable questioning. After revealing her measurements, contents of her wardrobe, and several other personal bits of information, Babe froze Martin when he turned his observations to George. As Martin recalled sheepishly, "In probing into the exact degree of her feeling for George, I suggested to Babe that he wasn't exactly a glamour boy. . . . She shot a withering glance at me and said, 'He's a glamour boy to me, mister.' I dropped that line of talk." In fact, Martin had trod on very sensitive turf. By 1947 George weighed 300 pounds. And "as many yards of cloth are required to fashion a sports coat for him as to make an ordinary-sized man a coat, vest, and pants. His neck bulges out below his hairline in a shelf of flesh, and his shirts are made to order. The stores simply don't carry them that big." But for Babe George was still beyond reproach.[66]

Babe much preferred to turn the focus to their domestic harmony. "Marriage woke the Babe's latent passion for domesticity," one reporter began. "When George bought a two-story, English-style home in Denver's Lakewood section, she made her own floral chintz curtains, complete with pleated valances, her own cream lamp shades with green ruffles, planted her own rose garden." This narrative was accompanied by another posed kitchen photo of Babe, in front of the stove, dressed in a gathered shirtwaist dress and apron. She's holding a fish over the frying pan for the photographer. George is in the foreground rinsing dishes at the sink. The caption reads: "With a few assists from her amiable husband, Mrs. Zaharias does all her own housework. Here she is frying trout which they caught in the Rockies."[67]

Through these articles and photos, Babe campaigned for her femininity with a vigilance exceeding that of reporters. Babe even vented her frustration with her youthful "Texas toughie" image. Snapped Babe, "I wish those people who always wanted to make a tough mug out of me could just get a look at me now." At the British Women's Amateur Tournament in 1947, she deliberately acted the part of a traditional woman in front of the cameras. "Like any other woman," she said later, "I'm forever freshening up my lipstick. Coming off the twelfth green I was putting new lipstick on. I was doing it automatically, not even thinking about it." In another instance she lamented about the weather saying, "My curls had come down. I never did get my hair to stay up right the whole time I was in England and Scotland."[68]

Her golfing contemporaries, though leery of discussing issues of femininity in detail, did notice that Babe at times "tried too hard." Peggy Kirk Bell recalled that by 1946, "she was not tough or manly. Sometimes she overdressed a little—she'd wear frilly blouses that didn't look right. She was best in tailored things." In the 1940s Ruth Scurlock described Babe thus: "Babe's skin was tanned and very soft; it was lovely skin, not like a lizard's, the way so many of those Texas women golfers get to be. She had that lovely skin and she also had smooth, rippling muscles. There was nothing knobby or knotted about her calves. She had a typical Norse grace. She was a classic, slender Norsewoman, not masculine at all." No one denies that as she aged "her physique took on more womanly proportions. . . . She became downright bosomy." As one chronicler noted, "This was an occurrence that she viewed as a mixed blessing; once when she missed a spare during a bowling game, she came back gesturing at her breasts and shouting, 'God*damn* these things! They sure do get in the way!' "[69]

Betty Hicks understood the line Babe walked and the game she'd learn to play. "To those of us who shared the country club locker rooms with her, Babe was conclusively female. She was not feminine by our culture's peculiarly warped definition of it, though she did acquire certain layers of the veneer of femininity. She painted her fingernails, curled her hair, put on high-heels, and wore lace-trimmed dresses." These were all "proofs" of a heterosexual woman's conscious appeal to men and to cultural norms.[70]

Even if the look was right, she still didn't quite act like other women. Babe's unlikely combination of athleticism and charisma drew big crowds, built gate receipts, and added color to an event. The dress-up "little woman" bit was a persona she mastered, but the wisecracks and the unwillingness to behave properly at all times were sheer Babe. She could dress up, but what happened next was anyone's guess.

Ole Didriksen, Sr., and his five children, circa 1916–17. Babe is standing in the center. (Courtesy of the Mary and John Gray Library, Special Collections, Lamar University, Beaumont, Texas, Doct. 11.2.22.1)

Employers Casualty Company basketball team, circa 1929-30. The arrow points to Babe. (Courtesy of the Mary and John Gray Library, Special Collections, Lamar University, Beaumont, Texas, Doct. 11.2.22.8)

Portrait, 1932. (© USOC Photo Library)

Babe competing in the 80-meter hurdles with her unorthodox "hedge-hopping" style, Los Angeles Olympics, 1932. (© USOC Photo Library)

This photo, taken privately circa 1932–33, is inscribed to Bill "Tiny" Scurlock, sportswriter and friend. (Courtesy of the Mary and John Gray Library, Special Collections, Lamar University, Beaumont, Texas, Doct. 11.2.6.6)

Babe in full football regalia circa 1931–32, mock punting at Southern Methodist University Stadium for the university's team. (Courtesy of the Mary and John Gray Library, Special Collections, Lamar University, Beaumont, Texas, Doct. 11.2.22.10)

Portrait, 1932-33. Stunningly androgynous and provocative, this image generated speculation about her sexual orientation. (Courtesy of the Mary and John Gray Library, Special Collections, Lamar University, Beaumont, Texas, Doct. 11.2.22.28)

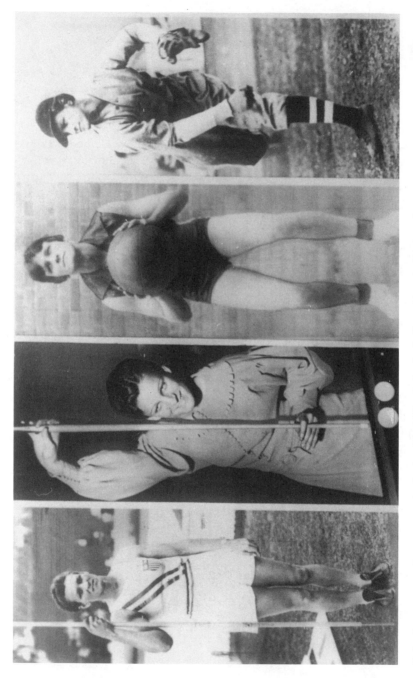

Babe demonstrates her prowess in the javelin, billiards, basketball, and baseball. This photo accompanied the Associated Press story of her death. (Courtesy of the AP/Wide World Photos)

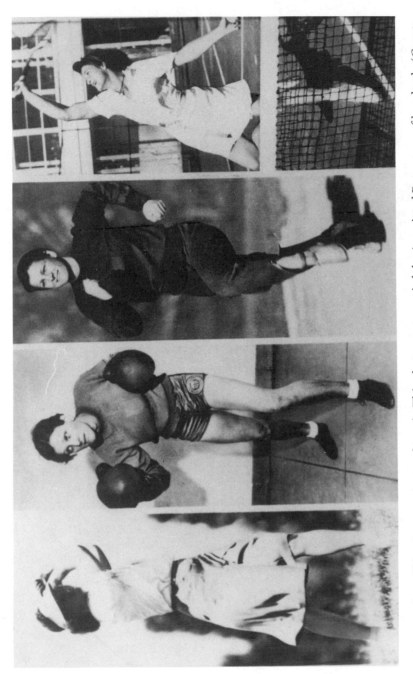

Babe poses for golf, boxing, running, and tennis. This photo accompanied the Associated Press story of her death. (Courtesy of the AP/Wide World Photos)

Amelia Earhart (*left*) with Babe. This photo was taken privately during a little informal target practice and did not run in the national press. They did not know each other well. (Courtesy of the Mary and John Gray Library, Special Collections, Lamar University, Beaumont, Texas, Doct. 11.2.23.18)

Babe, in evening gown circa 1933–34, intentionally constructing a feminine image. (Courtesy of the Mary and John Gray Library, Special Collections, Lamar University, Beaumont, Texas, Doct. 11.2.23.9)

Babe's brief stint as a stage entertainer, Palace Theatre, Chicago, Illinois, 1933. (Courtesy of the Mary and John Gray Library, Special Collections, Lamar University, Beaumont, Texas, Doct. 11.2.22.36)

Babe touring with the House of David Baseball Team, 1934. (Courtesy of the Mary and John Gray Library, Special Collections, Lamar University, Beaumont, Texas, Doct. 11.2.23.1)

George Zaharias in his wrestling prime as the "Crying Greek from Cripple Creek." (Courtesy of the Mary and John Gray Library, Special Collections, Lamar University, Beaumont, Texas, Doct. 11.2.23.16)

Babe, relaxed, at the peak of her game, circa 1947-50. (Courtesy of the Mary and John Gray Library, Special Collections, Lamar University, Beaumont, Texas, Doct. 11.2.24.81)

Babe competing in the first Babe Zaharias Golf Open in Beaumont. This annual event was established to raise monies for cancer research and education. George, Babe's sometime coach and companion, who eventually reached over 400 pounds, eyeballs her shot while enjoying one of his infamous cigars. (Courtesy of the Mary and John Gray Library, Special Collections, Lamar University, Beaumont, Texas, Doct. 11.2.24.25)

Babe and Betty on the road in April 1953. Babe is displaying the merchandise she endorses for Wilson Sporting Goods while the young Dodd looks on admiringly and graciously assists. (Courtesy of the Mary and John Gray Library, Special Collections, Lamar University, Beaumont, Texas, Doct. 11.2.24.15)

Babe, ever the image-conscious lady of the house, dons a dress and pearls to build the brick wall at Rainbow Manor, her dream house, in Tampa, Florida, circa 1954-55. (Courtesy of the AP/Wide World Photos)

Betty Dodd (*left*) and Babe belting out the tunes. The two eventually appeared on the "Ed Sullivan Show" and performed their duets for a wildly enthusiastic audience. (Courtesy of the AP/Wide World Photos)

Babe, aware of her importance as a symbolic survivor of cancer, freshens up before meeting the cameras at the Hotel Dieu Hospital, Beaumont, Texas. This photo was taken in April 1953, shortly after her colostomy. (Courtesy of the Mary and John Gray Library, Special Collections, Lamar University, Beaumont, Texas, Doct. 11.2.25.9)

An uneasy triumvirate. Betty, George, and Babe share a rare peaceful moment as Babe admires her bouquet in John Sealy Hospital, Galveston, 1956. Toward the end of Babe's life friction and separation were par for the course between husband and wife; Dodd was at Babe's side incessantly. (Courtesy of the Mary and John Gray Library, Special Collections, Lamar University, Beaumont, Texas, Doct. 11.2.26.10)

CHAPTER SEVEN

Dominating the
Fairways and the Greens

O nce she regained her amateur status, Babe entered a unique
world of lush, green, rolling hills, hushed whispers, and predictable decorum. Golf has a distinct history in the United
States that is perpetually interwoven with money, privilege,
exclusivity, and social class. Characterized by its good
manners, golf welcomed women with relative graciousness much sooner
than most other sports. "Golf was considered a man's game by the dour golf
fathers at St. Andrews," two historians noted, "and it remained so until the
Shinnecock Hills Club on Long Island let down the gates in 1891 and invited the ladies to tag along with their husbands." That it provided the same
rarefied atmosphere for women as it did for men, was not overly strenuous,
and could be enhanced by grace heightened its appeal in a rigid sex-typed
world of social interaction. Cultural dictates against upper-class women
"using their muscles for anything but household tasks" had previously re-
stricted their physical recreation to archery, croquet, and lawn tennis.[1]

By 1893, when the first women's golf course was opened, the sport had
already attracted a large following. By the 1920s, golf provided a showcase
for the talents of two superstar women athletes. The popularity, acceptability, and social pedigrees of Eleanor Randolph Sears (1881–1968) and Glenna Collett (1903–89) opened opportunities for recreation and vocation in
sports for women.[2]

Sears, the great-great-granddaughter of Thomas Jefferson and niece of
Richard Sears, first national tennis champion, became "The Belle of Boston."
An athlete rivaling Babe in versatility, Sears won the Pacific Southwest Ten-
nis Tournament in 1900 at age thirteen, the national championship in 1904,

and Wimbledon twice. She was a good rifle shot, a powerful swimmer, a fine golfer, and squash's national women's single champion in 1928 at age forty-four. The winner of some 240 trophies, she was "controversial because of her independent ways." She defied convention, "wore men's clothes when she felt like it, and challenged the boys to anything, especially automobile and motor boat racing." Her tomboyish ways appalled New England conservatives, but as one historian noted, "she demonstrated that a woman could play men's games like a man without causing a revolution." Her impeccable background clearly smoothed her acceptance just as surely as Babe's origins impeded hers.[3]

Glenna Collett, the best American woman golfer in the 1920s, was admiringly dubbed "the female Bobby Jones." Popular among sportswriters, she was labeled one of the "Golden People in the Golden Decade of Sport." She won six U.S. national amateur championships, more than any golfer, male or female, had ever won, and was the first woman to break 80 in national competition. Collett's defeat of Jesse Sweetser, a former national men's champion, at a country club in Fairfield, Connecticut, demonstrated that women could compete against men. Yet by wearing "proper" attire and playing with feminine charms and womanly elegance, she increased the game's popularity and visibility while not challenging societal norms. She was featured in magazines of the day as a popular hero and sweetheart wrapped into one. Collett married Edwin H. Vare, Jr., University of Pennsylvania graduate and member of the Pine Valley Club, in June 1931. Like Sears, her pedigree and selection of an "appropriate" mate sheltered her from potential critics.[4]

Although Collett and Sears made participating in many sports acceptable for upper-class women, golf's very nature limited it to play by the upper classes. "A golfer needed a set of clubs, private club memberships, sufficient leisure time to play eighteen holes, and frequently, a caddie."[5] By 1929 Americans spent $200 million per year on this most expensive of sports. The Women's Metropolitan Golf Association, founded in 1900 in New York City, sponsored tournaments that only members of private clubs could participate in. Membership in these clubs was expensive and thus became "a visible symbol of achieved success." Upper middle-class women looked upon golf as an opportunity to mingle with the upper class and thus better their social status. Golf became so equated with status that magazines advertised expensive items and posted social notices around articles on golf. One historian has argued that "much of the 'sports' coverage designed to appeal to rich women readers confirmed the view that social pedigree interested them more than athletic achievement."[6]

Despite their heavy participation in the sport, women's power within golf was elusive. Women had decision-making power only at the local, state, and sectional levels over their own competitions. The USGA, founded in 1894, refused to admit representatives from women's associations to the executive board, which governed men's and women's regional, sectional, and national play. This limit to women's decision-making authority caused one historian to comment: "The denial of control by women over men's affairs in a prestigious association was obvious and blatant."[7]

The highest echelons of golf alternately recognized women's abilities and punished them for their perceived shortcomings. These attitudes were mirrored in the press. A 1920 article in the *Star Weekly* joked, "Lady golfers who have been in the habit of picnicking on the fifth green will please move to the grove 50 yards to the right, where benches have been provided. Ladies with small children," the wit wrote, "must not have them accompany them on the round unless accompanied by a nurse or governess. Perambulators must not be taken around the course." Yet women's competitive championships met with serious coverage. *Literary Digest* in 1932 detailed the American team's capturing of the Diana Fishwick Cup followed by the women's defeat at the British women's championship.[8]

One Texan's Turf: Babe's Golf Game

Babe, as usual, generated her own coverage, though it was not necessarily the kind of public interest golf's leaders had hoped for. In the two years of tournament play after she regained her amateur status, Babe established herself as one of the dominant women competitors, and her game revolutionized women's golf. Herb Grassis, former sportswriter for the *Chicago Daily Sun* and a frequent contributor to *Esquire,* commented, "Before Babe it was a game for girls . . . after Babe, it was a business." She made it a business through her marketability and her powerful style of play. In the *Saturday Evening Post* Pete Martin said of her: "Not much has been made of the undeniable fact that the Babe has revolutionized the feminine approach to golf. Perhaps there isn't enough color in that kind of copy to make it provocative. When she told me, 'I was the first woman to play the game the way men play it—I mean to hit the ball instead of swinging at it,' it didn't seem egotistical, but merely a statement of fact. 'Now all the women do it that way.'" As two *Sports Illustrated* biographers wrote, "Babe Zaharias created big-time women's golf. She launched it as a legitimate sport and brought gusts of freshness and fun to a game too often grim. . . . Her booming power game lowered scores and forced others to imitate her."[9]

Babe's powerful drives were path-breaking. This, coupled with her "speed, strength, co-ordination and competitive temperament [and] stamina," made her a champion, according to Grantland Rice. Legends of her booming drives abound. The folklore tops out at a 408-yard wallop reported in *Time*. She did routinely hit 250-yard tee shots. One Beaumont sportswriter wrote, "She developed an aggressive, dramatic style, hitting down sharply and crisply on her iron shots like a man." Babe reveled in her power game and she lorded it over opponents. A male rival once chivalrously offered her the honor of teeing off, and "she withered him with, 'Naw, you better hit first cause it'll be the last time you get the honor—and you'd better bust a good one if you don't want to be out-drove 20 yards by a gal.'"[10]

A product of innate talent and ceaseless practice, Babe's game was honed relentlessly. And there was much more to it than strength. "She was an intelligent golfer," two aficionados wrote. She had elegant, tapered hands, and her short game became soft and certain. Both Babe and George knew that her greatest weakness was approach shots and putting. "So the Babe practiced," Lawrence Lader wrote in *Coronet* in 1948, "hour after hour, until she could chip to the pin and sink 20-foot putts as easily as she could slam the ball 275 yards." She also spent hours in the woods "learning how to commune with the trees, hooking and slicing her way around big oaks and tall pines" until it was too dark to play. But she also knew when to stop practicing. She told a *Golf World Magazine* reporter in 1947 that she suspended her minimum eight-hour practice "before a tournament round. I do not hit a ball. I do not wish to tire and leave my game on the practice tee."[11] Training became paramount, almost "a religious ritual." According to the press, "she still does calisthenics and flip-flops every morning. She sleeps at least eight hours a night, doesn't drink and smokes only in moderation." Again Didrikson was creating an image for herself; Betty Dodd asserted that Babe drank and smoked as she pleased.[12]

Didrikson was a student of the game's fine points. Compared with her scorn of the lengthy AAU rulebook, Babe held golf's regulations in reverence. After it got too dark to practice anymore, she said, "I went home and had my dinner. Then I'd go to bed with the golf rule book. I'll bet I have read that book through twenty-five times, line by line. Today when I'm playing with anybody and a rule question comes up, they say, 'Ask Babe.'"[13]

Although she practiced constantly, her studying did not extend to her own playing style. Betty Hicks, in her innovative golf book/cook book *Golf Tour Gourmet* (1986) explains Babe's "unconscious" game. Hicks, Gloria Armstrong, later an LPGA teacher of the year, and Greta Leone, a pro from Chicago, watched Babe hit some tee shots. Armstrong asked, "'Babe, does the weight go to the outside of the right foot on the backswing, or does it stay inside?' 'It goes outside,' Babe responded." Gloria turned and asked Hicks, "'Does it? Outside or inside?'" Hicks, a connoisseur of golfing mechanics answered Armstrong, "'Depends on how much a player lets her right knee straighten on the back-swing. Babe lets hers straighten.'" Babe looked at Hicks incredulously. "'I do?'" Here Hicks editorialized, "For Babe, a golf swing was a completely physical act; for her, the swing was reduced to its simplest denominator: there was no thought process involved. . . . Babe was not a classic swinger."[14] She was instead a natural talent, bettered by practice.

Her fierce competitive will carried her at times when sheer skill or fatigue would have let her down. George likened the tremor he had felt when he first held her to a tremor he felt many times afterward "during tournaments, when things were close." Babe thrived on competition. *This Life I've Led* pictures her working on a golf club handle, cocker spaniel beside her. The caption reads: "Male pros have been tinkering with and reworking their clubs for years, but most girls are satisfied to just swing them. Not me." Babe used any edge that might bring victory. The ritual of the game, the preparation, the obsession with detail, all led to consistent excellence.[15]

A relentless competitor, she gave the edge to no one, not even her closest friends in the most casual match. One time she "lent Betty Dodd a driver and another time let Peggy Kirk Bell borrow an eleven-iron. Both immediately used the new clubs with excellent results. In both cases, Babe said after a few holes, 'I believe I'll take that club back now,' and she did." Dodd emphasized how Babe couldn't stand to lose anything. They were playing for a dollar and Babe had missed several putts during the game. "She just stopped," Dodd recalled, "stood there and all of a sudden she snapped the putter over her knee like a toothpick. Then she hauled off and threw the pieces into the woods. She scared the rest of us to death. We didn't say one word the rest of the way in." Her aggressiveness did not end at the eighteenth hole. "She once claimed she won at gin rummy by watching the cards reflected in her opponent's glasses."[16]

In competition, any casualness disappeared. Lader wrote of Babe, "In practice she may look sloppy, even listless, but when she starts to play she is like Joe Louis, stalking her prey. She may allow a golf opponent to stay even during the first round. Then she turns on the heat." Her poise was unshakable. "She has the cold indifference to what people think or say about her that is essential to a champion. Even on the links, no heckler can disturb her."[17]

Despite her poise she remained an entertainer while playing. Peggy Kirk Bell said that Babe thought everything she did was news. "She was always on, always entertaining, always laughing. We'd sit down to eat and she would balance a spoon on her hand, whack it and jump it into a glass. She'd hit a cigarette and catch it in her mouth." This indefatigable part of Babe's spirit never faded. Bell recalled, "When she was dying in Galveston, she was still going to entertain you. I went to visit her and she said, 'See that Coke bottle over there?' And then she promptly flipped a cigarette into it. She was always doing the impossible. If she missed, no one remembered. When she made it work it became legend."[18]

For Babe, the larger the audience the better. Even the simplest adoring onlookers elicited an outstanding performance. Ginny Gravley recalled being at the all-girl Tamarack Camp in Sisters, Oregon, in 1945. It was a stunning setting replete with pine trees and snow-capped mountains. And on one day young Ginny would never forget, Babe dropped in unannounced. She had a full entourage with her and they, the campers, counselors, and everyone else nearby witnessed Didrikson at her best. Babe set her mind to driving a golf ball over the width of the camp's lake. On her first attempt she missed the ball. Then she chipped it into the lake. It was clear to Ginny that Babe wouldn't quit until she succeeded. On her third try she slammed it clear across the lake to land on the other side. Wild cheers. The next day Babe and her entourage played tag football with the campers. Ginny marveled that the game "was *very* athletic. I was such a tomboy—and I thought *I* could pass!"[19]

In 1949, Babe delighted a Boston Red Sox crowd with on-field antics during a rain delay. Ted Williams was the big draw, but when the rains came the umpire postponed the game "and Babe went out and entertained for an hour in the rain. The crowd stayed put and they gave her a standing ovation. The game ended up being canceled, but Babe had given the fans their money's worth." One-on-one at dinner with Bell, or in front of several thousand gallery fans, Babe was in her element.[20]

"I just love a gallery," Babe said in her autobiography. "It bothers some athletes to have people always crowding around them. I wouldn't feel right if the people weren't there. Even in a tournament, I like to kid around with the gallery." Not even the heat of competition quieted Babe's antics. In fact, it brought out her best tricks and one-liners.

To warm up a gallery, she'd put on dazzling displays of trick shots. She'd set up five balls on the tee, drive them in rapid succession, and get the fifth one launched before the first one had landed. "Or I'll shoot left-handed" she gloated, "I can hit a ball pretty good that way too. On the green I may stick my foot in the front of the ball, and make the ball hop over it into the cup. Then I'll throw down some clubs, like an ice skater setting up a row of barrels to leap across, and I'll hit the ball with my putter so that it jumps over all the clubs."[21]

These shows served several purposes: they made Babe the center of attention, they encouraged galleries to adopt her as their favorite, and they psyched out her opponents. A sportswriter remarked, "Babe stalks the fairway with a conscious sense of theater." He chronicled her impressive cigarette flips, in which she "catches them nonchalantly in her mouth, then lights her match with her fingernail." This is the same woman who so diligently campaigned to be called Mrs. Zaharias and shed her rowdy image. Contradictions abound, but Babe had one hell of a time confounding her onlookers.[22]

She packed a mighty warehouse of saucy one-liners that she regularly fired at the gallery. This lack of decorum bothered Babe's opponents and the lovers of golfing etiquette, but when Babe played to her audience, her critics were her last concern. When one of her tremendous drives would sail out of bounds she'd turn to the crowd and explain, "I hit it straight but it went crooked." When she sank long putts she often fell to her knees and thanked Allah; when she missed a short one she'd quip, "I feel like nuts and bolts rattling together." On another occasion, Babe used her sharp tongue to move the gallery out of her way: "I know I'm good, but not this good. I have to have room to hit the ball." The gallery, duly scolded, fell back and Babe smashed a mighty tee shot.[23]

Hicks says Babe entertained the galleries like no one else. "Oh, how she gave them a show! None of the others of us could have, would have dared. Only the Babe could rasp to our LPGA clinic galleries: 'Stand back, caddie! This ain't no kid hittin'.'" Or she'd call out, "'Watch close boys, 'cause you're watchin' the best.'" Or, Hicks marveled, "after a well 'busted' tee shot, hit shortly after surgery, 'They sure didn't cut that out.'" Not all of Babe's one-liners were in the best taste. Hicks lamented that other golfers described bad rounds with "innocuous tritisms" like "'I was a basket case today,' or 'Couldn't have hit a washtub with my putts.' Not so Babe Zaharias, ever seeking a more graphic phrase 'Couldn't hit an elephant's ass with a bull fiddle today,' Babe groaned."[24]

One of Babe's more outrageous acts was gathering a circle of women around her on the golf course on a very hot day and shedding her petticoat. In 1951 at the Western Women's Open in Philadelphia Babe halted her match with Patty Berg while three thousand spectators, "looking on bug-eyed," saw her "remove a white nylon slip and nonchalantly toss it to her caddy. 'Too hot,' she commented, striding to the next tee." Her all-time favorite wise-crack to galleries was "When I wanta really bust one, I just loosen my girdle and let 'er fly!"[25]

Even George got in on the act. His bad knees and weight often prevented him from walking the links with Babe, so "he cruises around the edge of the course in his auto," Babe told the *Saturday Evening Post* in 1947. "When the Babe knocks in a putt, he beeps his horn. 'When he does that, it means 'Nice going, honey.'" During one match on a blustery day, the wind kept shift-ing. As *Newsweek* reported in "The Versatility of Mrs. Z.," "before each shot, the Babe took careful note of the smoke from her husband's cigar, to see which way the wind was blowing. This gave her all the help she needed to win the tournament, and she romped home. Mr. Zaharias rushed to her side to congratulate her. 'Nice going,' he said affectionately. 'Thanks,' said the Babe veering away with a slight wince. 'Get rid of the cigar and tell me more!'"[26]

Babe's opinions on cigars impressed Red Gibson, who recalled how Babe playfully lectured him on his cigar-smoking style. She was determined to teach him to quit chewing the ends. "'A gentleman doesn't smash his cigars to a pulp,' she once said. 'It doesn't look good. Here, practice on these,' she said, snitching a couple from her uncomplaining husband." Didrikson, Gib-son recalled, thought the lessons funny. "George thought they were expen-sive." Gibson "thought they were magnificent, inasmuch as a $55-a-week sportswriter did not ordinarily fraternize with dollar cigars."[27]

Despite her clowning antics, which some interpreted as trivializing golf, there was widespread acknowledgment, as Patty Berg said, that "our sport grew because of Babe. She had so much flair, color and showmanship, we needed her. Her power astonished galleries." Her mighty game entertained galleries and her crafty psychological tactics could—and at times did—im-mobilize her competitors. Betty Hicks lamented Babe's favorite one-liner. "'Hi girls!' she'd shout as she entered a tournament locker room. 'Ya gonna stick around and see who'll finish second this week?'" There was no real question mark at the end of the taunt, and Babe didn't wait to hear any an-swers. She'd won that round. Yet when she lost after such taunting she would sulk and retreat from the locker room—solo—for a few beers. She was not a graceful loser. The same line haunted Betsy Rawls, another top pro. "'Babe intimidated her opponents,' Betsy recalled, as delicately as she could say it. 'Gentleness was not my recollection of it.'"[28]

And then Babe went beyond taunts to insults. Peggy Kirk Bell, self-described as "Babe's best friend," went on to tell a tale that would try any friendship. In the late 1940s "the Babe called us together and informed us we were the spear carriers and she was the star and no one paid to see spear toters." A press release from Wilson Sports echoed Babe's sentiments. "Mrs. Zaharias is the player they pay to see. And as long as the galleries trail her around the fairways, the walloping Babe from the Lone Star state will get the big money."[29]

Babe milked her psychological hold over the other women pros. Once, down by several strokes, she attached a child's exploding pistol cap to her own golf ball. When she drove the ball, the bang so rattled her opponents that Babe went on to win. Another time she invited Peggy Kirk Bell to be her partner in the Hollywood fourball tournament. Peggy was thrilled but fearful of playing with Babe. Babe "stared at me and said, 'Look, Peggy, I can beat any two of 'em. I'll let you know if I need you.' She won everything in sight. She was so confident," Bell said, "she was hard to compete against."[30]

The "Unbeatable Queen"

One of Didrikson's biggest years was 1945. In the fall she won her second Texas Women's Open title, beating Marge Becker by seven on the front nine and six on the back. Babe also won the Western Open, making her the first woman to win it three times. Many of Babe's matches pitted her against Joyce Wethered, the great English golfer. Babe proved her dominance of the sport in these matches. Her other accomplishments that year included defeating Betty Jameson in seventy-two-hole challenge matches at Los Angeles and San Antonio. Babe and Jameson first met at a Red Cross challenge match—the Benefit PGA Veteran's Rehabilitation Program—in Los Angeles. They had shared the sports page in Dallas on occasion, where they had both excelled in earlier years because Betty "was something of a nominal prodigy in golf." Quite alone, they recognized each other in the locker room of the Los Angeles Country Club before their match. Babe said immediately, "My, but you're a big girl!" Her knack for speaking her mind entertained Betty: "She never held back. I mean there was nothing ever. She was just a free spirit of the first order and didn't elaborate on stories. She was always just giving out." Jameson recalled the fun they had with the "marvelous gallery," loaded with film stars such as Gary Cooper. Babe, buddies with many celebrities, wowed Jameson with her acquaintances. Jameson, then earning her living as a reporter for the *San Antonio Light* newspaper, admitted, "I did not show too well, but it didn't take away from my confidence. I thought I was the best golfer living at that time and Babe no doubt thought she was, or was going to be."[31]

With admirable nonchalance Babe recalled, "And at the end of 1945 a nice thing happened. I was picked as the 'Woman Athlete of the Year' in the annual Associated Press Poll." She'd won it in 1932 and would win it a total of six times in her life. But the award in 1945 had special meaning because "during all those years in between, what with my troubles over professionalism and everything, I hadn't been able to compete enough to establish whether I was the No. 1 woman athlete." After the 1945 season when the AP honored her, her dominance over women's golf was firm. "She was its unbeatable queen."[32]

In 1946, Babe told *Coronet*, "I want to establish the longest winning streak in the history of women's golf." Although it was quite a goal, it was not a preposterous one for a woman who had already declared and satisfied her desire to win Olympic gold and be the greatest woman athlete of all time. A second goal for 1946, as she chose to soft-pedal it in *This Life I've Led,* was to win the national championship.[33]

"It started in August," Lader intoned melodramatically in *Coronet*. "For 17 straight major tournaments, the Babe ran roughshod over the world's greatest women golfers." After a June loss to Mary McMillin in the Western Women's Amateur about which Babe said, "That was the last losing I was going to do for a long time," the streak began. She won in Denver and Colorado Springs and then captured the All-American Championship held at the Tam O'Shanter Country Club in Niles, Illinois. She shot a four-round total of 310 strokes, an average of 77.5. As Babe correctly surmised, "That Tam O'Shanter competition was a happy hunting ground for me for many years, starting back there in 1947. . . . I've improved on that score considerably in later tournaments there."[34]

At the U.S. Women's Amateur national competition in Tulsa, Oklahoma, at the Southern Hills Country Club, Babe was ready. "I was pointing for this tournament, all right. You could say I'd been pointing for it more than thirteen years, from the time I first took up golf seriously." As she told Paxton in the *Saturday Evening Post* serialized version of her life, she'd been kept from the tournament first by her scrambled amateur status, then the war. She knew that she had a good chance to win her first national title because "it was a long course, a good tee-shot course. I always liked that kind." In the thirty-six-hole final she obliterated Clara Callender Sherman ten-and-nine. This was the same opponent she had beaten in her first tournament after her amateur status was reinstated in 1943. What satisfied Babe most, next to winning the tournament, "was that I had not played any bad golf at all."[35] She "didn't have a single narrow squeak." In detail she told *Post* readers how she yearned to feel in control of her game. Of lucky shots where you don't hit the ball well, but it goes on the green anyhow, Babe said, "I don't like it that way. I'm never really satisfied unless I can feel that I'm hitting the ball just right." And she was. She had found an indestructible groove.[36]

After the national, Babe won her fifth consecutive tournament, the Texas Women's Open. October saw her beat Betty Hicks five-and-three. Babe was ready for a break, but as she matter-of-factly told the *Post*, "George had other ideas." He said, "Honey, you've got something going here. You've won five straight tournaments. You want to build that streak up into a record they'll never forget. There are some women's tournaments in Florida at the start of the winter. I think you should go down there."[37]

Discord emerged as George commandeered her athleticism. Babe was already settled into their new home in Denver, the first true home they'd owned. It was a beautiful, old, English-style house and, Babe recalled, "When I came back there at the end of the tournament season in October, I was ready to take a long layoff from golf competition and just enjoy my home for a while." But George pushed relentlessly for her to continue competing. He was, after all, her manager and promoter as well as her husband, and the combined influence of the roles was overwhelming. George agreed to accompany Babe but backed out at the last minute to tend to his Denver-based wrestling and boxing promotions. They traveled to Pueblo together and spent the night with his mother and father. The next day George returned to Denver and Babe set out alone by car for Florida.[38]

Babe really did not want to go. She drove about 150 miles, turned around, and drove straight back home to Denver. George greeted her with, "What are you doing here?" Babe, in a candid moment, admits to saying, "The farther I got down the road, the more lonesome I got. I'm not going to go." In the loneliness and isolation of traveling, Babe had become quite dependent upon George in all of his roles. "Believe me," she said, "it helps to have him right there pulling for me, and it's nice to be able to talk with him after the day's play is over." Wrangling ensued, but George's will won out. Babe noted, without editorial comment, "But I finally did hit the Florida tournaments late in January." Babe claimed he joined her in Florida "for some of the tour," but she never reintroduced him in her narrative of it.[39]

As 1947 began Babe tackled her sixth tournament, the Tampa Women's Open. After three rounds of medal play she was up one stroke over Louise Suggs. In the fourth and final round she shot two under women's par to finish on top by five. Victory seven came at the Miami Country Club in the Helen Lee Doherty Women's Amateur. She was only one stroke off the men's record for the course. The following week brought her to Orlando and the Florida Mixed Two-Ball Championship. Partnered with Gerald "Gee" Walker, a big-league ballplayer, they beat their nearest challengers, Polly Riley and Joe Ezar. The match ended on the thirty-first hole for her eighth consecutive win.[40]

Number nine came at the Palm Beach Women's Amateur, one up, at the expense of Jean Hopkins. In the tenth tournament, the Women's International Four-Ball at Hollywood, Florida, Babe and her partner, Peggy Kirk Bell, beat Louise Suggs and Hopkins. This competition was remembered for a fluky finish. On the thirty-sixth and final hole, despite descending nightfall, the tournament officials had them tee off anyway. Then the match was called due to darkness. So a dramatic tie-breaker was replayed in total the next day. Bell and Didrikson won, four-and-two.[41]

One week's victory partner was the next week's victim. In the South Atlantic Championship at Ormond Beach, Babe beat Bell five-and-four. More than one writer noted how "Babe is at her best with her back to the wall." In another tournament Babe took the aggressive tactic that secured her the win. After her drive and approach on the eighteenth hole, Margaret Gunther "came within an inch of the cup." Babe's drive lay at the edge of the green. Eschewing the safe strategy of two-putting, which would have left them tied, Babe lined up her ball with the cup, 50 feet away, and knocked it in to take the hole and, ultimately, the tournament. Climaxes like this made her a heart-breaking opponent. Number eleven was in the record books. The last Florida tournament, and twelfth win, came at the Florida East Coast Women's Championship at St. Augustine, where she triumphed over Mary Agnes Wall in the finals, two-and-one.[42]

Leaving the Sunshine State and traveling north to Georgia, Babe posted a spectacular comeback at the Women's Titleholder's Tournament in Augusta, then the women's equivalent of the Masters Tournament. After two rounds of medal play Dorothy Kirby was up by ten strokes. But, Babe happily recalled, "at the end, I was on top by five strokes with 304. I pulled the tournament out with a seventy-one the third day and a seventy-four the last day."[43]

At this point Didrikson and other sources claim her streak went on to seventeen consecutive wins. Betty Hicks, however, contends Babe "buried her fourteenth tournament, which she lost, to keep the string alive. According to Hicks, "an amateur named Grace Lenczyk of Connecticut knocked Babe out of the National Open's first round at the Spokane Country Club, 1946. Babe sorta repressed that match as she counted to 17." In fact research reveals that Babe did lose at Spokane in the tournament, played August 26–September 1, 1946. She was eliminated in the first round, and Patty Berg won. The tale of seventeen consecutive wins became so entrenched that otherwise reliable sources mistakenly claimed she intentionally missed the National Open.[44]

Babe, the hustler, originated the myth and kept it alive. As Hicks wrote, "Contrary to an expansive legend, Babe did not win every tournament she played in. Two of every three of our championships were won by players named Rawls, Suggs, Berg, Jameson, Bauer, Hagge, and Hanson." That Hicks should deconstruct this particular myth of Babe's is fitting; Babe was her life-long nemesis. By challenging the seventeen consecutive wins, Hicks was attempting to rewrite other women golfers back into the sport's history of that era. Babe was so good on the links and so personally powerful with the press that she dwarfed or obliterated everyone else. Her peers became disgusted with headlines that read "Babe Loses by One" instead of "Suggs Wins."[45]

Didrikson's next win came at the North and South Women's Amateur at Pinehurst, North Carolina, where she beat Louise Suggs, but not without considerable drama. Jammed up against a tree trunk, Babe tried a pool-type angle shot off the trunk that went awry. She moved her ball trying to clear pine needles out of the ball's lie, which cost another stroke. This disastrous hole allowed Louise to square the match. "Well," Babe recalled, "that almost killed me, and George, who was there watching, was just going crazy. He told me after, 'I thought for sure you were going to lose one and break that string.'" But she knocked in a good putt on the first extra hole, "and then on the second hole I knocked a real good putt for a birdie to win."[46]

She had a month off before the next tournament, and her yearning for home returned. "I was really ready to go home and see my flowers and work around the house and garden," she said. She went on to win the women's division of the Celebrities Tournament in Washington and longed to take a break. But according to Babe, George was determined for her to continue: "'Honey,' he said, 'you want to go over to Scotland and play in the British Women's Amateur in June. You need something like that to top off your streak, the way Bobby Jones went over and played those British tournaments the year he made his grand slam.'" Winning the British Women's Amateur would be the ultimate feather in Babe's cap. No American had done it, and it would give her international exposure.[47]

A friendly argument ensued. Babe said she wouldn't go without George; he promised he'd accompany her if he possibly could. Babe knew this line. She challenged him with: "I know you. You're giving me some more of that old con. You won't go. You'll never be able to get away for it." George again prevailed with the help of Tommy Armour, a golf pro who'd tutored Babe in Medinah, Illinois, a decade before. Armour, a Scotsman, added his urgent voice, "Mildred, you go!" Her admiration for him persuaded her to go. As anticipated, "George wasn't able to make the trip with me, but I went anyhow."[48]

In retrospect, she acknowledged, "There was never any event that was more important for me in sports than the British Women's Amateur golf championship in 1947. . . . That British tournament was to land me on more front pages than the other fifteen put together." Babe was aware that her famous golfing peers Walter Hagen, Bobby Jones, Gene Sarazen, Sam Snead, and Ben Hogan had all nailed down their reputations by adding British championships. "I was trying to do the same thing—to show that I could beat the best on both sides of the Atlantic Ocean." And she wanted to be the first American woman to seize the brass ring since the tournament's inception in 1893. But most of all she wanted "to see the expressions on the faces of the Scotch when I connect with a tee shot." Her glee at orchestrating a new audience was palpable.[49]

The sea passage to Southampton, England, was smooth, but the second portion of her trip to Edinburgh, Scotland, on the boat train was hellish. Loaded with gear (two cameras, a knitting bag, a fur coat, and several pieces of luggage), unfamiliar with local customs, and unable to get a seat on a suffocatingly hot, ten-hour trip, Babe recalled, "I stood in the aisle with all my gear. It was hotter than ever. The windows were open—we'd have suffocated otherwise—and soot from the engine was blowing in. There was black specks all over my face and hair. I was dripping all over. My curls had come down."[50]

Luckily, she was soon able to get beyond this inauspicious beginning. A private car awaited her in Edinburgh that shuttled her to Gullane and the North Berwick Inn where she lodged. The desk clerk, a great fan of hers, greeted her warmly, and the inn's manager, despite wartime rationing, had laid in a supply of hard-to-get familiar foods for Babe.

Later, as she walked through the town's quaint streets to the links for her practice sessions, townsfolk recognized her constantly and would call out hellos, addressing her as "Mrs. Zaharias." Babe, eager to establish downhome Yankee rapport, admonished the newspaper reporters, "I wish you'd ask everybody just to call me Babe." Her persona decided upon, Babe delighted in being beckoned into cottages for tea. Constantly shadowed by a flock of reporters, Babe donned a pair of Stuart Clan kilts one night as the

British press immortalized her transatlantic friendliness in dozens of photos. She even considered wearing kilts in the finals—if she got that far—but found them too cumbersome.[51]

Pre-tournament days were busy ones for Babe. She had arrived early to familiarize herself with the course and took advantage of the time by practicing countless hours a day, sometimes as late as 11 P.M. because it stayed light in Gullane until 3 A.M. at that time of year. She concentrated on coping with the thick and tangled hedge-like rough while avoiding the sheep kept on the course to keep the grass short. To ease her adjustment, the club courteously provided Babe with a white-coated attendant who "scooped" where the sheep had been in front of her. The average golfer managed that gritty detail solo. Babe also adjusted to the custom of open use of the course by townspeople on Sundays; golf was suspended and picnicking and dog frolics took its place.

George phoned nightly and admonished Babe not to overdo her practicing. Despite his warnings, she was not careful enough. At the end of a long day of practice, Babe's ball lodged in tall grass off the fairway. As she was trying to dislodge it, the long wet grass wrapped around her club and the handle banged her left thumb, chipping a bone. She was befriended by a local doctor, who administered to Babe's thumb daily. Babe kept this injury, as she had the shoulder muscle tear in the 1932 Olympics, hushed. "I didn't want anybody to think I was trying to build up an advance alibi for myself," she said. She probably also did not want to give any opponent a psychological edge. Babe later speculated that the tender thumb had actually helped her game because she couldn't slug the ball so hard—it improved her control. She missed the fairway on only one drive all week.[52]

The volatile weather, however, caught Babe unprepared. "Before leaving the United States," she wrote, "I'd gone out and practiced like mad every time there was bad weather, just to help prepare myself for this tournament on a Scottish seaside course." Unfortunately, she hadn't counted on the several daily climatic changes when packing her suitcases. With no coupons to purchase warmer clothes and rationing still in place, Didrikson mentioned her dilemma to the press. Her charm worked its magic. As word of her discomfort reached the people, her hotel was deluged with packages of warm clothes, which Babe dubbed "Bundles for Babe." Didrikson rummaged through them and selected an old siren suit—"one of those things the British air-raid workers used to wear—and a pair of corduroy pants." She thanked these two donors personally, thanked the scores of others through the press, and returned the rest of the clothes. Hence her "lucky pants," or "slocks" as the Scots called them, were born and became her calling card on the links. She donned the siren suit and blue slocks, which she carried in her golf bag, whenever the chills set in. As one chronicler noted, "The Scots took her to their hearts, insisting that she change from her sweater and skirt into her lucky 'slocks' for her final victory."[53]

Ninety-nine women entered the tournament and were issued partners at random. The luck of the draw did much to determine one's fate in a sudden death tournament such as this. Beginning on Monday, competitors would play two eighteen-hole head-to-head matches a day. By Thursday the field would consist of two survivors for a thirty-six-hole final.

After Didrikson began playing, the "reserved British Press exploded with such adjectives as 'spectacular' and 'phenomenal.'" What caught the imagination of Britain was "Babe's flamboyance and ungirdled power." As she started her first match against Helen Nimmo, Babe was disconcerted by the gallery's silence. "I was saying to myself, 'Gee, you have to knock the ball in the hole off the tee to get a hand around here.'" After her handy victory, they did applaud, albeit sedately.[54]

Babe spoke to Helen Holm, past British Women's Amateur champion, who was acting as marshal, about the crowd's silence. "I wish these people would just holler and enjoy themselves the way the crowds do back home," Babe lamented. Holm described the Scottish tradition that assured players would not be disturbed. But Babe, not a fan of decorum on either side of the Atlantic, decided, "I was going to loosen up those galleries if I could. In my match that afternoon I began kidding them a little, and telling them they could make all the noise they wanted and it wouldn't bother me." After that, she began to consciously egg the crowd on.[55]

Her afternoon opponent, Enid Sheppard, played well but fell back by six strokes on the sixteenth hole. American tradition had golfers play out the rest of the match although the winner was decided, to please the gallery. Scottish tradition dictated that play stopped once a winner was determined. Babe overrode national etiquette and asked Sheppard and Holm if they could finish the course. Both agreed to play the by-holes, albeit reluctantly. She was, after all, Babe Didrikson.

Babe grandstanded unabashedly. She wowed them with the dazzling array of trick shots she had used during exhibitions in the States. She placed a kitchen match behind her ball on the seventeenth hole so when she teed off "it sound[ed] like a small cannon being fired, because the match goes off with a loud pop." Out of the trap on the same hole she placed one ball on top of another. Her shot launched one into her pocket and the other toward the green. It went right into the hole. Babe was in heaven. As she told the *Saturday Evening Post* upon her triumphant return: "By this time the gallery was in an uproar. When I finished out on the eighteenth green by turning around backwards and putting the ball between my legs into the cup, they didn't quiet down for a long time."[56]

Put off by her grandstanding, the tournament officials posted a sign on the bulletin board in the clubhouse the next morning: "Please do not play the by-holes." "So I didn't do that any more," Babe said. But she'd prevailed. Her galleries got bigger and friendlier on each successive day. They were boisterous and rowdy at her behest. She felt at home.[57]

After her first day's competition, a British golf writer gasped, "Mrs. Zaharias took practically all the spectators and crashed her way over the hills and dales of this testing, undulating course. She tore holes in the rough with tremendous recovery shots, and simply bettered her opponents in both her matches with the most tremendous exhibition of long driving ever seen in women's golf." Clearly, "the British had never seen anything quite like Texas' wise-cracking Mildred ('Babe') Didrikson Zaharias." As *Life* reported in "What a Babe!": "A disconsolate Scot, bug-eyed over the Babe's long drives," said, "It seems a shame to send our girls out against a game like that." " 'She must be Superman's sister,' one spectator whispered after the Babe whacked a whistling drive down the fairway."[58]

The British had certainly never seen the like of her behavior either. A *Time* article noted, "A few tweedy old ladies in the gallery were horrified" as Babe was "altogether lacking in refinement." Marshal Helen Holm supported Babe with, "You're speaking of the finest woman golfer that has ever been seen here." "And what if she does clown a bit?" asked the father of golf pro Jimmy Thompson. "That's just her way, and only an old tabby would object to it." The British press loved her. They called her "Tough Babe" and willingly complied with her directive that they drop the "Mrs. Zaharias."[59]

Her next opponents, Mrs. Val Reddan, Mrs. Cosmo Falcone, and Frances Stephens all fell prey to Didrikson. Her closest match was against Stephens, whom she beat three-and-two. After Babe got by Stephens on Wednesday morning, she faced Jean Donald, the Scottish champion, in the semifinals. This confrontation had been hyped in the press all week. Babe was well aware that Donald had the best chance of beating her and keeping the championship at home. But Babe thrived on the publicity: "Well, that kind of talk sort of builds me up. The bigger they make a match, the more I get fired up to go out there and show them." Babe soared and Donald plummeted. Babe shot one under men's par and roundly trounced her, seven-and-five, "a runaway score in an eighteen-hole match," as she characterized it. Ever the hustler, Babe convinced Donald to pose doing the "Highland Fling and everything with me after it was over." Donald went along with the gag, and the photo was printed worldwide.[60]

Despite her shenanigans, Didrikson was momentarily rattled before her final round. One Scottish competitor clearly resented Babe's attempt to win "their" championship and probably hated Babe's boisterous Yankee ways. "She'd buttonhole me in the club-house and start telling me how there was a jinx against American women in this tournament that had stopped . . . Glenna Collett and Virginia Van Wie." This psychological sparring came to a halt when "some of the other women found out what she was doing and got her to pipe down." Babe was unusually shaken by this encounter, and her thoughts kept returning to the jinx as she lay in bed struggling to sleep before the finals.[61]

Her last opponent was Jacqueline Gordon, the big surprise of the tournament. Although not considered a top British player nor on Britain's Curtis Cup Team, she'd been beating everybody all week regardless. Babe awoke feeling magnificent and recounted her choice of outfit with obvious pride and much self-satisfaction. She left her siren suit and lucky blue corduroys at the clubhouse. "I put on a light chartreuse skirt with a light sweater, and white golf shoes and white visor—oh, I was a doll that morning, I'm telling you!" But later she remarked, "'I should have kept my lucky pants on.'"[62]

The British press estimated the crowd for the championship round at five to eight thousand, which "was the largest of the season—far larger than the crowd which gathered to watch the British men's amateur at Carnoustie" just two weeks before. Babe began the afternoon with a much anticipated bit of clowning. When she saw the British flag, she stood at attention and saluted. The crowd applauded. Babe, realizing she was onto something here, spotted the American flag floating atop the clubhouse. As she delighted in recalling, "I turned around and got right down on the ground and salaamed three times. Everybody roared," and no doubt Babe's competitive heart felt an adrenaline rush.[63]

The morning round found them even at 75, four over men's par, Didrikson's measure of success. Babe had mounted a modest comeback by evening the score on the fifteenth hole after being down by two on the twelfth. She'd already quieted her eighty-year-old caddy who, in keeping with local tradition, insisted on advising her on club selection, wind velocity, and shot strategies. Legend has it that she asked for a younger caddy and was given a silent seventy-five-year-old who left the decision-making to her. Babe adamantly denied this breech of etiquette.

As they broke for lunch, fifty members of the gallery called out, "Babe, go git your slocks on. Go git your slocks on." Babe also needed a quick shoe repair; the wet grass had split the leather. When she located the cobbler shop, a sign read, "Sorry. Closed. Gone To See The Babe." True to legend, the shoemaker was located, graciously repaired Babe's footwear, and sent his idol, well-shod, back into combat. Dressed more warmly in her lucky pants, which she admitted had served her well, and wearing her favorite shoes, she felt her confidence rise.[64]

She broke the tie on the first hole, and things kept going her way. An eagle 3 on the second hole, followed by a par 5 to Gordon's 6 on the third had her in control to stay. With victory soon to be hers, Babe had energy for a few pranks. On one hole, Babe quipped, "I hit a tremendous tee shot. I really creamed it. Oh, that drive felt good!" Two kilted Scotsmen who'd been avid onlookers all week were overheard by Babe to say, "I've watched Walter Hagen and Bobby Jones and Gene Sarazen and all those Americans who've played over here, and none of them can hit the ball better than this girl can." Babe fell in step behind them and put her arms across their shoulders. "How'd you boys like to see me knock this little wedge shot right in the cup?" she said loudly enough for all to hear. So she banked it just a little bit and it stopped right on the cup's edge and almost went in. Babe recalled, "And you should have seen the expressions on the faces of those two Scotsmen. Their mouths were hanging wide open. Even the kilts had stopped bobbing for a moment. You could see they were thinking, 'She can do whatever she wants to with the ball!'" This fun distraction completed, Babe resumed the match. She was up five going into the back nine and finished up ahead by four strokes. The by-holes went unplayed.[65]

Babe spruced up her lipstick and rouge coming off the final green. This ladylike display was juxtaposed against her removing the bandage on her damaged left thumb and brandishing it to the press. "It caused something of a sensation," Babe noted dryly in her autobiography. But she wasn't done yet. The photographers asked her to pose in front of the clubhouse and on the way there, she "hurdled the brown brick wall that ran around it. There was another uproar over that." Everyone there was left to sort out this spectrum of femininity for themselves.[66]

The crowd gave Babe a wonderful ovation. Babe elicited accolades and high emotions from her fans. "It seemed like they stood for fifteen minutes and applauded," she recalled. More Highland Flings, flashbulbs, and clowning. She'd won her six matches with ease. The *Manchester Guardian* could not praise her enough: "Surely no woman golfer has accomplished in a championship what Mrs. Zaharias has achieved in this one. . . . She has combined in a remarkable way immense length with accuracy, reaching with a number-five iron holes at which others are content to be short with a wood. She is a crushing and heartbreaking opponent."[67]

Another London newspaper crowed, "We have not seen a fairway phantom like her—not in 47 years. What a babe!" *Time* chronicled the jubilant scene: "As she went into a victory jig, a bystander asked her the inevitable question about the secret of her success and got a far-from-inevitable answer. Cracked the Babe: 'I just loosen my girdle and let the ball have it.'" Britain was shocked. It crossed the line between charming and uncouth. Babe swore to the *Saturday Evening Post*'s Pete Martin that the comment wasn't made in Scotland, but in Washington, D.C., at the Celebrities Tournament. Despite her denials, so many press releases and personal testimonies credit her with the reutterance of this wisecrack that it has become fact.[68]

In *This Life I've Led* is a photo of Babe flanked by three other women with trophies on a table. Seated, in a skirt, ankles crossed, hair styled, smiling sweetly with a purse sitting on her lap, Babe looks the epitome of femininity and decorum. The caption reads, "The British liked me, I hope, almost as much as I loved them. Here, I'm receiving the big cup, the first American-born girl to bring it home." Babe had captured the British Women's Amateur title and the hearts of the United Kingdom. During the presentation of the championship trophy, Babe recalled, "I sang a little Highland song I'd learned from some of the Scottish golf pros in the United States—hoping I'd have this occasion to use it. And everybody seemed to like that touch."[69]

Before leaving Scotland, Babe spent three or four days playing other legendary Scottish golf courses. One day, she went to play Tommy Armour's old club, Lothianburn, where several thousand fans showed up to watch her. She was hosted by high society on this mini-tour, and was even allowed into the inner sanctums of an until-then all-male clubhouse at Muirfield for tea. She also played St. Andrew's hallowed holes. Originally, no spectators were to be allowed so Babe could play the historic course in peace and relaxation. But when she saw one thousand people crammed behind a railing some distance off peering at her, she said to herself, "'Oh Well! I looked back and waved to them, 'Come on!' So those people followed me around the entire eighteen holes." She bypassed a few other legendary courses because she was eager to get home. "I'd already been away from George longer than I ever had been since we got married. I wanted to get back home."[70]

Feted and toasted as she left Europe, Babe returned a conquering hero. Her last night was spent as a guest at the Ladies' Golf Union Building in

Edinburgh. As her train pulled out from the platform, hundreds of admirers sang "Auld Lang Syne." Two railroad officials saw her aboard and pampered her with a private compartment loaded with flowers.

In London, the royal treatment continued. The Ladies' Golf Union housed her, and she enjoyed special accommodations on the boat train to Southampton. She did not have to stand this time. Transported home in royal style aboard the *Queen Elizabeth*, Babe was met two hours and forty minutes outside of New York by a tugboat filled with seventy-one reporters, photographers, and newsreel camera operators plus one fleshy, beaming, white-shirted, easy-to-spot promoter-husband, George Zaharias. Babe hollered and waved to him and let loose with a two-fingered mouth whistle that coincided with a blast from the liner. George, handy with gag lines, quipped, "Honey, I could hear your whistle above the *Queen Elizabeth*'s." When George was the first to climb the rope ladder to board the ship, the liner gave a little lurch. Called Babe, "Hey honey, watch out! You're going to turn the Queen Elizabeth over!" Babe later remarked, "Seeing George again gave me a greater thrill than when I won the tournament."[71]

Ever eager to please, Babe catered to the press for two hours "for the interviewing and picture-taking and what not." When the "cameramen said they wished I was wearing kilts, I told them, 'Be right with you,' and went and changed. I got a Tartan cap and a pair of kilts for George to pose in, too, and got him to try the Highland Fling."

They stayed in New York for a couple of days while their phone rang off the hook. Offers poured in, "but we turned them all down." Fred Corcoran, promotional director of the Men's Professional Golf Association, made a personal visit, offering to represent her if she chose to turn pro. She signed with Corcoran in July 1947. He also represented Ted Williams, Stan Musial, and others.[72]

Amidst the glorious fanfare, Babe and George made time for an old friend, Grannie Rice. Rice had been laid up with a severe bout of pneumonia and had been unable to greet her immediately upon her return. She agreed to give him an interview, and Rice nostalgically recalled, "I spent a short half hour at their hotel quietly celebrating with Babe and George Zaharias—two wonderful kids, who I feel constitute an unusually warm and wonderful American love story."[73]

Then they headed for Denver—home—and she was feted again, lavishly. The celebrations capped off in early July with a city-wide parade, replete with floats commemorating her excellence at other sports. Babe rode atop the flower-filled last float and threw roses to the crowd. Mayor Quigg Newton and Governor Lee Knous attended, and at city hall Newton presented her with a giant key to the city. Babe remembered "there was a mob of people watching, about 50,000, according to the newspapers, and they just roared." The 250-pound key, towering 12–15 feet high, presented no problem for George Zaharias, the ex-wrestler, who, Babe announced to the crowd, would carry it home. She had bragged about George's muscularity in the past but in 1955 she admitted, "He didn't have to do that, but he did show that he was able to lift it off the ground."[74]

Despite her huge victory, Babe was committed to play yet again in the Broadmoor Match Play Tournament at Colorado Springs in mid-July. She beat Dot Kielty in the finals, ten-and-nine, to complete her streak. The victory entitled her to "permanent possession of the Broadmoor trophy, which was a big silver cup with a lot of beautiful handwork on it. I had cost them a lot of money." Generously, Babe sensed their lack of enthusiasm to relinquish the trophy, so she told them to make a plaque for her and keep the cup in competition.[75]

Gallant. Charismatic. Transatlantic celebrity. Unprecedented champion. Babe was on top of the world.

CHAPTER EIGHT

Cashing In

Babe Didrikson's popularity and recognizability soared. She was named among 1947's women of the year by the Associated Press along with Helen Hayes, Helen Traubel, and Ingrid Bergman. Enticed by "a fast half-million dollars if I'd turn professional again," Babe debated her options. She claimed in *This Life I've Led* that George could still afford to finance her yearly golf expenses of $15,000 through his sports promotions, hotel business, and other Denver investments. "But sometimes," she reasoned, "offers get so big you feel you just have to take them." While "it nearly killed me to throw over the amateur standing I'd struggled so hard to get," Babe said, "I couldn't see any other choice." On August 14 Babe announced she was turning professional.[1]

Babe took Fred Corcoran up on his offer to be her business representative. They had originally met in 1934 when he booked Babe's exhibition tour with Sarazen. His autobiography, *"Unplayable Lies,"* lists among his clients Ted Williams, Bob Jones, Sam Snead, Stan Musial, and Ken Venturi. Babe was in competent hands. How George reacted to Corcoran's usurping of his role is largely unknown, but Fred, Babe said, "consulted with George on everything." George continued to book Babe for appearances and exhibitions, obligations that she fulfilled alongside Corcoran's grueling schedule. Corcoran's role was a first step for Babe away from her economic dependence on George and his very different style of management. Babe later grew to realize that George was satisfied to get any amount for her to perform.[2]

Fred's job, in addition to lining up exhibitions, shows, and contracts, was to prepublicize Babe's doings, even a dinner out. Nancy Corcoran, Fred's widow, recalled that Fred would "tell the press that we were going to have dinner at such and such a place and of course they were his best friends—the press—and they would come and she would sit and talk to them at dinner and then they'd go home with a story." The constant invasiveness of the press was not an unwanted intrusion to Babe but rather served to keep her in print when sports feats lulled.

Nancy confirmed that Babe "was always 'on.'" When they went to dinner she would play her harmonica at the table. As Nancy recalled, "You couldn't dislike her. She was good company." But Babe was insensitive to Nancy, ten to fifteen years her junior. "She wasn't interested in me whatsoever. We were not close." They never exchanged a personal thought and Babe didn't even make polite inquiries about Nancy's life. As usual, she was too busy being the star and basking in her own limelight to take much notice of anyone else.[3]

Finally Didrikson was being offered phenomenal pay to match her phenomenal stardom. She claimed she was offered a firm $300,000 to make a series of ten short golf films. But when Pete Martin of the *Saturday Evening Post* pushed her to name the studio, Babe blanched. Martin questioned Fred Corcoran and was told Babe had been in conference with Spyros Skouras, president of 20th Century Fox. Skouras told Martin "negotiations were still in a highly tentative status—so tentative that no figure for the Babe's services had been set." The $300,000 offer, Martin reported, "may turn out to be more fabulous than any of the fables that have ever sprung up about the Babe." No athlete before her "ever claimed to have been offered such a colossal sum to turn professional." Although Didrikson had fabricated the provocative offer, it was reported widely as fact and enhanced Babe's marketability and stature. She eventually did make three movie shorts for Columbia Pictures, "but at nowhere near the fabulous price the first people had offered."[4]

Fred Corcoran, witness to this sleight of hand, called Babe "a grand showman. She had a flair for the dramatic and a raw, earthy sense of humor. She loved life and loved people. She loved the color and glory of the passing parade and wore her role of champion . . . naturally." She was a promoter's dream. When he signed her, there was no women's professional golf tour, so the only money was in exhibitions. He regularly booked her at major league baseball parks where she would "stand on the diamond and hit golf balls out of sight." One night at Yankee Stadium, as the home team took the field for infield drill, "she called for a glove and stepped in at third base where she handled herself like a big leaguer: Her barnstorming days were back! She was hobbled somewhat by her skirt," Corcoran recalled, "but that didn't faze her. She ripped it up the front and went back to scooping up ground balls and firing them across to the first base. The crowd went wild." Then she summoned Joe DiMaggio out of the dugout to bat against her pitches. Shy, he resisted, "but I took him by the arm," Babe recalled, "and I grabbed a bat and handed it to him. I walked Joe out to home plate and bowed low." Babe caught him in the ribs with one pitch, he popped up a few, took one big swing—missed—and sat down.[5]

On another occasion Babe put on a show at Briggs Stadium in Detroit before a Red Sox–Tigers game. Despite pelting rain, she did not cut her routine short by one pitch. The game was washed out, and few of the 55,000 sellout crowd, according to Corcoran, used their rain checks. They had gotten more than their money's worth with Babe. The Tigers' general manager had weaseled out of her usual $600 fee and agreed to pay only $450 at the last minute. His debatable rationale was that Ben Hogan and Sam Snead were getting only $500 and Babe wasn't putting a single extra person in the ballpark. What was not debatable is that she kept them there. Not surprisingly Babe exaggerated that for an exhibition, "the least I get is two thousand dollars. I'll play either on a flat guarantee basis or for a percentage of the gate."[6]

Because of her fame and his contacts, Corcoran was able to book Babe with the biggest names in sports. He set Didrikson up against the Red Sox slugger Ted Williams in a golf driving contest in Sarasota, Florida, where the Sox held spring training. Babe admitted that Williams could outdrive her on rare occasions from the tee, but she would always win the game. When he dribbled a ball just off the tee, she called to him, "Better run those grounders out, Ted! There may be an overthrow."[7]

Since she was a pro, she could accept endorsements for money with no fear of the consequences. Corcoran signed her to a lifetime contract with the advisory staff of Wilson Sporting Goods Company marketing Babe Zaharias golf equipment. She would offer her expertise and promote the equipment for $8,000 yearly. This new field of endeavors signaled yet another opportunity for Babe to revise her image. She told reporters: "I know that women's golf has a greater future in this country than men's golf. Golf is a game of coordination, rhythm, and grace. Women have this to a much greater degree than men, as dancing shows." She also signed with the Serbin dress manufacturers, who made golfing clothes for women. Babe co-designed a golf dress, a shirt with buttons on the sleeves to allow for a wider swing, and a golf shoe with removable spikes. Babe described them as "sensible for gals who want comfort with grooming." Here, she successfully promoted herself, femininity, and the product. In addition, she represented Weathervane women's sports clothes manufactured by Alvin Handmacher, who paid her $10,000 per year to wear his clothes. Not all of Babe's outfits, though, were conservative. She once appeared on the golf course wearing a pink shirt embroidered with black palm trees and matching pink socks.[8]

Didrikson also teamed up again with P. Goldsmith Sons sporting goods company. The advertising brochure for golf equipment carrying her name implores dealers to "Cash in on . . . This Powerful, Sales-Producing Publicity, Surrounding Babe Didrikson, the World's Greatest Athlete." The pamphlet promises, " 'Babe' Didrikson Coordinated Golf Equipment . . . will establish a new record in Sales for You." A persuasive pitch by Babe claims female golfers' coordination will be improved with the use of her clubs.[9]

She also endorsed Timex watches and a long-life automotive battery. The watch ad posed her washing dishes and driving a golf ball with the caption "Housekeeping and golf, I love them both." To manage both she kept her eye on her Timex Sportster. The pitch concludes, "Neither the shock of driving a golf ball nor the water from washing dishes can hurt your Timex Sportster." Her Prest-O-Lite Hi-Level Battery ad pictured her, midswing, saying, "I add water only three times a year." She also endorsed cigarettes along with big-name male athletes.[10]

Babe was not alone in patching together a living through golf and endorsements. Betty Jameson also turned pro when Spaulding Sporting Goods offered her $7,500 to put her name on their golf clubs in the late 1940s. Similarly, Peggy Kirk Bell was paid $10,000 plus travel expenses in the 1950s by Spaulding to endorse its products and give exhibitions. As Bell said, "If I hadn't gotten a contract with a company like that there was no way I'd have turned pro. There was no way to make a living. You wouldn't turn pro until you got that contract." And their opportunities for earning a living through athletics were few. Bell stressed that even though she was a college graduate, her salary as a physical education teacher would have been only $3,500 per year. All women golfers knew the economic facts and none did better than Babe, "who'd say to everybody, you girls want to play golf or you want to go home and work as a secretary?"[11]

But Babe's goading didn't take into account the inequality of the situation. As Bell said, "She'd get a thousand an exhibition just like Hogan and Snead and Nelson and all those men. No other women got a dime. She was the only one that they pay to have her come. Everybody else—all of us were doing them free and Babe was getting $1,000." This "frustrated some of the other girls because she got everything. She got everything she wanted. Wasn't anything she asked for she didn't get. I mean if there were any contracts out there she got them." Undeniably, other pros resented her monopoly of fees. And Babe's insensitive rationale for this to her peers, "I'm the star, you're the chorus," didn't help relations any.[12]

It was no secret Babe loved making money. Jameson recalled, "She loved economic rewards, but the sport was the game. The game was it, and all this other was extra." Maybe: the sport was the crop and the cash was the harvest. In 1948, although Didrikson was the leading money winner, she earned only $3,400 playing golf. Her endorsements, appearances, and exhibitions, however, totalled over $100,000. That equalled Ted Williams's take.[13]

And then there were the extras, the gifts that Babe requested, wheedled, and was flat-out given. Bell recounted gratis hotel rooms and said Babe and George "got everything pretty much free." She added, "They'd pay her for tournaments, and she'd get appearance fees, and lots of things." When they built their home in Tampa they had three deep freezes, "and everybody gave her all this stuff." In part, the gift givers "just wanted to say I gave Babe this. They were just glad for Babe to speak to them."[14]

But Babe often didn't wait to be offered. Bertha Bowen, devoted but a straight talker, said Babe was "manipulative, a very manipulative person and liked material things." Bowen recalled that if Babe "heard of some celebrity getting things she'd put in her bid for the same thing." This was the case when Maco Turner of Oklahoma gave Byron Nelson a horse. Babe called him and said, "Now I want one." He agreed, and unannounced on a Sunday Babe and Dodd arrived at Bertha's in Forth Worth followed by a horse trailer. Ever accommodating, Bertha cut through the fence of a friend's ranch gate so they could store the horse there.[15]

Dodd claimed Didrikson "was never charged anything and if you were with her you wouldn't be charged either. I never had so many free meals in my life. It was a glamorous life to be with Babe. There was always somebody wanting you to go somewhere and do something and it was going to be free." A case in point: Diamond Jim Moran, a casual friend of Babe's and a New Orleans restaurateur, invited a group of pro women golfers out to a temporarily evacuated house of prostitution at the end of a pier on Lake Pontchartrain, complete with numerous bedrooms with private showers. Unannounced, Moran sent two men in tuxedos with a limousine to pick Dodd and Babe up on the eighteenth green as they completed their game and bring them to the party. They were treated to a beer and food feast of broiled chicken, shrimp, every imaginable appetizer, and T-bone steaks. As the party progressed, several of the players decided to throw Babe in the shower. Said Dodd of this attempt, "We all got wet except for Babe. It was all in fun, but she wasn't going to be the one to get wet. . . . We started to pick her up and put her in the shower and the next thing I knew I was in it. She was very powerful and I'm not weak, I'm strong. I probably weighed 150 pounds— but she was quick, not only strong but quick." Mused Dodd as she recalled this night of revelry and pranks, "She really was a heck of a lot of fun." Dodd also spun tales of Babe's other pranks: leaving hairbrushes in beds and making phone calls with German accents were among her favorites. Said Dodd of the good times with Babe, "I would have walked underground to China for Babe in those days. She was the most famous person in the world and I was her protégé."[16]

Babe was a charismatic leader who instilled devotion among many. As Berg said, "You know people loved the Babe and they clung to her for her wit and her humor and enthusiasm and really for her love of life." She brought joy with her and "went along in life beautifully." Berg, savvy to Babe, captured and appreciated her simplicity: "She enjoyed winning, playing the harmonica for people, and making them happy. She was a very caring lady."[17]

Peggy Kirk Bell and Babe often flew together in Peggy's plane. Peggy proposed to Babe: "You learn to fly and Beach will give you a Bonanza and we'll have a real airplane and I'll fly that baby." Their plan was hatched: Babe took flying lessons in Tampa and soloed, but "then she got sick and never finished." In fact, Babe's interest in flying predated Bell's encouragement. According to one source Amelia Earhart had asked Babe to accompany her on a flight. The offer was motivated by the publicity and respect Babe's presence would lend; she declined.[18]

The fun and action Babe always brought with her often resulted in more gifts for everyone. Walking down the streets of New York with Dodd, in 1953, Babe spotted the newest model Rolex watch in a shop window. She told Dodd, "I've always wanted one of those." So Babe steered them toward a phone booth, looked up the address of a Rolex distributor, and rode there in a cab. They entered a narrow dark hallway and Babe spoke through a small window: "I'm Babe Zaharias and I want to see the boss." The clerk, baffled, hesitated. Babe repeated, "Tell your boss Babe Zaharias is out here and wants to see him." Out came the boss and everybody else. They ushered Babe in, chatted for fifteen minutes, decided to play a round over at Wingfoot, "and then they went through a big luncheon for her, at one of those big Italian restaurants." They presented her with a Rolex watch, gratis, and Babe bought two others, at cost, for Betty and George. Another "conquest" of Babe's, as Betty perceptively called it, was requesting—and getting—free recording equipment so they could tape their harmonica and guitar sessions. Thus accustomed to such "freebies" Babe became angry when representatives of companies did not give her free products.[19]

Another project that kept Babe in perpetual motion, print, and the limelight was a golf instruction book Corcoran had arranged with A. S. Barnes publishers. *Championship Golf* (1948), a 125-page volume, guides golfers on equipment, practice, concentration, and playing techniques. The book is generously illustrated with photographs. Numerous shots are close-ups of Babe's hands demonstrating proper technique. Her nails are polished red, she's wearing a bracelet on her right wrist, and the long cuffs of her dress's loose-fitting buttoned sleeves are feminine and graceful. Her shoulder-length hair and A-line skirt paint a portrait of feminine propriety. Her hands look strong, and her long tapered fingers, which many golfing peers recalled as the most beautiful hands they had ever seen, ripple with her flexes. She looks every inch the champion. The "teacher" Babe is a carefully crafted feminine figure.

Reviews of *Championship Golf* were mixed. *Book Review Digest* of 1948 wrote, "The author's name may create a demand for this book but it is not recommended as the best book on golf. Directions are meager as compared with those in other books by champions." Both the *New York Times* and *Kirkus* were more complimentary. The *New York Times* praised its format: "The book is profusely illustrated, and generally presented in a form that's easy to understand and assimilate." *Kirkus* compared it with Ben Hogan's instructional book and stuck to description: "Mrs. Zaharias introduces each section with a brief straight forward analysis of each phase, including fundamentals of mental attitudes, match play, etc.—and then includes a question and answer section based on experience. Photographs illustrate her points."[20]

Babe had one other short-lived writing project. She was commissioned to write a series of columns for McNaught Syndication entitled "The Babe Says—." Babe and George asked Hicks to ghostwrite this series of practical golf tips aimed at women golfers for her. Hicks, an accomplished author, "whipped out three snappy columns and air-mailed them off to the McNaught editor. Soon thereafter George called her and canned their deal. Her writings were too erudite for Babe's down-home style. 'The writing,' he grumbled, 'don't sound like Babe.' And I thought, Hicks editorialized wryly, 'that was the whole idea!'"[21]

Despite her perks and revelry, Babe had exceeded her physical limits: "The fees were good, but we probably booked too many of them. One month there were seventeen nights that I was on a plane. I'd play in one place, then go to the airport to fly to the next place." Because she was satisfying both George's and Fred's bookings the grind wore her down, although it was years before she would admit it. "I kept going at a heavy clip. It always has been hard for me to slow down." George, said Babe, had come to believe her indefatigable, too. Years later, after Babe's death, George told a *Look* reporter what he didn't realize then: "Nobody who has not had some experience in that kind of life can know how demanding it is." The schedule apparently dulled her tournament sharpness so that her streak snapped when she lost in the quarterfinals of the Texas Women's Open by one stroke to Betty Mims White.[22]

Angered that her streak had been broken, fatigue or no fatigue, Babe roared back in her very next tournament, the Hardscrabble Women's Open at Little Rock, Arkansas. Her seventy-two-hole total of 293 set a world's record for women's tournament medal play. In retrospect Babe often ruminated about the Texas Women's Open loss: "I honestly believe that if I had squeaked through [it] I'd have gone on and stretched my winning streak to twenty-five or thirty tournaments." No goal struck her as insurmountable; no defeat at number thirteen impaired this vision.[23]

The Ladies Professional Golf Association

By 1948 Didrikson was looking for other opportunities. As a professional there were only a few more tournaments than there had been when she played in the 1930s. Babe, frustrated by the lack of competition, tried to enter the men's National Open, but the USGA refused, saying the championship "has always been intended for men, [and] the eligibility rules have been rephrased to confirm that condition." Of this thwarted attempt Babe said, "I don't suppose I'd have finished around the top if they had let me in there. But I don't think I'd have been at the bottom either. I wouldn't have disgraced myself."[24]

Babe's frustration epitomized the limited opportunities available for skilled women athletes. Only the All-American Girls' Professional Baseball League (1943–54), founded by Philip K. Wrigley, offered any chance for a female professional athlete to make a living. Unfortunately, despite the economic benefits, the athletes were still constrained by cultural dictates. The highly skilled women played bare-legged in pastel skirts despite the necessity of sliding on dirt base paths. In the early years of the league they were also forced to attend makeup and charm classes at night run by Helena Rubinstein representatives and other fashion experts. The league's handbook, in its chapter "Femininity and Skill," instructed recruiters, "the more feminine the appearance of the performer the more dramatic the performance." In 1951, the players were cautioned: "*Always appear in feminine attire.* This precludes the use of any wearing attire of masculine nature," which was "BARRED AT ALL TIMES." Violators were fined. Thus teams like the Racine (Wisconsin) Belles, Rockford (Illinois) Peaches, Muskegon (Illinois) Lassies, and South Bend (Indiana) Blue Sox enjoyed eleven years of popularity. League officials stressed to journalists that "no freaks or Amazons" would permeate their ranks.[25]

Golf had no counterpart, but that was soon to change. Babe liked to credit George with the inspiration for a solution. "He started thinking about the problem . . . and once again George came up with an answer. He got the idea that there should be a professional tournament circuit for women, just as there was for men." Actually L. B. Icely, president of Wilson Sporting Goods, contacted Corcoran and asked him to organize a pro women's golf circuit. Babe claimed George brought the idea up with Corcoran and Icely and "George persuaded them that once we got the thing going, it would build itself up." George, somewhat instrumental in these early phases of organization, was later loath to relinquish control.[26]

Corcoran, as manager of Babe and the pixie-cute golfing Bauer sisters, Alice and Marlene, realized the blunted opportunities for women pros and agreed to begin organizing a pro circuit. Wilson agreed to pay Corcoran's $15,000 yearly salary, but wanted the other equipment firms to help support the tour. Both hoped their circuit would fare better than the Women's PGA, which had been incorporated in 1944. This organization, Corcoran noted, "stumbled along for a few years and then went into hiding after playing one tournament at Spokane." Betty Hicks served as president until the group "disintegrated violently in March of 1947" amidst self-interested golf stars' desires. When its founder, Hope Seignious, a North Carolina pioneer woman professional, refused to relinquish the organization's name and charter to Corcoran because much of her money was invested in a WPGA magazine, he side-stepped any infringement on her group by naming the new group the Ladies' Professional Golf Association. One founding member, however, despised the appellation "ladies." "It sounds," she said, "like the stuff that comes out of the insides of the lobster." As Corcoran wryly noted, "The announcement that we had formed the Ladies PGA touched off a national storm of indifference."[27]

Corcoran finally persuaded Alvin Handmacher of Weathervane sports clothes to put up money for a professional tournament. They conceived the Weathervane Trans-continental Tournament, with matches in four major cities and first prize awarded to the low aggregate scorer. There was, obviously, a "Weathervane suit promotion tie-in at each stop." Handmacher put up the original $15,000 in prize money and a $5,000 bonus for the winner. Later Helen Lengfeld, owner of *National Golfer* magazine, promoted the

Pacific Coast Spring Tour to begin at Pebble Beach, California, worth $15,000 in prize money. The circuit was taking shape, but they still needed players. As Corcoran was well aware, "there were a lot of women golfers who couldn't afford to go on playing amateur golf forever, but couldn't risk the uncertainty of a professional career without any prospect or hope of making it pay out. Handmacher's prize money and the additional tournaments at way stations gave them the courage to take the step."[28]

It was a risk, but it was going from the fire to the frying pan. Hicks's *Saturday Evening Post* exposé piece on women's golf revealed that economic survival as a touring pro was not feasible. For four months in 1953 she played tournament golf after turning pro. She collected $3,750 in prize money. "I spent $3,335 of it on hotels, meals, tips, airplane tickets, automobile tires, caddies and cab fares." She put 40,000 miles on her odometer, 1,000 miles on her spiked shoes, and sprouted new gray hair. Hicks's article, tellingly, is subtitled: "Next to Marriage We'll Take Golf." Some women pros were painfully aware that a "good" marriage would relieve them of their ceaseless economic grind. Prior to turning pro, it usually cost golfers money to play the amateur circuit.[29]

The original Ladies Professional Golf Association had only six members: Babe Didrikson Zaharias, Patty Berg, Helen Dettweiler, Betty Jameson, Betty Hicks, and Bea Gottlieb. Even when the LPGA was incorporated in the state of New York in 1950, there were only eleven charter members. Despite its small size the group had huge personalities. Hicks wrote, "Meetings of the LPGA invariably produce mild pyrotechnics." The level of chaos caused "a public stenographer hired to render minutes of one session [to throw] up her pad and pencil in hysterical resignation." There was also considerable discord over Babe's and George's heavy-handedness. "Women's golf belongs to me," George growled "on more than one occasion." "It's a racket, golf is, just like the wrasslin' and the boxin' racket. And it's gotta be run the same way." On another occasion, George announced to the LPGA Board, "I don't give a shit about them by-laws."[30]

Didrikson was even heavy-handed in chronicling the history of the LPGA. In *This Life I've Led* she claimed, "Patty Berg became president of the Ladies' PGA for the first year. I've been president since." Wilson's Women's Golf Information Guide, however, credits Berg with over three years at the helm. Berg was president in 1949, Babe acknowledged, but Berg was also in charge in 1950, 1951, and 1952, years Babe claimed she was president. Babe did not actually assume the presidency until 1953 and maintained it throughout 1954 and 1955. Louise Suggs took over in 1956.[31]

Perhaps she recollected being president longer than she was because she knew she was the centerpiece on the LPGA's table. Corcoran knew it too. "Babe Zaharias," he said, "made the women's tour go. She was the color, the gate attraction." On the first year of the tour she was one of four players who controlled the circuit. Babe won the Essex Fells, New Jersey, tournament by thirteen strokes, a $1,000 purse. By winning the World Championship and Eastern Open Babe pocketed $4,650. Considering that the total tournament purse for 1949 was only $15,000, she had done pretty well. But with her fame and her marketing skills, Didrikson propelled the LPGA into the limelight, and it became the richest women's sports organization of its era.[32]

Mostly, however, she concentrated on promoting herself. Her insistence on personal press coverage, undeniably egocentric, was powerful. Said Dodd, "She didn't like it very much if the press didn't write something. You can bet on that. She didn't like it one bit. She needed to look at the sports page and see her picture." And when the press wouldn't cover her, she staged her own newsworthy stunts. In 1948 at the National Women's Open in Atlantic City, Babe announced, "If somebody don't raise that prize money before I leave, I won't come back for the last two rounds." The committee faced a crisis: if Babe left, so did the gallery. A gallant and anxious club member came to the rescue and upped the ante $1,000 for anyone who could break 300 strokes for the 72 holes. Babe came into the last hole needing a birdie 4 to shoot 299. When she missed a six-foot putt, she rasped to the gallery, "It would have put me in a higher tax bracket."[33]

As a household name, Babe brought out the crowds—golf fans or not—because they had read so much about her. No one else did more for women's golf than she did. According to Peggy Kirk Bell, her color, humor, and sense of fun, while antagonizing a few, "didn't do anything but help the LPGA." Berg and Bell were adamant that Babe presented the "right kind of image for golf." "The USGA loved her," Bell maintained. "They pulled for her to win. She brought in the crowds. She was their star." Bell didn't mind. Like the time they'd teed off for a tournament practice round "and she'd walk over and pat me on the shoulder and say, 'You know Peg, it's always nice to play with you because you have such a nice gallery.' And everybody'd laugh because everybody knew they were out there to see her." This wasn't cockiness to Bell. In fact she found Babe particularly accommodating in attending LPGA-run parties and functions, which many of the pros avoided. Babe was always in attendance, harmonica ready to belt out a few tunes. No one would argue that golf "grew because of Babe Didrikson Zaharias," an assertion made by Berg and seconded by all.[34]

Other players were not so accepting of Didrikson as Berg and Bell. Louise Suggs, for example, clearly abhorred Babe's behavior. Once, when Suggs was putting, Didrikson and Dodd broke out in a hillbilly song. Suggs missed the putt. Commented Babe's biographers, "Babe played with Suggs like a cat with a mouse; and Louise Suggs didn't get the credit she deserved." Jameson acknowledged that Babe did not portray the image the LPGA wanted for itself. First, her personality was so dominant that members wanted her to have an arch rival so that other players could get some press. Second, some at the helm of the LPGA felt that a more feminine image would benefit the sport. They sure "didn't want everybody to be Babe," Jameson said, "they wanted some color in some other way."[35]

Despite her carefully crafted feminine appearance, Hicks wrote, "The Babe remained back-alley tough and barroom crude, seemingly with determined effort and obviously with her uninhibited repartee." Hicks was aghast at the lengths to which Babe went for a laugh. "She boisterously protected her reputation, as uncouth and rough, gloried in the gallery mirth at the primitive humor. 'Man!' she'd protest loudly after a bad shot. 'All that work and the baby's dead!' " Hicks scorned Babe's "five-year-old's hunger for attention" and her use of shock language. Didrikson, according to Hicks, received ample criticism and ridicule behind her back in locker rooms and barrooms, a subtlety Hicks believed escaped Babe. "Babe gave them the show they wanted, and she in turn was assured center stage. But in seeking the limelight in this way, she was helping to perpetuate a cruel myth about women athletes—the myth that they aren't quite women." This myth flourished in the 1930s and 1940s "and was to become an enormous burden to those of us who were Babe's contemporaries in golf in the '50s." Women's golf, she concluded, spent years attempting to come out from behind that shadow.[36]

Betsy Rawls, like Suggs, shared Hicks's viewpoint. "She really was a rather crude person. She added a lot of color to the tour at a time when it was needed, but she did not add any dignity to the game." Still, they tolerated her because, as Hicks wrote, "Babe Zaharias is Mrs. Golf. She's the big drawing card. . . . We can't compete with her in color. Even though she annoys us at times with her egocentric attitude, we have twice elected her president of our association. We grin at her antics, tolerate her demands for favors from sponsors, sincerely wish her speedy recoveries from illness, take our beatings from her routinely—and thoroughly enjoy beating her." Beating Babe was rare indeed. Rawls recounted Babe having a round of golf called off when it started to rain and she was playing badly. "She didn't always play by the rules," Rawls said. "I don't think she cheated, but she did bend the rules. Above all she wanted to win and she would sacrifice other things to win."[37]

Two Ways of Winning

Babe's fiercely competitive game was bolstered by her golfing style and her mental manipulation of opponents. Preparation, of course, was the key to her style. In October 1952, she wanted to compete in the Texas Women's Open in Fort Worth. The course had always given her problems—she cursed it for snapping her winning streak in 1947. She told George she wanted to beat that course. Not her opponents. Not her personal best on it. But the course. A new opponent. "So I went about a week ahead and practiced. I did whip the course, and I won the tournament. I felt wonderful."[38]

Most peers point to her strength as the secret to her success. Berg credited her with bringing power, hence lower scores, to the game. Bell, noting Babe's self-confidence, concurred that "Babe could hit the ball longer than most men could hit it," a feat she witnessed many times playing with Babe. Dodd agreed that "Babe didn't hit the ball very straight. She just hit it a long damn way. And a lot of times it was in the trees or in the rough." Wrote one golf historian, less glowingly, "No doubt Mrs. 'Babe' Zaharias can hit a ball as far as any average scratch man can . . . but not as far as the 'horizon drivers'. . . nor as far as the majority of men amateurs of international class."[39]

Others point to her incredible coordination. Berg considered her "one of the best putters from 3-4 feet." Babe's aim, she said, was very precise on short shots, which was very "unusual for a long hitter." Jameson, a true admirer of Babe's game, said, "her short game and her iron play were the strengths of her game." Betsy Rawls was unequivocal on her skill. "She was the most physically talented woman I have ever seen. . . . She was strongest around the greens, she had that very soft touch, but she often mis-hit her drives and she did not have a classic swing." No matter. Her strength and ability "as a great scrambler" got her out of trouble.[40]

If her strength and her coordination failed her, then Babe's sheer will took over. Bell, Bill Nary, and other opponents noted that Babe could raise the level of her game to suit the moment. "She played as well as she had to win," Bell said. "If she had to play harder, she could do it. That was the confidence she had in herself." Once at Santa Monica's Brentwood Country Club, Nary witnessed a fierce comeback by Babe. On the last hole Babe "needed a par to break the course record and she hooked a drive in the trap." She was so disgusted with herself for this errant shot that "she hit a full 7 iron from the trap and sank it. And had a 67 which of course was the women's record." She was, Nary beamed, "very aggressive. If she had to play safe she wouldn't play safe. She'd go for the green."[41]

According to Hicks, herein lay her greatest strength. Hicks said, "Babe Zaharias was openly, hostilely, aggressively, bitterly, laughingly, joking, viciously and even sometimes lovingly competitive." Coming from Hicks, this is both praise and lament. Hicks, ever articulate, admitted, "Babe Didrikson Zaharias was my personal Gargantua. She ate little girls who couldn't drive a golf ball more than 225 yards. In head-to-head match play she was awesome." "She loved to slug the ball," Betty once wrote, "and in exhibition matches she would often use this ability to embarrass her opponent. . . . Her boasting launched galleries into paroxysms, but scarcely endeared her to competitors."[42]

Her competitiveness led her to do nearly anything to win. Although she wasn't mean, her insensitivity helped her outsmart her opponents. Hicks chronicled a litany of offensive one-liners apparently meant to amuse the crowd but destroy the concentration of other players. Once at a posh East Coast club a member of the gallery asked, "Babe, what do you think about when you hit the ball out in the woods?" "Just wish to hell George was there so we could ———," Babe replied, providing an explicit description that propelled the horrified fan off to join the gallery of a more couth professional.[43]

Didrikson also openly reveled in herself and her accomplishments. In 1950 she won two-thirds of the LPGA tournaments and earned $14,800, making her the year's leading money winner. Her victories included the All-American Open, National Women's Open, Women Titleholder's, Weathervane Women's Open Golf Championship, and the Western Women's Open. And in winning her second National Women's Open title she scored a record-tying 291 at Rolling Hills Country Club in Wichita, Kansas. She shot seven birdies to win by nine strokes.[44]

In 1950 six women pros, under Fred Corcoran's auspices, challenged "any team of British male amateurs" to a match. Leonard Crawley, a British golf writer and former British Walker Cup player, accepted Corcoran's promotional idea, but he scorned the possibility that the women might pose a real challenge. When Babe heard of Crawley's attitude, "her eyes glittered and her mouth thinned to a slit." "Save him for me, son," she said to Corcoran. "I'll play in this h'yah match, but only if I can have Crawley." Crawley lined up six former Walker Cup players to face off against Didrikson, Jameson,

Bell, Berg, Rawls, and Betty Bush, the six low scorers in the Weathervane tournament.[45]

At the first tee, "Crawley gallantly pointed down the fairway and observed, 'There's the ladies' tee down there.' Babe, portrayed with 'Honeyesque' ferocity, smiled a cold, mirthless smile. 'Ah'm playin' with you, son,' she drawled." Babe obliterated Crawley, "out-gunning him from every tee." She shot a 74 on the championship course. All the American women played from the "tiger tees" and walloped the men, 6-0. Commented Corcoran, "That evening I was probably the most unpopular man in England." Once again Babe wowed British golf fans. A week later at Sunningdale the American women "steamrolled a team of British Curtis Cup Allstars, 9-0." Not only did the American women beat a team of men and women champions, but Didrikson made a stunning final hole victory over Philomena "Phil" Garvey, a former British Women's Amateur champ.[46]

Babe dominated the tour for 1951 as well. *Newsweek* chronicled her stupendous accomplishments in "Mrs. Golf." "Striding purposefully on good legs, the green-eyed, combative, but likeable Babe" made 1951 the year of her greatest single tournament. In Tampa in January she shot a women's world record of 288 for 72 holes. *Readers Digest* described this as "the first time in golfing history that a girl had posted a score which could be compared with that of ranking men players." In Dallas in April, "eight strokes behind going into the showdown stretch, she put on an astonishing 66." Her last round of 73 at Fresno gave her a first place 225 for the 54-hole event and $3,000 in prize money.[47]

Of her twelve 1951 starts she tallied seven victories. She won the All-American Open, World Championship, and the Ponte Verde, Tampa, Fresno, Richmond, and Texas Opens. She came in second at the Sacramento, Eastern, and Carrolton Opens and runner-up at the 144-hole Weathervane. She finished third in the National Open, where she lost to Patty Berg, 146-147, in a 36-hole playoff. She ended the year as the leading money winner with $15,087 and was elected to the LPGA Hall of Fame, which had been established the previous year. At this point in her career she tallied seventy-four championships for her sixteen years of amateur and professional golf.[48]

As *Time* proclaimed in June 1951, she had become "Big Business Babe." Her exhibitions (656 of them in one three-year stretch, roughly one every day and a half) paid $500 a round on weekdays, $600 on Sundays. Her tournament winnings were supplemented by her many lucrative endorsements. Babe declined to say how much she was making, but Corcoran proudly declared, "She has become the first woman athlete to bring her annual income up to six figures." *Time* estimated she had pulled in "an estimated $250,000 out of golf from prize money, sporting goods companies, movie and tv shorts, endorsements and royalties on equipment bearing her name. *Plus* investments."[49]

Babe reigned supreme. And for her, supremacy naturally led to self-congratulation: "Where I go the galleries go," Babe once crowed at a tournament. "Let the rest starve." This was often followed by: "Ah'm makin' it [money] fast'n Ah can spend it." Obsessed, Hicks claimed, with outearning her peers, Babe announced, "Ah don't go for this rule of no tournament appearance fees. Ah can't buy me them mink coats on just prize money, and where I go these days, Ah gotta have mink." This attitude did not go over well with her peers. As Hicks pointed out with notable ire: "Babe's supremacy would be much easier for us to [bear] if she didn't cram it down our throats." Dodd, speaking with refreshing candor, corroborated, "She made it very, very hard on a lot of these women golfers because she'd walk right up and say, 'What are you girls practicing for? You can't win this tournament.' And that kind of thing. . . . She did it all the time, and there were a lot of them that didn't like it one damn bit." In fact, a couple of women pros who later claimed to be friends with Babe actually had a very hard time with her. Dodd agreed, "I wouldn't say that Babe had a lot of friends. She was not a terribly popular person with her peers."[50]

Her friendship with each of her major competitors, according to Hicks, "was either feigned, superficial, or ceased entirely on the first tee. At one time or another," Hicks revealed, "she engaged in open verbal warfare with all of us, since all occasionally had the audacity to either beat her or to threaten her ill structured ego in an area other than golf." There was, she reiterated, an unspoken requirement to maintain a facade of friendship with Babe. Even Bell, another staunch ally of Babe's, admitted that "when I started to travel a little bit with Babe people would come to me and say, 'Look Peggy, you've got to get away from her, you know.'" Get away from what? Her tough reputation and swearing, she was cautioned, although Bell contends she "never, never heard Babe swear."[51]

Didrikson's will to win overshadowed any affection she held for her few friends. Whether at home or in public, Babe was cocky and wanted to be the star. "And she wanted to win," Dodd asserted. "I don't care what she was doing. Cards, pool, ping-pong, it didn't make any difference . . . and she was not a good sport about losing it either." Playing cards, a favorite pastime of theirs, could trigger Babe's temper if she lost. "I've seen Babe just act like a horse's ass about that," Dodd interjected. "We used to play canasta a lot down there in Tampa, and Patty Berg would come and she'd play with us and I'll tell you if Babe didn't win she'd quit. She'd say, 'I'm tired of playing this. I don't want to play anymore.' Now if she was winning, she'd stay up all night . . . [then] she didn't want anybody to quit."[52]

Sometimes these scenes turned ugly. On a Port Aransas, Texas, fishing trip Babe lost at canasta because Dodd and her sister Peggy "ganged up on her to keep her from winning, because that's part of the strategy and she knew it." "Well," Dodd recounted, "she blew her stack—she was losing. And she let me have it up one side and down the other. And I said, 'Well, Babe, that's the way you'd play.' Well, my sister was furious at Babe because she acted like such a jackass."[53]

In another instance Dodd, Babe, Yogi Berra, and Al Lopez planned to play against each other in Florida. A one-armed golf pro named Jimmy Nichols colluded with Babe to dupe Berra, who didn't know Nichols's skill as a pro. "So Babe said to Jimmy, 'Let's get old Yogi. You come out and I'm going to tell him that you're my caddy . . . and that you're trying to learn to play the game.'" Babe approached Yogi and said under her breath, "This guy, he's only got one arm and I really feel sorry for him, so I've been giving him some work . . . and he'd just be thrilled to death to say he'd played with you. So how about letting him hit some shots?" Agreed, the game began. Jimmy intentionally muffed his first two holes, then on the third tee Babe gave him the go-ahead. He slammed the ball "260 down the middle and then he took an iron and knocked it over the water and did the par 5 hole in two." Yogi was silent. Jimmy aced the next hole too, then Yogi said, "Hey, what's going on here?" Tickled, Babe introduced Nichols as "the finest one-armed player in the world." Commented Dodd, who'd loved the display and prank as much as Babe had, "I guess Yogi didn't mind too much."[54]

Didrikson's fierce competitive spirit sometimes led her to bend the rules. Jameson readily admitted that Babe falsified practice scores to "out-perform" Louise Suggs and fuel their rivalry. When she'd "come in from a practice round she'd give them [the press] a good newspaper score. And Louise would just be livid about it. She'd say 'Oh! that liar.'" But Jameson chuckled recalling Babe's motives: "Babe was just trying to get a little good press and get the people out there. . . . She'd say . . . 'They're not going to come see anybody shoot 80.'" Peggy Kirk Bell told of similar practice "score adjusting" incidents. Babe's grandstanding surfaced again during the Tampa Open. On the eve of the tournament, at a dinner party with about twenty golfers and friends, Jameson announced, loud enough for it to reach Babe's ears via George, "I think Joyce Wethered is the greatest woman golfer that ever lived."

As an arch rival, Betty was trying to antagonize and irk Babe. When Babe got up to the mike to accept her trophy she said, "I just want to thank the girls for not playing so well this week and letting me win so easily. And you know, there are 8 to 10 girls out on this tour that are better than Joyce Wethered ever thought of being!" Peggy Kirk Bell asked Betty, " 'What's she bringing Joyce Wethered up for?' Jameson answered, 'Oh something I said.' Nobody else got the gist of that . . . but I got a good laugh out of it." While her cohorts agreed that Babe didn't cheat, there's some consensus that she "would edge as close to illegality as she could to win a nickel in a golf match."[55]

But by the end of her 1951 Tampa tournament triumph over Berg, Didrikson's competitive spirit had paled. Even the effervescent Berg had a hard time convincing herself that the "routine of traveling, strange hotels, dreary dinners, and the Spartan life of a professional athlete" weren't exhausting. At the close of the tournament Babe resolutely announced to the *Time* reporter that she was "going home to pots and pans." Babe was spent. She was the world's dominant female athlete, comfortably well-off, bone-weary, and increasingly lonely.[56]

CHAPTER NINE

Mates

By 1950 Babe overwhelmingly desired one thing: a permanent home. For most of the year she'd been the playing pro at Grossinger's swank upstate New York resort. In October she became the teaching pro at the Sky Crest Country Club outside of Chicago, which paid her $20,000 annually. The club had become their temporary "permanent" residence, which was fine with George, but not okay with Babe. She and George "were really living high off the hog," she wrote later. There was still playfulness between them and he chided her on occasion about her humble origins. One night after a long day of teaching golf he told her to get dressed—they were going out. "I put on my new girdle and one of my best new dresses," Babe recalled, "and got myself all dolled up for dining and dancing and whatever else George had in mind." George drove them to a diner where he ordered two hamburgers, two bowls of chili, and two glasses of buttermilk—her standard "on the road" fare before she turned professional. He did this to resurrect her unpretentious roots and to balance the posh atmosphere and choice steaks that had been theirs at the club. This spontaneity and willfulness of George's still appealed to Babe in part.[1]

George's behavior did not alleviate Babe's restlessness, however. From her viewpoint Sky Crest was just another country club and not a home. In fact she was probably more unhappy there than she had been for some time. Although she claimed in *This Life I've Led* that the predominantly Jewish membership "means absolutely nothing to me . . . it's what you are and what you do that counts," the truth was it did make a difference. Babe wrote a letter to Bertha Bowen saying that she had to work with Jews and had been trying to get out of her contract because of it. "Ultimately," biographers found, "Babe was asked to leave the Sky Crest job because many of the members thought she was hustling them for extra money."[2]

Once she was free of her obligations to Sky Crest she increasingly nee-dled George to buy their own place. From George's perspective, Babe's de-sire for her own home had become "an obsession." In fact, several friends related George's hesitancy to "allow" Babe to settle down. The more she argued for it, the madder he got. Dodd described it thus: "He wanted her going. He wanted to push her as hard as he could. To the next tournament, the next exhibition, the next this, the next that. He didn't want her to be happy in one place where she might not want to go do those things." Final-ly, after much cajoling, she convinced George to take a huge step and invest their funds and futures in the purchase of the Forest Hills Country Club in Tampa, Florida. Once renamed the Tampa Golf and Country Club with its membership boosted to 375, it served as their base until 1955.[3]

Just because they had a house didn't mean George would stay in it, how-ever. His wanderlust was legendary amongst those who knew him well. Bowen, golf peers, family members, and Dodd all noted its disturbing reg-ularity. Bowen said simply, "George liked to ride the road." He'd pack him-self and his belongings into his Cadillac and drive off for weeks at a time, "seeing after his investments," viewing the countryside, or simply heading "places unknown." This conflicted terribly with Babe's love of domestic se-curity and signaled their growing dissatisfaction with the marriage.

Didrikson's affection and even tolerance for Zaharias had disintegrated considerably since the early days of their marriage. George's appearance was a source of constant friction between them. She "thought he was ugly as sin," Dodd said. He had grown increasingly obese since retiring from the ring, topping out at over 400 pounds. Babe would taunt him about his weight to his face and behind his back. "When I married George Zaharias," she would say, "he weighed 250 pounds and looked like a Greek god. Now he weighs 400 and looks like a gawddamned Greek." Babe, ever body-proud, found his eating habits repulsive. Bertha Bowen recalled him eating a stick of butter like a banana, and in his wrestling days he'd keep a gallon of olive oil in their refrigerator, dunk a whole loaf of bread in it, and gnaw the huge slab.[4]

According to Dodd, "they used to argue a lot about his appearance. She would say, 'George why don't you go clean yourself up.' I mean he was al-ways dripping stuff all over his shirts and we'd go into restaurants and he'd pick up the dern water pitcher off the table and drink out of it. It embar-rassed her." As his manners became unbearable, she'd leave him just sitting there as she table-hopped and talked with others.[5]

In the late 1940s Babe and George had dinner at the Dubsdred Country Club in Orlando, Florida. George, according to Hicks, dunked and soaked a hard roll "in his glass of milk with the apparent intent of softening it for more rapid consumption." Babe remonstrated him with: "'George! Don't you know that ain't polite?' 'What ain't polite?' growled George. George never merely spoke; he always emitted growls from his cavernous interior of his monstrous 300-pound body," Hicks editorialized. "'It ain't polite,'" announced Babe imperiously, "'to eat with your elbows on the table.'" Hicks's point is clear: they were an uncouth duo, especially George, and Babe was as appalled as Hicks at George's table manners.[6]

But, as Jameson commented, Babe pulled herself up, while George was not welcome anywhere. He was "just a big fat slob," she said. "I wouldn't want him to come in my house and sit down on the furniture—I don't think I have a heavy enough piece of furniture." His physique was so distorted that Jameson did not recognize his youthful portrait on the piano. Even Bell, ever loyal to the carefully crafted memory of the blissful union between George and Babe, conceded that "there were times when George drank too much [in public] and it used to embarrass Babe." He'd get "strong and loud" and "he was fat. . . . That bothered Babe." Yet Bell, like so many others, retreated from the truth by saying, "I think she lived a very happy life. She acted like she never had any trouble."[7]

Thelma Didriksen, observer to much of the trouble in the Zaharias marriage, remembered an incident at a Houston tournament. They were in the country club lounge and "George started drinking. And he drank so much and so fast until the waiters didn't even pick the glasses up. There was a row of glasses, one row after the other." On that occasion George was drowning his sorrows because he and Babe had fought bitterly, in front of Thelma, about Babe going on to the next tournament. Babe, who soaked frequently in hot tubs to quiet painful hemorrhoids, wanted a rest. "But he made her go," Thelma recalled.[8]

Babe, on most occasions, was not only dutiful but also appeared happy. Dodd emphasized how Babe had learned to act the part of the happy wife for the press. Their marital discord never made it into print, she said, because Babe wanted to present herself as a happily married woman. "I think she was afraid of him [physically]," Dodd said, so she didn't speak against him publicly. And while Dodd believed they were in love when they first got together, "after a while George got to be a burden to her. Here she was trying to climb up socially and he was dragging her down."[9]

George, once her greatest backer, had become her greatest liability. As Bertha Bowen said, "Well, he was an unattractive, big, fat Greek wrestler, and Greek wrestlers weren't members of country clubs." Early in their marriage, however, "he was a wonderful help to her because his knowledge of staging the wrestling matches and everything helped him a lot with public appearances for Babe. And he's due a lot of credit for that." Said Hicks, "George was a grunting grizzly bear of a man, with a deep vein of tenderness permitted to surface only if it did not interfere with a business objective." Similarly, Jameson grudgingly admitted, "he was faithful, agreeable, and 'never really got out of line.' They always took up for one another as far as I could see." In fact, George long fulfilled the role of "wife" for Babe until their relationship deteriorated. As Jameson noted, George took care of the mechanics of her life. "She was always nurtured. She could go out and do her thing. She was very fortunate. She had somebody there." Three men, McCombs, George, and Fred Corcoran, all played this role for her—but George did so the most proficiently—until Dodd came along.[10]

Hicks, in her 1954 journalistic foray, "A Lady Golf Pro Lets Her Hair Down: Next to Marriage We'll Take Golf," noted just how unusual it was for a female athlete to have a helpmate. Male pros generally had their wives to pack, unpack, read maps, wash, iron, and run errands for them. Female pros, she noted disgruntledly, did all their own "slave labor." Yet despite the unlikely prospect that a male spouse of a female pro would devote himself to her the way George did to Babe, Hicks noted that one-third of the female pros were married and that "most of the single pros admittedly are keeping one eye on the ball and the other peeled for a likely prospect to lure them from the circuit to the altar." Hicks's narrative reveals another point: even in golf, an upper-class, ladylike sport, female athletes' normalcy is measured by the degree to which they seek heterosexual partners.[11]

In addition to nurturing Babe, George also nurtured her golf game. Women pros are adamant on this point. Berg recalled in a *New York Times* interview, "I can remember her husband, George—who was Babe's biggest backer—watching Babe drive the ball hour after hour and then advising her, 'You're doing all this great driving, but let's see you chip and putt.'" Peggy Kirk Bell recalled that when George was on tour with Babe, "some nights he'd pound on my door and say 'Peg, you go over there and sleep in the room with Babe. I want her to win this tournament tomorrow and I snore.' And then he'd take my room." Bell said unequivocally, "I think his whole life was Babe. . . . All he wanted to do [was to] make her more famous than she was."[12]

At times his fawning devotion infantalized him and diminished Babe. Bertha Bowen recounted how George "loved to go down on the street corner and stand with Babe after she became famous to attract the public's attention. [He was] childlike, like that, he was an exhibitionist." Interviewers who were otherwise cautious in word selection vented ire and disdain toward George. He did not endear himself to many. Bill Nary shed his soft-spoken demeanor to call Zaharias boisterous, unscrupulous in business deals, and tightfisted. According to Nary, Zaharias swindled the golf pro he'd hired at Twin Orchard Country Club out of his salary by accusing him of stealing. He would lie, cheat people, and bet on his own golf game just to make a buck. Nary ascerbically declared, "George Zaharias still has his first dollar bill." "But the Babe," he beamed, "I can't say a word against her. She was the most wonderful gal you would ever want to meet. But George—people disliked him like mad. Like I say—number one on the hate parade." He "bragged for Babe" to promote her, but it rubbed people the wrong way. When Babe did it, it came across humorously, charismatically; when George aggrandized her, it turned sour.[13]

Despite his dislike Nary readily admitted that "George was wonderful to her and she loved George; they were a compatible couple in spite of George's personality." He, like many others, conceded that their loyalty to one another was ironclad. Betty Dodd recognized that Didrikson often felt ambivalence and hostility for her husband, but she never allowed it to show. "She was very loyal to George. She didn't want the world to know that she had those kinds of feelings about George because it had always been the other way." She wasn't merely worried about what others might think, however. Dodd concluded that "she didn't want to blow her cover" as a happily married woman.[14]

Those around Didrikson knew she wasn't happy despite appearances and they didn't like the way George treated her. Jameson acknowledged, "Oh, he wasn't really a great guy as far as a lot of us were concerned. He didn't let Babe run her life. I mean he was her manager. Always. She couldn't keep her own money, so she kept her own bank account that he didn't even know about. But mostly he had the purse strings." On a trip to New York with Betty Dodd, Babe singlehandedly wrangled a $6,000 miniwindfall in three weeks through television appearances, including the "Ed Sullivan Show." She negotiated $1,000 to $1,500 per appearance. Thrilled and proud, she phoned George in Tampa to tell him. Betty Dodd recalled, "George was furious and told her to get home. He knew he was losing control of her, that she didn't need him. She hung up the phone and said to me, 'Damn him! If he thinks I'm going to go home so he can book me for $300 in some exhibition, he's crazy!'" Several women on the tour were aware of how much George controlled the money even though Babe earned it, a financial arrangement unusual for the period. As a result,

George didn't treat her golfing peers well. His control of the money was "hard" on Babe, yet, Jameson commented, "Babe in a way liked that, she trusted him." In short, "she coped with George."[15]

Coping was about all she was able to do. In 1953, a reporter unknowingly revealed the distance between Babe and George. "The only door inside the house," he noted casually enough, "is to the bedroom where George sleeps in a double bed and Babe in a single bed." This symbol of marital distance elicited none of the speculation that their eight-foot first bed had.[16]

The Era of Conformity

By the 1950s the cultural retreat back into femininity for women was well under way. Despite notable changes in clothing (pants were first advertised in *Ladies Home Journal* in 1948) and a new acceptance of store-bought items (canned orange juice and Hydrox cookies), the average American housewife was living in an ever-narrowing world, as evidenced by the frustrations women expressed in their letters to advice columnists.[17]

The decade of the 1950s has been called "the era of conformity" and is seen by some historians as "a part of the legacy of the war experience." The war, as one scholar pointed out, "generated no ideological or institutional legacy that could aid in resolving the growing contradiction in women's lives." Others argue that the 1950s were also an era of "personal growth" for certain professional and creative women. These factors coalesced to produce the "feminine mystique." Striking middle-class women, it was loosely defined as a psychological malaise accompanied by feelings of purposelessness and dependency. Although caught between the two poles of career and home, Babe tried to— and wanted to—fit and conform. She embraced the 1950s rush to suburbia, yearned for togetherness with a spouse, and eagerly participated in the "do-it-yourself" craze that for women manifested itself as "redecorating their homes, planting gardens, and making their own clothes."[18]

The decade propounded "passivity, dependence, and the desire to raise children [as] the formula for female contentment." Far from passive, independent, and incapable of having children, Didrikson remained discontent despite her attempts at domesticity. She still yearned for someone to really share a home with her. When Babe met Betty Dodd, a nineteen-year-old with a captivating smile and eye-catching red hair and freckles, she found the partner she had longed for. When they met in 1950 at an amateur tournament in Miami, Dodd was twenty years Babe's junior and deemed the new rising star on the women's golf tour.[19]

When Babe approached Betty's father, General Dodd, after the 1950 Women's Titleholder's in Atlanta, she said, "I want Betty to go back to Tampa. I want to work with her on her game." Dodd soon found out this was not completely true: "Well, she just wanted somebody to play with." Dodd was totally and unabashedly enamored of Babe. "I sort of just admired her," she began cautiously in 1987. "She was my idol sort of." Soon caution was abandoned: "Not sort of—she was."[20]

When their relationship started, Dodd stayed with Didrikson for two or three tournaments; then Babe would return to her home in Tampa where George thought she belonged. "Well, no one stopped him from being on the tour," Dodd said, "but he blamed me if she didn't want to go home." Betty was in awe of Babe's talent and fame and smitten by Babe's attention. "I had such admiration for this fabulous person," Dodd recalled. "I never wanted to be away from her even when she was dying of cancer. I loved her. I would have done anything for her."[21]

What began as youthful admiration for a charismatic idol on Dodd's part and desire for a "running buddy" on Didrikson's grew into a mutually enriching and satisfying intimate relationship. She and Babe became constant companions. Dodd lived with the Zahariases in their converted clubhouse-turned-dreamhouse in the midst of the Tampa golf course from 1950 until Babe's death in 1956. Although a sexual relationship was never publicly acknowledged, they became each other's primary partner.

Their silence on this point is a matter of survival given the times. The conservative culture of the 1950s fostered a virulent homophobia alongside women's scripted return to domesticity. "An upsurge of media interest in sexual crime and 'perversion' intensified public hostility toward homosexuality. Police raids on gay bars, military purges, and the firing of homosexual government employees under Cold War security policies added to the homophobic atmosphere of the 1950s." Still, it's possible to learn about their life together. As one historian noted, "the methodological problem of how to find evidence about lesbianism when silence and invisibility have been integrated to lesbian experience" poses a challenge. Female narrators learn to "edit" their lesbian experience. Without "violating the limits set by narrators," one can listen to the use of language, and "even under these constraints, . . . learn valuable information about" their lives. Together, without George, Dodd and Didrikson built a complete life. "We always had a lot more fun when he wasn't around," Dodd said forthrightly.[22]

Happy at home, Didrikson was equally happy on tour. The year 1952 started off with athletic and economic splendor for Babe. "I was up around the top in every tournament I played," Babe happily recalled. She won the Women's Titleholder's in March and took the first two legs of the four-city Weathervane tournament. She was the women's leading money winner at the end of April.[23]

Then the bottom fell out. Babe's autobiography religiously chronicles a searing "trouble in my left side [that] was really getting to me. The pain and the swelling came more often. They were more severe, and I couldn't seem to shake off the attacks as fast as I had before." In each tournament city, according to Babe's narrative, "George was with me, and he was getting worried. He thought I should take some time off and find out what was wrong." At the Seattle leg of the Weathervane "those thirty-six holes were just agony for me," she said, uncharacteristically revealing her vulnerability. But not until she finished the final round did she admit, "the pain was so bad now that I couldn't stand it any longer. I told George, 'I think I'd better go to a hospital.' He said, 'I think so too.'" In "The Babe and I" (1957) George detailed his repeated efforts to get Babe to see a physician.[24]

Yet, according to others George pushed her to continue playing. Dodd, in particular, recalled it quite differently. Babe and George fought in front of Dodd over Babe's continuing on; he insisted that she do so. George, Dodd said, didn't want Babe's illness to interfere with his bookings for her or the tournament schedule.[25] George took off in one direction in their car and Babe drove with Dodd as far as Salt Lake City. In Salt Lake, Babe caught a plane to Beaumont to see Dr. W. E. Tatum. The pain had become unbearable.

Admitted into the Hotel Dieu Hospital, sans George, she was diagnosed with a strangulated femoral hernia, a protrusion at the top of her left thigh bone that stopped the circulation of the blood supply in the tissue. Tatum told her, "If I'd let it go another week I might have been a goner." She was anemic from overexertion and fatigue so much so that they postponed the surgery for several days until she was "built up." Then she came through the hernia surgery fine and returned to Tampa to recuperate.[26]

Sidelined, Babe was as restless as a grounded flier. She "chipped and putted" a little while she mended. As she wrote Tiny Scurlock, "I'm feeling fine now, but still won't do anything for a couple months and I got warning just today from The Doctor. Take it easy he says—I'm not ready." She loved to boast in later years how she hit the honorary "first ball" at the National Women's Open in Philadelphia in June. Too recently postoperative to play the whole tournament—or to risk swinging a driver—she took a three-iron "and smacked that ball out there 180 or 190 yards. And that was as long as most of the drives that were made off that tee the first day." When Tatum gave her the go ahead to reenter competition at the world championship, the Tam O'Shanter in Chicago, she was delighted. It had been dubbed by insiders "The Babe Zaharias Benefit" because she'd won it all four times it had been played. She was strong on days one and two then faded in the later rounds. She wound up third behind Betty Jameson and Patty Berg.[27]

She redoubled her efforts and stormed back to win the Texas Women's Open at her nemesis, the course in Fort Worth, in October. Yet despite ending on this high note the year was a disappointment for Babe. Though coming in second or third several times, she won only four of the twenty tournaments she competed in: the Titleholder's Championship in Augusta, the Fresno and Texas Opens, and the Miami leg of the Weathervane. She was the fifth money winner with $7,503.25.[28]

After the circuit ended for 1952, Babe retreated to Tampa and was plagued by chronic, bone-wracking fatigue. No sharp pain, just "no gas." The new year began with mediocre performances; a good round would be followed by a lousy back nine. As Babe lamented, "Those wonderful rubdowns that George gave me never seemed to reach quite deep enough any more to get all the tiredness out of my muscles." Noticeably absent is any mention of the physical attention given Babe by Dodd; to have acknowledged it would have insinuated lesbianism.[29]

In March she placed second to Berg in the Jacksonville Women's Open, sixth in the Women's Tiltleholder's, out of the running in the Peach Blossom–Betsy Rawls Tournament in Spartanburg, South Carolina, and second to Berg in the New Orleans Women's Open. At the Beaumont tournament created in her honor, the Babe Zaharias Open, Babe was determined to make as strong a showing as she could—and to see Dr. Tatum the morning after the final round. Her stamina was nil.[30]

Babe, up by one stroke over Suggs after two days, said, "The last day it was more of an effort to play than ever. I wasn't in command of my shots the way I'd been the first two rounds." It was at this point in her autobiography, on page 195 of 232, that Babe introduced Dodd, saying, "My buddy, Betty Dodd, a girl I encouraged to go into professional golf, had completed her own round and came out to root me home." At Babe's request Dodd told her that Suggs had finished with a 213 total, Berg with a 219. Babe managed a birdie on the eighteenth to capture the tournament with a 212. She was mobbed and cheered by the hometown gallery. Dodd, Berg, "and some of the other girls rushed onto the green and lifted me up in the air. They practically carried me off to the clubhouse. Television cameras were going and everything." But instead of feeling jubilation, Babe felt near collapse. She retreated to her bed and awaited her early morning appointment with Tatum at the Beaumont Hospital Hotel Dieu.[31]

The warning signs had been unmistakable. She had noticed blood in her stool a few months earlier. Relying on their ever-increasing intimacy, she confided only in Betty Dodd. Dodd persuaded Babe to see a doctor and suggested that it could be cancer.[32] Babe procrastinated but finally phoned Dr. Tatum of Beaumont, who gave her the leeway she'd been hoping for. He allowed her to wait to see him until the upcoming golf tournament that would bring her back into the area. Although relieved by the temporary reprieve, Babe still harbored secret fears and doubt as she became increasingly weary on the tour.

Babe, rarely one to share her feelings, confided her growing fear of cancer to Dodd alone. As she recalled in her memoirs, "I'd never even hinted at such a thing to George. . . . I continued to keep my cancer fears a secret from him."[33] This reluctance to turn to her husband reveals two critical trials Babe faced: the dwindling intimacy within their marriage and his inability to cope with her illness. Babe was not prepared to take care of George; it was abundantly clear to her that he was incapable of caring for her.

When Babe was diagnosed with colon cancer, journalistic speculation that her career was over began immediately. Tatum's prognosis, shared honestly only with Dodd and George and kept from Babe, was grim. Babe, erroneously believing her situation curable, positioned gallantly. George and Betty shared denial and despair. Unofficially quoting a doctor and a close friend, *Newsweek* reported "that a great athletic career was over." Deluged with over two thousand messages within a few days, Babe, the *Newsweek* reporters noted, "took the setback steadily." Refusing to join the emotional fray, Babe's only comment was " 'Tell everybody hello.' "[34]

Constructing a Unified Self

As Babe gained fame with a new and rekindled audience during her cancer bouts, she finally secured her feminine image. Her confidant on one occasion, Will Grimsley, snowballed Babe's ballyhooed love of home and hearth so greatly that as she battled her cancer he wrote, "If Babe Zaharias, the world's greatest all-around woman athlete, is forced by her present illness to give up all sports competition, she probably won't mind too much. She'll still have George and her roses." This patently absurd statement, given Babe's fierce competitiveness, desire to excel, and love of the limelight, is exceeded only by Grimsley's "insider" observation that "she has always regarded herself as first and foremost a housewife." But Grimsley was not delusional. He followed Babe's lead. As before in her life, genuine sentiment and hyperbole meshed to form myth.[35]

This myth became increasingly important as her relationship with Betty Dodd deepened. Babe wanted more than to distance herself from her problematic past. She chose to comply with definitions of appropriate feminine pursuits to deflect speculation about her liaison with Dodd and to distinguish herself as a beacon of respectable womanhood. In fact, she had internalized, at least in her public self, the need to denounce her hazy gendered past. She began by denouncing her own athletic achievements. Speaking in the 1940s, she editorially echoed the critics' condemnation of competitive team sports for girls: "And those individual, 'feminine' events are the best sports for women—some of the others are really too strenuous for girls." As one columnist commented, "It seems strange to note in dispatches that Babe, now Mrs. George Zaharias, frowns on almost all forms of strenuous athletics." She advocated limiting women's activities to golf and swimming. "Track and field, basketball and even tennis are too severe," Babe declared. "They age one terribly."[36]

Speaking in 1955 she recounted how she was often approached by parents who predicted athletic accomplishments for their daughter "because she's the biggest tomboy in the neighborhood." "That's fine," Babe would retort, "being a tomboy when you're a youngster. Because the years will take care of any girl who is a tomboy. When you get to a certain age, and you start growing in places where you weren't developed before, then nothing can stop you from changing. You've just got to go with it."[37]

The press, as always, went with this new image right along with Babe. When Dodd moved into the Tampa home with the Zahariases, the press didn't miss a beat. Biographers William Oscar Johnson and Nancy Williamson blandly noted only that "Betty Dodd came and stayed with them often, although she and George did not get along well." According to *Readers' Digest* Babe and George "had virtually adopted a 21-year-old San Antonio youngster, Betty Dodd, one of the finest of the new crop of players." And Paxton wrote of "the devoted friendship of her young golf protégé, Betty Dodd, who was in there helping at every step as the Babe and George settled into their new home." Minimization or invisibility often overshadowed more accurate portrayals of their bond.[38]

Characterizations of their relationship by others are a study in contrasts. They range from culturally induced homophobia to deep appreciation of their affinity. Peers and friends openly acknowledge Dodd's centrality in Babe's life. Hicks, who described Dodd as "the gangly Texas redhead and long-ball hitter," said "the companionship, competition, adulation, loyalty and solicitude of Betty Dodd were deeply meaningful to Babe." Jameson deemed them confidants who "had each other's ears." Bell felt Didrikson really needed Dodd and that Dodd was wonderful to her.[39]

Others who knew Dodd and Babe less well still knew their relationship was rumored to be lesbian. Nancy Corcoran said, "I heard lots of rumors, but I don't know anything really." Bill Nary, singularly hesitant to speak of their relationship, said, "I just heard about [Betty Dodd]. . . . You're probably aware of it, but I don't even want to mention it." Far later in the conversation, after much prodding, Nary admitted "that the girls on the tour said that they were lesbians, and I think from hearsay that I thought she [Dodd] was one of those mentioned. But as far as I know, Babe and Betty Dodd never—she was all woman."[40]

Always spoken in whispers, speculation on their relationship equated lesbianism exclusively with intimate sexual contact and the dreaded link with mannish/butch working-class athletes. It failed to acknowledge the intimate emotional and physical interdependence of the relationship. Defined as such it was taboo and thought to discredit and minimize them both.

Young Dodd's boyish appearance encouraged the link with working-class athletes. As Bertha Bowen said, "Betty would go around looking just awful." Babe, however, was attracted to Dodd's untamed ways. Through Dodd she could vicariously experience what she had felt when she was more in touch with herself and less schooled in feminine behaviors. Significantly, Babe tried to break Dodd of these masculinist ways much as she'd been broken. "You talk about being a girlish type," Bertha Bowen remarked. "Babe was more girlish than Betty Dodd in appearance. People didn't know if Dodd was a girl or a boy."[41]

Betty Dodd: Protégé, Buddy, Partner

Babe's coolness in introducing Dodd, her placement of her toward the very end of her life narrative, and the appellation "buddy," while apt, all minimize their bond. They had been virtually inseparable before the fateful April revelation from Tatum. Babe chose not to reveal their intimacy to the public until her illness made it unavoidable and more acceptable.

Leila J. Rupp, a historian writing on women's relationships, identified "the charismatic leader who attracts intense devotion" from those working with her. At times this devotion becomes almost hero worship. In many ways this characterizes the relationship shared by Didrikson and Dodd. The youthful Dodd, enamored of Babe's stature, rarely challenged her. In photographs Dodd is usually in the background gazing admiringly at Babe. And Babe, twenty years older, saw in Dodd a younger version of herself: untamed, boyish, and talented.[42]

But Dodd was not really Babe's protégé, despite attempts by the press and others to categorize their relationship that way. "She never taught me anything," Dodd said. "She wasn't interested in teaching me how to play golf, she was interested in winning her own deal." If Babe wanted to skip work and play cards, go fishing, go to the show, "that was the way it was." In fact, Babe's support and presence actively rattled Dodd on the golf course. At Sea Island, Georgia, Dodd led after two of three days, and Babe was way down the list. When Babe came onto the course and followed Dodd on the backside, it made Betty self-defeatingly nervous. Dodd knew Babe's was a gesture of support, and her reaction made no sense because "I'd only played 500 rounds of golf with her." Perhaps, Dodd theorized, "I was trying too hard to please her." Dodd played poorly and lost the tournament to Berg under Babe's watchful eyes. Tellingly, Hicks recalled that Babe intentionally pulled Dodd away from attentive reporters while Dodd held the lead. To many it appeared that Dodd's excellence and fledgling fame irked Babe.[43]

The relationship impaired Dodd's career as a golfer, according to Hicks. Dodd readily admitted that her own career was undercut due to her devotion to Babe. "I've been accused by a lot of other women golfers of just being so wrapped up in what Babe did that I didn't nearly reach the potential that I should have. . . . Babe just didn't take up with me because I was a cute kid. She thought I had a lot of talent. And in one way she wanted to help me and in another way she did not want me to beat her."[44]

Theirs, clearly, was not an equal relationship. Dodd consciously acquiesced to all of Babe's decisions and moods; she had sampled her disapproval and avoided it judiciously. When angered, Babe would become unpredictably cool toward Dodd, at times acting as if she didn't know her. Dodd confided, "I never would have wanted to have crossed her. I mean, that would have never occurred to me to cross her, but I think to myself a lot of times now that if I ever crossed Babe I don't know what she might have done or how she might have reacted. But there was no chance of that, because I just loved her. She was just something else as far as I was concerned." Despite these inequities and tensions, when I interviewed her in 1987 one fact emerged; she still missed Babe wholeheartedly and tenderly.[45]

Together they concentrated on the good times. Jameson noted Babe liked to play the harmonica, Dodd the guitar, and they'd do so by the hour. Said Hicks, they "are inveterate gin players, when they're not whipping up a new rendition of some folk tune." Even Wilson's Women's Golf Information Guide, distributed to journalists writing about Babe, noted, "she and Betty Dodd, who excels on the guitar, entertain frequently with Texas ditties." Their musical soirees brightened many a drab locker room and often provided them with their only socialization on the golf tour. The two of them would sometimes have a few beers with the other players in the locker room, but most often, particularly after her operation, Babe wanted to go back to the motel and get into her pajamas. They isolated themselves from the rest of the tour. The jam sessions were the exception. "There have been some times," Dodd said of often otherwise strained relationships with golfing peers, "when we all had a good time. Particularly when we were playing the harmonica and the guitar. We did that a lot. Everybody would sit around and listen to it. She was good on that thing. She could really blow that thing." Berg, too, fondly recalled their music making. On one "fun night" before a tournament, Berg sang accompaniment.[46]

In fact, Didrikson and Dodd were more than just casual entertainment; they had become a smashing musical duo. They frequently entertained medical staff at the hospital and Galvestonians in their homes. After Babe hustled top-notch recording equipment, in one of her infamous self-promoting deals, they cut a record with Mercury. Babe played "Detour" on one side, and Dodd "sang a song on the other side of it which was really bad," by her own admission. They did an impromptu jam session on the "George Jessel Show" in New York and "the audience was beating the place down, you know, screaming and clapping like audiences do now."[47]

Their most famous performance came on the "Ed Sullivan Show" in 1953. Sullivan, then connected with the American Cancer Society, invited Babe because she had become a national inspiration. He introduced her saying, "the whole nation was shocked to hear she had cancer." Babe strode out with a golf club and chatted with him for a few minutes. Didrikson had also wrangled the opportunity to play her harmonica, accompanied by Dodd's guitar. Sullivan originally wanted a walk-on appearance only because he said, "I want all the people to see how you've licked this thing." Not only did Babe get the musical spot, but she also negotiated a $1,500 fee for herself and $350 for Dodd. On that same trip Babe booked herself on two hidden identity shows, "What's My Line" and "Masquerade."[48]

After her RKO days, Babe was certainly no stranger to the entertainment stage. The "Ed Sullivan Show" appearance followed hard on the heels of her 1952 winsome cameo in *Pat and Mike,* a slick, upbeat movie starring Katharine Hepburn and Spencer Tracy. The plot featured a female college gym teacher turned golf and tennis pro whose career was nurtured and promoted by her business partner and odds maker. The plot is undeniably reminiscent of the Didrikson-Zaharias union in that Hepburn, a multi-sport athlete, works together with Tracy, the devoted promoter, to make her a star. Hepburn and Didrikson, amidst a star-studded field of women golfers (including Beverly Hanson, Betty Hicks, and Helen Dettweiler), were pitted against one another in the finals at the Women's National Match Play Championship. In the film, Babe was introduced by the public address announcer as "the Mighty Babe" and "Mrs. Babe Zaharias," who turned in "a sensational 73." She was surrounded by an impressive entourage and posed for photographers before striding off confidently.

The script originally called for Hepburn to beat Babe. But Babe, true to competitive form, refused to lose—even in the movies. In fact, Babe thought Hepburn was "double-parked with herself," hence she refused to be outshone. So it was rewritten for her to win by one on the eighteenth green. When Babe sank her winning putt, she scooped the ball out of the cup, kneeled on the grass behind the hole, "kissed" the ball up to heaven, and jogged off. Mobbed by appreciative fans, Babe in her permed hair and calf-length A-line skirt donned a fitted cardigan with top button undone. Hepburn, as she shakes the victor's hand, is the only pro wearing slacks. Hepburn scorned the usual pro attire and insisted on wearing jodhpurs, a silk blouse, and jodhpur boots.[49]

Hepburn's clothes played up the masculine-feminine tension in the film. When Hepburn repels thugs beating up Tracy, his ego is offended and he laments, "I've built you into some kind of Frankenstein monster. . . . I like a she to be a she and a he to be a he." Although they revert to "normal" sex roles by falling in love, Hepburn's athletic body and her appearance as a "mischievous boy" are reminiscent of Babe's bewildering physical and psychological image. This film was a historical anomaly. With the exception of swimming movies starring the lovely and curvaceous Esther Williams and Annette Kellerman and ice skating films featuring everyone's sweetheart, Sonja Henie, films about fiercely competitive female athletes were as rare as Babe Didrikson's personal history.[50]

In a closing repartee worthy of Babe and George, Hepburn jabs at Tracy the way he jabbed at his other clients: "Who made you?" "You," he sheepishly responds. "Who owns the biggest part of you?" she prods. "You," he acquiesces. "What'd happen if I ever dropped you?" "I'd go right down the drain." "And," she prompts. He, determined to triumph at least once, departs from the usual refrain "And stay there" by ending with a teasingly telling, "And take you right down with me, shorty." Their symbiotic interdependence echoes that of their real-life counterparts.[51]

Naturally, "just like Babe" stories emerged from this Hollywood escapade. Jim Backus and Henny Backus wrote about Jim's experience playing a golf pro in *Pat and Mike*. "What teed Hepburn off above all was the fact that Babe Didrikson was completely unimpressed by her. Hepburn did everything to get her attention." Her recent triumph in *African Queen* with Humphrey Bogart swayed Babe not at all. One day, as they were filming on the course, a mammoth Cadillac limousine lumbered across the fairways and out stepped Bogart in person. "Hoping to shake Miss Didrikson's tree and with a triumphant gloat in her voice, Miss Hepburn shouted, 'Look who's here? It's Bogie! Bogie! Bogie!'" Given this perfect opportunity, barked Babe as she spun around, "'Lady, never say that word on a golf course.' She then drilled a drive down the fairway 275 yards for Bogie! Bogie! Bogie!" Always the last word. Always the victor. Always the idol's idol.[52]

While Babe's antics in the movies reached epic proportions her feuding with George reached explosive proportions. Bertha Bowen confided that George summoned her to the hospital during Babe's 1953 illness in Galveston saying, "Babe wants a six-month separation. We're just not getting along." Bertha's conversation with him, the exact contents of which she can't remember, led them both to Babe's bedside. Bertha comforted Babe while George took her hand and said, "Goodbye Babe, I'm gone." Bertha interrupted, "Oh you darn fools, come off it. And that was all there was to it. It was all over." Bertha's simplistic version of temporary discord is contradicted by later statements by her and others recounting their continual disagreements.[53]

Dodd readily admitted that Babe discussed divorcing George with her. "Oh, many a time, many a time . . . [but] she never discussed it with him [until the Bowen incident] because she was afraid of that. See she was his meal ticket . . . and she was beginning to be a little disenchanted with George and the way he did things. She was not pleased with the way he was managing her career. And she felt he was mean to her. I've seen a lot of incidents where he treated her like dirt. . . . You'll never see any of that in print." Although Babe complained, she was still unwilling to leave George. Bowen acknowledged that Didrikson mentioned "many times" that she wanted a divorce, but "Babe could talk out of one side of her mouth then do the opposite."[54]

Bertha ascribed blame to Dodd for fueling the sore points in the Zaharias marriage: "She was just the oil of the misery. She just kept things going." Babe would complain to Betty about George, then Betty "would be on Babe's side and that causes friction." Although these dynamics certainly operated within their relationship, Bowen also minimized the possible intimacy between the two women when she said, "A close girlfriend can cause trouble between a couple, not meaning to." Actually, more often than not, Dodd was responsible for smoothing over the rough spots in the marriage. When George bumped into her intravenous stand at the University of Texas Medical Branch in Galveston, where she was later admitted, Babe started screaming at him thinking he'd done it intentionally. In that instance, Dodd "covered for them" in front of the nurses.[55]

Dodd scorned the press portrayals in this era of their marriage. "It was ridiculous," she said. "It was the furthest thing from the truth. She wanted to call a lawyer to come in, to divorce them." In 1953 when Babe told George she wanted a divorce, "he really got mean. He got meaner than a snake." It was then that Betty and George's strained tolerance for one another exploded. George cornered Betty one night and said, "Me and Babe has been together and nobody's gonna break us up." Dodd, intimidated but furious, lashed back, "I have no intention of breaking you up." George felt Dodd could do so by contacting lawyers and arranging sequestered funds at Babe's bidding. Bertha Bowen, sister Lillie, and hospital personnel were within earshot of this confrontation.

But George's jealousy of Dodd was modulated by his need of her. She buffered an otherwise intolerable marriage by being Babe's devoted intimate. And she was the only caretaker Babe allowed to perform her most private functions. "He was jealous of me," Dodd stated flatly, "but as time went by . . . he couldn't afford to be anymore. Because he wouldn't do anything for Babe. He wouldn't help her." In what surely irked George, "he needed me," Dodd said.[56]

As the illness progressed, Dodd's presence and effect on Babe became increasing vital. Bowen clearly recalled how "Babe would have been in the bluest funk you ever saw if Betty hadn't been in the hospital with her. She put Babe's clubs right in the room with her where she could see them after the colostomy operation." Babe's dependence on Dodd accelerated, as did George's strained tolerance of his nemesis. As Babe's health deteriorated he too became dependent on Dodd to take care of Babe. He "never gave her a shot. Ever. As a matter of fact he didn't go anywhere near that. He wasn't involved in that at all." Nor did he once irrigate the colostomy.[57]

After a week of intravenous feeding following the colostomy, Babe went back on solid food and her bowel functions became uncontrollable. Dodd recalled, "With this type of operation you have no control, you never know when something is going to happen. She had just gotten out of the bathtub and she sat down and everything let go. Instinctively I just put out my hands. It was not that big a thing but from then on she wouldn't let anyone take care of her but me."[58] Irrigating the colostomy was done every other day. Betty, wearing rubber gloves, helped Babe through this demanding and elaborate procedure. In a colostomy the cancerous part of the colon is removed. If possible the two cut ends are sewn together to maintain a passageway for digested food. When this is not feasible, as in Babe's case, an opening called a stoma is made in the abdominal wall, through which digested material can pass into a bag. Emptying and cleaning the bag was a painful routine, but a chore Betty and Babe withstood as a resolute team. When Babe was in the hospital "she wouldn't let the nurses take care of her. She had to irrigate that colostomy every other day. . . . She wouldn't let the nurses help her with any of that. I did it. I'd been doing it all along. From the very beginning."[59]

Peggy Kirk Bell and others in Babe's inner circle appreciated and acknowledged Dodd's nurturance. "Betty just sort of gave up golf and everything to go stay with Babe when she got cancer. She was a really good friend to Babe. . . . [She] just stayed there with her and did all that." Jameson, too, said that Dodd, as well as Bell and Bowen, "filled a much needed friendship role for Babe."[60]

Dodd and Didrikson became inseparable. Every project of Babe's interested Dodd and she eagerly followed. In Tampa, Betty and Babe arranged a comfortable life. Its ease was proportionately related to George's absences. They didn't go out to dinner very much. Babe finally had the homelife she cherished. "I like to cook," Dodd recalled, "so I did a lot of cooking and so we'd eat at home. We went out to dinner every night on the tour, so it wasn't a treat to go out." Although their bond was much more intimate than Betty let on, she was most comfortable seeing herself as Babe's caretaker, an appropriate role for one woman to play for another. Dodd, in a sense, became Babe's wife: she allowed Babe to be the dominant personality, catered to her needs, and oversaw the comforts of her daily living.

After the 1953 colostomy, Dodd maintained no other residence than with Babe. They were either on the road together or at their Tampa home. "I lived there with 'em," Dodd said, "And that was one of the things that I think [George] didn't like. He felt like that there—that well—you know what he thought. You know exactly what he thought." Although George recognized the extent of Betty's relationship with Babe, "he never talked about it. I think he was afraid to talk about it. I think he thought she'd kill him." And he didn't speak of his fear of lesbianism to Dodd either. "He just sort of acted like, you better—you're not going to take her away from me. Not that I was trying to," Dodd qualified it. "But the problem was," she continued, "that Babe did not have anybody except for Bertha and R. L. And they were an older couple; they couldn't go and do things with her and she needed a playmate." In a telling portrayal of a central aspect of their relationship, Dodd said, "I mean that's what Babe liked. She wanted someone to talk with her all the time, she wanted somebody to travel with her, she wanted somebody to go here, to go there, she wanted a playmate and a friend. And she didn't have anybody else."[61]

Dodd became Didrikson's playmate, friend, and ideal mate. Her love and admiration of Babe were unswerving. Dodd, privy to Babe's charms and idiosyncracies, loved her in all her complexities. She delighted in Babe's impromptu tap dances, shared her love of Bebe the poodle, arranged the dog's visits to Babe's apartment near the hospital, anguished with Babe when George had her tan and white cocker spaniel euthanized without Babe's consent while they were at the National Open in Atlanta, and listened to Babe's confidences, infrequent as they were.

Babe on several occasions told Dodd "that all her children were swimmers." In Babe's lexicon, that meant she'd miscarried. Although this implies Babe had several miscarriages, only one is known. Her interest in having these children remains unclear. Betty Jameson believed Babe wanted children, and Peggy Kirk Bell attributed a strong yearning for motherhood to Babe. When Babe learned of Peggy's pregnancy, "she went crazy, and said, 'Oh, I'd give up every trophy I've ever won to have a baby.'" When Peggy asked her why she and George didn't adopt, Babe said, "George won't let me. I tried to do that." Bell interjected her own insight that "that would have cramped their life and he was interested in promoting her and making her the greatest." Dodd, however, claimed, "She never did say that she wished she had a child. . . . It didn't sound to me like she was very upset about it. Ever."[62]

When Peggy's daughter was born, Babe rejoiced for Peggy, told everyone in town before Peggy had, and urged the new mom to "choose a name that would look great in print." Preferably "Babe." But the chosen "Bonnie" was good media copy to Babe's trained eyes and ears. Babe said of the infant, "I'm going to teach her how to play golf! It's great you had a girl. There are a lot of great men athletes but there are not many great women." The importance of childlessness to Babe remains an enigma. She loved other people's children, but whether, given the opportunity, she would have curtailed her own freedoms and self-centeredness for parenthood remains open to conjecture.[63]

In fact, conjecture was one of Dodd's only tools for understanding Babe. For example, after Babe lost weight, she wore bermuda shorts around the house (although never in public). Dodd surmised this was because Babe thought she looked good in them. Also, her Olympic medals, stuffed unsanctimoniously in a coffee can on the kitchen counter of her house, were hidden, Dodd knew, not because there was no room to display them, as Babe claimed, but because Babe wanted to disavow her track and field past.

Dodd alone was privy to Babe's feelings toward her siblings. Of her sister Nancy, the "fancy Didriksen," Dodd said, "I don't think Nancy understood one single thing that made Babe tick. . . . I don't think Babe would have gone twenty-five miles to see her." Conversely, Dodd reiterated Babe's love of "matronly Lillie," and of Louis, her next favorite, whom they often visited with his wife, Thelma, in Newton. Bubba and Jackie were within Babe's "inner circle," Dodd knew, as their trips to Baytown confirmed. And Dodd certainly appreciated Babe's sentimental attachment to a treasured ring with stones that had belonged to Hannah. That, and her prized Rolex, were the only pieces of jewelry that she wore; their meaning, unarticulated, was clear to Betty.

And Dodd knew Babe's dark side, too: the temper outbursts when losing, the ugly scenes, and, Dodd revealed, Babe would drink to numb her disappointment if she lost. "Babe could get pretty loaded," Dodd said. "And it was always on beer. I think that's why she got heavy. And she could drown her sorrows pretty good in a few bottles of beer." Despite these morose moments, though, Dodd wryly commented, losing "didn't make her feel like she was not still the star. I'll tell you that."

Given her own skirmishes with innuendo, it's not surprising that Dodd was particularly savvy about Babe's determination to appear feminine. Thus Babe's retrospective silence about the Olympics Dodd attributed to "Babe [doing] everything in her power to make people feel that she was a lady, she never did talk about any of her accomplishments except for golf." Said Dodd assertively, "As much as I was with her, as long as I was with her and as well as I knew her, I never heard her talk about the Olympics. She just didn't talk about it."

Making people "feel she was a lady" involved dressing the part too. Dodd maintained, "she definitely did it for the public image. No question about it. I think she was much more comfortable in tailored clothes. She looked better in tailored clothes. And when she started to put on some of this fru-fru stuff, which she did occasionally, to me it looked kind of ridiculous. [She'd do it] for this feminine thing that she was trying to make people think."

Equally culturally constructed was her happy marriage. Dodd realized that despite tense discord and soured hopes with George, Babe fueled the image of their harmonious union for the benefit of the press. Babe, Dodd believed, sheltered the press from their strife because "she felt that she was safe being married. She had already been through a lot of bad vibes with people when she was an Olympic star. And when she got to be a feminine person being married was part of it." To this end, Babe essentially abandoned using the name Didrikson. "She never used it. She signed the D. She signed Babe D. then Zaharias. Always. She never signed her name any other way." Babe's determination to keep the union intact, or at least its reputation intact, was, according to Dodd, because "she was interested in her public image. And being married to George was part of her public image."[64]

As always, Babe with one hand carefully sculpted the clay of her image while with the other hand engagingly enlisted the aid of others in her task. Her relationship with Dodd allowed her to shape her own legacy through her own words but also through Dodd's. Quite likely Dodd censored her telling of their relationship accordingly. The inducements for a woman to reveal a lesbian life to a national audience are few; the reasons for silence, many.

CHAPTER TEN

"I'm Not Out
of the Rough Yet!"

With cancer Babe was, more than ever, like a queen holding court. A national press corps, clustered around the edge of her bed in the Beaumont hospital, leaned in to catch every word. Her operation had been only hours earlier. Flash bulbs went off, as the subject of all this attention was coaxed to "give us a smile, Babe." She complied willingly. As always, Babe was center stage, using her charismatic wiles to engage and entertain the press. She was quick-tongued and ever able to provide a snappy one-line retort. And she used the media as her audience in her battle against cancer just as she used fans in the golf gallery to improve her competitive edge.

In *This Life I've Led,* Didrikson described her response to her cancer: "All my life I've been competing—and competing to win. I came to realize that in its way, this cancer was the toughest competition I'd faced yet. I made up my mind that I was going to lick it all the way. I not only wasn't going to let it put me on the shelf. I was determined to come back and win golf championships just the same as before."[1] This passage reveals the determination and unswerving competitive nature of the woman the Associated Press named the Female Athlete of the Half Century in 1950.

Didrikson needed and used all of her bravado to confront and manage the most demanding challenge of her life. Aside from her hernia operation in 1952, she had rarely been ill. In fact her body's natural athleticism and disciplined responses were her greatest source of pride and certainty. Since her childhood Babe had enjoyed a cohesiveness and confidence between body and mind that few ever know. The onset of cancer, then, was devastating indeed, more so for Babe because her body had always been her staunchest ally.

After consulting with Dr. Tatum in Beaumont and learning of her cancer, Babe called Dodd, weeping, and said, "I've got to be operated on. I've got to have a col . . . col . . ." Dodd recalled that Babe "couldn't say the word. I said 'Colostomy?' and she said, 'That's right.'" Babe had never heard of a colostomy. Dodd told Babe, "I didn't think it was so bad. Because she dreaded it. More than anything in the world. And I don't even think she was as upset about the cancer as she was the colostomy." Dodd recalled, "It took ten days to build her up for the operation. I moved into the hospital room with her. George was around, but he kept insisting that she *didn't* have cancer."[2]

In Babe's surgery the doctors removed the malignancies from her rectum and colon, sutured her anus shut, and resected her bowel so that her solid waste could pass through an incision in the left side of her abdomen. For an athlete whose physical prowess had been her most valued and honed attribute, the psychological anguish of such a procedure is undeniable. Didrikson voiced the often-heard lament "Why me?" and was temporarily overwhelmed with the irony of her condition given her earlier charity work on behalf of the Damon Runyon Cancer Fund.[3]

When Babe recalled her reactions to the diagnosis, she made Dodd invisible while centering on George. "We didn't talk much. Big George, three hundred pounds of man, had tears in his eyes, and he wasn't ashamed of them, either. And I, well, I guess I was numb. The real terror was to come later. Right then all I could seem to think of was—Why did it have to happen to me?"[4]

The operation was performed at the Hotel Dieu Hospital in Beaumont on April 17, 1953, with Dr. Robert Moore from the nearby University of Texas Medical Branch as surgeon and Tatum assisting.[5] Why Didrikson chose a small Catholic hospital in Beaumont for her surgery speaks volumes about her. She was of the stature and finances to seek care at any medical center in the world. It was a choice in keeping with her working-class, East Texas background. By returning to the region where she was implicitly understood in all her brazen complexities, Babe surrounded herself with reassuring familiarities.

After more than four hours of surgery, Dr. Moore conferred with Betty and George, who shared the waiting room in anxious anticipation. Dr. Moore told them, "She's got three strikes against her." The operation had gone well, but malignancy in the surrounding lymph nodes signaled doom.

"George," Betty recalled, "went into hysterics and walked out." Dodd asked Moore how long he thought Babe had to live "and he said, 'I don't know. I don't want to say,' but he said, 'I just don't think she can live.'"[6] The colostomy would ease her pain for the time being but he suspected that the cancer would spread within a year. He suggested not divulging this prognosis to Babe. Dodd recalled, "George was crying, I don't think he heard a word Moore said. I just put the whole thing out of my mind."[7]

Betty and George followed Moore's advice and concealed from Babe that some cancer remained despite the surgery; "not telling" was rather common practice in the 1950s. "We did not tell her because neither one of us thought she could handle it—the fact that she wasn't going to live," Dodd said. "Now, she could handle everything else. But she couldn't handle that. She never was told that—never, ever. Until she just knew it herself. . . . It was not more than a month before she died that she finally resigned herself to the fact that she wasn't going to live. She fought it tooth and nail." Beyond this "reading" of Babe, why each agreed to the silence is instructive: one from the innocence of youth, the other from the weakness of self-involved emotionalism. Neither could face her eventual death. She was the lead character in the play, they were supporting actors, and she provided strength and direction to both.[8]

Bertha Bowen, like Dodd, recalled Babe's concern with George's distress. They were all in Dallas awaiting the results of the biopsy. "She was so pale and drawn and she said, 'B. B. [her nickname for Bertha], I think I've got it'—when George was out of the room—and that's all she said about that. And then at eleven o'clock they got back from the doctor and George just collapsed. He went up to the front of the house and she was in the back room with me where I am now and she said, 'In all honesty I'm not worried about myself, I'm worried about George.' And she meant it, because she knew he didn't have the stamina that she has to meet reverses like that and of course George liked to parade Babe." A biographer of Babe's confirms this portrait of George. "George was a worrier, he was especially a worrier when it came to Babe. Babe meant more than anything else to this big hulk of a man. He would break down and cry at even the least thought that anything might be wrong with her."[9]

And yet, despite this portrayal of George's solicitous devotion, he often treated her brutally. His denial of the severity of Babe's illness coupled with his desire to keep her bringing in the dollars accounts in part for his actions. Although he had partially acquiesced to Babe's desire for a home, he still refused to purchase the dream house of her own design she still so desperately wanted "because he didn't want her settled down. He wanted her go-ing," according to Dodd. "He wanted to push her as hard as he could to the next tournament, to the next exhibition. . . . He didn't want her to be hap-py in one place where she might not want to do those things . . . but when she first got sick in '53 things turned around a lot. I mean they changed drastically because he was scared to death. And he didn't know how to cope with her cancer."[10] Only then did they get their dream house, but even after her diagnosis he didn't stop pushing her beyond her strength.

Bowen recalled Dodd's resiliency to the diagnosis, although it was mixed with denial. When Bertha, R. L., Babe, and George received the news, Babe's first move was to call Betty in San Antonio. Dodd agreed to head for Fort Worth right away to join them. Bowen said this was what any one of them would have done for Babe, but it was particularly fitting that Dodd be thus summoned, because "she did everything for Babe."[11]

After the operation, a steadfast network of female friends encircled Babe. Patty Berg and Bertha Bowen visited frequently, while Dodd and Thelma Didriksen, with her sisterly bond with Babe, attended to the most intimate aspects of Babe's illness. Immediately after the operation, Thelma picked up not only Babe at the Hotel Dieu but also Dodd, who'd had an unexpected appendectomy. It must have been quite the sisterly scene as Thelma "had them both in the bed to start with." Press coverage, the most well-researched adult biography, and the 1975 movie *Babe* show a saddened and support-ive George helping her home. But Thelma was emphatic about this detail. "The book says that George picked her up, but George did not. I picked her up. She hardly ever knew where he was. He was in and out." He resided al-ternately with Thelma and Louis or in Galveston "even though she was in Beaumont's Hotel Dieu." Other contemporaries including kin, friends, and acquaintances verify that George's unpredictable behavior and wandering continued during Babe's illness.[12]

Babe's early plan to take a cottage in Galveston for her recovery was aban-doned once Betty had surgery and as she realized that George couldn't be counted on to be in residence or to be a caretaker. So she called Thelma and asked, "'Have you got room for two invalids?'" Thelma said, "'I told you that I did.'" Babe instructed her sister-in-law to "try to find George and get a check so I can get out of here." Thelma had no idea where to look, but for-tunately George pulled up "and he handed me a signed check. He more or less kept Babe's money where she couldn't get to it, I'm sorry to say."[13] Babe's empty pockets were not new. On another occasion, Babe called Louis and Thelma to lend her cab money to get from the Hotel Dieu back to their house—this by a woman earning some $100,000 per year. Money matters between the Zahariases worsened dramatically in these years and left Babe in a grossly vulnerable and dependent condition.

During these early days following the surgery, Thelma modified the doctor's orders to aid Babe's recovery and to make her as comfortable as possible. Irrigating the colostomy was daily fare. This was before air conditioning, so in an attempt to beat the heat, Thelma tinkered with cleansing, bed covers, and bandages, all aimed at improving Babe's comfort. Dodd exclusively assumed these chores when they left Thelma's. Even nurses during later hospitalizations were kept from this task.

Thelma also performed another valuable function by answering Babe's mail, particularly the letters from cancer and colostomy patients who sought advice on how to take care of themselves. Babe made this information sharing and role modeling a priority throughout her illness. Nurtured by her select inner circle of female friends and their concealment from her of the remaining cancer, Babe felt reassured. The series of events that followed brought Babe fame of a different sort, as a medical humanitarian.

Her Biggest Contest

Even before her surgery, Didrikson had requested, through the Associated Press, "that instead of flowers, please send all contributions to the [Damon Runyon] cancer fund." Just two hours before surgery, Tiny Scurlock was summoned to her bedside. He found her "cheerful, courageous and smiling with her usual quips." Babe remarked to Scurlock, "I'm tired of being on the sports page, put me on page one." Her mortal battle removed the last vestiges of her freakish image and made her a vulnerable woman to be admired. As a result, she saw her opportunity to capture the unquestioning acceptance and regal glory she had never quite managed to attain. More altruistically, she used her celebrity status to educate and reassure the public about cancer.[14]

Put on page one she was. Dispatches from Beaumont sent out over the United Press and Associated Press wires reported her every move, meal, statement, and reassuring salvo. The *New York Times* followed her recovery devoutly, an interesting choice for a newspaper that had only intermittently reported her sports accomplishments. Because the *Times* has never been known for its sports coverage, its legion of journalists helped make her name and achievements nationally known to a new audience. April 11, 1953, found her plight described on page ten, as thousands of get-well wires were sent to her in the hospital where she underwent tests. "Three-Hour Operation on Mrs. Zaharias" on April 18 reported that the operation went well and she might be able to play golf again. An April 19 story, "Good Night Spent by Mrs. Zaharias," confirmed her condition and spirits and cited physicians saying she might be able to play again someday.

The press, on occasion, took notice of George too, who was known to be highly emotional. A statement released by the hospital "added laconically that the ex-wrestler George Zaharias, the star's husband, was all right, too." Dodd's inclusion in press accounts was erratic, but one reporter did note in particular that she always slept on a cot in Babe's hospital room. Babe makes special mention of this in an excerpt from her autobiography that appeared in *Cosmopolitan.* Betty, whom Babe described as "steady as a rock, . . . moved in with me, slept on a cot by my bed." Their intimacy had become accept-able to mention only once illness bound them.[15]

From the outset Babe was as concerned with saving her career as she was with saving her life. Before the operation she ruminated about "all the peo-ple I know and like and love, and who know and like me—would they ever see me alive again? The girls I've helped be better golfers, the girls I've beat-en, the girls who've beaten me. And me, dead. Maybe alive, but bedridden, helpless, *maybe I'd never play golf again!*" Amidst gloomy predictions prof-fered by Bertha Bowen that "Babe will never be able to play golf again" and Dr. Tatum's dreary speculation, "I don't know yet if surgery will cure her, but I will say that she never again will play golf of championship caliber," Didrikson's future seemed grim. Although national and international sym-pathizers poured in their good wishes, she found a couple of communica-tions "conspicuous by their absence, too. Namely, some of the people whose products I endorse. They didn't seem to feel my endorsement would mean that much again."[16]

True to her fighting spirit, Babe clutched at whatever hope she could find. Even George tried to help. As she went into the operating room he said to her, "All the championships and all the honors, all you have ever won—they were just preliminaries to this." "Remember," he said, trying to sound con-vincing, "you're the champion, at everything you've set your mind to. You're the best there is." Most of all, however, she clung to Betty Dodd's words. Perhaps sheer love, youthful enthusiasm, or naivete accounted for Dodd's reassurances. She told Babe, "If it hasn't spread too far, you can play golf again. You've got a chance Babe." Believing her cancer cured and trusting in Dodd, Babe publicly scoffed at Dr. Tatum's suggestion and others' pre-dictions. Privately, relatives remembered that on two occasions she ran her hands over her golf clubs in the trunk of the car and sighed, saying, "Well, I guess I won't be needing these anymore." Thanks to Dodd, they then became a fixture in all of her sick rooms.[17]

Once she was determined to fight, there seemed to be no stopping her. Babe herself set the tone for the press coverage of her ailment. For example, she compared her 1953 cancer diagnosis to the unsettling ruling in 1935 that she no longer qualified as an amateur: "I didn't do any sounding off myself. When you get a big setback like that, there's no use crying about it. . . . You just have to face your problem and figure out what to do next."[18]

The press, following her lead, covered both her physical recovery and her athletic recovery. The *Times* reported in early April that "physicians . . . would try to save her life and athletic career with a major operation," and "physicians who examined her refuse to guess about her future in golf." The press helped bolster, if not create, the sports metaphors that so informed her three-year struggle with the disease. Babe's cancer became, alternately, the "hole she couldn't birdie," the "hurdle she could leap," the "roughest contest of her life," the "course she must run," and, in her own words, the "biggest competitive round of my life."[19]

Following her lead, four months after the operation, a 1953 *Time* article, "The Babe Is Back," featured a photograph of Babe swinging a golf club with the caption "Golfer Zaharias: The muscle is spiritual." The article says that Babe took the news of her cancer "as calmly as she takes one of her rare setbacks on a golf course. 'I'll beat it,' she said. . . . Last week, with doctors marveling at her recuperative power (the Babe calls it 'spiritual muscle') she was back on the golf course playing in Chicago's Tam O'Shanter Tournament."[20]

It would trivialize Babe's psychic and athletic comebacks and her reentry into competitive golf to attribute them solely to her lack of knowledge of her cancer or to media hyperbole. Didrikson, because she viewed her recovery as a contest, was able to use the media to further her own ends, much as she had as a competitor. Further, by relying on the athletic model that stressed endurance, striving for "personal bests," and public approval, Babe knowingly surrounded herself with familiar and successful life strategies. Additionally, Peggy Kirk Bell recalled Babe reading a Bible that had been underlined by a mutual friend in Little Rock.[21] This lends poignancy to her use of the term "spiritual muscle."

In addition to exercising her spiritual muscle, she exercised her physical muscles too. The *Saturday Evening Post* reported that while she was recuperating, she occasionally got up, took a few golf swings with her four wood, and happily reported that her grip felt real good. She also began self-directed exercises five or six days after the surgery; she'd alternately tighten her leg and arm muscles. One photo showed her sitting up in bed, beaming, with golf clubs criss-crossed over her bedsheets.[22]

To aid her recuperation Didrikson also increasingly relied upon her activism on behalf of cancer education and fund-raising to bolster her well-being. This renewed zeal began on her forty-second birthday with the Babe Didrikson Zaharias Week Golf Tournament, June 22–28, 1953. The Beaumont Country Club along with nearly two thousand other cooperating golf courses nationwide donated all proceeds to the Damon Runyon Cancer Fund. Babe, true to her image, won the tournament.[23]

As a result of her conditioning routine, her superb physical shape, and her own powerful will, Babe returned to the professional links a mere fourteen weeks after her surgery. She finished third in the Tam O'Shanter Tournament. George, in Denver on business, encouraged Babe in her quick return to the limelight while cautioning her to take it easy. Her performance at the Tam O'Shanter enabled her to edge out Ted Williams, the left fielder of the Boston Red Sox (who had just returned from Marine duty in Korea), to win the Ben Hogan Comeback Player of the Year award.[24]

A week later Babe was paired, by request, with Dodd at the World Golf Championship at the Tam O'Shanter Country Club in Niles, Illinois. "She was familiar with my condition," Babe wrote, "and could step in and help if I had any trouble." Dodd recalled, "Everywhere that Babe went after her surgery, I went. . . . She needed someone to be with her. It made her feel more comfortable."[25]

Babe's goal was not just a "good showing." "To me," she wrote of her fourteen-week postoperative comeback, "shooting tournament golf doesn't just mean getting a respectable score and finishing up among the leaders. It means being able to win. That's the standard the public has come to judge me by. It's the standard I set for myself. I wouldn't want it to be any other way." While her fans thought these finishes remarkable, George told *Look* magazine in 1957 that "she was not much good in the All-America and came in third in the World," a comment that belies his gargantuan expectations. He echoed the expectations she set for herself. To her, that was like finishing last. Babe held herself to standards that exceeded reason, but not possibility.[26]

Babe had an emotional turning point during the third round of this tournament. When an important putt stopped just short of the cup, she told one journalist, "shattered, I stretched out my hands, still gripping the club, and buried my face in my arms and cried." This "blackest of moments" was triggered by the responsibility Babe felt toward the "thousands of others [cancer patients, who] would be on the losing side with me." Momentarily feeling terribly alone, Babe sensed Dodd and George approach. "I felt their comforting hands on my shoulder—and, in a wonderful way, the hands of many others. I whispered, 'Please, God . . . You've helped me this far. Give me the strength to go on . . . please.'"[27]

Dodd remembered the critical moment thus: "She was missing shots and fighting like mad. On the 5th hole she three putted from four feet. She walked off the green and sat down on a bench, put her head in her hands and sobbed. I told her, 'Quit, Babe, no one will care, they'll understand.' She looked up with tears streaming down her face and said, 'No, no, I don't want to quit. I'm not a quitter.'"[28]

Babe finished out 1953 as the sixth highest money winner with $6,345.42, winning only two of the twenty-four tournaments. After her stunning comeback win at the Babe Zaharias Week Golf Tournament, she tied for second in the Jacksonville and New Orleans Opens and tied for fifteenth in the All-American Open. Frustrating mediocrity began 1954 as she placed seventh in the Tampa Women's Open. She rebounded to tie for first with Bev Hanson in the St. Petersburg Open but lost in sudden death on the third playoff hole. She then came in fifteenth at the Tam O'Shanter Tournament and third at the World Golf Championship. Ten months after her operation, Babe knew "people were beginning to ask each other whether I'd ever be capable of winning tournaments again. And I was asking myself the same thing."[29]

Finally, in the Serbin Women's Open in February 1954, Babe caught her brass ring. Neck-and-neck with Berg after three rounds at 220, Babe won the tournament on the last hole with a par five, only a few months after the surgery. After so many losses, Babe's spirit soared. She said Serbin was her "biggest thrill in sports." Bowen, Bubba, Thelma, and Dodd all confirmed that Babe considered this her greatest triumph.[30]

Babe was hosted by the Eisenhowers to cap off her triumphant comeback. She opened the Cancer Crusade in a White House ceremony and flatteringly imitated Mamie's bangs for the occasion. "'Mrs. Eisenhower,'" she told her, "'I've fixed up my bangs tonight so I can be right in unison with you!' Mrs. Eisenhower replied, 'Oh, but your bangs look so nicely curled, and mine never do.'" Babe and "Ike," as she cozily called him in her autobiography, chatted golf after the photo session in which Babe mock-drove golf balls with the symbolic sword of the American Cancer Society. Just a year after her surgery, the April 18, 1954, edition of the *New York Sunday News* showed her comeback in all its glory: Babe smiling from her hospital bed, Babe smashing a golf drive, Babe and George smiling lovingly after a golf victory, and Babe and President Eisenhower in a ceremonial presentation of the American Cancer Society's Sword of Hope.[31]

In one of sports all-time dazzling ascents after adversity, Babe won five tournaments in 1954. She captured the All-American by eight strokes with a score of 294—only one stroke above her own seventy-two-hole women's record for the course—and added the U.S. Women's, Sarasota, Serbin, and National Capitol Opens. Her U.S. Women's Open victory alone, at the Salem Country Club in Peabody, Massachusetts, was a masterpiece. She shot a par 72 on the first day, never exceeded a five on any hole, and remained under par on thirteen of the final eighteen holes. As the press reported this victory, a crowd of six thousand watched her finish twelve strokes ahead of her nearest rival. Following her last putt and a roar from the crowd, Babe was immersed in a flood of hugs and kisses from George, Betty, and rival golfers.[32]

Babe phoned her doctors from the course, and when she thanked Dr. Robert Moore, her personal physician, for all he'd done, Moore replied, "You did it yourself, Babe. . . . It was your faith, Babe . . . that and your courage." Babe had developed close and meaningful relationships with her physicians and their families, so that sharing her victory with them was a natural extension of the bond between them. Peter Moore, a present-day Galvestonian and son of Dr. Robert Moore, remembered social and informal visits paid to his house by Babe, George, and Betty. Peter remembered Babe as warm, cheerful, and stoic; essentially no talk centered on her cancer. This was due, likely, to both her sense of "being cured" and the youthful ears of the listener, a teenager struck by the magnitude of the celebrity in his home. Similarly, Babe and George socialized frequently with Drs. Martin and Rose Schneider. The former, now deceased, was the head of Radio Therapy at the University of Texas Medical Branch (UTMB), where Babe was hospitalized repeatedly from 1954 to 1956. Dr. Rose Schneider, still on the faculty at UTMB when interviewed in 1985, remembered Babe as a charming, warm, and stoic woman.[33]

Seldom would she give credit to others, but of this July victory Babe contradicted Robert Moore when she said, "Actually *we* won it. *We* are the thousands of people whose faith helped make me strong. United through our prayers, we share our separate victories." Hicks, who came in second to Babe, quipped, "Thus [I achieved] the dubious distinction of going into the USGA record books as the most out-distanced runner-up in USGA history. I console myself that Louise Suggs was 4 strokes behind me, Betsy Rawls and Mickey Wright 5 strokes back, and Patty Berg 10 strokes in my debt." Babe obliterated her opponents.[34]

Babe's triumphant win obscured another crisis of hope. In April 1954, Babe told a *New York Sunday News* reporter that she intended to quit golf after two more tournaments. Apparently Babe's victory here and later dimmed any such plans. Her other finishes that year tallied $14,452 in earnings, placing her in the second-place spot. She won the prestigious Vare Trophy (originated by Betty Jameson in 1952 to honor past champion Glenna Collett Vare) for lowest scoring average. In April she received the William D. Richardson Trophy presented in memory of the former *New York Times* golf writer in honor "of her outstanding contributions to golf within the past year." Her 301 points in the voting edged out Dwight D. Eisenhower's 288. She also won the newly created Serbin Trophy, awarded on a point system reflecting high finishes in tournaments. The trophy, containing over $5,000 worth of diamond-studded gold, "became a prize target for the women professionals." To complete the coronation, Babe was voted Female Athlete of the Year for the sixth time by the Associated Press. She remains the only person ever to claim that honor so often.[35]

One other prize came her way in 1954. At the Ardmore Open in Oklahoma, where she battled to an unexciting tie for seventh, she was given a palomino horse named Superman. Never one to shun the spotlight, Babe rode the prancing showoff onto the eighteenth green as the announcer proclaimed, "Here comes Superman, ridden by Superwoman!"[36]

A true golden cyclone, Babe was surrounded by both glory and chaos in 1954. Her reelection to the presidency of the LPGA was a vote of confidence by her peers for her steady recuperation. Under her direction, the association changed its legal headquarters from New York to Florida, divided membership into three categories (active, associate, and honorary), and defined its goals and purpose more clearly. As a self-defined educational, recreational, and social organization of female golf professionals, the group, through its ruling body, the executive board, sought to enhance the status of the sport and its membership. Membership rose to a high of twenty-nine, of whom nineteen, including Dodd, attended the business meeting held in Evanston, Illinois.[37]

So far so good. Then, all hell broke loose. Fred Corcoran, Babe's and the LPGA's business manager, was "let go" because the golf equipment manufacturing companies would no longer pay his salary. Babe, a fiercely loyal friend, resigned the LPGA in support of Corcoran on January 21, 1954. Next came Betty Hicks's article, "A Lady Golf Pro Lets Her Hair Down: Next to Marriage We'll Take Golf," which appeared in the *Saturday Evening Post* on January 23. This insider's exposé infuriated Babe by quoting some of her less admirable one-liners such as "Why don'tcha girls all go home?"; reporting her insistence on the last-minute increase in prize money at the National Women's Open; characterizing her music-making with Dodd as "hillbilly"; recounting the tournament appearance fees granted to her and no one else; and including the unflattering concession that "even though she annoys us at times with her egocentric attitude, we have twice elected her president of our association."[38]

God hath no fury like an idol scorned. Babe told the *New York Times,* "I'm washing my hands of the whole thing, both as president and as a member." She turned in her LPGA membership card in a huff, talked of starting a new tournament group, and "said a few words about some of her sister pros" (that went unquoted). A frantic night of heated negotiations with other members and smoothing ruffled feathers ensued. The next day Babe agreed to resume her duties. Her price tag? The understanding that efforts would be made to reemploy Corcoran and that the newly formed tournament committee that had temporarily assumed his duties would be abolished. Babe acted as tournament director until Hicks was elected to fill the post that summer.[39]

Other organizational business that was discussed during the negotiations included increasing the number of tournaments from twenty-five to thirty-five, raising purses to $5,000 minimum, securing exclusive concession rights with Pepsi-Cola, and arranging radio and television broadcasts. Hicks also argued for increasing the fees for golf clinics from $300 to $500 (Babe was receiving $1,000 to $1,500) and establishing uniform pairing procedures for tournament play.[40]

Babe was a formidable opponent in the conference room or on the fairways. She was the LPGA's biggest drawing card, and secession from the group would have been a fatal blow to the neophyte organization. She knew this and used it as leverage to secure her desired aims. Not surprisingly, this entire series of events goes unmentioned in *This Life I've Led.* Her ire at Hicks was palpable and significantly contributed to Babe's decision to walk out; exposés like hers damaged the image Babe had so carefully crafted.

Most folks knew little of this mayhem. To the general public Babe was the recipient of awards, accolades, and adulation. Babe responded by giving of herself to countless cancer efforts. Remembering her pact with God, wherein she had promised that "if He made me well, I'd do everything in my power when I got out to help the fight against cancer," Babe devoted herself full-force to this new opponent. She "said yes to everything," opening a Babe Didrikson Zaharias chapter of the American Cancer Society and making personal appearances and radio and television spots for the American Cancer Society and the Damon Runyon Cancer Fund. Whenever she played in a tournament, noted Babe, "I generally did some cancer work there. A priest or somebody would ask me to visit cancer patients he knew, and try to raise their spirits, and I was glad to do it." As one journalist noted, "So Betty and Babe toured the wards [playing guitar and harmonica] and in trying to cheer others, Babe forgot her own uncertain future."[41]

Everywhere she went Babe symbolized hope. In March 1954, Babe attended an exhibition game between the New York Yankees and the Cincinnati Redlegs at Casey Stengel's invitation. Team members from both clubs came to the stands to greet her. Mickey Mantle, Yogi Berra, and Cincinnati manager Birdie Tebbets chatted with her. In the seventh inning her presence was announced over the public address system "and she received a heart-warming ovation from the near-capacity crowd. . . . She took her yellow straw hat off her head and waved it in response to the cheers."[42]

By late 1954, worn down and quite ill, Babe was forced to retreat from her cancer work. George finally agreed to let her have a permanent home of her own design. They built it across the street from the converted caddy house on a pond at the edge of the Tampa golf course. They moved into their dreamhouse, "Rainbow Manor," in March 1955. George waxed effusive describing Babe's design of it. "She planned every inch of it," he emoted to *Look* magazine in 1957, "making it just as she wanted it, remembering the rooms she had seen and liked as she traveled back and forth across the country." Babe adored the home, and George reveled in Babe's enjoyment. According to his idyllic portrayal, "We would walk through it," George mused, "and I would ask her if there was anything she would change, and she would say there wasn't a thing she would change." To accommodate George, Babe claimed, "I planned everything big and roomy, for George's comfort. He's a big man." Dodd, also a permanent resident, received no special mention or building concessions. Babe put in gardens, laid bricks—in full evening wear for the photographers' cameras—helped the carpenters and electricians, made curtains, and cooked meals.[43]

Despite their apparent happiness and energy, they were an unhappy and ailing couple. George's health, too, was frail; in 1954 he developed diabetes that necessitated strict diet regulation. Babe's physical condition deteriorated while on a fishing trip in the spring of 1955 with Dodd and Dodd's sister Peggy, down at Port Aransas, Texas. Didrikson's car became stuck in the sand.

Dodd recollected, "Well, it was stuck big and we had to figure out some way to get that car out of that sand because we were about twenty-five or thirty miles from where we were staying." The two approached a lighted shack and borrowed shovels from the two male inhabitants playing checkers. They dug out the wheels and used a long wharf plank under the back tires, "but we got it stuck right back again. So we had to do it all over again. And by that time these old gentlemen were down there watching us. Of course they weren't helping us but they were watching us. And one of them said, 'God, have you ever seen a woman shovel sand like that?' They were talking about Babe because she was just, you know, getting right in there." They eventually extricated the vehicle and headed home. Babe was awakened that night by a terrible back pain that she attributed to the shoveling. Dodd called Dr. Moore, who prescribed Demerol, a potent painkiller, to be injected by a nurse on the island. Retrospectively, Betty surmised, "Now that I look back, this was the beginning of the end. The cancer had returned but it took *months* to find it."[44] All the while, Babe thought it due solely to shoveling.

After the Port Aransas nurse gave Babe that first injection at Moore's instruction, Betty became Babe's sole inoculator. She gave Babe all of her shots. "We had . . . a little tin box that locked and that box went everywhere that [we] went." Slowed, often in great pain, Babe kept playing. In 1955 she won the Tampa Open, Serbin Women's Open, and Peach Blossom–Betsy Rawls Open and placed credibly in several others. She was reelected president of the LPGA.[45]

Yet at the Sea Island Invitational, Babe sank wordlessly on a bench on the sixteenth tee, "her scorecard, heavy with bogeys, speaking for her." Dodd, George, and her close associates painfully watched her fade. George recalled in 1955 that she left the Galveston hospital to spend Christmas with the Bowens. One afternoon they drove her to the Colonial Country Club. Bertha said, "I remember Babe bending down and putting her hand on the green, just feeling it." Hicks wrote of Babe's agonizing demise, "I realized that my passion for sports had made me the only witness to the now full circle of this incomparable athlete's career . . . from her immortality in the Olympics to the only out-of-the-money finish in her golf career."[46]

Bedside: The Final Round

The locus, of only the partial source, of Babe's pain is revealed in her records from John Sealy Hospital at UTMB, where she moved after tests in Beaumont brought neither answers nor relief. A June 17, 1955, medical chart entry states, patient "was doing well until October 1954 when severe pain in rt. buttock, leg and calf began following an apparent injury described as trying to move an automobile which was stuck, and after stamping a golf ball into the ground with her right foot. Pain has been intermittent since then becoming more severe and more continuous."

Her medical chart resounds with the doctors' growing concern with her drug use; one accused Babe of becoming addicted to the drugs while suffering psychosomatic pain. June 28: "Is under heavy medication"; July 6: "receiving novocaine blocks"; July 7: "PT groggy from thorazine; Dr. Ford helping handle her to wean her away from narcotics"; August 4: "requiring narcotics less often, seems to do much better with any barbiturates sedative"; September 11: "The PT has tolerated a narcotic withdrawal regime without undue difficulty the past 12 hrs." Dodd corroborates this: "All of these doctors said that she was addicted to the drugs and that it was all psychological. . . . They did say that." Fortunately, Babe was believed and befriended by a psychiatrist named Grace Jamison.[47]

According to Dodd, the accusations that Babe's pain was inorganic and psychosomatic made Babe "come unglued. She got furious." It was at this point that Dr. Jamison was called in to talk to Babe. When "she came out of Babe's room she came straight to me—I was in the solarium—and she said, 'She's no more addicted to drugs than I am. That girl is in pain.' And she was the one that stuck by Babe, until they found it [the cancer]. She believed her totally."[48]

Jamison's allegiance, though, failed to convince the attending medical staff immediately. Since no organic problem could be found, Babe was weaned from the painkillers. In a situation that can only be called maddeningly frustrating, Babe lived with pain for lack of "proofs." Dodd witnessed Babe writhe with pain and called Grace at home. Only Jamison's intervention persuaded Babe's prescribing physician eventually to rescind the order barring administration of painkillers.

In this second bout with cancer, Dodd noticed a definite shift in Babe's spirit. "When she got struck down the second time, I think that was emotionally disturbing to her. She was having all this pain and they couldn't find out what was the matter; she just sort of wasn't public after that." They played a lot of cards, watched television in the hospital room, and "she'd hit balls off the beach in Galveston. At her home in Tampa she would go out on the golf course occasionally and try to hit a few shots, but her interest was just gone." Bell also remembered Babe's sense of waning strength and vulnerability. "I can remember her sitting there in the bed and she'd put her leg up.

And she'd say, 'Look at that.' And here's this little calf on her leg, and she'd say 'This is what made me great and it's gone.'"[49]

On June 22, 1955, Babe was operated on by Dr. Snodgrass at John Sealy for the removal of a herniated disk in her back, then thought to be the sole cause of her pain. Thelma Didriksen still fumes when she hears about this surgery. Kenneth Miller, a surgeon friend of hers in Beaumont, studied Babe's medical records and confronted her physicians at Thelma's behest. "They admitted to him," Thelma claimed, "that they operated on her but in the papers they said they took this disk out, but they didn't because she didn't have anything wrong with her back."[50]

Despite Thelma's disbelief, it seems likely that Babe's pain did emanate from the herniated disk as well as from the undiagnosed return of the cancer. The medical chart entry states that the fourth lumbar disk left was removed and the lumbosacral disk left explored. The pathology report "revealed degenerated fibro cartilage of lumbar vertebra." No physicians signed any entries. Thelma insisted that "when that [cancer] ate a hole big enough that you and I could have seen it with our naked eye they found it." Her ally, Dr. Miller, reexamined the original medical X-rays and located the cancer, which was the size "of the sharp end of a pin." The disk surgery, Thelma insisted, was a red herring.[51]

On August 5, Babe was told she had "a small cancer lesion" in the pelvic area. "When they finally found the cancer," Betty said, "I think she was relieved. . . . It was almost like well, thank God, now they know I'm not just, you know [imagining it]." Warning signs of this second cancer, irregular vaginal bleeding that had occurred for at least the three preceding months, had not been noted in her medical chart until August 4. It is unknown whether Babe concealed this bleeding, thought it irrelevant, or refused to acknowledge its significance. On the day the cancerous lesion was found, an innovative X-ray treatment, designed to alleviate her recurring pain, commenced. George, ever the promoter/hustler himself, met members of the press at the hospital and told them that Babe "took the bad news like the mighty champion she had always been. . . . She's not giving up. . . . She never flinched when told she had another cancer."[52]

In an eerie twist of literary premonition, Babe's tape-recorded autobiography ends on August 5, the day the X-ray treatments began: "At the end of July I got some bad news. They spotted a trace of new cancer. . . . So x-ray treatments were started. The doctors said it would be three to six months before I could get back to the golf tournaments. And just as in 1953, a lot of people were doubting that I ever would get back in competition. As far as I was concerned, there was no doubt about my coming back again. With the love and support of the many friends I have made, how could I miss? They have helped me hurdle one obstacle after another, and any success I have had is due to a great extent to their devotion and consideration." She continued, "In the future, maybe I'll have to limit myself to just a few of the most important tournaments each year. I expect to be shooting for championships for a good many years to come. My autobiography isn't finished yet."[53] But it was, indeed, the last day she told her life story.

Babe's unswerving optimism in the face of the physical pain she endured is explainable in part by her belief in her own invincibility and denial of her mortality. She also had a strong desire to return to competition, her life's blood. Yet Babe also realized that her medical treatment would attract national attention. Her stated goal throughout in going public with her ailment was to minimize the fear, uncertainty, and sense of isolation experienced by others in her condition. More important, her attitude reflected her commitment to serve as a role model for other cancer patients. Bubba Didriksen recalled in the summer of 1988, "She wanted so desperately to get well and to help relieve tension and fear in others of this dreaded disease."[54]

In response to the oft-asked question, why didn't she just quit pro golf, fade from public life, and take it easy in 1955, Babe responded, "There are several reasons why I didn't retire from golf after that 1953 cancer business— and still don't intend to retire—in spite of my 1955 ailments. One reason is that every time I get out and play well in a golf tournament, it seems to buck up people with the same cancer trouble I had." Only fifteen or sixteen days after her colostomy operation in 1953, Babe held a bedside press conference from the hospital. In a *Saturday Evening Post* interview in the summer of 1955 Babe recalled how she set her hair in preparation for the posed photos. "I knew that it would encourage other cancer patients if they saw me get well. I wanted the public to know I was alright."[55]

A smaller, but equally significant example of Babe's influence and resolve occurred when a patient at the Hotel Dieu, a nun named Sister Tarsisis, refused a colostomy. At Babe's urging the sister relented and permitted the surgery to be performed; her bowel was later resected and reconnected. During Didrikson's own hospitalizations and tournament play she at times dropped into the local sick rooms of other cancer patients. The "The Girl Who Lived Again" captured this moving scenario: "The faces of anxiety-torn men and women turn hopefully towards her. She looks and is the picture of vibrant health. She discusses cancer with them as casually as she discusses her golf score. If they are facing an operation, she sits down and gives them words of encouragement from her own experience." In short, Babe had a profound impact on other cancer patients as one who "went public" with the disease in an era when this was rarely done.[56]

Her influence on cancer education and fund-raising was similarly immense; from her hospital bed in John Sealy Hospital in Galveston, on September 12, 1955, Babe and George announced the formation of the Babe Didrikson Zaharias Cancer Fund. As one news release characterized the scene: "A bit weak from her long hospital stay . . . Babe was smiling big as she announced the establishment of the fund . . . from a sun porch at the hospital." As Babe stated, the purpose of the fund was "to help the needy people who are not able to pay to find out if they have cancer."[57]

"Those who were not financially able to undergo long periods of examination and observation" were a special concern to Babe. In fact, Dr. Rose Schneider of UTMB, whose husband served on the original cancer fund board of directors, remembers Babe's gratitude to UTMB, where Ole Senior, who also died of cancer, was treated. This gratitude toward UTMB, whose teaching hospital treats people regardless of ability to pay, largely accounts for Babe's sentimental decision to receive her own treatment at the university as well as to establish her cancer fund there.[58]

The non-profit fund's first project was the establishment of a tumor clinic at UTMB. Beyond that, "funds were to be used to assist established tumor clinics and cancer treatment centers in employing well-trained technicians and financing most of the advanced equipment." At the fund's opening day ceremonies John W. McCullough, one of the board's directors and chairman of the Sealy-Smith Foundation that donated John Sealy Hospital to the university, contributed the first $1,000. George matched this gift on behalf of Babe and himself.[59]

Two days after the fund was established, on September 14, Babe left the hospital with Betty Dodd, who had stayed by her side during the hospitalization. George accompanied them to their home in Tampa. A notation on her medical chart the day she left the hospital says, "From a psychologic viewpoint, I think it would be preferable to allow her to ret. to her own home for a time, with sufficient narcotics to remain comfortable. When symptoms become worse, chorodotomy [severing the spinal nerves] or some other procedure could be performed."[60]

Throughout 1955 and 1956 Babe and George continued their efforts on behalf of the Babe Zaharias Open, which had become an annual fund-raising event in Beaumont after the full-week tournament in 1953, and remained active in the cancer fund. A June 4, 1956, letter addressed to sports editors nationwide, printed on the fund's letterhead, explained that the fund's board, as well as Governor Allan Shivers of Texas and the governor of Florida, "has honored me by designating the month of June Babe Zaharias Cancer Fund Month, as my birthday is June 26." In previous eras, she had hustled sportswriters in a quest for self-aggrandizement, but this was a genuinely altruistic act. The letter requested that the editors publicize and cover tournaments in their area. Babe concluded the personally signed letter with "I believe the Fund can help a great deal in the fight against cancer, and I will personally appreciate your cooperation in this effort." The letterhead sports the initials BDZ superimposed on a key, signaling, perhaps, her desire to unlock the mysteries of the disease.[61]

When Babe and Dodd left John Sealy Hospital, Dodd was instructed in dispensing and injecting Babe's Demerol, codeine, and sleeping pills. "They showed me what kind of dosage to give her and when," Dodd matter-of-factly recalled, "and I was pretty good." Only if the pain became unbearable did Dodd contact Didrikson's Tampa physician. Throughout the remainder of 1955 Babe resided in Tampa with Betty and George. Although at times she felt well enough to play golf, on occasion she was unexpectedly overwhelmed with pain. The pain centered in her left foot as "the cancer had affected the sciatic nerve that ran down her leg." Dodd recalled that "her foot hurt all the time. The only relief was to squeeze it. I used to lie on the end of her bed for hours and just mash her foot." Dodd completed her recollection with: "My hands became strong. I could even have strangled George." Babe, unable to bear the pain in her leg and foot, returned to John Sealy Hospital in December 1955 and stayed there until the end of January 1956.[62]

Returning to Tampa in February, Babe used her waning strength to travel to Sarasota to watch Dodd on the eighteenth green of a tournament she had a chance to win; Dodd lost by one stroke. In March 1956, Babe asked to return to John Sealy, where she remained until her death. Babe's sister Lillie moved to Galveston and acted as her helpmate until Dodd could rejoin Babe. At an LPGA tournament in June 1956, held in honor of Babe's forty-third birthday, Dodd raised approximately $5,000 for the cancer fund. Less than a month later, Babe underwent a chorodotomy to relieve her pain.[63]

As covered by the press, Babe's personal struggle took on Olympian proportions in the public eye. Newspapers, who had slacked off their watchdog postures since the colostomy in 1953, followed her diligently when the cancer returned. There was a flurry of coverage when Babe and George set up the cancer fund. And when Babe returned home the press was there to greet her.[64]

In late November her return to Texas for a medical check-up seeking diagnosis of recurring hip pain was covered in detail. Here, Dodd, described as "a close friend and golfing companion," was Babe's only traveling companion and spokesperson. Article titles alone give ample evidence of the role she had come to play as a symbolic survivor of cancer: "The Girl Who Lived Again"; "Cheerful Babe Continues Stubborn Battle against Cancer as Forty-second Birthday Nears"; "Babe Loses Strength, Weight but Continues to Put up Fight"; "Babe's Grit Praised by Physicians"; and "Tributes from World Pour Down on Babe at Birthday Party." The press coverage of Babe's decline, cloaked as it was in sports metaphor, was made palatable to an American public all too prone to deny the ugly realities of the disease.[65]

Babe chose the tenor of these portrayals; she was never quite at ease or totally self-revealing in discussing her pain or dying. In private and in public Babe refrained from emotionalism. Her life narrative contains conspicuously few in-depth accounts of her feelings about her illness. Insights into her innermost thoughts were spared even her closest friends. Peggy Kirk Bell and Patty Berg, when they would phone or visit her, would be told briskly "I'm doing all right" and then conversation would shift to tournaments and better times and places. Dodd, in closest proximity, recalled similar conversations, although the help she gave Babe with physical functions necessitated a greater recognition of Babe's frailty. Yet even this recognition was not verbalized. Infrequent outbursts of crying and frustration on Babe's part quickly receded into controlled determination to overcome the next obstacle.

Two cases in point: Dodd said Babe's "mental and emotional state was terribly rocky when the subject of the colostomy came up. She cried a couple of times and kept asking people, 'Do you think they'll *really* have to do it?' Then, after it was done, she accepted it." Dodd affirmed that after the surgery "she didn't have any trouble with that colostomy at all. She never did. Most people would have been afraid to go outside . . . but after she found out that it wasn't that big of a deal . . . she just forgot about it and went on her merry way and did whatever she wanted to do." In fact, Babe bordered on being cavalier: "I mean," Dodd stressed, "she didn't have any more problem with that colostomy than if she'd had a toothache." In a second incident, when Babe and George left Dr. William Tatum's office in Fort Worth, having been told of the need for the colostomy, Babe recalled, "I was crying when we went down on the elevator. George was all distressed. He had never seen me cry before, and I don't believe he saw me do it any more after that." Silent stoicism soon followed, as Didrikson put on a brave face not just for George and for her fans, but also for herself.[66]

Although Babe won seven tournaments after her 1953 colostomy, neither sports metaphor, spiritual hope, public adoration, nor medical science could help her lick "the black beast of cancer." Peggy Kirk Bell, who played with Babe during her last-ever round of golf at the Tampa course, remembered Babe wearing loafers because her foot was too painful for golf shoes. On their nine-hole outing, Babe managed a good wisecrack on the third hole. She slapped Peggy on the back and said, " 'You're just great. I don't know how you girls break 80 only hitting it this far.' Her leg hurt too much to really hit and at her weakest point she hit the ball about where I hit it at my best," Bell said.[67]

Even without employing sentimentality Didrikson knew how to mobilize the public. She understood fans' infatuation with an athlete and she used that love to involve her fans in her cancer fight. The American public became the audience for her struggle through carefully orchestrated press conferences from her bedside. At times the press coverage seemed invasive and almost circus-like, particularly upon her death. Her shriveling body size, emaciated features, physical frailty, and exhausted state were captured in verse and on film. As one biographer remarked of this coverage: "Babe deserved better. Her death was so agonizing, so public, so sensationally reported it is only now possible to see her in perspective."[68]

Through this mutually caring yet exploitive relationship between Babe and the press, cancer became mentionable and tolerable to the American people. Her personality, coupled with the media's packaging of her illness, coalesced to make her symbolic, to many, as the one who could beat what others couldn't. But it was one challenge she couldn't conquer. Babe Didrikson Zaharias died at John Sealy Hospital on September 27, 1956, at age forty-five. Bubba, following Babe's wishes, went alone with her body to Houston for her cremation. He said, "Her ashes are in Forest Park Cemetery in Beaumont, directly across from the Beaumont Country Club where she played golf a lot."[69]

Fred Corcoran told a chronicler that "her funeral was surprisingly small. Not many reporters. Frankly, there were very few people outside of her family." Patty Berg, one of the few pro golfers who attended, remembered differently. She recalled a sizable crowd. And curiously, an AP dispatch from Galveston on September 29, 1956, picked up by the *New York Times,* read "Throng Attends Zaharias Rites." It was a full and well-attended service, according to this account, as "hundreds of residents of her home town joined with celebrities of the sports world for the funeral service."[70]

Indicative of the heroic portrayals of her death is the following excerpt from the *New York Times* editorial of September 26:

> Babe Didrikson Zaharias has finally lost the big one. It was after the greatest and most gallant struggle of her great and gallant career. This one was the hardest to lose, but she knew that "you can't win them all" and that there is one antagonist against which even the stoutest heart is not quite defense enough. . . . She didn't know the meaning of the word quit, and she refused to define it, right to the end. Her tragic death must spur us to renewed efforts to fight the foe that cut her down. But her own terrific fight against that foe can also be an inspiration to all those who must face and overcome handicaps. It is not only the annals of sport that her life has enriched. It is the whole story of human beings who somehow have to keep on trying.[71]

For those closest to her, her final days were agonizing. Bubba and Jackie Didriksen recalled that Babe weighed "170-something that last time she got sick and when she was in her casket, Dale Broussard [a journalist and friend] told us that the whole thing weighed 76 pounds." Peggy Kirk Bell also remembered with painful clarity Babe's wasting away. She'd been going to visit Babe frequently until she spoke with George, who said, "You won't even know her, Peg. She got so bad." Bell never went back after that, but she by chance ran into a nurse of Babe's who told her, "If it had been anybody else but the Babe they wouldn't have kept her alive. They kept her alive with needles. It was stupid. She weighed 62 pounds when she died and she didn't know what end was up, they had her drugged so." The nurse went on to explain to Peggy that her spinal cord had been severed to stop the pain, "and all she was was a vegetable. It was terrible what they did." Dodd, too, believed Babe's life was prolonged because she was Babe Didrikson. Each day that Babe lived bolstered public hope and notions of her invincibility. Her doctors' determination to prolong her life reflected their medical aspirations for treatment breakthroughs. Dead, she was only a memory. Alive, she was a unique inspiration.[72]

George, in addition to his personal grief and despair, faced the odd omission that he and Babe had no medical insurance, only accident coverage. Thus all of Babe's medical bills were paid from their savings. Peggy Kirk Bell recalled that these hospital and medical costs were very high, but paying them did not bankrupt George. Bell said, "Babe had money. . . . Babe made plenty of money. She had good contracts with different companies and they didn't spend it big."[73]

The funeral itself was a spectacle. According to Bubba, George, "distraught and very sad," essentially fell apart. "He was at the casket on his knees and he's such a big guy and he was crying and he was just shaking that casket. It was terrible." Tellingly, this was not reported by the press in an era when most journalists still protected their sports subjects from questionable coverage. Jackie added to Bubba's account that George "was a very emotional person anyway. He could bring on the tears." In fact, the Associated Press report of her death began: " 'Babe never really asked God for too much,' Big George sobbed. 'She never asked Him to win any tournaments for her. . . . She just prayed [to] Him to let her get well.' " And the most incredible memory came from Bertha Bowen, who vividly remembered George trying to crawl into the coffin. Bertha told Dodd, "George really made a jackass out of himself. He tried to get in the coffin—I mean he just went to pieces. Put on the biggest show you could possibly imagine, in the church."[74]

Each person close to Babe recalled her last days differently, some tenderly, some angrily, and some sadly. Berg, who'd taken to calling her once a week in the hospital, recalled their banal chitchat. Babe asked about the tour, told stories of the medical staff, and would say only, "Oh, I feel a little better today." Lillie began the gruesome habit of sitting by Babe's grave site, wailing to her lost chum and inspiration.[75]

George had lost his center. Immediately after Babe died, he sought refuge with Florence Chadwick, the first woman to swim across the English Channel and back again. He had known her when he wrestled in Los Angeles and then later on his many travels. Chadwick, who'd met Babe twice, thought highly of her. During his two solid days at Chadwick's apartment George spent hours "talking to me about it, he seemed to want to tell me all about it." Chadwick learned of Babe's last thoughts expressed to George. Babe was all business. "She called him into her room to discuss business details, 'get this settled and get that settled and sign these papers and that papers,' and . . . finally she said she had to conserve her energy. So she just whispered and then she stopped talking and the next thing you know she was gone." These impersonal last words between the Zahariases would baffle the public suckled on tales of endless romance. Babe had tried to ferret away $14,000 for Lillie. George, rummaging through her hospital night table drawer, discovered the check and confiscated it. Because Babe left no last will and testament, leaving checks was the only way she could provide for her loved ones. This may speak to her sense of physical invulnerability and outright denial but likely reflects her great physical weakness and economic domination by George.[76]

George's interest in Chadwick eventually became more intense. Months later he asked her to marry him, his attraction to strong and independent women apparently still intact. But, Chadwick quipped matter-of-factly, "I wasn't interested in him." He offered her Babe's golf clubs, which she refused, saying, "No, George, you keep them because no one could do justice to them like the Babe did." But he did give her a bathrobe with a beaver collar that Babe had worn in the hospital. "It was very beautiful. It was a lovely form-fitting robe that she had and I kept it as a souvenir for many years."[77]

Dodd, at Babe's request, did not attend the funeral. Banished by Babe in a generous act of protectionism and an unadmitted attempt at ego mainte-nance (Babe knew full well how emaciated and pained she looked), Dodd saw Babe for the last time eleven days before she died. Babe protected the youthful Dodd from the anguish of witnessing her death; perhaps she want-ed Dodd to remember a more robust and appealing version of herself. Keep-ing her promise to forgo the funeral, Dodd collapsed into a week-long slum-ber aimed at recuperating, remembering, and forgetting.[78]

Amidst this personal turmoil for those closest to her, her public image remained untarnished. The New York Times reported her death on page one on September 27, 1956, incorrectly, but typically, stating her age as forty-two, not forty-five. Inside there was a lengthy four-column story capped by two photos, one a face shot of Babe looking healthy in 1955, the other, her now-famous hurdling stride as she propelled her way to the 1932 Olympic gold medal. The front-page story recounted her life history and accomplish-ments, while that same day's editorial, devoted to Babe, paid tribute to her athletic career, life, and fight against cancer.[79]

This prominent coverage of her death was rivaled by two other tributes. The London Times obituary stated that the "all around sportswoman and breaker of many records, died peacefully in her sleep at Galveston, Texas, yesterday at the age of 42 after a series of operations for cancer." The narra-tive, several inches long, went on to describe her athletic career, medical setbacks, and sports comeback. This coverage of her death confirmed her international fame and appeal.[80]

President Eisenhower, in a gesture that some relatives and friends can repeat nearly verbatim, honored her on the day of her death. He began his news conference with a heartfelt and moving tribute to her: "Ladies and gentlemen, I should like to take one minute to pay a tribute to Mrs. Zahari-as, Babe Didrikson. She was a woman who, in her athletic career, certainly won the admiration of every person in the United States, all sports people over the world, and in her gallant fight against cancer she put up one of the kind of fights that inspired us all. I think that every one of us feels sad that finally she had to lose this last one of all her battles."[81]

A champion's ashes were laid to rest on September 27, 1956. The closing line of her narrative, "My autobiography isn't finished yet," written mere days before her death, had a prophetic ring. In her death Babe achieved a level of public approval, purposefulness, and valor that transcended all of her athletic honors. Her earthly achievements were stupendous but her dying, despite and beyond her emaciated physique, had been magnificent.

CHAPTER ELEVEN

Legacy

Babe's death left thousands of admiring fans, many loving friends and family members, and two devoted mates devastated. Most worked in some way to preserve her memory either for themselves or for others. Bubba and Jackie Didriksen represented Babe at many ceremonies honoring her. They graciously accepted awards on her behalf at the Texas Sports Hall of Fame in Willis, Texas; the University of the American Academy of Sport in Mobile, Alabama, which grants a yearly courage award in Babe's name; and the centennial golf celebration in 1988 hosted by Golf World in New York City. Bubba presented an apple tree trophy commemorating Babe as golf's Player of the Decade, 1938–47, to a museum later built to honor her. Bubba, of Crowley, Texas, died in May 1989 after surgery following a heart attack. Jackie said when interviewed on his death, "He was quite proud of her. He always wanted to do everything he could [to represent Babe]." He actively participated in the Babe Zaharias Open and remained a member of the board of directors of the Babe Didrikson Zaharias Foundation, Inc., which oversaw her museum. "He helped keep her memory alive his whole life," Jackie said.[1]

Bertha Bowen, like Bubba and Jackie, devoted much of her life to fanning the legacy of Babe. In 1988, Bertha was still an organizer of the Texas Women's Open. The first Sunday of every state tournament in Texas is played to benefit Babe's cancer fund, and on one day when we spoke she was excitedly awaiting a photograph of a new bronze statue of Babe to use in her souvenir program. "That's the way things go now," she said. "I'm going to be 90 years old if I make it to January. And so I'm doing all of these things—it keeps me busy all the time. Promoting, just promoting." Perpetuating the Babe legend was full-time work.[2]

Betty Dodd finally came into her own as a golfer on tour. Dodd won her first tournament the month after Babe died. "And then I won some more," she recalled. "I didn't win a lot but I played well—I was in the top five, ten a lot. And I never was when Babe was alive. I just didn't do that well." Released from Babe's overwhelming shadow, Dodd realized a modicum of her athletic potential.

Her social world changed dramatically, too. Blunt and candid, Dodd said, "The minute she was dead—now I don't want to sound like I was relieved—but the minute she was out of the picture I was back on that tour on my own. Boy, I was very close friends of everybody." No longer seen as Babe's alter ego, Betty developed friendships with pros who had shunned her before. "I didn't really get to be as good friends with a lot of them until after Babe was gone because they just figured that I probably wasn't a very friendly person either. . . . [They figured] I didn't want to be with them because I just wanted to be where Babe was." In particular, Betty developed a close friendship with Louise Suggs, Babe's arch rival and recipient of playful unkindnesses. After Babe's passing Dodd became "just one of the big gang."[3]

Dodd went on to devote her life to golf as a player as well as a teacher. Although she never tires of telling Babe stories and in no way regrets the immense impact Babe has had on her life, she is rarely recognized for her central and intimate role in Babe's life. In 1988 Bertha Bowen recounted Dodd being "just thrilled to death" that she was elected to unveil a bronze memorial statue of Babe in San Antonio. That same year she was featured in Olympic televised coverage focusing on Babe. But these public recognitions are too few and too inadequate considering the depth of their relationship. While she speaks honestly of her love for Babe, she never loses sight of the line of appropriate femininity Babe tried to walk. Their bond was both rich and limited. Their closeness remains shrouded in silence long after Babe's death. This is due in part to Babe's carefully constructed autobiography that grossly marginalized Dodd, the highly fictionalized 1975 movie *Babe* that fueled visions of the Zahariases' wedded bliss, and concerted efforts by contemporaries to disavow the sustaining intimacy in their relationship lest it posthumously resurrect innuendos of lesbianism and thus, by our culture's particularly warped definitions, "discredit" Babe.[4]

George, after being refused by Florence Chadwick, did remarry twice. His second wife, Betty, an actress, was a mutual friend of his and Babe's. This union was short-lived. Dodd recalled Peggy Kirk Bell's ire at seeing this new wife, who "had on all of Babe's jewelry." His third wife, Harriet Apostolos, a woman who nursed him through his failing health, was described by Peggy as "a Greek woman who'd flipped over him when he was a wrestler." He was, by all accounts, a pathetic figure in his last years. Peggy, who saw George every two to three years, the last time six months before he died, recalled that George wanted her to raise money for him. He was terribly sick with a kidney problem, had become emaciated, and "cried and talked about the old times." George's sole claim to fame remained the old times with Babe. His 1984 obituary names neither his second nor third spouse and instead refers to him as "husband of athlete Babe Zaharias." One obituary closes with "Now, George is at her side again."[5]

Even after Babe's death, this "sentimental guy who did her bidding," as one reporter tagged George, continued to hustle on Babe's behalf and on his own. George's need for an economic livelihood, and his determination to keep the myth of their perfect union intact, produced some notable results. George swore immediately following Babe's death that he would "continue the fight that Babe started against cancer. I plan to do everything that I can in this fight." Thus he remained director of the Babe Didrikson Zaharias Cancer Fund and regularly accepted charitable proceeds on its behalf. With his aggressive help her accomplishments continued to be recognized; in 1957 she received the Bob Jones award for sportsmanship and her "fight for life in the name of golf." He also began negotiations with officials in Beaumont to build a permanent facility to house Babe's sports honors.[6]

Most of all, however, George claimed he left three legacies in Babe's name. The first was the Babe Zaharias Junior Golf Tournament for teenagers he said he originated and later sponsored in Tampa "for the children he and Babe could never have." Yet correspondence with Thad Johnson, for forty years sportswriter and editor of the *Beaumont Enterprise* during Babe's heyday and thereafter, reveals this is a total fabrication. Johnson, in 1993 a seventy-eight-year-old "devotee to newspaper, community and state," was the only living active charter member of the Texas Sports Writers Association and Texas Sports Hall of Fame. He followed her career with "dutiful intensity" as a professional, not a friend. He shared a letter from George Zaharias about the proposed tournament dated February 1970. In it, George urged Thad to "get some stationery up with Babe's name on it . . . and I think you and I can get this off the ground and make it real." To this letter Johnson appended a note reading, "never heard from him again. This took *work* . . . not talk."[7]

As Johnson wrote, "One thing I learned the agonizing way about awards: Somebody always was dreaming up an award. In most cases, these such recognitions died on the vine." Johnson's contempt for Zaharias's braggadocio is palpable: "I lost confidence in him. I found that in no way could I rely on his claims of origination in the awards area of sports. For example, he declared himself to have inaugurated the Texas Sports Hall of Fame. He had *absolutely nothing* to do with this. He credited himself as beginning other entities pertaining to sports, but didn't. I found that I could place no credence whatsoever in his babbling over matters relative to the ultra-greatness of his personable and talented wife."[8]

Second, he was "instrumental in the creation of the Associated Press' Woman Athlete of the Year Award, called the Babe Zaharias trophy." This distinct award, created in 1956, is not the same award Babe won six times. George promoted the newer award's implementation. Standing four feet high (the winner receives a two-foot bronze replica), the trophy, shaped like an Olympic torch and flame, has action poses of women competing in diverse sports carved into the flames. George claimed he presented the first one, in 1955, to Patty Berg. Yet in January 1957, the *New York Times* reported that Pat McCormick, an outstanding swimmer, received the first trophy in 1956 established by "Babe and her husband . . . to stimulate interest by women in amateur athletics." George presented the trophy to each and every recipient (including tennis champion Evonne Goolagong in 1971), as long as his health allowed.[9]

In 1990, a new award, the Babe Zaharias Female Amateur Athlete Award, was presented by Olympic gymnast Mary Lou Retton, who acted as director of ceremonies for the awards banquet sponsored by the Beaumont Convention and Visitors Bureau. This award did not replace the 1956 award George originated. Harriet Apostolos last presented "his" award to Wilma Rudolph in 1981. The 1990 recipient of this award, Suzy Favor, a superb amateur swimmer from the University of Wisconsin, received the trophy as well as a $10,000 scholarship.[10]

The third legacy, however, was the one that George, and probably Babe too, would have considered the greatest. In 1975, the movie *Babe*, starring Susan Clark and Alex Karras (who met making the movie and ultimately wed) cemented her image as a doting wife and George's image as a devoted husband. *TV Guide* promoted it thus: "She was one of the greatest female athletes of all time—he was the one who loved her and spurred her on." This double billing as a sports/love story was George's ultimate sleight of hand. In 1973 George told a reporter in Tampa, "They want to make a movie of our life. But all they want to do is Babe's records. That's not the story. The story is Babe and me. But 'Love Story' already has been done and that's our story."[11]

Thanks to George, their bond was portrayed idyllically. As Babe struggled with the diagnosis of cancer, George reassured her, "You're going to get well." Gloomily, Babe rejoined, "It's easy for you to say. It isn't happening to you." George retorted, "The hell it's not." At every opportunity George fueled this depiction so that by the time the movie was made, the public believed it. In a piece entitled "George Zaharias Says 'Thank You' " he eulogized, "Babe and I were close, very close, in our social and business lives. We always consulted each other and talked things out. There were few misunderstandings. Babe's one regret was that she would leave me alone. I will certainly miss her." And, in 1973, when asked to highlight a favorite memory they shared he emoted, "My fondest memory was every minute I was with her. Just for her to touch me. She had big, beautiful hands and long fingers. She had a touch that would electrify you."[12]

Bell, Dodd, Bowen, and Louis and Bubba Didriksen were not consulted on the film. Bell said, "It was a love story. It wasn't as honest as it could have been. The truth would have been a better story. . . . They never called any friends like myself or Betty Dodd or Patty Berg or anybody like that about Babe. They just talked to George and made a love story out of it." A *Beaumont Enterprise Journal* reviewer, upon the film's release, clucked, "The romance changes Babe from a surface hard, cocky, wise-cracking athlete into a woman providing a home for her man." The reviewer highlighted Babe's remarkable accomplishments and ended with "Babe loved to win—but she loved George Zaharias more." Another reviewer correctly perceived that "sports isn't the real story of 'Babe.' This is a story of love between two very nice people. . . . You will see their love develop, and finally the marriage of the athlete and the wrestler." Given her selection as Woman Athlete of the Year an unprecedented six times, George truly pulled off an astounding marketing feat.[13]

The *TV Guide* copy that promoted the film, Melvin Durslag's "Trying to Catch the Babe," chronicled George's historical unwillingness to cooperate on Babe's life story until 1974, when finances forced him to acquiesce to a pair of MGM executives, Norman Felton and Stanley Rubin. Felton recalled, "He said he would make the deal but emphasized, 'I want to see a check. I don't want conversation.' " In fact, George withdrew his permission until specific scenes were rewritten portraying their relationship more amiably. Durslag acknowledged that the film addressed and dismissed premarital rumors of Didrikson's "abnormalcy." According to an MGM executive, "'before she married him, there were whispers that she might be a lesbian. . . . We touch on this in the film. It is clear before her marriage that her sexual experience was limited. She seemed almost totally occupied with sports and training.' "[14]

Durslag presented a moving and realistic portrayal of the rigors Susan Clark underwent in converting herself into a credible athlete. She trained under a coach's tutelage at UCLA with the university's women's track team from 8:00 A.M. to 2:00 P.M. daily, sprinting, hurdling, throwing the javelin. Then she went to the gym to shoot baskets. From the campus she went to the driving range to hit upwards of three hundred balls per day until calluses appeared on her hands. Her eating and sleeping habits changed to withstand this regimen and "her back, arms and legs burned from pain." She melted away ten pounds on a frame with little excess and cut her brown hair to match the short-cropped Dutch boy of Babe's youth. Although the *Daily News Tribune* noted that she "collected a series of sore muscles, pulled tendons and assorted contusions," Clark claimed she felt healthier and more confident than ever before.[15] The training and contact with female athletes opened her eyes and made her "really respect female athletes" who took themselves seriously "even though most people do not take them seriously for doing it." She also tasted what it was like for Babe to play with pain. One day she cut her leg going over a hurdle, fell, and had it land on top of her. The coach, who would not let her quit practicing, told her she would get used to the pain. And she did, although her knee remained swollen for a month. Clark quipped, this film "proves that if I can learn to hurdle, women are capable of anything."[16]

Yet despite some realism, the movie was woefully inaccurate, "filled with factual mistakes and fraught with soap-opera cliches." First and foremost, Dodd does not appear in the film. One scholar surveying portrayals of women athletes in films declared this a common omission. "There are few, if any, scenes of female camaraderie or support among female athletes in films, yet anyone who has observed or participated in sports activities would find it difficult to believe these women's lives didn't include a female sports community or important female friends." Although male bonding within sports is seen as crucial to team success, it casts no aspersions of homosexuality because male athletes epitomize heterosexual ideals of competitive manhood. But because female athletes in no way embody ideals of femininity, female bonding would imply lesbianism and hence besmirch the accomplishments and "normalcy" of all involved. In fact, more than one historian has noted the dual proclivities in portraying female athletes. They are either surrounded by guiding and loving coaches, husbands, or male friends and therefore not homosexual or they are "handicapped or die young" and therefore have little or no sexuality in Hollywood's dangerously limited lexicon.[17]

No Dodd, no cutting one-liners, no prickly locker-room confrontations, no braggadocio, but instead, as Peggy Kirk Bell noted irritably, flat-out errors in golfing history. The film portrays a tense moment when the announcer whispers, "If Babe makes this putt she'll win the U.S. Open." In reality she won it by thirteen strokes and smashed the record. Nor did she meekly surrender to her doctor with "Whatever you say . . ." followed by a whimpering "Oh! Don't touch my body." To those aware of her athletic greatness and physical resiliency, these characterizations still rankle.[18]

In addition, the film portrayed her as a gender-conscious analyst of the difficulties facing women athletes. Babe, erroneously portrayed as nearly single-handedly establishing the LPGA, delivers the following monologue: "No one encourages women to compete at all. If you're born with a talent for athletics and you're a female, you either apologize for that talent and drag it out at family picnics, or, if you're serious about it, you sneak around to the back doors to practice while men go in the front. In schools, you get the courts and field only when the boys are done using them. You're second class all the way down the line. And, if in spite of that you make a name for yourself as a female athlete, the world calls you a freak!"[19]

In fact, Babe was not articulate about sports, gender, or sex discrimination. Nor was she a conscious role model for other women athletes. She acted in keeping with the behavior and values of most exceptional professional women from the 1930s through the 1950s. Believing that "individual merit" would win out, most women listened to the "equality of opportunity" rhetoric and did not align themselves with feminism or become involved in women's issues. Babe believed completely in herself and seemed not to think much beyond her own accomplishments. What she was concerned about was winning and "herself. Really. I mean I hate to say that," Dodd confided, "but it's true. . . . As far as golf was concerned I think she felt that golf would just fold [without her]. I think she really thought that." Her lack of reflection on her Olympic victories and refusal to confront cultural responses to her speak to her utilitarian, self-protective, categorically unanalytical, nonintrospective, and typically poor southern female character. As Dodd surmised, "I think that she didn't think that anybody could ever be as good as she was. I mean that was probably her attitude exactly."[20]

Her bullying of LPGA board members on trivial points to benefit herself attests to her lack of a larger mission. In this regard, she was unlike politically motivated women athletes such as Billie Jean King, whose personal accomplishments and posturing have benefited tennis as well as her own career. King won numerous championships but perhaps is most famous for her 1973 "Battle of the Sexes" with Bobby Riggs, staged in Madison Square Garden after Riggs claimed any man could beat a woman. Evaluating her tennis accomplishments King said, "Winning at Wimbledon a fifth time gave me the most personal satisfaction last year . . . but the Riggs match put tennis on the map. It was great for tennis, and I'm proud of that, too." It was, in fact, a turning point in women's sports history. The dignity and feminist motivation with which King beat Riggs and dismissed his posturing uplifted all women athletes. This public stance as a woman's rights advocate was never embraced by Didrikson, although her behavior inspired others.[21]

Babe was at all times at the center of her universe; she did not see herself as a pathbreaker for others. Not one friend or family member could name someone Babe idolized, although Dodd noted she admired Amelia Earhart and Katharine Hepburn. Earhart, Babe conceded, had "the most beautiful hands that she'd ever seen." And while Babe was fond of Hepburn, she never went to see her movies. Babe loved meeting President and Mrs. Eisenhower in 1954 and considered her White House visit a thrill. But no one approximated Babe's admiration of herself. "I think she was probably her own idol," Dodd said.[22]

When Babe, sentimental, riveting, inaccurate, and legend-building opened in Beaumont, a local entrepreneur staged a premiere worthy of P. T. Barnum. Ben J. Rogers, who together with three brothers ran Texas State Optical and Rogers' Brothers investments, multimillion-dollar corporations, set his considerable talents on enshrining Babe. "I'm a mover," Rogers said in 1975 with a candor and bravado worthy of Babe. "Always have been and always will be. When I start a project, I can't stop until it's completed." The first president of the Babe Didrikson Zaharias Foundation, Inc., which was established to raise funds for a museum and to further promote Babe, Rogers orchestrated an entourage of fifteen black limousines for the premiere that "sped through the night along Interstate 10 of this Texas gulf city snaking its way past farm houses and oil derricks toward a theatre downtown."[23]

The fifty-dollar-a-head gala included the movie, dinner, and dancing at the Parkdale Mall. Clark and Karras were there, as were former heavyweight champion Joe Louis, who later recalled the numerous times Babe had bet she'd beat him playing golf: "She was a great lady . . . and she got a lot of my money, too." Also in attendance were Walter Cunningham, astronaut; Steven Mills, executive producer of programs for CBS; Stanley Rubin and Norman Felton, Babe's co-producers; David Goldsmith, executive producer for CBS; Frank Glicksman, MGM executive producer; Jack Brooks, member of Congress; Pike Powers and Carl Parker, state representatives; Ken Ritter, mayor of Beaumont; Joe Fisher, federal judge; John Gray, president of Lamar University; and Lillie Grimes, ever-loyal sister. Betty Ford, first lady, was the honorary national chairperson for the premiere, and Rogers read a letter from her. Conspicuously absent was George Zaharias. Sixty-seven years old and recovering from a stroke, he said, "I would've been there if possible, but I just couldn't make it." Ill health and the stormy process of filmmaking kept him away. "We had a few squabbles working out details on the picture," he admitted, "but it all turned out good."[24]

Babe was extremely well received. The *Los Angeles Times* reviewer wrote, "Watching her story unfold in flashbacks, I was profoundly stirred. Not only by Babe but the era in which she outran the world." Kudos went to Clark "who we always knew could act" and to Karras. "The big man will break you up. It's not only the best acting job he's ever done, it's hard to imagine anyone doing George Zaharias better. There's not only the wrestler, the athlete, the emotional Greek that he shows us, but also the promoter, the crafty manager of his wife's career." In fact, before the shooting Alex Karras saw George briefly "and asked his advice on playing the part. Zaharias' answer was brief. 'Love her,' he said." The critic for the *Houston Post* concurred: her athletic feats and "one of the world's great love stories" were "portrayed sensitively." Clark's performance earned her an Emmy. The movie also received an Emmy nomination for outstanding special.[25]

Babe would have reveled in the film's impact. "She was angular and unattractive, and the greatest woman athlete of her time. Perhaps all time," one reviewer began. But he, like others, switched tones abruptly. As the *Los Angeles Times* critic wrote under the telling subheading "Just a Regular Woman," "A freak Babe was not. Early on in the film, a nurse murmurs, 'Why, she looks like a regular woman.' That's the portrait Susan gives you—a regular woman, a little shy and distant, more at home in the field than the drawing room, but a regular woman who loved her guy." And "her guy" loved the film. Babe's normalcy was reaffirmed for the thousandth time, his devotion impeccably portrayed. In fact, George, believing he'd given Peggy Kirk Bell his only copy of the film, cried when he learned she didn't have it.[26]

In addition to her film legacy George wished to maintain Babe's real sports legacy. He pledged that her trophies would be brought to Beaumont for permanent display "if a suitable place for the trophies is provided." Mayor Jimmie Cokinos promised such a facility "as soon as Babe's trophies are catalogued" and as soon as the space needed was known. As early as 1956, discussion began about a "shrine" (George's word of choice) to house Babe's trophies, medals, awards, citations, equipment, photos, press clippings, and sports clothing. The first shipment of trophies and medals arrived in Beaumont in October 1956. In a historical irony, Babe's greatness was invoked around that time to counterbalance the negative publicity the town received when a newly organized White Citizen's Council hustled two black students off the Lamar campus while "100 white persons . . . formed the picket line . . . and some 30 police patrolled the campus but made no effort to disperse the pickets." Apparently Babe's memory as a sports hero overshadowed any realistic account of her views toward blacks and Jews.[27]

After this flurry of publicity her awards gathered dust until a chamber of commerce committee co-chaired by Ben Rogers and Thad Johnson restarted plans for a memorial in 1969. Johnson had argued for a museum, including a life-size statue at the main entrance, in the fall of 1968. The committee proposed a memorial costing between $8,000 and $10,000, but when the plans were sent to George he proposed a much larger structure costing about $100,000 and offered to donate the first $10,000. The city council finally gave ten acres of land to the committee along the I-10 freeway for construction of the museum and agreed to George's grander scheme.[28]

Plans were underway, but the thirteen-year lull between 1956 and 1969 earned Beaumont officials a few rebukes. True, "Babe Zaharias Drive" had been named on March 13, 1956, "in honor of a distinguished citizen and the world's greatest woman athlete," but that was the total homage paid in her hometown. In 1964 the Southwestern Historical Wax Museum in Dallas installed a full-size, smiling wax figure of Didrikson in dress and golf hat swinging a club. In 1976 the Zaharias cancer fund was responsible for purchasing a $60,000 top-of-the-line radioactive cobalt machine for the University of Texas Medical Branch. A plaque was unveiled "memorializing Babe's . . . fight against cancer." When the Texas Historical Marker was placed at Babe's grave in 1967, a columnist wrote, it "represents commendable state and local interest in one of the most fabulous sports figures of all time, and we are deeply grateful to the sponsoring organizations."[29]

"But this is not enough," the columnist scolded. "We direct observation, perhaps reprimand is a better word, to the world-famous athlete's home city and her old neighbors." The irate author concluded, "Unless we come up soon with a plan for adequately housing and displaying Babe's trophies, Beaumont has lost them forever. And that loss we could blame on no one but ourselves." Pictured alongside this impassioned account is Bebe, Babe's fifteen-year-old poodle who lived with Lillie. The pooch is gazing at a blown-up chart of Babe's accomplishments with a jar beside her that says "Give to Help Keep Babe's Memory Alive." Also in 1968, Thad Johnson implored locals: "What a pity. She gave so much to this city and received so little in return."[30]

Yet despite the exhortations of Babe's supporters and their fledgling attempts at preserving Babe's memory, her birthplace home was razed in spring 1970. Criticizing this as a short-sighted and ahistorical move, boosters redoubled their efforts at erecting a museum. The "Babe Memorial Drive" began that very May. "Operation Kickoff," sponsored by the chamber of commerce and based at I-10 and Gulf Street, the future home of the museum, started fund-raising efforts for the $100,000 memorial. Proclamations were read declaring it "Babe Day" in Texas by Governor Preston Smith and in Beaumont by Mayor James D. McNicholas. Babe's trophies were proudly displayed by her sister Lillie. Prior to the 1975 opening of the Babe Didrikson Zaharias Museum, a special exhibition, aptly entitled "The Lady and the Legend: The Babe Didrikson Zaharias Memorial Collection," was temporarily set up by the Babe Didrikson Zaharias Foundation, Inc., and the chamber of commerce for the inaugural exhibition of the Beaumont Sports Museum at Finger's Furniture Center.[31]

The *Beaumont Enterprise Journal* devoted several pages to Babe Didrikson Zaharias Sports Week due to begin in mid-May 1975. The six-day salute "to the memory of the greatest athlete . . . aimed to raise $4,000 to aid the cancer fight." Babe's supporters also hoped the publicity might generate more funds for the museum. Later that year Ben Rogers announced he had raised about $50,000 for the museum and building should commence. He masterminded the ground-breaking ceremonies for the construction of the Babe Didrikson Zaharias Museum (replete with gold shovels) and the establishment of the John Gray–Babe Zaharias Scholarship Fund to coincide with the movie premiere of *Babe*. The $52,000 in funds raised at the premiere went toward the building of the museum as well as to Lamar University. John Gray accepted the money to establish a scholarship for an outstanding woman athlete at Lamar. The award, designed to go to a qualified student athlete with an "unbeatable spirit," was a gender-conscious sports legacy bestowed in Babe's honor.[32]

When the museum was finally opened on November 27, 1976, almost eight years to the day after its construction was begun, visitors were treated to an architecturally unique structure that was aesthetically appreciated by the community. The round museum, with the five interlocking Olympic rings in the center, was presented a beautification award by the Beaumont Women's Club in May 1979, and in 1983 the facility received the Public Attractiveness Tribute. Despite the completion of the building, the foundation was $45,000 in debt. Undaunted, Ben Rogers reported, "Donations to erase that deficit keep pouring in. People will not forget Babe Zaharias. They cannot forget her."[33]

In 1985, an auction held in conjunction with the Babe Zaharias Open raised $12,000 for the museum by selling off sports memorabilia including a shirt signed by Dallas Cowboys head coach Tom Landry, a golf glove autographed by Lee Trevino, and Willie Shoemaker's Kentucky Derby horse racing boots. The field of 288 players raised an additional $18,000, "money that will cover 60 percent of the operating expenses" of the museum for that year.[34]

The same year ground was broken for the museum and *Babe* premiered provided a turning point for the Beaumont-hosted Babe Zaharias Open too. When Althea Gibson, a tennis marvel and a black woman, entered the tournament, the Rotary Club withdrew its financial support. The tournament was canceled the following year. Later the Babe Zaharias Open moved to Cleveland but Beaumonters lamented the switch in locale.[35]

Although the first Cleveland tourney was given some legitimacy by the appearance of Patty Berg, who had been playing in it for five decades and won in four of them, the event was plagued from the onset with leadership and financial problems tinged with scandal. Ed Haddad, a Cleveland attorney with two previous skirmishes in shady fund-raising, assumed its helm and announced his hopes to parlay the money raised from it into a $50 million cancer research center honoring Babe in Cleveland. Additional proceeds were promised to the American Cancer Society; the Babe Didrikson Zaharias Cancer Fund; the Babe Didrikson Zaharias Foundation, Inc.; and Bob Hope's charity, the Eisenhower Medical Center in Palm Springs, California, among others. The $100,000 in prize money wasn't secured until two to three days before the tournament commenced and Haddad went $20,000 in debt to tournament suppliers. The tourney was a resounding financial flop. Of all the charities promised donations, only Babe's cancer fund, which received $1,600, and some high schools saw any money. Worse yet, no one filed for tax-exempt status as a charity for the Babe Didrikson Zaharias Foundation, Inc., so outsiders assumed that the foundation was profiting from the tournament. The credibility of the foundation was left tarnished while the tourney's future, taken away from the protective hands of devoted Beaumonters, was uncertain.[36]

What remains certain is Babe's powerful legacy as a medical humanitarian. Her efforts were recognized in awards from the American Cancer Society in 1954 and the Public Health Cancer Association of America in 1956.

And on January 22, 1957, a resolution was passed in the Texas House of Representatives paying tribute to "the memory of this gallant Texas lady . . . for her athletic career" and "her dramatic fight against cancer." As always, Babe's renown in this area was largely fostered by herself in collaboration with the press. A press release circa 1955 credits not her athletic accomplishments but her cancer fund as "Babe's big gift to the world."[37]

During her battle with cancer, Babe evolved from a self-centered athlete to a bona fide humanitarian. Yet, despite her substantial financial assistance in the fight against cancer Babe's real legacy to the American public was mixed. She surely provided much-needed awareness about cancer but at the same time she posed as one ready, and perhaps even able, to emerge victorious over any foe, including cancer. The very bravado that sheltered her adoring public from her uncertainties and distress cloaked the precise sentiments and isolationism that she shared with other cancer patients. As a result, rather than offering to them a realistic model of genuine communicativeness, introspection, and resolution, Babe offered instead a conqueror's independent stoicism laced with denial, courage, good humor, and distorted hope. This model, though tempting, demanded unrealistic behavior for cancer patients and ultimately deceived an American public all too eager to deny this frightening and bewildering disease. Yet the subtlety of this contradiction eluded her contemporaries, as so much of her contradictory life did. To them, she was a haloed hero.[38]

The Sports Legacy

She ended her sports career with dignity. There were no disappointing and minimizing comeback attempts, no promises left unkept. Unlike Jim Palmer, Mark Spitz, and Bjorn Borg, who tried desperately in the 1990s to overcome their inactivity and age, Didrikson was in peak form almost to the end of her competitive days. Her exit can be compared with Ted Williams's 1960 eighth-inning final at-bat in the last home game at Fenway Park. Williams delivered his 521st career homer beyond the center-field wall. After that, he laid down his bat forever. As one sports journalist remarked, "He never went to the plate again. Ted Williams quit right there, on the spot. . . . Now *that* is the way to do it, on the day forever comes." As one children's book said of her, "When she died, no one considered that she had lost, just that time had run out on her game."[39]

Babe went out on top with eighty-two tournament wins in her eighteen-year dominance of women's golf. She was inducted into the Texas Sports Hall of Fame by the Texas Sports Writers Association (December 1954); the LPGA Hall of Fame (1968); the National Track and Field Hall of Fame (August 30, 1974); the Texas Golf Hall of Fame (August 23, 1978); the International Women's Sports Hall of Fame; the Helms Athletic Foundation Hall of Fame (for basketball), and the PGA Hall of Fame (January 1977). She received literally dozens of awards, including the Graham McNamee Memorial Award as the greatest woman athlete in history, voted by the Sports Broadcasters Association (February 2, 1956); the Academy Awards of Sports Courage Award for "showing great courage in overcoming tremendous physical hardships" (April 27, 1987, Mobile, Alabama); the Associated Press Female Athlete of the Half Century (1950); the William D. Richardson Memorial Trophy for outstanding contributions to golf by the Golf Writer's Association of America (1953); the American Cancer Society Certificate of Appreciation "for notable assistance in the Crusade to Conquer Cancer" (1954); two *Los Angeles Times* Merit Awards; the Philadelphia Sports Writers Association Most Courageous Athlete of 1953 Award (January 25, 1954); the Greater Tampa Chamber of Commerce Outstanding Woman Athlete of the Half Century Award for track, basketball, and golf (December 14, 1954); the Brith Shalom National Sports Award for sportsmanship, fair play, and courage (February 27, 1956); the Greatest Female Athlete of the Past Fifty Years by the nation's Associated Press sportswriters, sponsored by the *Washington Post* (1950); the Greatest Sportswoman of All Time by the Zonta Club of Fort Worth, Texas (1956); Player of the Decade, 1938–47, on the occasion of the centennial of golf in America (1988); and the Optimist International Award. She is also one of a handful of sports women to be honored on a commemorative stamp, issued September 22, 1981.[40]

Her awards and her effect on others continue even more than thirty years after her death. In 1992 Thad Johnson devoted himself to posthumously awarding Babe with a gold medal in the high jump. After the 1988 Summer Olympic Games, Thad Johnson and Ben Rogers, who viewed Didrikson's half silver, half gold medal an egregious injustice, filed an appeal with the Olympic Committee seeking co-championship for Babe with Jean Shiley since each cleared 5 feet ¼ inch. In a thirty-four-page brochure they compiled details about the event, stressing that her "jumping style was well-known and accepted in track circles. Canada's Duncan McNaughton used the same form as Babe to win the men's gold medal." Johnson, a zealot in the tradition of Scurlock, likens this campaign to the sixty-year struggle to have Jim Thorpe's Olympic medals restored after charges that he was a professional stripped him of them. "So we mustn't lose faith if we are turned down in our first appeal."[41]

As Patty Berg testified in 1980, Didrikson's impact on sports went far beyond her personal awards. "The tremendous results of the doors she [helped] open for women in sports" are astounding. These include the federal implementation of Title IX, which guarantees equal funding for girls' and women's sports at all public institutions (which has, ironically, caused a severe decrease in the number of female coaches and presents numerous problems of enforcement); the comparative good health of the women's pro golf, tennis, and bowling tours; and the cultural support for physical fitness and competition for women at the leisure, community, high school, collegiate, professional, and Olympic levels.[42]

This legacy clearly establishes her as a once-in-a-lifetime athlete and personality. Said Gallico, erstwhile hangman and idolater, "She was probably the most talented athlete, male or female, ever developed in our country. In all my years at the sports desk I never encountered any man who could play as many different games as well as the Babe." As an elderly man in one of her galleries commented: " 'Take a good look at her, bub. There was never anybody like her until she started to play this game. She may lose a match here and there; but when she stops playing, nobody'll see her like again for a hundred years. She's the Hogan, Nelson, and Locke of her sex all rolled into one!' Commented chronicler Pete Martin, 'Even Annie Oakley couldn't have asked for a finer tribute!' " Her excellence inspired Pete Martin to write in 1947, "The word to describe Babe is 'frabjuous'—used by Lewis Carroll in *Alice in Wonderland*—This is fabulous raised to a high degree, and fits the Babe as snugly as the running pants she wore in the 1932 Olympics, which hugged her boyish figure as if they were sprayed on."[43]

Her athletic excellence combined with her personality led kin, friends, golf peers, and Beaumonters to care deeply for her, almost revere her. She was unshakably loyal, caring, and forthright. And while she never missed a chance to praise her own talents, she also never felt above helping or reaching out. As Herb Grassis, a Chicago sportswriter, said, this "celebrated girl would help do the dishes in your home." She bad-mouthed no one, although she could, and did, taunt competitors to tears. Hence her name always comes up when her golf peers gather. Betty Jameson remarked, "If we're at our reunion we'd like to have The Babe. At the Hall of Fame we're always talking about Babe." Berg, too, noted the special qualities of Babe: "There was always something distinctive about her. . . . She was not only a popular, gifted athlete but also a champion as a woman and as a human being." These intangible qualities inspired Ben Hogan and Sam Snead, while participating in the Canada Cup in 1956, to suspend the tournament to pray for her. Players from thirty countries observed a moment of silence on her forty-fifth birthday.[44]

As one writer described her in her earlier years, "She has an irresistible legend-generating quality. . . . She has become a part of our national folklore." Sure, she tooted her own horn, Pete Martin giddily admitted, but there was always that Midas touch. When "she blew out of Texas in 1931 like a whirling twister giving her competitors her dust, she was gutsy and bumptious, not to say cocky."[45]

Few other athletes inspired journalists to such heights—and depths. Granny Rice wrote a poem praising her in 1935. The adoration for her shines through sixty years later:

> From the high jump of Olympic fame,
> The hurdles and the rest,
> The javelin that flashed its flame
> On by the record test—
> The Texas Babe now shifts the scene
> Where slashing drives are far
> Where spoon shots find the distant green
> To break the back of par.[46]

She knew how to be a champion. Although she never used Ali's phrase, she said "I am the greatest of all time!" in a thousand ways. She postured like a champion. Truly, "she never let people down with what they expected of her." In fact, Babe's refusal to ever blame a loss on anyone or anything except herself is still a refreshing attitude amidst whining athletes who lean on injuries, opponents, or personnel issues as scapegoats. She did this to her own detriment at times, for she forsook genuine expressions of fear, love, and despair. But her character enabled her to cope with her own disappointments and depression at the end of her life by cheering those around her. As one observer wrote, from "her big bear of a husband to the youngest janitor who mopped the hospital corridors . . . Babe was an uplifting example." Babe's good cheer, masking inner pain and physical distress, "was sincere," wrote one who visited her in her last days. "It was characteristic. For she believed in showing emotions, . . . especially if the emotion was happiness. She lived life for what it was worth, and she made her 42 years on earth memorable ones for everyone who knew her." Babe's personality, as distinctive and unparalleled as her sports accomplishments, did not elicit neutral responses: she was adored or abhorred, but always a force to be reckoned with.[47]

The tributes continued after her death, mixing fact with fiction. As recently as 1990 *Women's Sports and Fitness,* the leading publication in the field, ran a story entitled "The Babe Is Here: Greatest Woman Athlete of All Time," which was a flattering rehash of all the old triumphs, myths, and lies. Most, not surprisingly, bought into the myth Babe and George had created about themselves. Arthur Daley's "A Remarkable Woman" (1959) said, "But behind that steel-sinewed, square-jawed facade was feminine softness and gushy sentimentality. . . . This was no mere muscle girl who died the other day." George Zaharias's death in 1984 occasioned more resurrections of their ideal union and her wifely side. "The most important thing in George's life," the reporter asserted, "was his bride Babe, the one-time tomboy of Beaumont. 'She was a beautiful person, a wonderful wife,' he said on more than one occasion."[48]

Despite the tributes from supporters, contemporaries and historians continue to debate the sum total of Babe's contribution to women's sports. The most frequent critical charge is that she fueled negative stereotypes of women athletes, making it difficult for those who followed to live down and begin to change that image. "Babe herself became a symbol of the negative effects competitive sports could have on women." While some observers contended that "Babe outlived her mannish track and field days," many claimed Babe later became a caricature of herself. According to Hicks, "Babe Zaharias . . . allowed herself—indeed, pleaded—to be stereotyped, mimicked, mocked, whispered about and exploited." Even in the midsixties Carol Mann, a professional golfer, tried to live down this part of Didrikson's legacy. Her self-consciousness about her 6 foot 3 inch frame was mitigated by her determination to be "particularly careful to look as feminine as possible." Mann admonished, "We should all try to look more ladylike on the course. Being thought of as anything but a woman absolutely frosts me." Like Babe, she cared deeply about how she was perceived.[49]

Another interpretation suggests Babe instead acted as an affirming role model for women.

> The association between masculinity, lesbianism and sport may have had a more positive outcome for some women. In the dominant culture, lesbianism formed a category of deviance internal to womanhood, a dangerous 'no-man's land' between 'real' womanhood and male sexual privilege. Sport too formed a 'no-man's land' situated at the border between new definitions of womanhood and old domains of male power. Because of this confluence of meanings and possibilities, the lesbian athlete was most likely not only a figure of discourse but a living product of women's sexual struggle and cultural innovation.[50]

Perhaps more obviously objectionable for her peers was Babe's willingness to ingratiate herself to officials, sponsors, and reporters. And while she courted public approval, some criticized her for "using" men. Pete Martin wrote in 1947 that there were two kinds of men to Babe: those who would help her and those who wouldn't. "She confronted [the latter] by looking them bleakly in the eye and telling them how good she was. If she said she was good loud enough, it made the papers." Although many pros were unwilling to sell themselves to reporters or partake in the cocktail party socials, Babe's absence made that ever more necessary. More than one pro commented that "after Babe's death the tour hit the skids for a few years." By 1958, cocktail parties, under the watchful eye of the LPGA, were held at half the tournaments and scheduled events so that pros could improve their public image and express their appreciation to country clubs, reporters, and radio broadcasters.[51]

Additionally, Babe left a legacy of devastating comments for her opponents to remember years later. Wrote Hicks candidly, "I withered on confrontation with a living legend." Twice runner-up to Babe at the Texas Open (1940, 1946), Hicks recalled, "Forty-five years is a long time to remember exact feelings of pain, anger, frustration." Hicks was up by four with eleven holes to play, yet lost on the thirty-sixth hole. Babe's expression of concern still irks Hicks: " 'Ya got tired, d'ntcha?' Babe asked, as we shook hands late that October afternoon in 1940. I nodded," Hicks laments, "but I did not agree. I was only 19, and 36 holes were a stroll in the country for me then. Naw, Babe, I thought, I just began dreaming of the ecstasy of beating you, and the joy of it got in the way of my swing."[52]

Babe tried diligently to purge these criticisms of her masculine and aggressive image. Early on, "the Babe accepted the popular concept of herself as a tomboy and muscle moll with a grimly set jaw. Her temperament and the body nature had given her made her a 'loner.' Her remarks about women were corrosive." But in telling *This Life I've Led* she deconstructed "unflattering" episodes. For example, she denied scaling outside walls at the Olympics to snag souvenirs. "It wasn't just me doing it," she said. "It was a bunch of us girls. And we didn't scale any outside walls. We went up inside the buildings to where we could reach out and grab what we wanted." Similarly, she denied to national magazines ever wrestling, boxing, or playing football. This denial came despite nationally circulated AP wire photos showing her pursuing all three sports.[53]

These denials aside, one sports historian convincingly argued:

Babe Didrikson Zaharias, more than any other female athlete of her day, embodied the new female athlete. Zaharias changed cultural perceptions of the physical limitations of womanhood using her body as a weapon. She ignored those who attempted to bar her from opportunity because of her class origins and aggressive style. And although she eventually knuckled under to society's dictates, for many years she stood in direct defiance of sex and class prejudice in the world of sport and in society at large. Guided only by her desire to be the best at whatever she did and her determination to take care of herself, and her family, Babe Didrikson Zaharias became the standard for excellence in women's sports for several decades.[54]

The standard Didrikson set was complicated by her pressuring of other women athletes to "be normal" (heterosexual and feminine). As a personal role model, then, Didrikson remains carefully constructed yet controversial, but as an economic role model, she remains unparalleled. In 1948 Babe was the leading money winner on the LPGA tour with $3,400, but she made much more than this. In the late 1940s and early 1950s, "her income from endorsements, exhibitions, and appearances totalled $100,000 annually." In Babe's era, "healthy though the LPGA was, not even the most successful players could live in any high style on prize money alone." Babe's greatest single tournament cash prize was $2,100. Her best year earned her only $15,087 playing golf. "Everyone on the tour had to keep hustling up extra jobs, exhibitions, endorsements. Babe was better at this too, than anyone on the tour."[55]

She embodied the American dream: from the street to stardom and wealth. Thanks largely to her popularity and her hustling the LPGA's economic strength grew in leaps and bounds. By 1954 the total LPGA tour's purse exceeded $100,000 over twenty-three tournaments, and eighteen women pros additionally served on the staff of nine sporting goods companies with an average income of $15,000 each. In 1956, Marlene Hagge earned $20,235. In 1969 Carol Mann became the first pro to earn $50,000 in one year from playing golf. Yet despite these significant increases, "the money earnings of women golfers nowhere approached the prize monies awarded to the men." Worse yet, the attendees at the LPGA's annual business meeting in 1956 lamented the decrease in actual take-home purse money from $154,000 in 1955 to $139,000 in 1956. The 10 percent fee subtracted from winners' earnings by the LPGA club treasury for operating expenses was to blame. This problem was solved by adding a 12 percent service fee to contracts negotiated with tournament-hosting country clubs so that winners' earnings went untouched.[56]

Earning less money had made a difficult living impossible. As Hicks told *Golf World* in "Why I'm Quitting Tournament Golf" in 1956, "If you're below sixth in money winnings on the LPGA list, you aren't paying your freight." Annual expenses averaged $7,000 to $8,000 (including such things as automobile expenses, caddie fees, hotels, meals, golf equipment, clothes, cleaning, and laundering), which forced 75 percent of the players to survive on other incomes or live frugally "in hopes that they would be able to deduct the loss from their income tax." Hence Hicks resigned as a touring pro because the $20,000 she'd earned in her two and a half years of play "did not offset the amount of money necessary to cover her expenses."[57] Hicks was not alone. These financial difficulties forced "some of the most promising stars such as Betty MacKinnon, Jackie Pung, Pat O'Sullivan, Carol Bowman, and Lesbia Lobo" into retirement. To help remedy these myriad problems Fred Corcoran was rehired in 1958 as tournament director of the LPGA.[58]

As early as 1956 the LPGA suffered attendance problems, blamed on not enough "publicity which might build each woman as a personality." Hence, sportswriters were furnished with participants' biographies two weeks prior to tournament play. At that time Patty Berg suggested that "a committee of five girls should be designated to entertain the sports writers and sponsors at each location." So it was done. And Mickey Wright, in another attempt to fuel interest in the sport, suggested that "interest in the game might be enhanced if the women played from the ladies tees. The scores would thus be lowered; and the game, more exciting." This too was implemented. Babe abhorred playing from the shorter women's tees because she thought it capitulated to presumed male superiority. She would have detested this decision, but she would have dominated the tour even more. "Had Babe been playing on these truncated layouts, she would be scoring many rounds in the low sixties. Since she died, no one has come remotely close to matching her dominance of women's golf."[59]

Thanks in part to these attempts to buoy the LPGA, by the midseventies, as Babe's biographers noted, "the days of Babe Didrikson Zaharias are far behind us. . . . Since then, the condition of women in sport has improved—but perhaps less than one might have hoped." At the 1976 Babe Zaharias Open Berg reminded a reporter of just how much purses had changed. In the first Babe Zaharias Open Didrikson won $875 of a total $3,500 purse. Come 1976, the tourney was a full-fledged LPGA tour stop with a $100,000 purse. The winner would receive $15,000. In 1975, thirty-six tournaments generated $2,200,000 in prize money, offering winners a chance at earning $50,000 per year.[60]

Still, purses lagged behind those for men. In an ironic example of re-discovering the wheel, leaders in and commentators on women's golf again suggested that purses would only increase when the women pros became less "nameless and faceless" and developed media-ready personalities like those on the men's tour. Although the LPGA had secured corporate sponsorship from Colgate, S&H Green Stamps, Sealy-Faberge, and Sears, people were not interested in watching. As two chroniclers noted, "The Ladies Professional Golf Association is rich and successful, though lacking in color and charisma." Carol Mann argued in a 1991 newspaper column that the LPGA's mission was more media exposure. According to one essayist, the LPGA has "got some good-looking women who can play, and this needs exploitation." Increased media exposure might increase interest, but the LPGA no longer had a charismatic centerpiece. The intangible electricity that Babe exuded cannot be packaged. The precise attributes that rankled so many also helped her sport immeasurably; she has yet to be replaced in that realm of leadership.[61]

Babe's other positive legacy to women's sports was the combination of her ground-breaking physique with her skill and her fierce competitive spirit. She was a first, and as such, her own disavowals aside, she eased the way for those who followed. Because she stretched the parameters of acceptable body form, single-sport expertise, and aggressive approaches to sports for women, she expanded the range of behaviors and opportunities open to them.

These traits still set her apart from other women athletes and serve as an inspiration for other female competitors. Upon being named Athlete of the Year for 1988, the track and field star Jackie Joyner-Kersee singled out Babe as the finest all-around athlete. And sportswriters, lacking a contemporary parallel, resurrect tales of Babe when fanciful comparisons between male and female athletes surface. In a 1990 column a writer for the *Los Angeles Times* speculated that Babe was the only female athlete capable of throwing a baseball from third to first in time to get a runner out.[62]

As her athletic prowess still echoes, so does her physique. Since Babe's track and field days a fifty-year lull ensued until the 1980s explosive interest in female bodybuilders triggered opinionated debate over women athletes' physiques. Dubbed "The Unprecedented Women," these sleek, muscular, strong women confront the same dilemmas Babe faced. Chronicled in the 1985 documentary film *Pumping Iron II: The Women,* they receive the same gender-restricted imperatives Babe confronted in the 1930s. One especially muscular competitor heard "the judges declare that femininity is the goal, not muscles." Still seen as freakish, these athletes struggle with self-esteem and others' damning opinions, as did Babe. Said one competitor, "When a woman walks in who has a radically different look it challenges you to decide what you think about it. Some people think I look beautiful. Some people are disgusted." In a statement reflecting the strength one garners from a cultural context informed by feminist consciousness she added, "I have to detach myself from their opinions; I feel good about my muscles and about myself." Yet this athlete, the first to reject wearing high-heeled shoes during competitions, closed the interview by discussing her boyfriend in great detail.[63]

So the old question of "normalcy" hovers around these body-building groundbreakers, too. As Gloria Steinem observed, the entire contest resembles a traditional beauty pageant. "Most of all, there is a fervent ongoing debate about what 'femininity' is. . . . Their pleasure in their own strength is limited by a constant need to point out that muscles are feminine, that body balance and symmetry are the point, and that they *themselves* are real women." Then Steinem strikes at the heart of the issue when she says of Australian Bev Francis, by far the most muscularly developed competitor, "Unlike the other contestants she looks no more conventionally beautiful than, say, Billie Jean King or Babe Didrikson." The cultural response to these "boundary-breakers," as Steinem called them, takes the same toll on them as it took on Babe.[64]

This cultural response in some arenas leads to hormonal testing. Spain's high hurdler Maria Jose Martinez Patino, the first woman to publicly protest the sex test ruling that excluded her from competition for three years, said after the reversal in 1991, "I feel like I've been given license to be a woman again." As former Olympic heptathlete Jane Frederick observed about the IOC, "I think they're saying, 'You're so good, we can't believe you're a woman, so prove it.'"[65]

Even today female athletes feel they have to prove themselves and thus experience stress and feelings of anxiety over "balancing" their conflicting sports and gender roles. Homophobia encourages women to espouse heterosexuality and deny very real same-sex attachments. Martina Navratilova's public posturing as a lesbian athlete and role model for women with same-sex orientations provides an example of what Babe might have been. Navratilova, an unabashedly self-avowed lesbian athlete, has served as a beacon for generations of lesbians and lesbian athletes. Her straightforwardness, public display of female lovers, and uncurtailed muscularity has signaled a breakthrough in discussions of lesbianism in sports.[66]

Despite her strength and her accomplishments Navratilova is not completely accepted by the public. A culture that necessitates silence and invisibility from lesbians and lesbian athletes in particular deems her existence and any self-assertion on her part as excessive. For this culture, to be a lesbian and an athlete is to be the epitome of the female antihero. Her awkward endorsement of feminine blouses and her scanty opportunities to sell products designed exclusively for men or women speak to the discomfort the public feels in embracing her as an acceptable role model. Others, however, are most comfortable in labeling her a hero. As one California-based gay paper wrote of Navratilova in 1993, "For the lesbian and gay community, Navratilova is not only a living tennis legend, she's also a walking revolution, a human symbol of pride."[67]

Many lesbians of the 1940s and 1950s may have seen in Didrikson what Navratilova shows the world. Seeking public images of themselves, these lesbians may well have searched for familiar signs, read silent texts, and found in Babe what they were looking for. Babe could have chosen to speak out about her life in her own generation, but she deliberately rejected doing so. The historical text shows she camouflaged any indication that she might have been anything other than the feminine persona she constructed. The cost of being that other role model was too high. The cost of her silence and self-negation lies buried with her, ensconced in codes barely readable even to the trained eye. Historically, personally, she abhorred approximating the Navratilova of her generation. She sought acceptance and normalcy beyond all else. Neither the hostile culture nor her private yearnings led her to publicly avow her relationship with Betty Dodd. Her lack of self-acceptance and articulation was a loss to a generation of lesbian women who yearned for a self-proclaimed lesbian hero. But that was not a burden she chose to bear. She cannot be faulted for this—she bore so many other mantels so magnificently. This silence does not make her less of a person. It simply makes her a survivor of a generation and a culture constrained by unrealistic images of men and women and sometimes violent homophobia. In this arena she was human, vulnerable, and afraid. For all her courage, bravado, and fiercesomeness, she ultimately chose silence. Her silence, like her fiercesomeness, was her own creation; it informed her self-definition and muted her true identity. She was as entitled to it in life as she is in death. She does not owe us; rather, her silence teaches once again the enforced lessons of self-preservation. In this final context, her voice will forever be heard.

A V-shaped walkway surrounded by perfectly manicured grass leads to the graves of Babe's parents and siblings, buried under simple ground plaques, and on to Babe's date-blurred monument at the apex. She is placed, rightly so, at the helm of her family in death as she was in life. The declaration that the greatest athlete of all time lies buried beneath the lawn overhung by cypress trees is chilling. To one prone to doubt it, Babe herself might have said, "Who's the competition?" George, according to the wishes of his family, is buried in Pueblo, Colorado, thus placing a chink in his carefully constructed Cinderella/Prince Charming script.

Babe's grave marker stands chest high on a four-foot pedestal in sculpted granite. An open book engraved with the time-worn motto of good sportsmanship reads: "It's not whether you win or lose, it's how you play the game . . ." That was not how Babe lived or played, but it was how she insisted on being remembered. It is a eulogy created by local boosters to honor the Babe they so cherish. Yet in the decades of her purest excellence she often quipped to reporters, "I don't see any point in playing the game if you don't win, do you?"[68]

Babe never did. And that's what made her a national treasure, a press hound, a legend, a path-breaking athlete, a hustler, a sometimes cautious sometimes reckless woman, and the ultimate queen/king trickster holding court.

Notes

Introduction

1. Carroll Smith-Rosenberg, "The New Woman as Androgyne: Social Disorder and Gender Crisis, 1870–1936," *Disorderly Conduct* (New York: Alfred A. Knopf, 1985), 291–92. Yet as Smith-Rosenberg points out, the trickster's inversion of order is transitory. It suggests but does not effect an alternative order. Whether Babe constitutes "the ideal feminist hero," an achievement attributed to female tricksters in the 1920s and 1930s, is open to question.

2. The comments of Benjamin G. Rader were most helpful in framing this section.

3. Susan Kathleen Cahn, "Coming on Strong: Gender and Sexuality in Women's Sport, 1900–1960" (Ph.D. diss., University of Minnesota, 1990), 233, 330.

4. Ibid., 233–34; quotation on 234.

5. Ibid., 329, 7.

6. Carolyn G. Heilbrun, *Writing a Woman's Life* (New York: Ballantine Books, 1988), 28; Lawrence C. Watson and Maria-Barbara Watson-Franke, *Interpreting Life Histories: An Anthropological Inquiry* (New Brunswick: Rutgers University Press, 1985), 166–67.

7. Heilbrun, *Writing,* 13. May Sarton's *Journal of a Solitude* (New York: Norton, 1973), is the acknowledged work that breaks the mold and silences by mentioning the "unmentionables."

8. Mary Catherine Bateson, *Composing a Life* (New York: Penguin, 1989), 5–6; Heilbrun, *Writing,* 23, 27.

9. Watson and Watson-Franke, in *Interpreting Life Histories,* 161–84, argue both are crucial ingredients to the interpretation of life histories. See also William Oscar Johnson and Nancy Williamson, *"Whatta-Gal": The Babe Didrikson Story* (Boston: Little, Brown, 1975).

10. Sherna Berger Gluck and Daphne Patai, *Women's Words: The Feminist Practice of Oral History* (New York: Routledge, 1991); Susan Ware, *Partner and I: Molly*

Dewson, Feminism, and New Deal Politics (New Haven: Yale University Press, 1987). Ware underscores the value of "reading" photographs as historical sources; quotation from Personal Narratives Group Staff, *Interpreting Women's Lives: Feminist Theory and Personal Narratives* (Bloomington: Indiana University Press, 1989), 4.

11. A telephone conversation with Ron Didriksen, Louis's son, in 1994 confirmed that Dodd died in July 1993.

12. Heilbrun, *Writing,* 30–31; Personal Narratives Group, *Interpreting,* 5; and Bateson, *Composing a Life,* 8.

13. Personal Narratives Group, *Interpreting,* 5; James Clifford, "Partial Truths," in *Writing Culture: The Poetics and Politics of Ethnography,* ed. James Clifford and George E. Marcus (Berkeley: University of California Press, 1986), 17. Clifford comments upon the "partial truths" that are revealed when gender is not fully explored in ethnographic research.

14. Personal Narratives Group, *Interpreting,* 5; Heilbrun, *Writing,* 18, 30–31.

15. Virginia Lou Evans, "The Status of the American Woman in Sport, 1912–1932" (Ph.D. diss., University of Massachusetts, 1982), 117–18, 232–33, quotation on 233.

16. Donald Spivey, ed., *Sport in America: New Historical Perspectives* (Westport: Greenwood Press, 1985), 207.

17. Helen Lenskyj, *Out of Bounds: Women, Sport, and Sexuality* (Toronto: Women's Press, 1986), 179.

18. Barbara Jane Walder, "Foremothers: Mrs. Hoover's Holy War on Athletics," *womenSports,* Sept. 1974, 23–24.

19. Tracy Mehr, "Quest for Justice," *North American Society for Sport History: Proceedings and Newsletter* 4 (June 1976): 10; Mary L. Remley, *Sport History in the United States* (Washington, D.C.: Organization of American Historians, 1983).

20. Cindy Himes, "The Female Athlete in America, 1860–1940" (Ph.D. diss., University of Pennsylvania, 1986), 149.

21. Ibid., 195. See also 190–220.

22. Lenskyj, *Out of Bounds;* Yvonne Zipter, *Diamonds Are a Dyke's Best Friend: Reflections, Reminiscences, and Reports from the Field on the Lesbian National Pastime* (Ithaca: Firebrand Books, 1988), 33; quotation from Donald J. Mrozek, "Sport and American Mentality, 1880–1910," *Journal of American History* 71 (Dec. 1984): 662–63.

23. Remley, *Sport History,* 21; Martha H. Verbrugge, *Able-Bodied Womanhood: Personal Health and Social Change in Nineteenth-Century Boston* (New York: Oxford University Press, 1988); Walder, "Foremothers," 23.

24. Walder, "Foremothers," 23.

25. Ben B. Lindsay and Wainwright Evans, *Companionate Marriage* (New York: Boni and Liveright, 1927).

26. Billie Jean King, *Spectators No More: Women in the Olympics* (n.p., n.d.).

27. Ibid.; Pamela Feinsilber, "Women Olympians: In the Running at Last," *Ms.,*

Feb. 1984, 25–27; Mary Leigh, "Women's Entry into the Olympic Games in the Twentieth Century," *North American Society for Sport History: Proceedings and Newsletter* 4 (June 1976): 12–13.

28. Feinsilber, "Women Olympians," 25.

29. Ibid., 16; Jim Jennings, "Female Track Athletes Given Cold Shoulder," n.p., 1932, Scrapbooks, Babe Didrikson Zaharias Museum, Beaumont, Tex.; Stephanie L. Twin, "Women and Sport," in *Sport in America,* ed. Spivey, 205; Evans, "Status," 116; Leigh, "Women's Entry," 12–13.

30. Jennings, "Female Track Athletes," 26.

31. Peter Arnold, *The Olympic Games: Athens 1896 to Los Angeles 1984* (London: Hamlyn, 1983), 50; Evans, "Status," 154; King, *Spectators No More,* 62.

32. William Oscar Johnson and Nancy Williamson, "Babe," part 1, *Sports Illustrated,* Oct. 6, 1975; Evans, "Status," 232.

33. Michelle Kort, "The Year of the Team: Going for the Gold Together in Four Olympic Sports," *Ms.,* Apr. 1984, 44–48; Leigh, "Women's Entry," 13.

34. Twin, "Women and Sport," 209.

35. Ibid., 204.

36. Cited in Evans, "Status," 76–77, 205.

37. "How Much Competition Is Good for Girls?" *Literary Digest,* Apr. 17, 1926, 74.

38. Frederick Rand Rogers, "Olympics for Girls?" *School and Society* 30 (Aug. 10, 1929): 190–94, quotation on 192; Donald A. Laird, "Why Aren't More Women Athletes?" quoted in Lenskyj, *Out of Bounds,* 39; Debrah Larned and Cheryl McCall, "Mighty Mead Strikes Out at Sports," *womenSports,* Aug. 1976, 40.

39. Nancy M. Theirot, "Towards a New Sporting Ideal: The Women's Division of the National Amateur Athletic Federation," *North American Society for Sport History: Proceedings and Newsletter* 4 (June 1976): 15; Himes, "The Female Athlete," 146; see also Himes, 147–48, 83, 87, and her discussion of the organization, homosociality, and goals of the Women's Division; for a discussion of the importance of Smith College's (1895) basketball game between freshmen and sophomores, see Himes, 94–95; Walder, "Foremothers," 24.

40. Evans, "Status," 236, 237.

41. Feinsilber, "Women Olympians," 25.

42. Himes, "The Female Athlete," 224–25, 228, quotation on 224; Cahn, "Coming on Strong," 234–35, 339.

43. Randy Roberts and James Olson, *Winning Is the Only Thing: Sports in America since 1945* (Baltimore: Johns Hopkins University Press, 1989), 100; quotation from Himes, "The Female Athlete," 228.

44. Himes, "The Female Athlete," 256, 236.

45. Ibid., 237–43. Himes chronicles similar aspects of Wills's accomplishments: her privileged class status; her desire to be more than just a wife; the negative press she received as "Little Miss Poker Face" occasioned by her unemotionalism and in-

tellectual snobbery; and the image of her "unquestioned beauty, innocence and morality"; for Glenna Collett see Paul Gallico, "The Golden Decade," *Saturday Evening Post,* Sept. 5, 1931, 12, and Evans, "Status," 160; Himes, 224–37, discusses "Trudy" Ederle's athletic accomplishments, her image as a domestic and pure daughter, her socioeconomic status exceeding that of most immigrants, and her soothing link as a German American in post–World War I America. Mismanagement of publicity and poor packaging of her as a "commodity" relegated her to a life of teaching swimming to children. Gallico chronicled her athletic attempts and successes in "The Golden Decade," 115. Earhart and Didrikson did know one another. The extent of their friendship was not, apparently, deep. Ann Tibbets of San Antonio, Texas, Amelia Earhart's niece, recalls no mention of Babe by her aunt. Similarly, of those interviewed for this book, a few recall her mentioning Earhart, though not as a friend. Katherine A. Brick, "Amelia Earhart," *Notable American Women: 1607– 1950: A Biographical Dictionary* (Cambridge, Mass.: Belknap Press, 1971), 538–41; correspondence with Ann Tibbets, 1987.

46. Aileen Riggin, "Woman's Place," *Collier's,* May 14, 1932, 11, 46. Riggin was the former Olympic fancy diving champion. Robinson's time in the 100 meters was 12.12 seconds. For Walsh's records see Ellen W. Gerber, Jan Felshin, Pearl Berlin, and Waneen Wyrick, *The American Woman in Sport* (Reading: Addison-Wesley, 1974), 133; Betty Hicks interview, Mar. 8, 1989. The ethnicities of Copeland (Jewish) and Walsh (Polish) were widely featured in the press.

47. Himes, "The Female Athlete," 53, 63.

48. Ibid., 80. The term "invert" was also applied to two other "new women": the feminist and the intellectual.

49. Mary P. Ryan, *Womanhood in America from Colonial Times to the Present* (New York: New Viewpoints/Franklin Watts, 1975), 288.

50. Ibid., 287–91, 369–71; Peggy Kirk Bell interview, Oct. 3, 1989.

51. Donald Mrozek, "The 'Amazon' and the American 'Lady': Sexual Fears of Women as Athletes," in *From 'Fair Sex' to Feminism: Sport and the Socialization of Women in the Industrial and Post-Industrial Eras,* ed. J. A. Mangan and Roberta J. Park (Totowa: Frank Cass, 1978), 282–98, especially 293.

52. B. F. Boller, "Physical Training," *Mind and Body* 7 (Apr. 1900): 25–26, and Dudley Allen Sargeant, *An Autobiography* (Philadelphia, 1927), 36, as quoted in Mrozek, "The 'Amazon,'" 282.

53. Amram Scheinfeld, as quoted in Mrozek, "The 'Amazon,'" 288; Caryl Rivers, "The Girls of Summer: All the Dirt on the American Tomboy or Why Girls Say to Heck with the Prince—I'll Keep the Frog," *womenSports,* Aug. 1977, 49.

54. Susan Cahn, "From the 'Muscle Moll' to the 'Butch Ballplayer': Changing Concepts of 'Mannishness' in Women's Sport, 1900–1960," paper presented at the Eighth Berkshire Conference in the History of Women, Douglass College, New Brunswick, New Jersey, June 1990, and Cindy Himes, chair's comments.

55. Babe Didrikson Zaharias as told to Harry Paxton, *This Life I've Led: My Autobiography* (New York: A. S. Barnes, 1955), 103; hereafter cited as *TLIL.*

56. Bubba Didriksen and Jackie Didriksen interview, Aug. 11, 1988.

57. Johnson and Williamson, "*Whatta-Gal*," 91.

58. Benjamin G. Rader, *American Sports* (Englewood Cliffs: Prentice-Hall, 1990), 115. A 1930s survey revealed that 80 percent of all men read at least portions of the sports page regularly.

59. Ibid., 115, 116.

60. Ibid., 118; See also Kathy Peiss, *Cheap Amusements: Working Women and Leisure in Turn-of-the-Century New York* (Philadelphia: Temple University Press, 1986); Lewis A. Erenberg, *Steppin' Out: New York Nightlife and the Transformation of American Culture, 1890–1930* (Chicago: University of Chicago Press, 1981); Larry May, *Screening Out the Past: The Birth of Mass Culture and the Motion Picture Industry* (New York: Oxford University Press, 1980); John Kasson, *Amusing the Million: Coney Island at the Turn of the Century* (New York: Hill and Wang, 1978); and Roy Rosenzweig, "Middle Class Parks and Working Class Play: The Struggle over Recreational Space in Worcester, Massachusetts, 1870–1910," *Radical History Review* 21 (Fall 1979): 37–48.

61. Roberts and Olson, *Winning*, xi, 103.

62. Ann Fears Crawford and Crystal Sasse Ragsdale, "The Texas Babe," in *Women in Texas: Their Lives, Their Experiences, Their Accomplishments*, ed. Ann Fears Crawford and Crystal Sasse Ragsdale (Burnett, Tex.: Eakins Press, 1982), 273; "Babe Zaharias Open This Week Honors Beaumont Gal Who Rocked Sports World," *Time*, Feb. 2, 1953, and *Beaumont Journal*, Mar. 31, 1953, Doct. 11.1.6.18, Babe Didrikson Zaharias Papers, Mary and John Gray Library, Lamar, Tex.; *TLIL*, 62. Hereafter all references to documents in the Didrikson collection at the Mary and John Gray Library will include only the author, title, date, and document number.

63. Vin Burke, "Former Enterprise Sports Editor Tells Story of Babe Didrikson," *Beaumont Sunday Enterprise*, May 3, 1970, Doct. 11.1.12.3; Frank G. Menke, no title, *Dallas Daily Times*, Aug. 7, 1932, 1.

64. *TLIL*, 223.

65. Mrozek, "The 'Amazon,' "; see also Lois Banner, *American Beauty* (New York: Knopf, 1983), 276.

66. Glenda Riley, *Inventing the American Woman: A Perspective on Women's History, 1865 to the Present* (Arlington Heights: Harlan Davidson, 1986), 87; Banner, *American Beauty*, 210–13.

67. Patsy E. Neal and Tomas A. Tutko, *Coaching Girls and Women: Psychological Perspectives* (Boston: Allyn and Bacon, 1975), 43.

Chapter 1: The Texas Tomboy

1. These dates are corroborated in Johnson and Williamson, "Babe," part 1, 116.

2. News release, biographical, n.d., Doct. 11.1.2.13; Notes with information about Didriksen family, Doct. 11.1.16.14.

3. *TLIL*, 8; Alfred C. Nielsen, *Life in an American Denmark* (New York: Arno

Press, 1979), 75; see also Margaret Jarman Hagood, *Mothers of the South: Portraiture of the White Tenant Farm Woman* (New York: Arno Press, 1972), 69.

4. Caulton C. Qualey, *Norwegian Settlement in the United States* (Northfield, Minn.: Norwegian-American Historical Association, 1938), 198–214. Population statistics for the 5,543 Norwegians in Texas and their counties of residence come from *Fifteenth Census of the United States, 1930,* vol. 2, *Population* (Washington, D.C.: GPO, 1933); see also Leola Nelson Bergman, "After Three Generations," *Americans from Norway,* People of America Series (New York: J. B. Lippincott, 1950); see also Torben Krontoft, "Factors in Assimilation: A Comparative Study," *Norwegian-American Studies* 26 (1974): 188–96; Nielsen, *Life in an American Denmark,* 57.

5. Odd S. Lovoll, *The Promise of America: A History of the Norwegian American People* (Minneapolis: Norwegian-American Historical Association, 1984), 175; Ted Deford, "Only Memory Remains of House in which Babe Didriksen Was Born," *Beaumont Enterprise,* Apr. 12, 1970, Doct. 11.1.13.24.

6. *TLIL,* 22; Christen T. Jonassen, *Value Systems and Personality in a Western Civilization: Norwegians in Europe and America* (Columbus: Ohio State University Press, 1983), 267–68.

7. "The Babe's Favorite Poem," n.p., n.d., Scrapbooks.

8. George M. Stephenson, "The Mind of the Scandinavian Immigrant," *Norwegian-American Studies and Records* 4 (1929): 67; Gunnar J. Malmin, trans. and ed., *America in the Forties: The Letters of Ole Munch Raeder* (Minneapolis: University of Minnesota Press, 1929), 38, 80; Krontoft, "Factors in Assimilation," 185, 189; Lovoll, *Promise,* 141; Evon Z. Vogt, Jr., "Social Stratification in the Rural Middlewest: A Structural Analysis," *Rural Sociology* 12 (1946): 373.

9. Lillie Didriksen Grimes interview, Doct. 11.1.16.8.

10. Kathy Kahn, ed., *Hillbilly Women* (New York: Avon, 1972); Hagood, *Mothers of the South.*

11. Bubba Didriksen and Jackie Didriksen interview; *TLIL,* 11; Nielsen, *Life in an American Denmark,* 38.

12. Bubba Didriksen interview, Aug. 11, 1988; Bubba was also a skilled athlete. He played professional baseball for the Cincinnati Reds from 1933 to 1937, although by his own retrospective evaluation, "I never developed the perfection necessary to get to the top as [Babe] did." Quotation from Johnson and Williamson, *"Whatta-Gal,"* 39–40.

13. Morrison and Fourny Directory Co., *Beaumont (Texas) City Directory, 1921–1922* (Houston, 1921), 12–15. Steamers pulled in and out of Beaumont daily (372 entered in 1910); a yearly tonnage by steamers during that same year was over two million. The city's assessed value increased from $48 million (1921) to $62 million (1929). Morrison and Fourny Directory Co., *Beaumont (Texas) City Directory, 1929* (Houston, 1929), 12–16.

14. Judith Walker Linsley and Ellen Walker Rienstra, *Beaumont: A Chronicle of Promise* (Woodland Hills: Windsor Publications, 1982), 94, 95.

15. Ibid., 96–98. The chapter disbanded out of fear because *The Crisis* (the NAACP's magazine) had erroneously reported a lynching in Beaumont that actually occurred in Tyler, Texas. Beaumont did have a Jewish community. It dated back to 1878, built a synagogue in 1901, and counted noteworthy residents. National Park Service, *Portrait of a People: An Ethnic History of Beaumont, Texas* (n.p., n.d.), 11, Tyrrell Historical Library, Beaumont, Tex.

16. Ole Didriksen, Aug. 18, 1947, 2, Doct. 11.1.1.22.

17. *TLIL*, 7; Bubba Didriksen interview; Nielsen, *Life in an American Denmark*, 102, 130, and "Scandinavians in America," *American Scandinavian Review* (Summer 1955): 187–91.

18. Jonassen, *Value Systems*, 77.

19. An article appearing in the *American Scandinavian Review* in 1932 discussed six outstanding Norwegian women leaders who were assertive and independent. But the female author assured the reader of their femininity, support by husband and family, motherly hearts, and warm nurturing despite outward appearances. See Kari Sjonsberg, as cited in ibid., 80.; Susan Sontag, as quoted in ibid., 82–83.

20. Krontoft, "Factors in Assimilation," 191; Malmin, *Letters*, 40; Lovoll, *The Promise of America*, 200.

21. Carl G. O. Hansen, "Contributions to Sports," in *Norwegian Immigrant Contributions to America's Making*, ed. Harry Sundby Hansen (San Francisco: R and E Research Associates, 1921); Frank Elkins, "Norwegian Influence on American Skiing," *American Scandinavian Review* 35–36 (Winter 1947): 337–39; Lovoll, *The Promise of America*, 190–91; Leola Nelson Bergman, "Sports," in *Americans from Norway*, 292–93; quotation from Jonassen, *Value Systems*, 83–84.

22. Elliot J. Gorn, *The Manly Art: Bare Knuckle Prize Fighting in America* (Ithaca: Cornell University Press, 1986), 132. Gorn analyzes boxing in particular, but the insights into working-class sporting behavior are generalizable.

23. Ibid., 134, 140.

24. Ibid., 192–93.

25. Ibid., 141; for further discussion of social class differences in sports see Himes, "The Female Athlete," 18–19, 245–46. Shirley Sommerour, from Auraria, Georgia, in southern Appalachia, was a poor white woman who proudly recalled that when neighbor kids beat her she always fought back. "My grandpa," she said, "always taught me to fight. And I didn't take nothin' off of nobody. Me, I fight." Growing up in a town nicknamed Knucklesville, she recalled getting beaten, beating back, and reaching truce status through superior blows. See Shirley Sommerour, "My Grandpa Always Taught Me to Fight," in *Hillbilly Women*, ed. Kahn, 101–10; see also Shirley Dalton, "Someday Us Poor Is Going to Overrule," in *Hillbilly Women*, ed. Kahn, 37.

26. *TLIL*, 23. For further evidence of Babe's atypical behavior, see Julia Kirk Blackwelder, *Women of the Depression: Caste and Culture in San Antonio, 1929–1939* (College Station: Texas A&M University Press, 1984) and Donald Worster *Dust Bowl: The Southern Plains in the 1930s* (New York: Oxford University Press, 1979).

27. Johnson and Williamson, "*Whatta-Gal*," 43.

28. *TLIL*, 22; Hagood, in *Mothers of the South*, 142, asserts that most disciplining, including whipping, is done by mothers.

29. Sigrid Hill (born Hansen, Norway, 1903) interview, Apr. 8, 1989, conducted by Sarah F. Fleming.

30. Ibid.; *TLIL*, 26–27.

31. Johnson and Williamson, "*Whatta-Gal*," 45–46.

32. Lillie Didriksen Grimes interview.

33. Mrs. Emma Andress interview, 820 Doucette, Neighbor of the O. N. Didriksens, n.d., Doct. 11.1.1.20.

34. Ibid.; Carol Schlueter, "Remembrance of Babe: Her Friends Remember Babe Was Always Athlete," *Beaumont Journal*, Oct. 10, 1975, Doct. 11.1.12.13.

35. Reagan Baker interview, constable Jefferson County, Tex., former Beaumont High School all-state center, Doct. 11.1.1.19; Burke, "Former Editor."

36. Mildred (Babe) Didrikson, no title, Jan. 11, 1933, North American Newspaper Alliance, Inc., Scrapbooks.

37. Theresa M. Wells, "Greatness for Mildred Didriksen Indicated in 1923 Clippings Kept by Theresa Wells," *Beaumont Sunday Enterprise*, Apr. 27, 1969, Doct. 11.1.12.2.

38. E. W. Jackson interview, 825-22nd St., Beaumont, Insurance man, Doct. 11.1.1.19; Mrs. George Urquhart interview, 2608 Hazel, Beaumont, played baseball against Babe in junior high, knew her in high school, Doct. 11.1.22.

39. Edwina Lockhart interview, teammate in junior high school, Aug. 18, 1947, Doct. 11.1.1.22; John Lockhart interview, 1511 Avenue A, Beaumont, Aug. 18, 1947, Doct. 11.1.1.22; Burke, "Former Editor."

40. Mrs. Clyde D. Jones interview, Doct. 11.1.1.19; quotation from Sam Blair, "In Homberg's Mind, Babe Didrikson Is Still Alive," *Dallas Morning News*, Sept. 7, 1980, Doct. 11.1.10.9. Not surprisingly, early tutors disagree. Babe's high school physical education teacher, Beatrice Lytle, adamantly claimed being the first to introduce Babe to golf and teach her; later, others made similar claims.

41. *Pine Burr of 1929*, 144, 145, Babe Didrikson Zaharias Museum, Beaumont, Tex.

42. Roger Reese interview, Doct. 11.1.1.19.

43. Miss Thelma Hughes interview, 2668 Liberty, Beaumont, Tex., Aug. 18, 1947, 1, Doct. 11.1.1.22; quotation from R. R. Knudson, "Babe Didrikson: No More Ms. Nice Guy," *womenSports*, Dec. 1977, 54.

44. Baker interview; Mrs. David Hearn interview, 1936 Liberty, Beaumont, Tex., "With Babe in High School," Aug. 18, 1947, 2, Doct. 11.1.1.22; Mrs. H. M. Whitaker interview, 2333 Harrison, Beaumont, Tex., Aug. 18, 1947, Doct. 11.1.1.19.

45. Miss Beatrice Lytle, personal testimonies, Doct. 11.1.1.21; "A-Razz-A-Ma-Tazz: Jazz Age Grads Return for Reunion," *Beaumont Sunday Enterprise-Journal*, May 22, 1977, 3-B, Doct. 11.1.13.1.

46. Lytle, personal testimonies. This may have encouraged her pursuit of one-on-one competitions with men in later years.

47. Johnson and Williamson, "Babe," part 1, 122.

48. Ibid., 122; "A-razz-a-ma-taz."

49. Rivers, "The Girls of Summer," 27, 30, 49–51, 56, 61, quotations from 30 and Sigrid Hill interview.

50. Will Grimsley, "Tidbits," first in a series, n.d., Doct. 11.1.2.18. No identification of the speakers is available.

51. Burke, "Former Editor"; Whitaker interview; Bill Scurlock, "Fabulous Babe Descends on Beaumont," *Beaumont Journal,* Apr. 12, 1953, Doct. 11.1.5.5; Statements of Mrs. A. J. Harmon, Doct. 11.1.1.20.

52. Mrozek, "The 'Amazon,'" 286.

53. Gene Schoor, *Babe Didrikson: The World's Greatest Athlete* (Garden City: Double Day, 1978), 26.

54. Hearn interview; Whitaker interview.

55. Nielsen, *Life in an American Denmark,* 58, 78; Osland Birger, *A Long Pull from Stavanger: The Reminiscences of a Norwegian Immigrant* (Northfield: Norwegian-American Historical Association, 1945), 250–51.

56. Whitaker interview.

57. Hearn interview

58. Jackson interview.

59. Hagood, *Mothers of the South,* 70–71; Johnson and Williamson, "Whatta-Gal," 61; Betty Dodd interview, Oct. 13, 1987.

60. *TLIL,* 27, 28.

61. Ibid., 28, 29; Bubba Didriksen interview.

62. *TLIL,* 29.

63. Hicks interview, Mar. 8, 1989; Schoor, *Babe,* 22; *TLIL,* 20.

64. *TLIL,* 15, 16–17. Hagood, in *Mothers of the South,* notes the continuous and hard labor required to do laundry. The children and husband oftentimes participated to ease the task.

65. *TLIL,* 24; Lovoll, *The Promise of America,* 210–11. The Didriksens' disdain of charity is echoed in the sentiments of other poor people. See Dalton, "Someday," 32. See also Jacquelyn Dowd Hall, James Leloudis, Robert Korstad, Mary Murphy, LuAnn Jones, and Christopher B. Daly, *Like a Family: The Making of a Southern Cotton Mill World* (Chapel Hill: University of North Carolina Press, 1987). The chapter "From the Cradle to the Grave" discusses the influences of kinship and common culture in forming identity and hedging against poverty in southern textile mill towns of the Carolinas (see xviii and 114–236). While Beaumont was not a manager-run mill town, similarities exist amongst the experiences of these two white, poor, working-class regions.

66. *TLIL,* 18.

67. Hill interview; *TLIL,* 26, quotations on 27; Schoor, *Babe,* 17. For further dis-

cussion of factory women's paid work see Ruby Green, "You Don't Need to Be in That Mill," 121–28, and Artie Chandler, "I Really Know What It Means To Do Man's Work," 61–66, both in *Hillbilly Women,* ed. Kahn. In "Child Raising," 128–56, Hagood discusses how these "extra-home experiences" are seen as part of child-raising. See *Mothers of the South.*

Chapter 2: One Golden Cyclone

1. Bill Scurlock, "Babe Is Warm Personal Memory," *Beaumont Journal,* Sept. 28, 1956, 24, Doct. 11.1.10.1; Bill Scurlock to Harris Shevelson, editor of *Coronet,* Aug. 18, 1947, Doct. 11.1.1.22.

2. Employers Casualty Company, "Company Athletes Prove Good Workers," *Office Manager,* Sept. 1932, Scrapbooks; quotations from Johnson and Williamson, "Whatta-Gal," 63.

3. *TLIL,* 37; Roxanne M. Albertson, "Basketball Texas Style, 1910–1933: School to Industrial League Competition," in *A Century of Women's Basketball: From Frailty to Final Four,* ed. Joan S. Hult and Marianna Terkell (Reston: National Association for Girls and Women in Sport, 1992), 163; Mildred (Babe) Didrikson Zaharias as told to Harry T. Paxton, "The Story of a Valiant Woman: This Life I've Led," *Saturday Evening Post,* June 25, 1955, part 1, Doct 11.1.13.17.

4. Bill Cunningham, "The Colonel's Ladies," *Collier's,* May 23, 1936, 60–61, 62; Himes, "The Female Athlete," 200–201.

5. Employers Casualty, "Company Athletes"; Col. M. J. McCombs Photo, Employers Casualty Company Track Team, 1930, Scrapbooks; Jack Copeland, "Looking 'em Over," *Dallas Dispatch,* n.d., Scrapbooks.

6. Roxanne M. Albertson and Jean Pekara, "Golden Cyclones, 1931 National Basketball Champions," *North American Society for Sport History: Proceedings and Newsletter* 13 (May 1985), 31; Sylvia F. Nadler, "A Developmental History of the Hutcherson Flying Queens of Plainview, Texas, from 1910–1979" (Ed.D. thesis, East Texas State University, 1980). This is a thorough study of the development of women's collegiate basketball. In 1948–49 the team gained a company sponsor, Harvest Queen Mill. It went on to become a powerhouse dynasty in the 1950s and a mainstay of international competition. See also Albertson, "Basketball Texas Style," 157, 158, 159.

7. Albertson, "Basketball Texas Style," 165.

8. Ibid., 161.

9. Ibid., 161, 162–63.

10. Gerber, Felshin, Berlin, and Wyrick, *The American Woman in Sport,* 94; quotation from Scurlock to editor of *Coronet;* Babe Biographical by Tiny Scurlock, 4, Doct. 11.1.1.2; Johnson and Williamson, "Babe," part 1, 124.

11. *TLIL,* 36.

12. Spivey, *Sport in America,* 206; Gerber, Felshin, Berlin, and Wyrick, *The American Woman in Sport,* 36.

13. Evans, "Status," 70; "A-Razz-A-Ma-Tazz."

14. *TLIL,* 37.

15. Ibid., 39; Cyclones Basketball, Wichita, Kansas, Jan. 16, 1931, Dallas, Dec. 1933, Employers Casualty Scrapbooks, 1931–32, Babe Didrikson Zaharias Museum; "Pap," "Cyclones Run Over Kittens in 46–25 Tilt," n.d., Scrapbooks.

16. Johnson and Williamson, "*Whatta-Gal,*" 74.

17. *TLIL,* 36; Golden Cyclone individual team photos inscribed to Babe, 1930–31, Scrapbooks. For further clarification of teammates see "Golden Cyclone All Americans," team photo with full names and positions, Scrapbooks, and Charlisle Bocell, "The Territory Traveler," *Malakoff News,* Sept. 3, 1965, wherein the 1929, 1930, and 1931 teams reunited "to renew those wonderfully exciting memories."

18. Johnson and Williamson, "*Whatta-Gal,*" 110.

19. *TLIL,* 44; B. D. Zaharias, "Valiant Woman," part 1.

20. *TLIL,* 43; R. R. Knudson, *Babe Didrikson: Athlete of the Century* (New York: Puffin Books, 1986), chap. 3.

21. *TLIL,* 41, 27; Knudson, *Babe,* 22.

22. Johnson and Williamson, "*Whatta-Gal,*" 29; *TLIL,* 42.

23. Johnson and Williamson, "*Whatta-Gal,*" 138; Stan Kertes said the same of her; quotations from *TLIL,* 11, and Johnson and Williamson, "*Whatta-Gal,*" 141.

24. Babe Didrikson to Tiny Scurlock, June 23, 1930, handwritten on Employers Casualty Company letterhead, Doct. 11.1.14.8; "Didrikson High Point Scorer When Cyclones Capture A.A.U. Crown," n.d., n.p., Doct. 11.1.13.4.

25. Contract between Babe Didrikson and Tiny Scurlock, Sept. 15, 1931, Doct. 11.1.3.1.

26. Didrikson to Scurlock, July 7, 1930, Doct. 11.1.14.9; Didrikson to Scurlock, May 21, 1930, Doct. 11.1.14.6.

27. Didrikson to Scurlock, June 8, 1930, Doct. 11.1.14.7.

28. Ibid.

29. Didrikson to Scurlock, June 8, 1930, Doct. 11.1.14.7; Didrikson to Scurlock, May 9, 1930, Doct. 11.1.14.5.

30. *TLIL,* 39, 65–67; Johnson and Williamson, "*Whatta-Gal,*" 77.

31. Ibid., 68.

32. Ibid., 64; Nancy Corcoran interview, Oct. 14, 1989.

33. Ironically, her marriage in 1938 to George Zaharias—which on the surface promised financial security—also eventually became a financial burden she bore alone: she supported them both.

34. Didrikson to Scurlock, Apr. 25, 1931, Doct. 11.1.14.10.

35. Didrikson to Scurlock, Oct. 5, 1931, Doct. 11.1.14.12.

36. Didrikson to Scurlock, Nov. 6, 1931, Doct. 11.1.14.13.

37. Didrikson to Scurlock, Dec. 28, 1931, Doct. 11.1.14.14.

38. Johnson and Williamson, "*Whatta-Gal,*" 79.

39. *TLIL,* photo caption, photo section following 34; "The 'Babe': A Record of

Achievement, Mildred (Babe) Didrikson Zaharias, 1914–1956," distributed by Babe Didrikson Zaharias Foundation, Inc., Beaumont, Tex., reprinted from W. R. Schroeder and Thad S. Johnson, "WHO in Sports." Didrikson won the Associated Press's award Female Athlete of the Year in 1932, 1945, 1947, 1950, and 1954. She was voted Female Athlete of the Half Century in 1950. See "Table of Associated Press Female Athletes of the Year," *Information Please Sports Almanac* (Boston: Houghton Mifflin, 1994), 458. Thad Johnson's pamphlet circa 1985 erroneously listed 1931 as a year in which she'd won the award.

40. In track and field individual winners get points that accrue to the team's total. The highest team total determines the winner.

41. Didrikson to Scurlock, Mar. 9, 1930, Doct. 11.1.14.4; Didrikson to Scurlock, Oct. 5, 1931, Doct. 11.1.14.12.

42. *TLIL*, 39.

43. Johnson and Williamson, *"Whatta-Gal,"* 75; Knudson, "No More Ms. Nice Guy," 54–56.

44. Mildred (Babe) Didrikson, "I Blow My Own Horn," *American Magazine,* June 1936, 102.

45. Lawrence Lader, "The Unbeatable Babe," *Coronet,* Jan. 1948, 157, Doct. 11.1.17.1.

46. Ibid., 156.

47. Red Gibson, "Babe Didrikson Zaharias—Now THERE Was an Olympic Champion," n.p., Aug. 27, 1972, 3, Doct. 11.1.13.32. Just thinking about the crowds' response still gave her goose bumps in the 1950s; *TLIL*, 47.

48. Knudson, "No More Ms. Nice Guy," 27.

49. BDZ Foundation, "The 'Babe,'" 1; Gibson, "Now THERE Was a Champion," 3; quotation from Johnson and Williamson, *"Whatta-Gal,"* 83.

50. "Didrikson, Unaided, Wins National Track Championship," *Dallas Morning News,* July 17, 1932, Scrapbooks; *TLIL*, 50.

51. Arthur Daley, "Sports of the Times: A Remarkable Woman," n.p., 1956, Doct. 11.1.10.4; "What a Girl!" *Chicago Tribune,* 1932, Doct. 11.1.1.21.

52. "The Weaker Sex?" n.p., n.d., Scrapbooks; James Roach, "Women in Sports," *New York Times,* Aug. 2, 1931, sec. 10, p. 6.

53. *TLIL*, 51; Mildred (Babe) Didrikson Zaharias as told to Harry T. Paxton, "The Story of a Valiant Woman: This Life I've Led," *Saturday Evening Post,* July 2, 1955, part 2, 34, Doct. 11.1.13.18.

54. Johnson and Williamson, "Babe"; Paul Zimmerman, "Babe Didrikson Plans Three Championships," n.p., Aug. 5, 1932, Scrapbooks.

55. "Didrikson Girl Sports Marvel," *New York Times,* n.d., Scrapbooks.

56. *TLIL*, 52.

57. Johnson and Williamson, *"Whatta-Gal,"* 84.

58. Ibid., 80.

59. Babe Didrikson, Identity Card 7119, Tenth Olympiad, Los Angeles, 1932, Doct. 11.1.4.1.

60. Bud Greenspan, *Time Capsule: The Los Angeles Olympic Games of 1932* (Lorimar: USA Home Video, 1982–84); quotation from *TLIL*, 53; B. D. Zaharias, "Valiant Woman," part 2, 34; "Babe Didrikson Teaches Foreign Girls U.S. Slang," n.p., July 30, 1932, Scrapbooks.

61. Bubba Didriksen and Jackie Didriksen interview; "Parents May Go to Dallas To Greet Babe: As Dallas Acclaims Local Girl Athlete, Hitch-Hiking Brother Missed Olympics," *Beaumont Journal*, Aug. 10 or 11, 1932, Doct. 11.1.4.12.

62. "Parents May Go To Dallas."

63. *TLIL*, 54–55. This mark held until the 1936 games.

64. *TLIL*, photo caption, photo section following 34. This record also held until the 1936 Olympics; Hicks interview, Mar. 8, 1989; *TLIL*, 55; Greenspan, *Time Capsule*. This Olympic mark of 11.7 seconds stood for sixteen years, and it was the best U.S. effort for twenty-three years. BDZ Foundation, "The 'Babe.'"

65. Kim Q. Berkshire, "A Look Back: Evelyn Hall Adams, Now Seventy-eight, Remembers Controversial Loss to Didriksen in '32 Olympics," *Los Angeles Times*, 1988, 1–2.

66. Knudson, "No More Ms. Nice Guy," 54.

67. Berkshire, "A Look Back," 1–2; Knudson, "No More Ms. Nice Guy," 54. My repeated reviewing of the actual race and finish shows the tape on both their outstretched craning necks simultaneously. The winner is undiscernible to the naked eye. See Greenspan, *Time Capsule*.

68. Johnson and Williamson, *"Whatta-Gal,"* 105; Knudson, "No More Ms. Nice Guy," 54.

69. Johnson and Williamson, *"Whatta-Gal,"* 84.

70. Knudson, "No More Ms. Nice Guy"; quotations from Johnson and Williamson, *"Whatta-Gal,"* 84, 85, and Dodd interview, June 17, 1987.

71. Johnson and Williamson, *"Whatta-Gal,"* 85.

72. Evans, "Status," 152. At the 1932 AAU track and field nationals (that doubled as Olympic tryouts) the two women "tied for first place and set a world record." They jumped 5 feet ³⁄₁₆ inch. See BDZ Foundation, "The 'Babe'"; quotation from Johnson and Williamson, *"Whatta-Gal,"* 106; see also "In Preparation for Your Track Meet," *Sportswoman*, May 1932, 11–12. The magazine had run an article about this style, also called the Western Jump, in May 1932, three months prior to the Olympics, wherein it was deemed acceptable. A photo caption explained: "Remember the horizontal position of the body, practically parallel to the bar, when practicing this event."

73. Greenspan, *Time Capusle*; BDZ Foundation, "The 'Babe' "; quotation from Johnson and Williamson, *"Whatta-Gal,"* 107. Countless reviews of the Olympic film footage by this biographer reveal Shiley topped the bar with an upright scissor kick. Babe, parallel with the bar, did not conclusively go over head first. Frame-by-frame replay shows a possible feet-first jump.

74. Betty Hardesty, "Women's Record Breaking Feats in Olympic Games," *Sportswoman*, Sept. 1932, 10.

75. Ibid.

76. *TLIL*, 57. Yet, as the Babe Didrikson Zaharias Museum in Beaumont, Tex., quickly points out in a flyer given to all visitors upon entering, "The International Amateur Athletic Federation sanctioned Miss Didriksen's jump as the world record, which she held jointly with Miss Shiley for six years." Later she was given a first place tie. See "The 'Babe.'" In the 1990s, local Beaumonters devoted themselves anew to securing a posthumous first-place gold for Babe's jump.

77. Evans, "Status," 164; "Mid-Week Pictorial," *New York Times*, n.d.; "Babe Didrikson," cartoon, Metropolitan Newspaper Feature Service Inc., n.p., n.d.; "America's Hopes in 1932 Women's Olympic Games," n.p., n.d.; "How About a Women's All-Around Championship?" n.p., n.d., all in Scrapbooks. Arnold, *The Olympic Games*, 65, 164. Her closet rival was Helen Madison, "the outstanding Olympic swimmer, who received 45 votes."

78. "Personal Glimpses: The World-Beating Girl Viking of Texas," *Literary Digest*, Aug. 27, 1932, 26.

79. "Current Events, USA," *American-Scandinavian Review* 20 (Aug.-Sept. 1932): 448; Bergman, "Sports," 292–93; Hansen, "Contributions to Sports," 164–65.

80. Post-Olympic coverage, Scrapbooks; Johnson and Williamson, "Whatta-Gal," 5; Knudson, *Babe*, 36; Scurlock, "Fabulous Babe."

81. Johnson and Williamson, "Babe," part 1, 126.

82. Arnold, *The Olympic Games*, 47; Johnson and Williamson, "Whatta-Gal," 6–7.

83. "Welcome Home, Babe," *Dallas Journal*, Aug. 11, 1932, 5, Scrapbooks; "Dallas Welcomes Babe Didrikson Home," *Dallas Dispatch*, Aug. 11, 1932, 1, Scrapbooks; "Parents May Go to Dallas."

84. *Dallas Journal*, Aug. 11, 1932, 1, Aug. 12, 1932, 1, Scrapbooks; Johnson and Williamson, "Babe," part 1, 127.

85. "Parents May Go to Dallas"; "Dallas Welcomes," 1; See Testimonial Citation from the Citizenship of Dallas, Aug. 11, 1932, Scrapbooks. The signing mayor was Charles E. Delaney. "Babe Honored by Ad League," n.p., n.d., Scrapbooks; Johnson and Williamson, "Babe," part 1, 127.

86. Johnson and Willimson, "Babe," part 1, 49; Johnson and Williamson, "Whatta-Gal," 109.

87. "Parents May Go to Dallas."

88. "Crowds Cheer 'Babe' in Welcome Parade: City Turns Out to Pay Girl Honor," *Beaumont Journal*, Aug. 16, 1932, 1, Doct 11.1.4.17; Merita Mills, "Beaumont Places Her Laurel Wreath on Brow of 'Babe', Returning Heroine," *Beaumont Journal*, Aug. 16, 1932, Doct. 11.1.4.19.

89. Mills, "Beaumont Places Wreath."

90. Ibid.; Didrikson to Scurlock, Aug. 25, 1932, Doct. 11.1.14.16.

91. Cartoon, *Amarillo Globe*, Aug. 15, 1932, 1; "Babe," n.p., n.d., Scrapbooks.

92. "Girl Star's Plea Heeded: Court Gives Miss Didrikson Right to Handle Own Business Affairs," *New York Times*, Aug. 30, 1932, 15.

Chapter 3: A Sportswriter's Dream

1. Riley, *Inventing*, 109; Ethel Klein, *Gender Politics* (Cambridge, Mass.: Harvard University Press, 1984); Carol Ruth Berkin and Mary Beth Norton, eds., *Women of America: A History* (Boston: Houghton Mifflin, 1979); Marjorie Rosen, *Popcorn Venus: Women, Movies, and the American Dream* (New York: Avon, 1974), 139–258. Hepburn later starred in the film *Pat and Mike*, in which Babe appeared.

2. Evans, "Status."

3. See, for example, Doris Watts, "Changing Conceptions of Competitive Sport for Girls and Women in the United States from 1880–1960" (Ph.D. diss., UCLA, 1960); Mrozek, "The 'Amazon,'" 59; quotation from Sally Fox, *The Sporting Woman: A Book of Days* (Bulfinch Press, 1989), p. opposite Mar. 13–18; John Durant and Otto Bettman, *A Pictorial History of American Sports from Colonial Times to the Present* (New York: A. S. Barnes, 1952), 84.

4. Durant and Bettman, *Pictorial History*, 49, 98, 100, 147; see P. Vertinsky, "The Effect of Changing Attitudes towards Sexual Morality upon the Promotion of Physical Education for Women in Nineteenth-Century America," 165–77; Mary-Lou Squires, "Sport and the Cult of True Womanhood: A Paradox at the Turn of the Century," 98–140; and Karen Kenney, "The Realm of Sports and the Athletic Woman, 1850–1900," all in *Her Story in Sport: A Historical Anthology of Women in Sports*, ed. Reet Howell (New York: West Point, 1982).

5. Durant and Bettman, *Pictorial History*, 147.

6. Mrozek, "The 'Amazon,'" 286.

7. Ibid., 286–87; See Peiss, *Cheap Amusements*.

8. Kenney, "The Realm of Sports," 107–9; Barbara N. Noonkester, "The American Sportswoman from 1900–1920," in *Her Story in Sport*, ed. Howell, 181.

9. Susan Ware, *American Women in the 1930s: Holding Their Own* (Boston: Twayne, 1982), 1–24; Riley, *Inventing*, 99. In 1937 women's annual yearly wage was $525, while men averaged $1,027. Domestics earned $312. The average family had "$20 to $25 a week to feed, clothe and provide shelter for itself."

10. Hagood, in *Mothers of the South*, 243, defines survival and achievement as women's two primary life values.

11. Crawford and Ragsdale, "The Texas Babe," 274.

12. *TLIL*, 21. This sense of invincibility, albeit tinged by denial, came to play a major role in her ability to maintain hope amidst bouts with cancer.

13. Ibid., 33.

14. B. D. Zaharias, "Valiant Woman," part 2, 34.

15. "Works as Clerk in Office and Devotes Spare Time to Training, Babe Didrikson of Dallas, Olympic Prospect, Holds Eight Track Records," n.p., n.d, Doct. 11.1.4.6; "Babe Doing Heavy Thinking," n.p., n.d., Scrapbooks.

16. Scurlock, "Fabulous Babe," 4; Johnson and Williamson, "*Whatta-Gal,*" 9; Scurlock to editor of *Coronet*.

17. Scurlock, "Fabulous Babe," 4.

18. "Miss Didrikson Buys First Hat for Trip to U.S. Title Games," *New York Times,* July 11, 1932, 19.

19. Evans, "Status," 78–79; see also Grantland Rice, "Leading Ladies," *Collier's,* Apr. 6, 1929, 16; Grantland Rice, "Our Glorious Sports Girls," *Ladies Home Journal,* Nov. 1930, 22–23; and Grantland Rice, "Women with the Wallop," *Collier's,* July 11, 1925, 14.

20. Grantland Rice, "The Sportlight," July 23, 1932, Scrapbooks; Grantland Rice, "For Men Only?" *Collier's,* Sept. 24, 1932, 19.

21. Grantland Rice, *The Tumult and the Shouting: My Life in Sport* (New York: A. S. Barnes, 1954), 240.

22. Ibid., 238–39; Grantland Rice, "'Babe' Athletic Marvel: Miss Didrikson's Feats Hard to Believe until You See Her in Action," 1932, North American Newspaper Alliance, Scrapbooks.

23. B. D. Zaharias, "This Life I've Led," part 2, 34.

24. Johnson and Williamson, *"Whatta-Gal,"* 91, 237.

25. Herb Grassis interview, Mar. 15, 1987. The Golf Writer's Association collected money for Babe's cancer efforts.

26. Evans, "Status," 79–80.

27. Westbrook Pegler, "That Didrikson Babe Is a Sissy: And, According to Mr. Pegler, It Seems She Can Sew," Feb. 6, 1933, Doct. 11.1.13.10.

28. Paul Gallico, "The Texas Babe," *Vanity Fair,* Oct. 1932, 36, 71, reprinted in *The Thirties: A Time To Remember,* ed. Don Congdon (New York: Simon and Schuster, 1962), 73–78; Paul Gallico, "Women in Sports Should Look Beautiful," *Reader's Digest,* Aug. 1936, 12–14.

29. Alfred Einsenstaedt, photographer, "Beautiful Skeeter: Pat Laursen Is National Champion," *Life,* Sept. 16, 1940, 54, 57.

30. Ethel McGary, "Ethel McGary Favors Competitive Sports for Women if Wisely Supervised," *Sportswoman,* Nov. 1931, 11–12.

31. Cunningham, "The Colonel's Ladies," 62.

32. Lenskyj, *Out of Bounds,* 78.

33. Paul Gallico, "Frisking for Sex," 48, within "The Little Babe from Texas Turned Out to Be One of the World's Greatest Athletes," *Esquire,* Mar. 1955, 48, Doct. 11.1.13.16. Gallico suggested in 1955 that any "oversized women" (he mentions a 6-feet-2-inch, 185-pound Russian high jumper) be forbidden to compete against other women. "She is unquestionably a female," he wrote, "but since she is so far from the norm of the average woman in height and weight (5 feet 4 inches, 135 pounds), it seems to me . . . silly and unfair to let her compete against average women." Here, Gallico's definition of normalcy creates another method by which women athletes can be deemed abnormal: size. This is the same year Babe claimed her eighteen-year-old frame had been 5 feet and 100 pounds.

34. Lenskyj, *Out of Bounds,* 77; Laird as quoted in Lenskyj, *Out of Bounds,* 39; Geoffrey Theobald as quoted in Lenskyj, *Out of Bounds,* 38.

35. Esther Newton, "The Mythic Mannish Lesbian: Radclyffe Hall and the New Woman," in *Hidden from History: Reclaiming the Gay and Lesbian Past,* ed. Martin B. Duberman, Martha Vicinus, and George Chauncey, Jr. (New York: New American Library, 1989), 287, 282–83; Also see John D'Emilio and Estelle Freedman, *Intimate Matters: A History of Sexuality in America* (New York: Harper and Row, 1988), 288–95.

36. Smith-Rosenberg, "The New Woman," 271, 289–90; The ultimate fear, that she would usurp male enjoyment of women's erotic love, lurks in the foreground.

37. Johnson and Williamson, *"Whatta-Gal,"* 20, 56, 58; quotation from Dodd interview, June 17, 1987, and Betty Jameson interview, May 19, 1988.

38. "Statements Describing Babe"; "Works as Clerk in Office."

39. Johnson and Williamson, *"Whatta-Gal,"* 74.

40. B. D. Zaharias, "Valiant Woman," part 2, 34.

41. Jameson interview; Dodd interview, June 17, 1987.

42. Johnson and Williamson, *"Whatta-Gal,"* 51.

43. Ibid., 74.

44. Ibid., 133.

45. Ibid.

46. Westbrook Pegler, "Babe Didrikson—A Real Champion," *Journal American,* Oct. 9, 1956, Doct. 11.1.10.7.

47. Gallico, "The Little Babe from Texas," 48; Betty Hicks, "Babe Didrikson Zaharias: 'Stand Back! This Ain't No Kid Hittin,' " *womenSports,* Nov. 1975, 27.

48. Gallico, "The Little Babe from Texas," 71.

49. Paul Gallico, "Honey," *Vanity Fair,* Apr. 1933. Gallico was not alone in his disdain for flat-chestedness. Some physical educators also believed that women with small breasts needed development. Certain high schools adopted rules that discouraged two-handed basketball passes because they supposedly cultivated flat chests and round shoulders. As one historian noted, "The flat-chested woman, after all, would fare poorly beside her buxom sister in the marriage selection process." Himes, in "The Female Athlete," 133–34, discusses the "Newcomb" style of basketball as espoused by Clara G. Baer, physical educator at Newcomb College, and physical educator Henry S. Curtis.

50. Gallico, "Honey."

51. Johnson and Williamson, *"Whatta-Gal,"* 20.

52. Gallico "The Little Babe from Texas," 48.

53. Smith-Rosenberg, "The New Woman," 295–96.

54. King, *Spectators No More,* 62; Lenskyj, *Out of Bounds,* 76–77.

55. Lenskyj, *Out of Bounds,* 77, 80.

56. Gerber, Felshin, Berlin, and Wyrick, *The American Woman in Sport,* 418.

57. Evans, "Status," 133, 155–56; Hicks interview, Mar. 8, 1988.

58. Hicks, " 'Stand Back,' " 27; Bertha Bowen interview, May 5, 1988.

59. Didrikson, "I Blow My Own Horn," 104.

60. Ruth Putnam, "Girl Can't Get Ahead by Getting Married, Declares Babe Di-

drikson, Visiting Akron," n.p., circa 1932, Scrapbooks; "Mildred (Babe) Didrikson, 'Babe' Sure She Will Marry," n.p., Jan. 19, 1933, Scrapbooks.

61. Michelle Kort, "Is She or Isn't She?: Women Athletes and Their Gender Identity," *Chrysalis* 9 (1979): 76.

62. Ibid., 77. Inspection of nude athletes was used only once as a test of sex identity before it was replaced with a chromosome test. The chromosome test required examining a plucked hair follicle or tissue scraping from inside the cheek.

63. King, *Spectators No More*, 62.

Chapter 4: Trials, Triumphs, and Sideshow Trickery

1. "Congratulations, Mr. Chrysler! Congratulations, Mr. Dodge!" *Chicago Daily Times,* Feb. 1, 1933, Scrapbooks. Later, this controversial disputed endorsement was resurrected as "The Famous Babe Didrikson Dodge on Display." "She exchanged her Dodge Coupe for a Dodge Six Sedan, and gave the latter to her fond parents as a Christmas present." The "ORIGINAL DIDRIKSON DODGE," billed as "the most famous Coupe in the world!" was for sale. Babe, pictured alongside the auto, said, "It's a spiffy car—would you like to own it?" See "The Famous Babe Didrikson Dodge on Display," n.p., n.d., Scrapbooks; Johnson and Williamson, *"Whatta-Gal,"* 115.

2. Jane Seeley, "Amateur or Professional," *Sportswoman,* Oct. 1928, 14–15.

3. Lader, "The Unbeatable Babe," 160; *TLIL,* photo section following 98.

4. "Will Seek Reinstatement: Firm Employing Miss Didrikson to Act on Her Behalf," *New York Times,* Dec. 6, 1932, 29; "Will Back Olympic Star: Miss Didrikson's Employers Confident She Will Be Cleared," *New York Times,* Dec. 7, 1932, 30; quotation from Flint Dupre, "Glancing Around," n.p., 1932, all in Scrapbooks.

5. "Grossly Unfair," *New York Times,* Dec. 14, 1932, 28.

6. "Miss Didrikson Now Suspended," *New York Times,* Dec. 14, 1932, 28; "Release Produced in Didrikson Case: Dallas Dealer, Showing Copy of Telegram, Says Star Did Not Authorize Advertisement," *New York Times,* Dec. 15, 1932, 28.

7. "Data Is Forwarded in Didrikson Case," *New York Times,* Dec. 17, 1932, 24.

8. "Miss Didrikson Resigns," *New York Times,* Dec. 21, 1932, 27; "Miss Didrikson Joins Pro Ranks," *New York Times,* Dec. 22, 1932, 23; "Babe Didrikson Turns Pro: A.A.U. 'Too Slow,'" *Reformatory Pillar,* Dec. 27, 1932, 5; "Amateur Status of Miss Didrikson, Star Girl Athlete, Is Officially Restored," *New York Times,* Dec. 23, 1932, 24; also see "Babe Didrikson Is Reinstated By A.A.U.," *Chicago Daily Tribune,* Dec. 23, 1932, 1. Babe's departure hastened the team's collapse. When the Cyclones disbanded in 1932, a unique chapter in women's basketball history closed with it. Depression-induced company retrenchment reduced the advertising budget and Babe's assumption of the role of "company's publicist eliminated the need to support an entire basketball team." That the Cyclones lost the 1932 AAU finals signaled the end of their reign. After 1932 fewer companies provided funds for women's teams, but they did sponsor commercial and recreational league teams. In its heyday, which

Babe rode high, industrial league play was a rare opportunity for women to be taken seriously as post-school athletes. See Golden Cyclone Basketball and Track File, Texas Employers' Insurance Association Archives, Dallas, Texas, and Albertson, "Basketball, Texas Style," 164.

9. *TLIL*, 68.

10. "Camera-Shy but Carefree, Miss Didrikson Moves on toward Career as a Pro," *New York Times*, Dec. 24, 1932, 19.

11. "Say Star Is in Chicago," *New York Times*, Dec. 23, 1932, 24; "Greeks Were Right, Brundage Believes," *New York Times*, Dec. 25, 1932, sect. 3, pp. 1–2.

12. "Miss Didrikson to Do Movie, Radio Work," *New York Times*, Dec. 27, 1932, 18.

13. *TLIL*, 69; "'Twas a Comedy of Errors,—But Babe Didrikson Has Gone Pro," *Literary Digest*, Jan. 7, 1933, 33.

14. *TLIL*, 70.

15. Ibid., 71.

16. Ibid., 72–73. This $2500 stage-performer paycheck was another "truth" that Babe fabricated. Babe was ever the financial self-promoter, and here again biographers followed suit.

17. Arthur J. Daley, "Babe Didrikson, Visiting Here, Hopes to Box Babe Ruth in Gym," *New York Times*, Jan. 5, 1933, 25.

18. Scurlock to Shevelson.

19. *TLIL*, 75–79.

20. Ibid., 80; Johnson and Williamson, *"Whatta-Gal,"* 14.

21. Johnson and Williamson, *"Whatta-Gal,"* 127, 130. They dub this woman "Jane" Mitchell. I believe this is Jackie Mitchell, at the time a nineteen-year-old minor leaguer/barnstormer who, like Babe, pitched exhibition innings against men pros. See Barbara Gregorich, *Women at Play: The Story of Women in Baseball* (New York: Harcourt, Brace, 1993). Also see Barbara Gregorich, "Not Every Issue Holds the Feature: Baseball, Women, and Research," *Wilson Library Bulletin* (May 1993): 41–43.

22. "Babe Didrikson to Show Versatility Here Tuesday," n.p., n.d.; Haps Frank, "Sports Reflections," n.p., n.d., both in Scrapbooks. In cities across America headlines charted her team's doings: "Babe Didrikson and Her All-Americans vs. Harlem Globetrotters in Minnesota"; "'Babe' Didrikson to Lead All-Americans against Erie Police"; "'Babe' Didrikson Leads Cage Team into Flint Today"; "All-Americans Give Policemen Sound Drubbing—'Babe' Didrikson Stars for Invading Passers in 35-27 Victory." See "World Famous Girl Athlete to Get in Fray," n.p., n.d., and "Babe: All-American's (Pro) Basketball," n.p., n.d., both in Scrapbooks.

23. *TLIL*, 81; quotation from William Oscar Johnson and Nancy Williamson, "Babe," part 2, *Sports Illustrated*, Oct. 12, 1975, 52, and "Famous Woman Athlete Pitches for Whisker Team," *New York Evening Post*, n.d., Scrapbooks.

24. "Yoicks! The Babe Rides to Hounds," n.p., n.d.; George A. Barton, "Sportographs," n.p., n.d., both in House of David section, Scrapbooks.

25. "'Babe' Didrikson, World's Greatest Woman Athlete, Just a Real Girl," *Detroit Evening Times*, 1933, sect. 2, p. 90, Scrapbooks.

26. *TLIL*, 82; Johnson and Williamson, "Babe," part 2, 52.

27. Johnson and Williamson, *"Whatta-Gal,"* 129, 121.

28. Hill interview.

29. Johnson and Williamson, *"Whatta-Gal,"* 130; D'Emilio and Freedman, *Intimate Matters*, 281–82.

30. *TLIL*, 82; Didrikson to Scurlock, Sept. 21–22, 1934, Doct 11.1.14.17.

31. *TLIL*, 83.

32. Ibid., photo section following 34; "Girl Athlete Now Sparkles as a Pitcher," Hot Springs, Ark., Mar. 14, 1933, Scrapbooks.

33. Rice, *Tumult*, 240; *TLIL*, 84; Gene Farmer, "What a Babe: Babe Is a Lady Now," *Life*, June 23, 1947.

34. Bill "Baby" Stribling, photo, Scrapbooks; Red Gibson, "Now THERE Was an Olympic Champion," 4.

35. Himes, "The Female Athlete"; B. D. Zaharias, "Valiant Woman," part 1, photo caption, 46.

36. Johnson and Williamson, "Babe," part 2, 52; William Baucher, "Why Doesn't Babe Swim the Channel," n.p., Aug. 24, no year, Scrapbooks.

37. Didrikson to Scurlock, Sept. 21–22, 1934.

38. *TLIL*, 83–84.

39. Lader, "The Unbeatable Babe," 162.

40. Ibid., 162. This occurred in the late 1940s, early 1950s; Johnson and Williamson, *"Whatta-Gal,"* 21.

41. Johnson and Williamson, *"Whatta-Gal,"* 23; King, *Spectators No More*, 62.

Chapter 5: Painful Transitions

1. *TLIL*, 85; Herbert Simmons, "Babe Didrikson, Still Eyeing Golf Titles, in Comeback Drills Here," *Chicago Sunday Times*, Oct. 14, 1934, 40.

2. Johnson and Williamson, "Babe," part 2, 51.

3. Charles E. Parker, "Good as a Man Is She?" n.p., 1932–33, Scrapbooks.

4. "Babe Relinquishes Title of Outstanding Woman Athlete to Helen Jacobs, Tennis Champ," n.p., n.d., Scrapbooks. Jacobs received 64 of the 180 votes; Babe received 2.

5. *TLIL*, 86.

6. Johnson and Williamson, *"Whatta-Gal,"* 144; Crawford and Ragsdale, "The Texas Babe," 276; see also Banner, "The Culture of Beauty in the Early Twentieth Century," in *American Beauty*, especially 203, 208, 213, 216, and 224.

7. Banner, *American Beauty*, 276–77; Nancy F. Cott, *The Grounding of Modern Feminism* (New Haven: Yale University Press, 1987), 215–25, 276.

8. Mirian Pitters, "An Analysis of the Humor Pertaining to Sportswomen in

American Newspapers, between 1910–1920," in *Her Story in Sport*, ed. Howell, 223–33; Thomas Craven, ed., *Cartoon Cavalcade* (New York: Simon and Schuster, 1943; rpt., Chicago: Consolidated Book Publishers, 1944). The cover of the *New Yorker* for the March 7, 1942, issue pictures a woman bowling in a long red evening gown with male bowlers laughing and smirking at her.

9. *Ladies Home Journal*, Jan. 1935 through May 1950, and *Vogue*, May 15, 1932, to 1950; "Our Marriage Comes First," *Ladies Home Journal*, Jan. 1943, 50; "Everything to Make Him Happy," *Ladies Home Journal*, Jan. 1947, 42.

10. "Home for the Holidays," *Ladies Home Journal*, Jan. 1935, 11; "What Does He See In Her?" *Ladies Home Journal*, Mar. 1935, 14, 64.

11. *Ladies Home Journal*, Apr. 1933; *Ladies Home Journal*, Apr. 1923, 8; *Ladies Home Journal*, May 1933, 24; *Vogue*, May 15, 1932, 13; "Dictated by Fashion," *Ladies Home Journal*, Apr. 1933, 130. From 1933 onward women's magazines housed a flood of "Sub Deb" (pre-debutante) articles and clubs. These articles counseled popularity, attractiveness, hostess skills, and marital appeal. This genre continued well into the 1940s. See Elizabeth Woodward, "The Sub-Deb," *Ladies Home Journal*, June 1933, 70, and Jan. 1933, 25; and "Journal Reference Library for the Sub-Deb," *Ladies Home Journal*, May 1943, 48.

12. "Thank Mother Nature . . ." *Vogue*, May 1, 1932; "Sportocasins," *Vogue*, June 1, 1932; "Exercise in Every Spoonful of Saraka," *Ladies Home Journal*, Feb. 1937; "Alice Marble," *Harper's Bazaar*, July 1937; "Setting Up in Bed," *Ladies Home Journal*, Apr. 1935.

13. *Collier's*, May 14, 1932; *Literary Digest*, June 18, 1932; "Helen II, New Queen of the Courts," *Literary Digest*, Sept. 3, 1932, 25–26.

14. See *Ladies Home Journal, Harper's Bazaar*, and *Vogue* throughout the 1930s, 1940s, and 1950s.

15. Bill Nary to Susan Cayleff, Sept. 22, 1989.

16. *TLIL*, 91; Grantland Rice, "The Sportlight," n.p., July 28, 1932, Scrapbooks.

17. Babe Didrikson, "How I Got Started at Golf," North American Newspaper Alliance, Inc., 1933, Scrapbooks; *TLIL*, 58.

18. *TLIL*, 58; Didrikson, "I Blow My Own Horn," 103.

19. Didrikson, "I Blow My Own Horn," 103.

20. Johnson and Williamson, "*Whatta-Gal*," 59.

21. Arthur J. Daley, "After Six Trying Years," *New York Times*, Sept. 30, 1956, 1, Doct. 11.1.10.4.

22. "National Women's Golf Title In Three Years, Babe's Goal," n.p., July 16, 1933, Scrapbooks.

23. Lader, "The Unbeatable Babe"; Gene Sarazen interview, Nov. 30, 1989.

24. *TLIL*, 88; Daley, "After Six Trying Years," 1.

25. Lader, "The Unbeatable Babe," 160; *TLIL*, 78.

26. Lader, "The Unbeatable Babe," 160. Kertes also noted her bleeding hands and ten-hour practice days.

27. Johnson and Williamson, "*Whatta-Gal,*" 138; *TLIL,* 79.

28. Sarazen interview; *TLIL,* photo caption, photo section following 98; Didrikson, "I Blow My Own Horn," 104.

29. Johnson and Williamson, "*Whatta-Gal,*" 148; Sarazen interview. Then in his nineties, Sarazen played only three to four charity tournaments per year, as well as the June Classic in Japan; back trouble kept him from playing more. He'd been an honorary member of the Marco Island, Florida, Country Club for twenty-six years.

30. *TLIL,* 101; Johnson and Williamson, "*Whatta-Gal,*" 149, 141.

31. Simmons, "Still Eyeing Golf Titles," 40; Eda Squire, "Didrikson Hits Long Golf Balls," n.p., June 28, 1934, Scrapbooks.

32. Sarazen interview; "Didrikson Panics Them at Beverly: Babe Loaded with Color in Match with Sarazen, Nies, and Mahan—Calls Her Shots," *Washington Post,* July 15, 1935, Scrapbooks.

33. Johnson and Williamson, "*Whatta-Gal,*" 172; Didrikson, "I Blow My Own Horn," 104.

34. Didrikson, "I Blow My Own Horn," 104.

35. Ibid.; William Oscar Johnson and Nancy Williamson, "Babe," part 3, *Sports Illustrated,* Oct. 20, 1975, 50; *TLIL,* 101.

36. Johnson and Williamson, "*Whatta-Gal,*" 150–51.

37. *TLIL,* 101; Didrikson, "I Blow My Own Horn," 104.

38. Johnson and Williamson, "Babe," part 3, 48–49.

39. Ibid., 49; Crawford and Ragsdale, "The Texas Babe," 276.

40. "Two Up Margin of Win," Independent News Service, Apr. 27, 1935; "Former Olympic Games Star Defeats Mrs. Dan Chandler of Dallas," n.p., 1935, Scrapbooks; "'Best at Everything' Babe Garners Another Trophy," *Newsweek,* May 4, 1935, 18.

41. *TLIL,* photo section following 34.

42. "Miss Didrikson Barred by U.S.G.A. from National Title Golf Tourney," *New York Times,* May 15, 1935, 29.

43. Ibid.

44. *TLIL,* 97.

45. Ibid.; "Uncertain on Next Step," *New York Times,* May 14, 1935.

46. *TLIL,* 98; "Golf Pros Joined by Miss Didrikson," *New York Times,* June 2, 1935, sect. 5, p. 1.

47. "Golf Pros Joined"; Babe lost in the semifinals to Elaine Rosenthal Reinhardt of Winnetka, Ill. Opal Hill of Kansas City won. See "Babe Says She Will Take Western Open," n.p., n.d., Scrapbooks; and "Western Women," *Time,* July 8, 1935, 42.

48. "Golf Pros Joined."

49. Betty Hicks, *Travels with a Golf Tour Gourmet: A Cookbook and More by Betty Hicks* (Palo Alto: Group Fore, 1986), 83.

50. *TLIL,* 91. The Walker Cup is awarded to the winner of the contest between men's British and American amateur teams. The Curtis Cup is the women's counterpart.

51. Johnson and Williamson, "Babe," part 3, 50; quotation from Bowen interview, May 17, 1988; Rhonda Glenn, *The Illustrated History of Women's Golf* (Dallas: Taylor, 1991), 137; quotation from Johnson and Williamson, "Whatta-Gal," 146.

52. Bowen interview, May 17, 1988; *TLIL*, 119.

53. Bowen interview, May 17, 1988.

54. Hicks interview, May 17, 1989; Jameson interview; Bubba Didriksen and Jackie Didriksen interview; Thelma Didriksen interview, Feb. 24, 1989; *TLIL*, 90.

55. Bowen interview, May 17, 1988.

56. Johnson and Williamson, "Babe," part 3, 50.

57. Crawford and Ragsdale, "The Texas Babe," 276; Johnson and Williamson, "Babe," part 3, 50.

58. Bowen interview, May 17, 1988. Sometimes, after 1938, George joined in; after 1947, Dodd was included. Johnson and Williamson, "Whatta-Gal," 152.

59. Bowen interview, May 17, 1988.

60. Ibid.; Johnson and Williamson, "Whatta-Gal," 202; Hicks interview, Mar. 8, 1989.

61. Johnson and Williamson, "Whatta-Gal," 153, 154.

62. Gallico, "The Little Babe from Texas," 48, 100, 102.

63. *TLIL*, 103.

64. Frank Menke, *Daily Times Herald*, Aug. 7, 1932, 1, Scrapbooks.

65. *TLIL*, 34, 104; and Mildred (Babe) Didrikson Zaharias as told to Harry T. Paxton, "The Story of a Valiant Woman: This Life I've Led," *Saturday Evening Post*, July 9, 1955, part 3, 43, Doct. 11.1.13.19.

66. *TLIL*, 104; Cott, *Grounding*, 145–74.

67. Simmons, "Still Eyeing Golf Titles," 40; Johnson and Williamson, "Whatta-Gal," 154, photo section.

68. Pete Martin, "Babe Didrikson Takes Off Her Mask," *Saturday Evening Post*, Sept. 20, 1947, 27.

Chapter 6: Romance

1. *TLIL*, 105, 104.

2. Crawford and Ragsdale, "The Texas Babe," 270–83; Lader, "The Unbeatable Babe," 160.

3. Paul Gallico, *The Golden People* (Garden City: Doubleday, 1965), 247–49; *TLIL*, photo section following 98.

4. *TLIL*, 105.

5. George Zaharias, "The Babe and I," *Look*, 1957, 88.

6. Ibid.; Joe Heiling, "Zaharias Rejoins Beloved Babe," *Beaumont Enterprise*, May 23, 1984, Doct. 11.1.21.3. And her 82 to his 81—the actual score—may signal yet another feminine lesson learned by Babe.

7. *TLIL*, 105; "Husband of Athlete Babe Zaharias Dies," *Beaumont Enterprise*, May 23, 1984, 2D, Doct. 11.2.21.4.

8. *TLIL,* 106.

9. Richard Corliss, "The Hype and Hullabaloo of Pro Wrestling," *Houston Post,* Apr. 10, 1985, 2H; see Gerald W. Morton and George M. O'Brien, *Wrestling to Rasslin: Ancient Sport to American Spectacle* (Bowling Green: Bowling Green State University Popular Press, 1985).

10. Harry Brundridge, "Ex-Bootblack Makes $100,000 Wrestling: Zaharias Won't Hunt Because He Hates to Hurt Animals but He Is Wild Man when He Gets Angry in Ring" (Star-Chronicle Publishing, 1932); Bryan Morse, "Londos Defends Title at Stadium Tonight: Zaharias to Tackle Champion on Herald Food Fund Mat Card," *Washington Herald,* June 15, 1933; Charles Bartlett, "Boo! Hiss! Boo! And It's All Money in Bank for Zaharias," n.p., 1934, all in Scrapbooks.

11. Franklin Lewis, "Cleveland Is Luck 'Spot' for Zaharias: Greek Mat Star Likes City Despite 'Bird' Fans Give Him," n.p., n.d., Scrapbooks; Morse, "Londos Defends." For further information on Zaharias's mat career see "Shovelling Piles of Slag in Pueblo, Colorado, Steel Mill Developed George Zaharias' Perfect Statue Like Physique," n.p., n.d., and "George Zaharias Makes Sensational Debut in Ottawa Ring," *Ottawa Journal,* Jan. 16, 1932, both in Scrapbooks.

12. Elliot J. Gorn, *The Manly Art: Bare-Knuckle Prize Fighting in America* (Ithaca: Cornell University Press, 1986), 136, 138, 144.

13. Ibid., 141, 129, 145.

14. Jim Murray, "The Other Babe," n.p., n.d., Doct. 11.1.12.18; Brundridge, "Ex-Bootblack."

15. Brundridge, "Ex-Bootblack," 108–9.

16. Paul Gallico, "Babe Didrikson," in *The Golden People,* 241. This sentiment, wanting a spouse as able as she was, is echoed by hillbilly women. As one said, "I want a man that's as big as I am. A man I can't walk over. Someone who is willing to share the good and the bad. When I find him, I don't care if he digs outhouse holes for a living. I'm going to live with him." She also swears she'll have good sex with him to keep him—a vow similar to Babe's brag of great sex. See Donna Redmond, "I'm Proud to Be a Hillbilly," in *Hillbilly Women,* ed. Kahn, 120.

17. *TLIL,* 110.

18. Ibid., 111.

19. Ibid.; Johnson and Williamson, *"Whatta-Gal,"* 163; G. Zaharias, "The Babe and I," 88.

20. "'Babe' Didrikson to Wed Geo. Z.: Wrestler Wins Heart of Beaumont Gal Athlete," n.p., July 22, 1938, Scrapbooks; Schoor, *Babe,* 97.

21. *TLIL,* 111; G. Zaharias, "The Babe and I."

22. G. Zaharias, "The Babe and I"; *TLIL,* 113. Leo Durocher married Grace Doxier in 1934.

23. Murray, "The Other Babe"; *TLIL,* xii. This was a stunning comment for a 1955 source when evidence of marital discord abounded. See also G. Zaharias, "The Babe and I."

24. John Lardner, "Strong Cigars and Lovely Women," *Newsweek,* June 1949,

75; Pegler, "A Real Champion," 1; Will Grimsley, "Babe and George Happy Two-some," n.p., Apr. 16, 1953, Doct. 11.1.6.8.; Johnson and Williamson, "Whatta-Gal," 163.

25. D'Emilio and Freedman, Intimate Matters, 177, 265–67.

26. TLIL, 19; Johnson and Williamson, "Whatta-Gal," 168. The caption empha-sized George's gargantuan appetite and his ballooning to 400 pounds; see also TLIL, photo section following 162.

27. TLIL, 113, 115.

28. G. Zaharias, "The Babe and I."

29. TLIL, 116.

30. Ibid., 117.

31. Ibid., 118; "Babe and Her Golf," 1939, n.p., Scrapbooks.

32. G. Zaharias, "The Babe and I." "Zaharias took time out in talking about his wife's golf to remind us that he won 18 straight wrestling matches in Australia and was booked to meet Jimmy Londos for the world's championship in Sydney when the war prevented it." See "Babe and Her Golf."

33. G. Zaharias, "The Babe and I," 119.

34. Ibid.; Didrikson, "I Blow My Own Horn." Yet only two tournaments of any importance were open to her—the same two as in 1935: the Western Women's Open and Bertha Bowen's "gift," the Texas Women's Open.

35. Johnson and Williamson, "Whatta-Gal," 168; TLIL, 120; Karol Stonger, "George Goes on without Babe," Beaumont Enterprise and Journal, Jan. 17, 1973, 1, Doct. 11.2.21.2.

36. G. Zaharias, "The Babe and I."

37. TLIL, 120.

38. Ibid., 120–21.

39. Ibid., 122.

40. Ibid., 124.

41. B. D. Zaharias, "Valiant Woman," part 3, 44, 45

42. TLIL, 125.

43. Ibid.; Johnson and Williamson, "Whatta-Gal," 169–70. The tournament name was substantiated by John Nettles, San Diego Hall of Champions; Pat Yeo-mans, Los Angeles Tennis Club; and Kathy Willette, Tennis Patrons Association.

44. Gordon Macker, "The Big Thumb," Beaumont Journal, Mar. 15, no year, Scrapbooks; Morton Moss, "Amazing Babe Bowling! Mrs. Zaharias Seeks New Lau-rels," n.p., n.d., Scrapbooks; Johnson and Williamson, "Whatta-Gal," 169–70; "Sun-set Bowling Center, '41–42," n.p., n.d., Scrapbooks; George Main, "Classic Pin Loop Opens at Western," n.p., n.d., Scrapbooks.

45. Arthur Daley, "A Remarkable Woman," Sports of the Times (New York: E. P. Dutton, 1959), 204; TLIL, 129–30.

46. Crawford and Ragsdale, "The Texas Babe," 278; TLIL, photo section follow-ing 98. This is after her 1947 British victory.

47. Bill Nary interview, Sept. 20, 1989.

48. Johnson and Williamson, *"Whatta-Gal,"* 164; Johnson and Williamson, "Babe," part 3.

49. "Whatta Woman," *Time,* Mar. 10, 1947.

50. Didrikson, "I Blow My Own Horn."

51. B. D. Zaharias, "Valiant Woman," part 2, 92; Grimsley, "Happy Twosome"; Cott, *Groundings,* 139, 183, 187–89, 209–10; B. D. Zaharias, "Valiant Woman," part 3, 45.

52. B. D. Zaharias, "Valiant Woman," part 3, 45.

53. Ibid.; Johnson and Williamson, "Babe," part 3, 50.

54. Johnson and Williamson, "Babe," part 3, 50.

55. *TLIL,* 136.

56. William H. Chafe, *The Paradox of Change: American Women in the Twentieth Century* (New York: Oxford University Press, 1992), 175; *Ladies Home Journal,* Mar. 1941.

57. Chafe, *Paradox,* 183–84.

58. Ibid., 73–75, 109, 154. In 1938 over 80 percent of Americans were against married women working; by 1943 over 60 percent of Americans approved of it.

59. *Ladies Home Journal,* Jan., Feb., Mar. 1941; "Nobody Loves a Phi Beta," *Ladies Home Journal,* Apr., 1941, 19; *Ladies Home Journal,* Jan. 1943, 31.

60. Leslie B. Hohman, "As the Twig Is Bent: Girlish Boys and Boyish Girls," *Ladies Home Journal,* Feb. 1941, 59.

61. *Ladies Home Journal,* Nov. 1944; Marynia F. Farnham and Ferdinand Lundberg, "Men Have Lost Their Women," *Ladies Home Journal,* Nov. 1944. Farnham, a psychiatrist, and Lundberg, a journalist, went on to publish *Modern Woman: The Lost Sex* in 1947. The book, like their 1944 article, was a reaction against the freedom gained by women during World War II. It called for a return to the home and women's dependency. This book was widely circulated and was an influential factor in the mental health profession's treatment and counseling of women. Women's mental health, they argued, depended on remaining in the home.

62. B. D. Zaharias, "Valiant Woman," part 3, 45.

63. Mrozek, "The 'Amazon,'" 292–93; Lenskyj, *Out of Bounds,* 57.

64. Martin, "Mask," 27; Quentin Reynolds, "The Girl Who Lived Again," *Reader's Digest,* Oct. 1954, 50–55, Doct. 11.1.17.2.

65. Martin, "Mask," 27.

66. Ibid.

67. Ibid.

68. Lader, "The Unbeatable Babe," 158; *TLIL,* 167, 152.

69. Johnson and Williamson, *"Whatta-Gal,"* 175, 13, 20–21. Johnson and Williamson note, "Though she dressed with good taste usually, her only errors in the selection of clothes occurred when she wore things too frilly. For years after most women on the golf tour wore Bermuda shorts, Babe stuck with skirts," 20.

70. Schoor, *Babe,* 97; Cott, *Groundings,* 174.

Chapter 7: Dominating the Fairways and the Greens

1. Durant and Bettmann, *Pictorial History*, 76, 94, 138, quotations on 139 and 149. See also Mehr, "Quest for Justice," 42. The first golf match was played on U.S. soil in 1888 at the St. Andrews course in Yonkers, New York. In 1892 Shinnecock Hills on Long Island became the first golf club in the country to be incorporated and have a clubhouse and a waiting list.

2. Ibid., 139; Remley, *Sport History*, 27–28.

3. Joanna Davenport, "Eleonora Randolph Sears, Pioneer in Women's Sports," *North American Society for Sport History: Proceedings and Newsletter* 4 (June 1976): 17; Durant and Bettman, *Pictorial History*, 148.

4. Evans, "Status," 158, 160; John Lucas and Ron Smith, "Women's Sport: A Trial of Equality," in *Her Story in Sport,* ed. Howell, 239–65.

5. Durant and Bettman, *Pictorial History*, 148.

6. Roberta J. Park, "Sport, Gender, and Society in a Transatlantic Victorian Perspective," in *From "Fair Sex" to Feminism*, ed. Mangan and Park, 58–93, quotation on 82; Donald Mrozek, "Sporting Life as Consumption, Fashion, and Display—The Pastimes of the Rich," *Sport and the American Mentality, 1890–1910* (Knoxville: University of Tennessee Press, 1983), 106. See also Evans, "Status," 105, 107–8.

7. Evans, "Status," 219.

8. Pitters, "Analysis of Humor," 228; "Our Lady Golfers Take the Cup, but Let the British Title Go," *Literary Digest,* June 18, 1921, 34. The American victor of the qualifying round was Maureen Orcutt. She was eliminated in championship play. The Fishwick Cup is presented to the winner in the qualifying round.

9. Grassis interview; Martin, "Mask," 137; Johnson and Williamson, "Babe," part 3, 48.

10. Rice, *Tumult,* 242; "Babe Zaharias Open This Week."

11. Lader, "Unbeatable Babe," 160–61; "Women's Golf: Remarkable Mildred," *Golf World,* June 18, 1947, reprinted as a commemorative issue, June 19, 1987, 9.

12. *TLIL,* 9; Lader, "Unbeatable Babe," 162; Dodd interview, June 24, 1985.

13. *TLIL,* 89.

14. Hicks, *Golf Tour Gourmet,* 56.

15. G. Zaharias, "The Babe and I," 89; *TLIL,* photo section following 157.

16. Johnson and Williamson, "*Whatta-Gal,*" 192, 193; Johnson and Williamson, "Babe," part 3, 51–52.

17. Lader, "Unbeatable Babe," 161.

18. Johnson and Williamson, "*Whatta-Gal,*" 18.

19. Ginny Gravley interview, Dec. 10, 1989, and Oct. 12, 1994. Ginny Gravley is now Ginny Muhlenberg of Philadelphia, Pa.

20. Johnson and Williamson, "*Whatta-Gal,*" 184.

21. *TLIL,* 100.

22. "Babe Zaharias Open This Week."

23. Ibid.; "Whatta Woman."

24. Hicks, *Golf Tour Gourmet*, 117, 18.

25. "Babe Zaharias Open This Week"; Will Grimsley, "Colorful, Wisecracking Babe," third in a series, n.p., Apr. 15, 1953, Doct. 11.1.6.7; Johnson and Williamson, "Babe," part 3, 50.

26. Martin, "Mask," 137; John Lardner, "The Versatility of Mrs. Z." *Newsweek*, June 1947, 75.

27. Gibson, "Now THERE Was an Olympic Champion," 5.

28. Johnson and Williamson, "Babe," part 3, 51; Hicks, *Golf Tour Gourmet*, 87, 117.

29. "Women Pros of the Decades—Babe Zaharias," *Golf World*, June 19, 1987, 36; Wilson Women's Golf Information, 1954, Doct. 11.2.20.3.

30. Hicks interview, Mar. 8, 1989; The tournament locale is unknown, but apparently Babe was not disqualified because it was her *own* ball, not an opponent's, with which she had tinkered. Johnson and Williamson, "*Whatta-Gal*," 174–75.

31. Quotations from Jameson interview.

32. *TLIL*, 138, 139; Johnson and Williamson, "*Whatta-Gal*," 175.

33. Lader, "Unbeatable Babe," 161.

34. Ibid., 161; *TLIL*, 140; BDZ Foundation, "The 'Babe.'" At the Trans-Mississippi in Denver, she beat Polly Riley in the finals, six and five. In the Broadmoor Invitational Match Play Tournament in Colorado Springs, she beat Dorothy Kielty, six and four. *TLIL*, 140.

35. *TLIL*, 140–41; B. D. Zaharias, "Valiant Woman," part 3, 46.

36. *TLIL*, 141; B. D. Zaharias, "Valiant Woman," part 3, 46.

37. B. D. Zaharias, "Valiant Woman," part 1, 46, part 3, 45.

38. *TLIL*, 142.

39. Johnson and Williamson, "Babe," part 3, 46; *TLIL*, 143. In later years, friends and relatives witnessed and willingly told how George badgered Babe to perform. Not surprisingly, they spoke much more freely after George's death in 1984.

40. BDZ Foundation, "The 'Babe'"; *TLIL*, 143. She won twelve and ten over Margaret Gunther.

41. Johnson and Williamson, "Babe," part 3, 50. The four competitors were all even after thirty-five holes in the finals. In a four-ball match, two players are matched against the other pair. On each hole, the low score of a two-person team is compared with the low score of the other team. The team with the lowest score on the hole is then "one-up." If the one-up team loses the next hole, the teams are "even." Play continues to the end of eighteen or thirty-six holes, when the team who wins the most holes wins the match. The scoring is the same in regular match play, in which only two players face off.

42. Lader, "Unbeatable Babe," 161.

43. *TLIL*, 145.

44. Hicks, *Golf Tour Gourmet*, 23; phone interview with Sandra Lynch, account-

ing assistant, Spokane Country Club, Feb. 15, 21, 1991. Lynch found the information in a scrapbook kept by the Ladies' Golf Association of the Spokane Country Club. See also Billye Ann Cheatum, "A History of Selected Golf Tournaments for Women with Emphasis upon the Growth and Development of the Ladies Professional Golf Association" (Ph.D. diss., Texas Women's University, 1967), 430; Jameson interview. The Spokane Tournament was under the auspices of the quickly defunct Women's Professional Golf Association, chartered by Hope Seignious of North Carolina. Despite the short life of the WPGA, the Spokane tournament did "count." See Fred Corcoran, *"Unplayable Lies:" The Story of Sport's Most Successful Impresario* (New York: Meredith Press, 1965), 167.

45. Hicks, *Golf Tour Gourmet,* 117.

46. Ibid.

47. Ibid.; *TLIL,* 146–47.

48. *TLIL,* 147, 148.

49. Ibid., 149–50; "Golf World: A Weekly Golf Newspaper," *Golf World,* June 18, 1947, reprinted as a commemorative issue, June 19, 1987.

50. *TLIL,* 152.

51. Ibid., 154.

52. Ibid., 157.

53. Ibid., 169, 159; Crawford and Ragsdale, "The Texas Babe," 279.

54. Lader, "Unbeatable Babe"; Johnson and Williamson, "Babe," part 2, 51; Mildred (Babe) Didrikson Zaharias as told to Harry T. Paxton, "The Story of a Valiant Woman: This Life I've Led," *Saturday Evening Post,* July 16, 1955, part 4, 107, Doct. 11.1.13.20.

55. B. D. Zaharias, "Valiant Woman," part 4, 107.

56. Ibid., 108.

57. *TLIL,* 163.

58. Ibid., 163–64; Gene Farmer, "What a Babe!" *Life,* June 23, 1947; "The Babe in Britain," *Time,* June 23, 1947.

59. "The Babe in Britain."

60. First names are unavailable for Redden and Falcone. Their given names, like those of most other women golfers of the forties and fifties, were not used in reports of the games despite their great accomplishments. Marge Dewey of the Ralph W. Miller Golf Library/Museum, City of Industry, Calif., to Susan Cayleff, 1994. Quotation from B. D. Zaharias, "Valiant Woman," part 4, 108; BDZ Foundation, "The 'Babe.'"

61. B. D. Zaharias, "Valiant Woman," part 4, 108.

62. Ibid.; "The Babe in Britain."

63. *TLIL,* 167, 109.

64. Ibid., 171, 173.

65. Ibid., 173, 174.

66. Ibid., 174–75.
67. As quoted in Johnson and Williamson, "Babe," part 3, 51.
68. Farmer, "What a Babe!"; "The Babe in Britain."
69. *TLIL*, photo sections following 98, 175.
70. Ibid., 175, 176, 177.
71. Ibid., 178; Grimsley, "Happy Twosome."
72. *TLIL*, 178.
73. Rice, *Tumult*, 242.
74. *TLIL*, 179.
75. Ibid.; BDZ Foundation, "The 'Babe.'"

Chapter 8: Cashing In

1. *TLIL*, 180; Crawford and Ragsdale, "The Texas Babe," 279; see also *World Almanac*, 1948.
2. *TLIL*, 181; Corcoran interview.
3. Corcoran interview.
4. Martin, "Mask," 26; *TLIL*, 180; see also Lader, "Unbeatable Babe," 161, wherein he reported the $300,000 movie deal as a fait accompli.
5. Corcoran, *"Unplayable Lies,"* 180, 181; *TLIL*, 181.
6. Martin, "Mask," 26; Corcoran, *"Unplayable Lies,"* 181.
7. *TLIL*, 182.
8. Crawford and Ragsdale, "The Texas Babe," 276, quotation on 277; quotation from *TLIL*, photo caption, photo section following 162; Corcoran interview.
9. Commericial brochure with Babe Didrikson endorsement, the P. Goldsmith Sons, Inc., Cincinnati, Ohio, Doct. 11.1.16.5.
10. Timex ad, *Good Housekeeping*, Apr. 1954, 281; "Prest-O-Lite" ad, *Saturday Evening Post*, Aug. 12, 1950.
11. Jameson interview; Bell interview.
12. Bell interview; Johnson and Williamson, *"Whatta-Gal,"* 190.
13. Jameson interview; Johnson and Williamson, *"Whatta-Gal,"* 185.
14. Bell interview. The Tampa home was built in 1950.
15. Bowen interview, May 17, 1988.
16. Dodd interview, Sept. 16, 23, 1987, Oct. 13, 1987; Johnson and Williamson, *"Whatta-Gal,"* 195, 19.
17. Berg interview.
18. Bell interview; Schoor, *Babe*, 63.
19. Ibid., June 17, 24, 1987.
20. Review of Mildred Babe (Didrikson) Zaharias, *Championship Golf*, *Book Review Digest* (1948): 952; *New York Times*, Aug. 29, 1948, 23; Virginia Bookshop Service, *Kirkus Review*, Apr. 15, 1948, Review of *Championship Golf*, 212.
21. Hicks, *Golf Tour Gourmet*, 7–8, 9; Crawford and Ragsdale, "The Texas Babe," 279.

22. Zaharias, "Valiant Woman," part 4, 110; George Zaharias, "The Babe and I."

23. *TLIL*, 183.

24. Ibid., 184.

25. The league entertained a "war-weary public as an interim measure to pick up the slack in major league attendance while some of baseball's best players served in the military." Susan M. Cahn, "No Freaks, No Amazons, No Boyish Bobs," *Chicago History* (Spring 1989): 27–41, quotations on 34, 35, 36; AAGPBL Photograph Collection, National Baseball Library, Cooperstown, New York.

26. *TLIL*, 185.

27. Corcoran, *"Unplayable Lies,"* 167; Betty Hicks, "A Lady Golf Pro Lets Her Hair Down: Next to Marriage We'll Take Golf," *Saturday Evening Post,* Jan. 23, 1954, 95; Patty Berg interview, Oct. 3, 1989. Wilson Sporting Goods paid Corcoran's salary for six years until other manufacturers joined in.

28. Corcoran, *"Unplayable Lies,"* 170, 171.

29. Hicks, "A Lady Golf Pro," 36.

30. Ibid., 95; Betty Hicks, "Foremothers: Babe Didrikson Zaharias; Part II—Babe Craved Attention; She Got It," *womenSports,* Dec. 1975, 22, 20; Cheatum, "A History of Tournaments," 225; Seven women had broken away from the WPGA to help found the LPGA. The original eleven members were Zaharias, Berg, Jameson, Dettweiler, Louise Suggs, Alice Bauer, Marlene Bauer, Sally Sessions, Bettye Danof, Shirley Spork, and Marilyn Smith. See Elinor Nickerson, *Golf: A Women's History* (Jefferson: McFarland, 1987), 55.

31. *TLIL*, 187; Wilson Information, 110; Cheatum, "A History of Tournaments," 222–23, 228, 237, 239, 241, 244, 254, 267.

32. Corcoran, *"Unplayable Lies,"* 178; Cheatum, "A History of Tournaments," 227–28.

33. Dodd interview, June 24, 1987; Hicks, "A Lady Golf Pro," 36.

34. Bell interview; Johnson and Williamson, "Babe," part 3, 48.

35. Johnson and Williamson, *"Whatta-Gal,"* 187; Jameson interview.

36. Hicks, " 'Stand Back,' " 27, 28.

37. Johnson and Williamson, *"Whatta-Gal,"* 189, 117.

38. *TLIL*, 193.

39. Bell interview; Dodd interview, June 24, 1987; Robert H. K. Browning, "Sex Equality on the Links," *A History of Golf* (London: J. M. Dent and Sons, 1955), 193.

40. Berg interview; Johnson and Williamson, *"Whatta-Gal,"* 191; Jameson interview.

41. Bell interview; Nary interview.

42. Hicks, "Foremothers," 18; Hicks, " 'Stand Back,' " 28.

43. Hicks, "Foremothers," 20, 27.

44. Cheatum, "A History of Tournaments," 230.

45. Corcoran, *"Unplayable Lies,"* 174, 175.

46. Ibid., 175.

47. Reynolds, "The Girl Who Lived Again," 53.

48. Babe Zaharias Golf Records, n.d., Doct. 11.1.2.12; Cheatum, "A History of Tournaments," 238; "Mrs. Golf," *Newsweek,* May 14, 1951.

49. "Mrs. Golf," 2; "Big Business Babe," *Time,* June 11, 1951, 66–68.

50. Hicks, "Foremothers," 18, 20, 22; Dodd interview, June 17, 1987, Sept. 16 and 23, 1987.

51. Hicks, "Foremothers," 22; Bell interview.

52. Dodd interview, June 24, 1987.

53. Dodd interview, Sept. 16, 23, 1987.

54. Dodd interview, Oct. 13, 1987. This match occurred in 1954.

55. Jameson interview; Bell interview; Hicks, "Foremothers," 21.

56. "Big Business Babe," 67–68.

Chapter 9: Mates

1. *TLIL,* 188.

2. Ibid., 133–34; Johnson and Williamson, "*Whatta-Gal,*" 197. As illustrated in the portrait of Beaumont, Babe matured in an era and a region particularly hostile to blacks and Jews. Part of Babe's deliberate Americanization process (e.g., the changed spelling of her surname, the family's detachment from ethnic activities, and her total self-identification as a Texan and an American versus that of a first-generation Norwegian-American) reflects her conscious shedding of any "ethnic taint."

3. G. Zaharias, "The Babe and I," 92; Dodd interview, June 17, 1987; *TLIL,* 189.

4. Dodd interview, Oct. 13, 1987; Bowen interview, May 17, 1988; Johnson and Williamson, "*Whatta-Gal,*" 200. Babe's comment about George's looks was also quoted by several other interviewees and in the press.

5. Dodd interview, June 17, 1988.

6. Hicks, *Golf Tour Gourmet,* 183.

7. Jameson interview; Bell interview.

8. Thelma Didriksen interview, Feb. 24, 1989.

9. Dodd interview, June 17, 1987.

10. Bowen interview, May 17, 1988; Hicks, "'Stand Back,'" 28; Jameson interview.

11. Hicks, "A Lady Golf Pro," 37, 92.

12. Patty Berg, "Babe Graced Sports with Her Skill and Courage," *New York Times,* July 15, 1984; Bell interview.

13. Bowen interview, May 17, 1988; Nary interview.

14. Nary interview; Dodd interview, June 17, 1987.

15. Jameson interview; Johnson and Williamson, "Babe," part 1, 57; Hagood, in *Mothers of the South,* 161, discusses men controlling the monies.

16. "Babe Zaharias Open This Week."

17. Betty Friedan, *The Feminine Mystique* (New York: Dell, 1963).

18. Karen Anderson, *Wartime Women: Sex Roles, Family Relations, and the Status of Women during World War II* (Westport: Greenwood Press, 1987); Eugenia Kaledin, *Mothers and More American Women in the 1950s* (Boston: Twayne, 1984), 182–83; Chafe, *Paradox,* 186.

19. Chafe, *Paradox,* 179.

20. Dodd interview, June 17, 24, 1987.

21. Johnson and Williamson, "Babe," part 3, 57.

22. Cahn, "Coming on Strong," 225, 350–51; Dodd interview, Oct. 13, 1987. In "Beauty and the Butch," 301–47, and "Play It, Don't Say It," 348–92, Cahn explores the factors that coalesce to silence lesbian athletes.

23. *TLIL,* 190.

24. Ibid., 190–91; Zaharias, "The Babe and I."

25. Dodd interview, June 17, 1987.

26. *TLIL,* 190.

27. Babe Didrikson Zaharias to Tiny and Miss Francis Scurlock, July 1, 1952, Doct. 11.1.14.19; Babe's postscript read: "P.S. George sends his regards. He hasn't lost a pound." *TLIL,* 192.

28. Cheatum, "A History of Tournaments," 239–40; Babe Zaharias Golf Records, 2.

29. *TLIL,* 194.

30. Ibid.

31. Ibid., 195; "Mrs. Zaharias' 212 Best at Beaumont," *New York Times,* Apr. 6, 1953, 27; *TLIL,* 196.

32. Dodd interview, June 17, 1987; Johnson and Williamson, "*Whatta-Gal,*" 205.

33. *TLIL,* 199.

34. "Tell Everybody Hello," *Newsweek,* Apr. 20, 1953, 93.

35. Grimsley, "Happy Twosome."

36. Wray's column, "Listen to Babe," circa 1940, n.p., Scrapbooks.

37. *TLIL,* 104.

38. Johnson and Williamson, "Babe," part 2, 57; Reynolds, "The Girl Who Lived Again," 53; *TLIL,* xii.

39. Hicks, "Foremothers," 24; Jameson interview; Bell interview.

40. Corcoran interview; Nary interview.

41. Johnson and Williamson, "Babe," part 2, 57; Bowen interview, May 17, 1988.

42. Leila J. Rupp, "Imagine My Surprise: Women's Relationships in Historical Perspective" *Frontiers* 5 (1980): 61–70. While examples are drawn from the political activist arena, I believe the model applies well to the Dodd-Didrikson relationship.

43. Dodd interview, Sept. 16, 23, 1987; Hicks, "Foremothers," 24.

44. Hicks, "Foremothers," 24; Dodd interview, June 24, 1986.

45. Dodd interview, June 17, 1987.

46. Jameson interview; Hicks, "A Lady Golf Pro," 92; Wilson Information; Dodd interview, June 24, 1987; Berg, "Babe Graced Sports."

47. Dodd interview, June 24, 1987.

48. Dodd interview, June 17, 1987, Oct. 13, 1987.

49. Johnson and Williamson, "*Whatta-Gal*," 15; Don Freeman, "Point of View," *San Diego Tribune,* Jan. 16, 1991.

50. Michelle Kort, "Women Athletes in Reel Life," *Chrysalis* 8 (Summer 1979): 38–41; Rosen, *Popcorn Venus,* 198–99.

51. Kort, "Women Athletes," 39.

52. Jim Backus and Henny Backus as quoted in Freeman, "Point of View."

53. Bowen interview, May 17, 1988.

54. Dodd interview, June 17, 1987; Johnson and Williamson, "*Whatta-Gal*," 203.

55. Bowen interview, May 17, 1988; Dodd interview, June 17, 1987.

56. Dodd interview, June 17, 1987.

57. Bowen interview, May 17, 1988; Dodd interview, June 17, 1987.

58. Johnson and Williamson, "*Whatta-Gal*," 207.

59. See Jeffrey R. M. Kunz, *The American Medical Association Family Medical Guide* (New York: Random House, 1982), 482. Equipment for colostomy irrigation includes an irrigation set with a drain, bag, and clamp; a catheter; lubricant; an ostomy belt; 1,000 ml of water warmed to 100°–105°F; a plastic or paper bag; a washcloth and a towel; soap and water; and the ostomy appliance. See Helen Klusek Hamilton, ed., *Procedures,* Nurse's Reference Library (Springhouse, Pa.: Communications, Inc., 1983), 565–68. Quotation from Dodd interview, June 17, 1987.

60. Bell interview; Jameson interview.

61. Dodd interview, Oct. 13, 1987.

62. Jameson interview; Bell interview; Dodd interview, June 24, 1987. The implication of more than one miscarriage remains unsubstantiated.

63. Bell interview.

64. Dodd interview, June 17, 24, 1987, Sept. 16, 1987, Oct. 13, 1987.

Chapter 10: "I'm Not Out of the Rough Yet!"

1. *TLIL,* 5.

2. Johnson and Williamson, "*Whatta-Gal*," 206; Dodd interview, June 24, 1987. See also William E. Tatum, *Saddle-Bag Surgeon: A Doctor's Autobiography* (Waco: Texian Press, 1978).

3. *TLIL,* 204–5.

4. Babe Didrikson Zaharias as told to Booton Herndon, "I'm Not Out of the Rough—Yet!" *Cosmopolitan,* Oct. 1953, 79–83, Doct. 11.1.13.23.

5. "Babe Zaharias Goes under Knife at Hotel Dieu Here Today," *Beaumont Journal,* Apr. 17, 1953, Doct. 11.1.6.19; "Final Hospital Pix," n.p., May 18, 1953, Doct. 11.1.6.13.

6. Dodd interview, June 17, 1987.

7. Johnson and Williamson, "*Whatta-Gal*," 206.

8. Dodd interview, June 17, 1987. See also Dennis H. Novak, Robin Plumer, Raymond L. Smith, Herbert Orchitill, Gary R. Morrow, and John M. Bennett, "Changes in Physicians' Attitudes toward Telling the Cancer Patient," in *Medical Ethics: A Clinical Textbook and Reference for the Health Care Professions,* ed. Natalie Abrams and Michael D. Buckner (Cambridge, Mass.: MIT Press, 1983), 187–90.

9. Bowen interview, May 17, 1988; Schoor, *Babe,* 134.

10. Dodd interview, June 17, 1987.

11. Bowen interview, May 17, 1988.

12. Thelma Didriksen interview.

13. Ibid.

14. "Babe Goes under Knife"; "Final Hospital Pix."

15. "Messages Pour in to Mrs. Zaharias," *New York Times,* Apr. 11, 1953, 10; B. D. Zaharias, "Rough," 79–82.

16. B. D. Zaharias, "Rough," 82, 83; "Mrs. Zaharias Is Ill at Beaumont: Athletic Career Appears at End," *New York Times,* Apr. 10, 1953, 26.

17. G. Zaharias, "The Babe and I," 94; Reynolds, "The Girl Who Lived Again," 52; B. D. Zaharias, "Rough," 83.

18. *TLIL,* 98

19. "Major Surgery Set for Mrs. Zaharias," *New York Times,* Apr. 12, 1953, sect. 5, p. 1.

20. "The Babe Is Back," *Time,* Aug. 10, 1953.

21. Bell interview.

22. Mildred (Babe) Didrikson Zaharias as told to Harry T. Paxton, "The Story of a Valiant Woman: This Life I've Led," *Saturday Evening Post,* July 23, 1955, part 5, 98–102, Doct. 11.1.12.21.

23. B. D. Zaharias, "Rough," 79–83.

24. Babe Biographical, 4; "Wilson Information, Press, Radio, TV; (Babe Zaharias Only)," 1954, Doct. 11.2.20.3.

25. *TLIL,* 217; Dodd interview, Oct. 13, 1987.

26. *TLIL,* 217; G. Zaharias, "The Babe and I."

27. Babe Didrikson Zaharias, "Spiritual Muscle," in *Faith Made Them Champions,* ed. Norman Vincent Peale (New York: Guideposts Association, 1954), 109.

28. G. Zaharias, "The Babe and I," 53.

29. *TLIL,* 219. Her other win came at the Sarasota Open. Elinor Nickerson, *Golf: A Women's History* (Jefferson, N.C.: McFarland, 1987), 48.

30. Ibid., 221.

31. Ibid., 221–22; "The Babe a Year Later, *New York Sunday News,*" 28, Doct. 11.1.13.14.

32. *TLIL,* 224; Joe Heiling, "Babe Zaharias: Great Athlcte and a Beautiful Lady," *Beaumont Sunday Enterprise-Journal,* Nov. 9, 1980, 2-H, Doct. 11.1.13.34.

33. "Fund for Detection of Cancer Established by Babe Zaharias," *Beaumont Enterprise,* Sept. 12, 1955, 11, Doct. 11.1.7.2; Peter Moore interview, Feb. 20, 1985; Dr. Rose Schneider interview, Feb. 20, 1985.

34. B. D. Zaharias, "Spiritual Muscle," 109; Hicks, *Golf Tour Gourmet,* 86.

35. Pete Coutros, "The Babe a Year Later," *New York Sunday News,* Apr. 18, 1954, 26, Doct. 11.1.13.14; Cheatum, "A History of Tournaments," 250, 240, quotation on 253; "Mrs. Zaharias Honored," *New York Times,* Apr. 9, 1954, 5; *TLIL,* 223–24. Wins in 1954: Serbin Women's Open, Sarasota, National Capitol, National, and All-American Tournaments; runner-up: Babe Zaharias Open, St. Petersburg Tournament; tied for second: Inverness Four-Ball Tournament; third: Women's Titleholder's Tournament and Betsy Rawls, Carrolton, and New Orleans Opens; fourth: World Championship and Wichita Tournaments; fifth: Fort Wayne Open; seventh: Tampa Open; tied for seventh: Ardmore Open; tied for fourteenth: Sea Island Open. Babe Zaharias Golf Records, 2. Berg won top-dollar honors with $16,011. To win the Vare Trophy, Babe shot an average of 75.48 over 66 rounds.

36. *TLIL,* 224.

37. Cheatum, "A History of Tournaments," 242–45; The officers were Jameson, vice-president; Betsy Rawls, secretary; Betty MacKinnon, treasurer; and Alice Bauer, member-at-large. See "Mrs. Zaharias Re-elected," *New York Times,* July 31, 1953, sect. 13, p. 2.

38. Hicks, "A Lady Golf Pro," 36–37, 92, 94.

39. "Ladies P.G.A. Blasted: Mrs. Zaharias Quits as Head and Talks of New Group," *New York Times,* Jan. 22, 1954, 33; "Ladies P.G.A. Feud Ends," *New York Times,* Jan. 23, 1954, sect. 17, p. 1; Cheatum, "A History of Tournaments," 246.

40. Cheatum, "A History of Tournaments," 247–49.

41. *TLIL,* 224, 225; Reynolds, "The Girl Who Lived Again," 54.

42. "Babe Visits Red Bombers in Tampa," n.p., Mar. 18, no year, Scrapbooks.

43. G. Zaharias, "The Babe and I," 92, 93; *TLIL,* 226, 227.

44. Dodd interview, June 24, 1987; Johnson and Williamson, "*Whatta-Gal,*" 211; Babe Biographical, 4.

45. Dodd interview, June 24, 1987. In 1955 Babe finished fourth in the Los Angeles and St. Petersburg Opens, ninth in the Serbin Women's Open, and thirteenth in the Babe Zaharias Open and tied for seventh in the Women's Titleholder's Tournament. See Babe Zaharias Golf Records, 2. In her autobiography, Babe called the Serbin Women's Open the Serbin Diamond Golf Ball because she won a diamond-studded putter there.

46. Hicks, "Foremothers," 25; G. Zaharias, "The Babe and I," 54.

47. Tumor Record, History No. 5554-K, Zaharias Mrs. Mildred, John Sealy Hospital, University of Texas Medical Branch, Galveston, Texas, 4721-105.0, Treatment Sheet, June 17, 1955. Babe's chart runs from Apr. 22, 1954, through June 22, 1955. A notation in the upper-right front page corner reads: "Exp. 9-27-56."; Dodd interview, June 24, 1987.

48. Dodd interview, June 24, 1987.

49. Dodd interview, Oct. 13, 1987; Bell interview.

50. Tumor Record, 5554-K, Treatment Sheet, June 22, 1955; Thelma Didriksen interview.

51. Tumor Record, 5554-K, Follow-up Notes, June 22, 1955; Thelma Didriksen interview.

52. Dodd interview, June 24, 1987; Tumor Record, 5554-K, Chart Entry, Aug. 4, 1955; "Babe Zaharias Gets Treatment for New Cancer," n.p., Aug. 5, 1955, Doct. 11.1.8.1. See also "Babe Rests in Second Bout with Cancer," Aug. 7, 1955, Doct. 11.1.8.2.

53. *TLIL*, 232.

54. Bubba Didriksen and Jackie Didriksen interview.

55. *TLIL*, 228–29; B. D. Zaharias, "Valiant Woman," part 5, 101.

56. *TLIL*, 214; Reynolds, "The Girl Who Lived Again," 55.

57. Zaharias Cancer Fund Story (Sports Guide), Doct. 11.1.1.18; The Babe Didrikson Zaharias Cancer Fund Information, Doct. 11.1.7.1; quotations from "Fund for Detection of Cancer Established by Babe Zaharias," *Beaumont Enterprise*, Sept. 12, 1955, 11, Doct. 11.1.7.2.

58. Zaharias Cancer Fund Story, 1; Schneider interview. See also "Fund for Detection," 11. The fund's board of directors included Dr. Robert Moore, Babe's surgeon; Fred Corcoran of New York, her manager and personal friend; Drs. John Otto, John Childers, Hyman W. Paley, and Martin Schneider of the Galveston Medical Branch; V. W. McLeod, Galveston attorney; Judge C. G. Dibrell of Galveston; and John W. McCullough, president of Galveston's Hutchings Sealy National Bank and chairman of the Sealy-Smith Foundation that donated John Sealy Hospital to the university.

59. Zaharias Cancer Fund Story, 1; Cancer Fund Information.

60. Tumor Record, 5554-K, Chart Entry, Sept. 14, 1955; her physician at this time was Dr. Snodgrass.

61. Zaharias Cancer Fund Story; form letter to sports editors on The Babe Didrikson Zaharias Cancer Fund, Inc., letterhead, June 4, 1956, Doct. 11.1.17.3; Babe Biographical. Babe won the Babe Zaharias Open in 1953, placed second in 1954, and finished thirteenth in 1955.

62. Dodd interview, June 24, 1987; Johnson and Williamson, "*Whatta-Gal*," 213; Johnson and Williamson, "Babe," part 3, 48–54; Tumor Record, 5554-K.

63. Johnson and Williamson, "*Whatta-Gal*," 216–17; "Pain Relief Operation Done on Babe," n.p., July 13, 1956, Doct. 11.1.8.5; "Babe's Pain Easing after Operation," n.p., July 14, 1956, Doct. 11.1.8.6.

64. "Mrs. Zaharias Improving," *New York Times*, Apr. 22, 1953, 40; "Mrs. Zaharias Is Fit," *New York Times*, Apr. 24, 1954, 22; "Mrs. Zaharias Tallies 291 for Third Open Golf Title," *New York Times*, July 4, 1954, sect. 5, p. 3; "Mrs. Zaharias Stricken," *New York Times*, Aug. 7, 1955, 11; "Mrs. Zaharias Resting," *New York Times*, Aug. 7, 1955, sect. 5, p. 10; "Mrs. Zaharias Expected to Return to Golf Play," *New York Times*, Sept. 11, 1955, sect. 5, p. 8; "Cancer Fund Set Up by Babe Didrikson," *New York Times*, Sept. 13, 1955, 6.

65. "Mrs. Zaharias to Fly to Texas Today for Check-up in Hospital," *New York Times,* Nov. 26, 1955, 16; Reynolds, "The Girl Who Lived Again," 50–55; "Cheerful Babe Continues Stubborn Battle against Cancer as Forty-second Birthday Nears," n.p., June 26, 1956, Doct. 11.1.8.3; "Babe Loses Strength, Weight but Continues to Put Up Fight," n.p., Aug. 25, 1956, Doct. 11.1.8.8; "Babe's Grit Praised by Physicians," n.p., Aug. 29, 1956, Doct. 11.1.8.11; "Tributes from World Pour Down on Babe at Birthday Party," n.p., June 27, 1956, Doct. 11.1.8.4.

66. Johnson and Williamson, *"Whatta-Gal,"* 205; Dodd interview, June 24, 1987; *TLIL,* 201.

67. Scurlock, "Warm Personal Memory"; Bell interview.

68. Johnson and Williamson, "Babe," part 3, 54.

69. Bubba Didriksen and Jackie Didriksen interview.

70. Johnson and Williamson, *"Whatta-Gal,"* 220; Berg interview; "Throng Attends Zaharias Rites: Lutheran Service Held in Beaumont, Tx., Church for Famed Athlete," *New York Times,* Sept. 29, 1956, 19. All agree that there was a dearth of women golfers in attendance.

71. "Babe Didrikson Zaharias," editorial, *New York Times,* Sept. 28, 1956, 26.

72. Bubba Didriksen and Jackie Didriksen interview; Bell interview; Dodd interview, June 24, 1987.

73. Bell interview.

74. Bubba Didriksen interview; Johnson and Williamson, "Babe," part 3, 7; Bowen interview, May 17, 1988; Dodd interview, June 17, 1987.

75. Berg interview.

76. Florence Chadwick interview, Apr. 3, 1989; Conversations with clerks at the Jefferson County Registry of Deeds and Probate Court, Beaumont, Tex., May 23, 1991; conversation with Richard Aye, clerk of Circuit Court, Hillsborough County, Tampa, Fla., May 24, 1991.

77. Chadwick interview.

78. Johnson and Williamson, *"Whatta-Gal,"* 19.

79. "Babe Zaharias Dies: Athlete Had Cancer," *New York Times,* Sept. 27, 1956, 1; "Mrs. Zaharias, Forty-two, Is Dead of Cancer: Eisenhower Expresses Sadness," *New York Times,* Sept. 28, 1956, 1, 30; "Babe Didrikson Zaharias," 26.

80. "Mrs. Zaharias," *London Times,* Sept. 28, 1956, 13c.

81. "The Transcript of Eisenhower's News Conference," *New York Times,* Sept, 28, 1956, 14.

Chapter 11: Legacy

1. Seventeen players received the honor; among them were five women: Babe, Patty Berg, Mickey Wright, Kathy Whitworth, and Nancy Lopez. See David Widener, "Babe's Brother Puts Trophy into Museum," n.p., Aug. 18, 1988, Scrapbooks; "Arthur Didriksen Dies in Fort Worth," *Beaumont Enterprise,* May 13, 1989. He was seventy-three years old.

2. Bowen interview, May 17, 1988.

3. Dodd interview, Sept. 16, 23, 1987.

4. Bowen interview, May 17, 1988.

5. "Husband of Athlete Babe Zaharias Dies," *Beaumont Enterprise*, May 23, 1984, Doct. 11.2.21.4; Bell interview; Heiling, "Zaharias Rejoins Babe." George and Harriet were married from 1981 to 1984. She now lives in Colorado Springs, Colorado.

6. Heiling, "Zaharias Rejoins"; "Golf Tribute Paid to Mrs. Zaharias," *New York Times*, Jan. 27, 1957, 1.

7. Karol Stonger, "George Goes On without Babe," *Beaumont Enterprise Journal*, Jan. 17, 1973, p. 1, Doct. 11.2.21.2; Thad Johnson to Susan Cayleff, Jan. 7, 1993; "Career Wrap-up," 1; George Zaharias to Thad Johnson, Feb. 10, 1970, on Skyview Lakes Golf Club, Lakeland, Florida, stationery; Thad Johnson to Susan Cayleff, Mar. 22, 1993, on Babe Didrikson Zaharias Foundation, Inc./Beaumont Chamber of Commerce stationery. Johnson was chairman and chairman emeritus of the Babe Didrikson Zaharias Foundation, Inc., as well as chair of the Beaumont Chamber of Commerce.

8. Johnson to Cayleff, Mar. 22, 1993. The only two awards Johnson considered of "sound and lasting quality" were the new Babe Didrikson Athlete of the Year Award and the original Associated Press Female Athlete of the Year Award.

9. "Husband Dies"; Stonger, "George Goes On," 1; "Diving Star to Get 'Zaharias' Trophy," *New York Times*, Jan. 6, 1957.

10. Apostolos interview.

11. *Babe* ad, *TV Guide*, July 9, 1985, Houston ed., A-59; Stonger, "George Goes On," 1.

12. Alvin Marill, *Movies Made for Television* (New York: Zoetrope Publications, 1987), 3; "George Zaharias Says 'Thank You,'" *Beaumont Journal*, Oct. 2, 1956, Doct. 11.1.10.6; Stonger, "George Goes On," 1.

13. Bell interview; Lela Davis, "'Babe' Is Moving Chronicle of Love," *Beaumont Sunday Enterprise-Journal*, Oct. 12, 1975, Doct. 11.1.12.16; Stonger, "George Goes On," 1.

14. Melvin Durslag, "Trying to Catch the Babe," *TV Guide*, Oct. 18, 1975, Houston ed., 11, 12.

15. Durslag, "Trying to Catch the Babe," 12. Years before, Esther Williams, swimmer turned actress who made twenty-six films between 1942 and 1961, had been considered to star in a film version of Babe's life, but that project never materialized. Vernon Scott, "Greatest Woman Athlete to Be Seen on TV Screen," *Daily News Tribune*, June 2, 1975, B-2, Doct. 11.1.12.19.

16. Lynn Ramsey, "From Lipstick and Lashes to Joysticks and Dashes: Is Hollywood Getting the Picture?" *womenSports*, Nov. 1976, 30; Durslag, "Trying to Catch the Babe," 12.

17. Johnson and Williamson, *Whatta-Gal*, 223; Michele Kort, "Women Athletes," 41. *Little Mo* (1978) about Maureen Connolly (tennis) and *The Other Side*

of the Mountain (part 1, 1975, part 2, 1978) about Jill Kinmont (skier), like *Babe,* are about women "whose careers were ended by gruesome catastrophe." While this same pattern appears in films about male athletes (e.g., *Brian's Song* about football players Brian Piccolo and Gale Sayers—also directed by Buzz Kulick who did *Babe*— and *The Lou Gehrig Story*), the movies about death and illness give the women a tinge of identifiable normalcy for the viewers. See Kurt B. Anderson, "Celluloid Heroines: Lights! Camera! Traction!" *womenSports,* Jan. 1979, 38; and Ken Hey, "Cultural Metaphors: Athletes and Athletics in American Films," *North American Society for Sport History: Proceedings and Newsletter* 4 (June 1976): 41.

18. Bell interview.

19. *Babe,* 1975, directed by Buzz Kulick, screenplay by Joanna Lee, producers Stanley Rubin and Norman Felton; Cecil Smith, "Gold Medal for Susan's 'Babe,'" *Los Angeles Times,* Oct. 15, 1975, Scrapbooks.

20. Cott, *Grounding,* 234, 239, 275–76. Nor was Babe involved in "voluntarist politics," a common gender-conscious activism for women of this era. Dodd interview, June 24, 1987; Hagood, in *Mothers of the South,* 75, notes poor southern women's intolerance for imagination and introspection "in the thinking and acting of the women."

21. "Billie Jean Named the King of the Ms.," 1973, Doct. 11.1.13.15.

22. Dodd interview, Oct. 13, 1987.

23. Bob Mazza, "'Babe' Bows in Home Town," *Hollywood Reporter,* Oct. 14, 1975, 3, 19. Rogers's presidency was followed by those of W. L. Pate, Sr., and Dr. John E. Gray. See "Career Wrap-up," 3.

24. Mazza, "'Babe' Bows," 19; Lela Davis, "Gala Premier Thronged," *Beaumont Sunday Enterprise-Journal,* Oct. 12, 1975, 1, Scrapbooks; Don Jacobs, "George Zaharias Grateful," *Beaumont Sunday Enterprise-Journal,* Oct. 12, 1975, Scrapbooks.

25. Smith, "Gold Medal for Susan's 'Babe'"; C. W. Skipper, "Love Story, Babe and Zaharias," *Houston Post*'s T.V. Week, Oct. 19, 1975, 3, Scrapbooks; Marill, *Movies Made for Television.* Kulick, the director, and Lee, the screenplay writer, were also nominated for their work, as were Jerry Goldsmith, composer, Charles Wheeler, cinematographer, Henry Berman, editor, and William Tuttle, makeup artist.

26. Skipper, "Love Story," 3; Smith, "Gold Medal for Susan's 'Babe'"; Bell interview.

27. Bill Scurlock, "Newly Created Babe Zaharias Trophy to Go to Top Fem Athlete of Year," *Beaumont Journal,* Oct. 2, 1956, Doct. 11.1.10.6; "Babe's Medals Suggested for Lamar," editorial, n.p. Oct. 11, 1956, Doct. 11.1.13.30.

28. Thad Johnson, "Sports World," *Beaumont Enterprise,* Sept. 27, 1968, 25, Scrapbooks; Edythe Capreol, "City Council Okays Land for Babe Zaharias Center," n.p., n.d., Scrapbooks. In 1971, the city council authorized a fifty-year lease for use of the ten acres. The lease stipulated that the building had to be completed within five years and opened to the public at no charge.

29. "Babe Zaharias Drive," n.p., Mar. 13, 1956, Scrapbooks; AP wire photo, Aug.

11, 1964, *Beaumont Journal*, Doct. 11.1.13.31; "Babe Zaharias Plaque Marks Cancer Fight," *New York Times*, Sept. 10, 1967, 7. The historical marker incorrectly lists her date of birth as 1913.

30. "Beaumont and the Babe," n.p., Oct. 10, 1968, Scrapbooks; Dan Wallach, "Johnson Preserves Babe's Champion Spirit, Memory," *Beaumont Enterprise*, Oct. 8, 1985. Johnson's contribution and inspiration were significant. When the museum finally opened, John Gray and Ben Rogers both paid tribute to Johnson's efforts.

31. "Port Arthur Landmark: Babe Zaharias' Birthplace Razed," *Houston Chronicle*, Apr. 3, 1970, sect. 1, p. 24; "Babe Memorial Drive Opens," n.p., May 5, 1970, 11, Doct. 11.1.12.6; "Babe Drive Kicks Off Today," *Beaumont Enterprise*, May 4, 1970, 13, Doct. 11.1.12.4. Mark Steinhagen, as president of the chamber of commerce, and Howard Hicks, as executive vice-president, "endorsed the Zaharias drive as a top asset to the community." See "Babe Memorial Drive Opens"; Thad Johnson, "The Lady and the Legend: Special Exhibition, Babe Zaharias Foundation," n.d., Doct. 11.1.12.22.

32. Bob Osius, "Babe's Fierce Competitiveness Remembered by Ruth Scurlock," *Sunday Beaumont Journal*, May 4, 1975, Scrapbooks. Ruth Scurlock, then eighty, emerged to praise Babe and support the sports week. Dan Green, "Betty Ford Chairperson for Premiere of 'Babe,'" *Beaumont Enterprise*, Sept. 1975, Scrapbooks; Lela Davis, "Gray Sets 'Babe' Award Standard," *Beaumont Journal*, Oct. 10, 1975, 3A, Scrapbooks.

33. Awards were displayed in trophy cases at the museum in January 1991. The beautification award was received May 1, 1979; the attractiveness tribute, Sept. 29, 1983. See Johnson, "The Lady and the Legend." Schoor, *Babe*, 169. Berg, along with other intimates, attended the opening. Berg interview. One source estimated construction costs at $154,000. See Crawford and Ragsdale, "The Texas Babe," 271.

34. "The Babe's Memory Still Vivid," Freeman File, *Galveston Daily News*, June 2, 1985, 4-C.

35. Johnson and Williamson, "*Whatta-Gal*," 223.

36. Bill Nichols, "Patty Berg, Babe's Rival, in Tourney," *Cleveland Plain Dealer*, June 22, 1976, sect. D, pp. 1–2. Berg struggled against cancer in 1971 and gladly paid homage to Babe's efforts years earlier. "Zaharias Golf Special," *Beaumont Journal*, June 24, 1976; Mike Marcellino, "Tournament Financial Flop: All Miss Tourney Green," *Chagrin Herald Sun*, Aug. 5, 1976, 32, all in Scrapbooks. The foundation did receive some good news in 1976, however. In the scrapbooks are oversized copies of two checks made out to the Babe Didriksen Zaharias Foundation, Inc., from the Babe Didriksen Zaharias–Red Carpet Inn Second Annual Invitational Golf Tournament. The first is for $5,000; the second, for half that amount.

37. House Simple Resolution no. 41, State of Texas House of Representatives, Doct. 11.1.11.2; Zaharias Cancer Fund Story. In a fitting epilogue to Babe's larger than life accomplishments, a 1985 interview with Dr. James Belli, chairperson of Radiation Therapy at UTMB, revealed that the radioactive cobalt machine purchased by the

Zaharias fund in the early 1950s was shipped to Tanzania, Africa, in February 1985. Prior to this it was in constant use at UTMB. In a joint effort by the United Nations, the World Health Organization, the International Atomic Energy Commission, Harvard University, UTMB, and Varian Corporation, the cobalt machine was transferred to the Tanzanian Cancer Center in Dar es Salaam; this qualified the facility as one of the best-equipped cancer treatment centers in Africa.

38. See, e.g., Scurlock, "Warm Personal Memory," 24; Lelia Scarborough Carroll, "Babe Didrikson Zaharias," poem about Babe written at the precise time of the funeral, Sept. 28, 1956, Doct. 11.1.10.10; Lorraine Good, "The Gallant Heart," Doct. 11.1.10.11; "Mrs. Zaharias Cremated: Ashes of Noted Athlete Are Buried at Beaumont, Tex.," *New York Times,* Sept. 30, 1956, sect. 5, p. 2.

39. Doug Cress, "Father Time's Latest Victim," *National Sports Daily,* Apr. 24, 1991, 5; Mark Kreidler, "Clearly, Someday They'll See Forever," *San Diego Union,* Mar. 17, 1991, H-12; Joan Ryan, *Contributions of Women Series—Sports* (Minneapolis: Dillon Press, 1975), 27.

40. Hicks, "Foremothers," 24. Bobby Jones's stamp was issued the same year. All inductions and awards are displayed in the fifteen trophy cases at the museum.

41. Joe Heiling, "A Gold-Medal Tribute to Babe: Effort Begins to Appeal Disqualification of Olympic Jump," *Beaumont Enterprise,* May 27, 1988, Scrapbooks.

42. Heiling, "Great Athlete."

43. Phyllis Hollander, *One Hundred Greatest Women in Sports* (New York: Grossett and Dunlap, 1976), 44–47; Martin, "Mask," 137, 16. The word Carroll actually ly used was "frabjous" in *Through the Looking-Glass.*

44. Grassis interview; Jameson interview; Berg, "Babe Graced Sports"; Johnson and Williamson, "Babe," part 3, 53.

45. Martin, "Mask," 27, 26.

46. Grantland Rice, as quoted in Johnson and Williamson, "Babe," part 3, 48.

47. Heiling, "Great Athlete"; Gibson, "Now THERE Was an Olympic Champion," 7. Take, for example, long-distance runner Mary Decker's poor treatment of Zola Budd, South African competitor, when Decker tripped and fell in a 1985 race. When Decker blamed Budd for the collision and refused to shake her hand, one journalist said Decker "fell from Olympic grace with a thud." She earned that reporter's sarcastic "Our Mr. Nice Guy Award." See also Melvin Durslag, "Boy, Was She Upset!" *TV Guide,* Feb. 2, 1985.

48. David Roberts, *Women's Sports and Fitness,* Nov.-Dec. 1990, 43–45. In the next issue, a representative of the U.S. Amateur Confederation of Roller Skating submitted a team photo and erroneously claimed Babe played women's roller polo in the 1930s at Lowes Rink in San Antonio. Hence the legend grows. See also Arthur Daley, "A Remarkable Woman," in *Sports of the Times,* ed. James Tuite (New York: E. P. Dutton, 1959), 204–6; Heiling, "Zaharias Rejoins Babe."

49. Johnson and Williamson, "Whatta-Gal," 132; Jameson interview; Hicks, "Foremothers," 20; Hollander, *One Hundred Greatest Women in Sports,* 50.

50. Cahn, *Coming on Strong*, 339.

51. Martin, "Mask," 135; Hicks, "A Lady Golf Pro"; Cheatum, "A History of Tournaments," 283.

52. Hicks, *Golf Tour Gourmet*, 106.

53. Martin, "Mask," 135; *TLIL*, 62. The last disclaimer, that she never played football, is belied in *This Life I've Led*, where Babe admits she and Lillie played with her brothers. She denied she played it post-adolescence, but there are photos of her punting—albeit staged—at Southern Methodist University's stadium. While in Spokane, Washington, for the 1946 National Women's Open Golf Championship, Babe and Hicks were hitting exhibition tee shots between halves of an exhibition game between the New York Giants and New York Yankees at Gonzaga Stadium. They had downed a few drinks at the Greek-American Club before dinner. Babe lobbed football passes to Hicks and kept exhorting her, "'G'wan, move back. This ain't no kid tossin.' I kept moving, because the Babe had commanded, and when I finally emerged from my trance, there I was at midfield, in the center of a stadium crammed with people, grabbing Zaharias passes thrown from 50 yards away." Hicks, *Golf Tour Gourmet*, 27.

54. Himes, "The Female Athlete," 254.

55. Cheatum, "A History of Tournaments," 282; Himes, "The Female Athlete," 253.

56. Hicks, "A Lady Golf Pro," 94; Hollander, *One Hundred Greatest*, 150, 50; Cheatum, "A History of Tournaments," 269.

57. Betty Hicks, "Why I'm Quitting Tournament Golf," *Golf World*, Oct. 26, 1956, 10; Cheatum, "A History of Tournaments," 270, 271.

58. Hicks, "Why I'm Quitting," 10; Cheatum, "A History of Tournaments," 282.

59. Cheatum, "A History of Tournaments," 269–70; Johnson and Williamson, *"Whatta-Gal,"* 221.

60. Johnson and Williamson, *"Whatta-Gal,"* 197, 221; Thad Johnson, "Cleveland Taking Over Zaharias Golf Tourney," *Beaumont Enterprise Journal,* July 4, 1976, 7-DD; "Zaharias Golf Special," *Beaumont Journal,* June 24, 1976. In the first tourney Suggs won $630 for second and Berg $490, for third.

61. Cheatum, "A History of Tournaments," 270; Carol Mann, "LPGA Mission: More Media Exposure," *Houston Post,* Jan. 6, 1991, B-17, B-19; Hollander, *One Hundred Greatest*, 50.

62. Bert Rosenthal, "Joyner-Kersee Named Athlete of the Year," *UCLA Daily Bruin,* Jan. 26, 1988, 32. Joyner-Kersee had seen Babe's story on television. Jack Smith, "Striking Out with a 'Sexist' (?) Counterprediction," *Los Angeles Times,* Jan. 30, 1990, sect. E, p. 1.

63. The athlete is Australian Bev Francis. See Louis B. Parks, "'Pumping Iron' Strong Contender for Year's Most Entertaining Film," *Houston Chronicle,* Oct. 5, 1985, sect. 4, p. 1; Carla Dunlap as quoted by Roger Ebert, "Flex Appeal: Articulate Woman Bodybuilder Stars in 'Pumping Iron II: The Women,'" *Houston Chronicle,* Oct. 6, 1985, 29.

64. Gloria Steinem, "Coming Up: The Unprecedented Women," *Ms.,* July 1985, 84.

65. Alison Carson, "When Is a Woman NOT a Woman?" *Women's Sports and Fitness,* Mar. 1991, 28, 26.

66. Patsy Neal and Thomas A. Tutko, *Coaching Girls and Women: Psychological Perspectives* (Boston: Allyn and Bacon, 1975). See Martina Navratilova with George Vecsey, *Martina* (New York: Alfred A. Knopf, 1985); Mike Downey, "She Succeeds as a Person, as an Athlete," *Los Angeles Times,* July 16, 1990, C1-C11. A new text, Mariah Burton Nelson's *Are We Winning Yet? How Sports Are Changing Women and How Women Are Changing Sports* (New York: Random House, 1991), explores lesbianism in women's sports and the LPGA Tour. It is an important first step toward breaking the silence around lesbianism and women athletes. See also Mariah Burton Nelson, "A Silence So Loud It Screams," *Golf Illustrated,* May 1991, 33–34, 37–41, 95.

67. For an extremely homophobic portrayal see "New Gay Sex Scandal Rocks Tennis: Lesbian Stars Stalk Young Players in Showers; Teens Lured to All-Girl Hot-Tub Parties," *National Enquirer,* July 31, 1990, 20–21; Keith Clark, "Martina Drives 'em Wild," *Gay and Lesbian Times,* Nov. 25, 1993, 16.

68. Joseph Gustaitis, "Babe Didrikson: America's Greatest Athlete?" *American History Illustrated,* Apr. 1987, 35; "Babe Zaharias Open This Week."

Index

Susan E. Cayleff has coedited *Wings of Gauze: Women of Color and the Experience of Health and Illness* and has written *Wash and Be Healed: The Water-Cure Movement and Women's Health* as well as numerous articles on women, medicine and health, and women's social history.

Books in the Series Women in American History

Women Doctors in Gilded-Age Washington: Race, Gender,
and Professionalization
Gloria Moldow

Friends and Sisters: Letters between Lucy Stone and Antoinette Brown
Blackwell, 1846–93
Edited by Carol Lasser and Marlene Deahl Merrill

Reform, Labor, and Feminism: Margaret Dreier Robins and the Women's Trade
Union League
Elizabeth Anne Payne

Private Matters: American Attitudes toward Childbearing and Infant Nurture
in the Urban North, 1800–1860
Sylvia D. Hoffert

Civil Wars: Women and the Crisis of Southern Nationalism
George C. Rable

I Came a Stranger: The Story of a Hull-House Girl
Hilda Satt Polacheck
Edited by Dena J. Polacheck Epstein

Labor's Flaming Youth: Telephone Operators and Worker Militancy, 1878–1923
Stephen H. Norwood

Winter Friends: Women Growing Old in the New Republic, 1785–1835
Terri L. Premo

Better Than Second Best: Love and Work in the Life of Helen Magill
Glenn C. Altschuler

Dishing It Out: Waitresses and Their Unions in the Twentieth Century
Dorothy Sue Cobble

Natural Allies: Women's Associations in American History
Anne Firor Scott

Beyond the Typewriter: Gender, Class, and the Origins of Modern American
Office Work, 1900–1930
Sharon Hartman Strom

The Challenge of Feminist Biography: Writing the Lives of Modern
American Women
Edited by Sara Alpern, Joyce Antler, Elisabeth Israels Perry,
and Ingrid Winther Scobie

Working Women of Collar City: Gender, Class, and Community in Troy, New York, 1864–86
Carole Turbin

Radicals of the Worst Sort: Laboring Women in Lawrence, Massachusetts, 1860–1912
Ardis Cameron

Visible Women: New Essays on American Activism
Edited by Nancy A. Hewitt and Suzanne Lebsock

Mother-Work: Women, Child Welfare, and the State, 1890–1930
Molly Ladd-Taylor

Babe: The Life and Legend of Babe Didrikson Zaharias
Susan E. Cayleff

Books in the Series Sport and Society

A Sporting Time: New York City and the Rise of Modern Athletics, 1820–70
Melvin L. Adelman

Sandlot Seasons: Sport in Black Pittsburgh
Rob Ruck

West Ham United: The Making of a Football Club
Charles Korr

Beyond the Ring: The Role of Boxing in American Society
Jeffrey T. Sammons

John L. Sullivan and His America
Michael T. Isenberg

Television and National Sport: The United States and Britain
Joan M. Chandler

The Creation of American Team Sports: Baseball and Cricket, 1838–72
George B. Kirsch

City Games: The Evolution of American Urban Society and the Rise of Sports
Steven A. Riess

The Brawn Drain: Foreign Student-Athletes in American Universities
John Bale

The Business of Professional Sports
Edited by Paul D. Staudohar and James A. Mangan

Fritz Pollard: Pioneer in Racial Advancement
John M. Carroll

Go Big Red! The Story of a Nebraska Football Player
George Mills

Sport and Exercise Science: Essays in the History of Sports Medicine
Edited by Jack W. Berryman and Roberta J. Park

Minor League Baseball and Local Economic Development
Arthur T. Johnson

Harry Hooper: An American Baseball Life
Paul J. Zingg

Cowgirls of the Rodeo: Pioneer Professional Athletes
Mary Lou LeCompte

Sandow the Magnificent: Eugen Sandow and the Beginnings of Bodybuilding
David Chapman

Big-Time Football at Harvard, 1905: The Diary of Coach Bill Reid
Ronald A. Smith

Leftist Theories of Sport: A Critique and Reconstruction
William J. Morgan

Babe: The Life and Legend of Babe Didrikson Zaharias
Susan E. Cayleff

Stagg's University: The Rise, Decline, and Fall of Big-Time Football at Chicago
Robin Lester

REPRINT EDITIONS

The Nazi Olympics
Richard D. Mandell

Sports in the Western World
Second Edition
William J. Baker